Signs of Salvation

Signs of Salvation

A Festschrift for Peter Ochs

EDITED BY

Mark Randall James

AND

Randi Rashkover

CASCADE *Books* · Eugene, Oregon

SIGNS OF SALVATION
A Festschrift for Peter Ochs

Cascade Books
An Imprint of Wipf and Stock Publishers
199 W. 8th Ave., Suite 3
Eugene, OR 97401

www.wipfandstock.com

PAPERBACK ISBN: 978-1-7252-6168-6
HARDCOVER ISBN: 978-1-7252-6167-9
EBOOK ISBN: 978-1-7252-6169-3

Cataloguing-in-Publication data:

Names: James, Mark Randall, editor. | Rashkover, Randi, editor.

Title: Signs of salvation : a festschrift for Peter Ochs / edited by Mark Randall James and Randi Rashkover.

Description: Eugene, OR : Cascade Books, 2021 | Includes bibliographical references.

Identifiers: ISBN 978-1-7252-6168-6 (paperback) | ISBN 978-1-7252-6167-9 (hardcover) | ISBN 978-1-7252-6169-3 (ebook)

Subjects: LCSH: Ochs, Peter, 1950–.

Classification: BX4827.O24 S57 2021 (print) | BX4827.O24 S57 (ebook)

Manufactured in the U.S.A.   03/26/21

Contents

Abbreviations

CP   Charles Sanders Peirce. *Collected Papers of Charles Peirce.*
Edited by Charles Hartshorne, Paul Weiss, and A. W. Burks.
8 vols. Cambridge: Harvard University Press, 1931–58.

PPLS   Peter Ochs. *Peirce, Pragmatism and the Logic of Scripture.*
Cambridge: Cambridge University Press, 1998.

Introduction ─────────────────────

The Wisdom of Peter Ochs

From Common Sensism to Scriptural Pragmatism

—MARK RANDALL JAMES, Independent Scholar
—RANDI RASHKOVER, College of William & Mary

IT IS A GREAT honor to present this collection of essays to Peter Ochs on behalf of his colleagues and students. These essays by scholars in a wide range of academic disciplines are a testimony to the generative potential of Ochs' distinctive pragmatic philosophy.

Ochs' pragmatism revitalizes the Jewish wisdom tradition within the context of modernity. Classical Jewish sages adopted the ordinary language term "wisdom" to refer to a practical mode of rationality concretely realizable in individual habits and communal life. So too Ochs identifies the locus of our deepest human wisdom in common sense beliefs implicit in everyday practices. The sages also believed, however, that to speak adequately about wisdom requires speaking about its relation to God as the ultimate source of wisdom and life. In the same way, Ochs speaks of God's Word which, through scripture, can repair our common sense, bringing life-giving wisdom to communities on the brink of death.

In this introduction, we aim to show how Ochs' pragmatic reappropriation of the classical wisdom tradition emerges in the confrontation between Judaism and modernity. We offer these words with trepidation. To represent any thinker's thought in a finite string of words inevitably involves selecting and freezing elements of an infinite living process of thinking. In Ochs' case, the task is especially difficult because of the remarkable range, subtlety, and

1

generativity of his thought. Nevertheless, we hope that this introduction can serve as one possible entry to the world of Ochs' philosophy.

We begin in section I by tracing the genealogy of Ochs' thought to two philosophical traditions that correct modern philosophy by appealing to the rationality implicit in practice. From German and American Jewish philosophers, Ochs learned to respond to modern challenges to the intelligibility of Jewish life by seeking the rationality implicit in Jewish practices. In the American pragmatist Charles Peirce, Ochs found a method of appealing to the logic of scientific practice to correct modern philosophy itself.

In section II, we sketch the common-sensist and scriptural dimensions of Ochs' pragmatism. In response to the Cartesian anxiety that plagues modern thought, Ochs appeals to the deep wisdom of common sense—vague but indubitable rational commitments implicit in our everyday practices and ordinary language. But in light of the recurring crises of Jewish history that threaten the intelligibility of Jewish life and practice, Ochs also recognizes occasions when common sense may fail and ordinary methods of pragmatic repair prove inadequate. Ochs' scriptural pragmatism describes how, through scripture, God's Word can heal communities in crisis, transforming their common sense and renewing their language.

If practice is the locus of rationality, then a philosophical theory's full meaning can only be determined, and its validity tested, with reference to its practical fruits. Section III examines the ways that Ochsian wisdom has borne fruit in communities of practice. Through the practices of Textual Reasoning and Scriptural Reasoning, modern readers are habituated in a distinctively scriptural wisdom governed by a pragmatic logic. In the Scripture, Interpretation, and Practice program at the University of Virginia, Ochs has built an academic community that shows how this wisdom can correct modern academic practices. In his Hearth to Hearth peacebuilding work and his recently developed method of Value Predicate Analysis, Ochs puts the wisdom of scriptural pragmatism to work creating conditions for interreligious peace.

In section IV, we introduce the essays offered to Ochs in this volume as a small sample of the many ways Ochs' wisdom has borne fruit in his colleagues and students. As is fitting for a man who preferred to practice "face-to-face theology,"[1] these essays reflect not only the influence of his thought but, above all, the force of his person as a teacher and friend. We offer these essays in the hope that the wisdom of Peter Ochs will be more apparent as it is refracted in the words of those who have learned from him.

---

1. Ochs, *Another Reformation*, 19.

I. Genealogy of Ochs' Common-Sensism

> λόγον σοφὸν ἐὰν ἀκούσῃ ἐπιστήμων αἰνέσει αὐτὸν καὶ ἐπ' αὐτὸν προσθήσει.

> If a man of understanding hears a wise word, he will praise it and add to it. (Sirach 21:15a)

Since the ancient world, Jews have frequently faced a double existential danger from their neighbors: the challenges, we might say, of Gentile *wisdom* and Gentile *swords*. Modern Jews in particular must come to terms with what Ochs calls "the two fires, metaphorically, of modernity and, literally, of the Shoa."[2] Jewish philosophy emerges in response to this double challenge to the intelligibility of Jewish life. Its primary task, as Ochs put it in an early essay, is to redirect "the dislocated Jew back to the speech community of Israel."[3] The Jewish philosopher can be a guide to the perplexed because she bears the perplexity of her people within herself. She participates in two traditions at once—the tradition of Israel, with its ultimate origin in the Torah, and the tradition of Western philosophy—and for this very reason, she tends to dwell at the margins of both.

It is characteristic of Ochs' pragmatism that he not only recognizes "influences" on his thought, but explicitly situates himself within both Jewish and Western philosophical traditions of inquiry and refers his thinking to problems that arise within these traditions. For this reason, Ochs' work frequently takes the form of *commentary,* clarifying or correcting the words of his teachers. The basic logic of commentary was aptly formulated by Jesus ben Sirach, himself a figure situated between Jewish wisdom and Greek philosophy, in the aphorism quoted above: the wise person *praises* the wise words she inherits (affirming their rational intelligibility) and then *adds* to them (clarifying their implications for her own time and place). To understand Ochs' pragmatism, then, we must begin with the traditions in dialogue with which his thought emerges.

1. Modern Jewish Philosophy

Like many of his contemporaries, the young Ochs identified himself with the critique of modern philosophy's tendency to erase Judaism's textual and civilizational resources launched by late nineteenth and early twentieth century Jewish thinkers including Hermann Cohen, Franz Rosenzweig,

---

2. Ochs, "Wounded Word," 155.
3. Ochs, "Torah, Language and Philosophy," 115.

and Martin Buber. Most noteworthy was their collective focus on the philosophical significance of the everyday linguistic practices of rabbinic Jews, in which these thinkers discerned an operative rationality that could not be adequately modeled in terms of modern logical systems. The "aftermoderns," as Ochs calls them,

> perceived in the grammar of everyday practices, including the everyday practices of the traditional rabbinic Jew, certain norms of reasoning of which the logical systems of the modern philosophers provided no adequate model. These systems did not offer . . . adequate tools for identifying the rationality or rule-governed character of "sound common-sense" or of the hermeneutical, legal-ethical and liturgical practices of traditional Judaism.[4]

According to these thinkers, thinking happens in and through Jewish language. They discerned in Jewish linguistic practice implicit rational norms for how we speak to others, how we relate to the world, and how we speak to God. Thus Cohen, for example, sought to describe a "religion of reason" implicit in the "sources of Judaism."[5] So too Rosenzweig identified a "new thinking"[6] embodied in dialogical relations that unfold over time. In conversation with these aftermoderns, Ochs' early work offered a dialogical response to this new thinking in which Ochs discerned "a critique and extension of Kant's transcendental philosophy that looks to us today like the foundations of a rabbinic semiotics."[7] Yet despite their attention to Jewish linguistic practices, Cohen, Rosenzweig, and Buber each retained residual elements of the modern philosophical approaches from which they sought to distance themselves and paid insufficient attention to the particulars of rabbinic linguistic practice and the context-specific character of their normative speech activity. In Ochs' view, aftermodern Jewish thought needed to develop a more ethnographic approach to language and "locate practices of speech-thinking in their social, or at least literary contexts."[8]

4. Ochs, "Scripture and Text," 219.

5. Cohen, *Religion of Reason*.

6. The term comes from Franz Rosenzweig, but it provides a useful description of the pragmatic approach shared by all three of these thinkers. See Rosenzweig, "New Thinking."

7. Ochs, "Rabbinic Semiotics," 35. This essay is reprinted, with slight modifications, as Ochs' discussion of "rabbinic pragmatism" in Ochs, *Peirce, Pragmatism and the Logic of Scripture* (hereafter cited as *PPLS*), 290–305.

8. Ochs, "Scripture and Text," 220.

The thinkers who, for Ochs, came closest to practicing this empirical recovery of rabbinic speech-thinking were not part of the canon of German Jewish thinkers, but rather two of his teachers at the Jewish Theological Seminary: Max Kadushin and David Weiss Halivni.[9] In Kadushin, Ochs found a thinker committed to providing a thick description of the logic of rabbinic thought exhibited by rabbinic texts. Rabbinic reading practices, Kadushin held, display and perform "value-concepts," the normative elements or units of a rabbinic *derash* or interpretation. As Ochs explains, Kadushin's value concepts have both "cognitive and valuational components."[10] This is because they are normative concepts that operate as hermeneutical rules to guide interpretive acts of text study and halakhic action. Throughout rabbinic literature one can find "haggadic statements" that display the outcomes of these interpretive acts and serve as evidence of the rabbis' use of value concepts to resolve interpretive questions. The rational potential of rabbinic hermeneutics lay, Kadushin argued, in the network of haggadic statements woven throughout rabbinic literature, since as Ochs puts it, "they imply the reason for the judgment they express."[11] These haggadic statements instantiate normative rules or value concepts that may be used to resolve other interpretive questions or problems. Since these rules are determined only in relation to particular cases, value-concepts are vague, their full meaning contingent upon their determination across a range of possible contexts. While value-concepts thus sustain a "drive" toward "concretization," they are "not tied to any particular manifestation. . . . [E]ach one of them suggests an identifiable, though not a definable idea or notion."[12] Value-concepts are not determinate propositions but "literary embodiments" that sponsor readers' open-ended but nonarbitrary deployment of them.

Kadushin's work was focused primarily on the relation between the Bible and the rabbinic logic it generated. Consequently, as Ochs has argued, Kadushin was "less attentive to the pragmatic force of rabbinic interpretation, or how it reformed rules of conduct in some particular community."[13] Ochs saw this problem as a product of the limits of Kadushin's method. In order to secure the objective validity of his thought, Kadushin tended to hypostasize value-concepts, abstracting them from the conditions of their ongoing use. But if interpretation, as Ochs has repeatedly maintained, is

9. Ochs has published volumes engaging in detail with both thinkers. See Ochs, *Understanding the Rabbinic Mind*; and Halivni, *Breaking the Tablets*.

10. Ochs, "Rabbinic Text-Process Theology," 148.

11. Ochs, "Rabbinic Text-Process Theology," 149.

12. Ochs, *Understanding the Rabbinic Mind*, 182.

13. Ochs, "Rabbinic Semiotics," 56.

a context-specific, historically conditioned activity, then value-concepts must function in relation to particular communities who use them to guide their interpretive judgments. Which value-concepts assume significance and in what systemic order depends upon the particular historical conditions of existing reading and speaking communities. What Ochs comes to call "rabbinic pragmatism" would seek not only to explicate the operative norms of rabbinic rationality, but also to offer an account of how these norms might be taken up to address the specific problems troubling particular Jewish communities.

If Kadushin modeled a pragmatic method for reconstructing rabbinic rationality, it was his teacher David Weiss Halivni who showed how to bring rabbinic rationality to bear on the defining catastrophe of modern Jewish life: the Shoah. For Halivni, a Talmud prodigy and a Holocaust survivor, the event of the Shoah is (in Ochs' words) "a condition of ultimate disruption that calls into question every level of Judaism, every Jewish habit of study, belief, and action in the world."[14] In theological terms, it constitutes a radical rupture in the covenant. Halivni's holocaust memoir *The Book and the Sword* begins with a midrash:

> The sword and the book came down from heaven tied to each other. Said the Almighty, "If you keep what is written in this book, you will be spared this sword; if not, you will be consumed by it" (Midrash Rabbah Deuteronomy 4:2). We clung to the book, yet we were consumed by the sword.[15]

As a sign of this rupture, Halivni describes how the relief he found through Torah study during the intensifying sufferings of his community in the ghetto of Sighet reached its limits in the concentration camps. "I had no desire or ability to study Torah amid people ready to kill us."[16]

Yet in the years that followed his liberation, Halivni charted a path forward that profoundly shaped Ochs' own response to the Holocaust. Halivni discerned in rabbinic sources a pattern of divine response to the traumas suffered by the Jews throughout their history in which communal restoration comes by way of the interpretive activities of the great sages. For Halivni, the prototype of this activity was the work of Ezra in the post-exilic Jewish community. Drawing on rabbinic traditions about Ezra's work of correcting the Torah,[17] Halivni argues that as a consequence of Israel's

---

14. Ochs, "Editor's Introduction," 47.

15. Halivni, *Book and the Sword*.

16. Halivni, *Book and the Sword*, 47.

17. B. San. 21b, Bemidbar Rabbah 3.12. See Halivni, *Peshat and Derash*, 136–46.

sin during the prophetic period, the post-exilic community found itself with a *maculate* text, a text wounded by textual errors and corruptions. As both prophet and scribe, Ezra repaired the text by making emendations (*tikkunot*) and by transmitting interpretive traditions that diverge from the plain sense, enabling the written text to continue to guide Israel after the exile. Halivni takes Ezra's correction of the written Torah as a proto-type for his own scholarly labors, which use academic methods of study to repair the oral Torah, those living traditions of interpretation and practice that we might call the deep common sense of the rabbinic community. Halivni realizes that academic methods are necessary to this process, but deployed *for the sake of* healing the wounded community, what Ochs calls "pragmatic historiography."[18]

Underlying Halivni's proposal is the theological insight that the wounds of the Jewish community are intertwined with wounds afflicting its texts and interpretive traditions. The wounds of interpreters mirror the wounds of the text, with the surprising result (though a result at the heart of Jewish life) that the apparently impractical work of reinterpreting troubling texts can become the means by which the divine Word heals troubled read-ers. As Ochs describes this process,

> When I bring my suffering to the text of scripture, I notice its wounds, first; I am drawn to tend to them; and, only after being engaged in the work of "mending" them do I realize that my own wounds correspond to the text's and that the more deeply I care for the text's wounds, the more deeply my own wounds are healed.[19]

Scriptural revelation is the process by which God's Word heals his people through reparative scriptural reading—not by delivering a collection of clear propositions ("the meaning" of scripture) but by transforming the lin-guistic practices by which the community derives meaning from its scrip-tures, effecting what Ochs calls a "radical change in the relations that bind the words of a language together."[20] Ochs' scriptural pragmatism will offer a theory that explains how this process works.

18. Ochs, "Talmudic Scholarship," 120–43.

19. Ochs, "Bible's Wounded Authority," 117.

20. Ochs, "Talmudic Scholarship," 133.

2. Charles Peirce

As a Jewish *philosopher*, Ochs participates not only in the Jewish linguistic community but also in the tradition of Western philosophy. Inheriting the problems of modern philosophy, Ochs sought methods for internally critiquing modern philosophy that can also guide dislocated modern Jewish communities. It was through Max Kadushin that Ochs first encountered the work of Charles Peirce, the founder of pragmatism.[21] Over time, Ochs came to regard Peirce's pragmatism as one of the best instruments for articulating the rationality displayed in the classical sources of Judaism using the language of Western philosophy.

One of the core insights of pragmatism is that the locus of rationality is not consciousness but practice. According to Peirce, a belief is not primarily a mental entity, but rather a habit or rule of action, of which our self-consciousness is only a fallible sign.[22] Clarifying the content of our beliefs thus requires explicating their implications for practice, as expressed by Peirce's pragmatic maxim:

> Consider what effects, that might conceivably have practical bearings, we conceive the object of our conception to have. Then, our conception of these effects is the whole of our conception of the object.[23]

For Peirce, a practicing laboratory scientist, this maxim implicitly guides the practice of modern science, for which concepts are only meaningful insofar as they have implications for a possible experiment.

Because practices are the locus of rationality, pragmatic inquiry, on Peirce's view, begins with problems that arise within our practices, registered to consciousness as doubt provoked by irritation or suffering. As Peirce says, "The irritation of doubt is the only immediate motive for the struggle to attain belief. . . . With the doubt . . . the struggle begins, and with the cessation of

---

21. Kadushin spent many an afternoon strolling down Riverside Park rehearsing his knowledge of Charles Peirce's pragmatism. Ochs writes, "According to the biblical scholar and philosopher, Yohanan Muffs, Kadushin rarely referred to Peirce in writing, but I think you might like to know that Kadushin was a careful reader of Peirce's writings and talked of them at great length. We used to walk down Riverside Drive together [in the 1960s], coming home from the [Jewish Theological] Seminary. One of us would hold a volume of Peirce's *Collected Papers*, and we would discuss his philosophy in detail" (Ochs, "Rabbinic Text Process Theology," 155).

22. Peirce, *Collected Papers* (hereafter cited as *CP*), 5.397–402. See Ochs, *PPLS*, 194–95.

23. *CP* 5.402.

doubt it ends."[24] Pragmatic inquiry is guided by the problems that give rise to doubt, and on Peirce's view, it can have no purpose beyond the fixation of some new belief, some new rule of action according to which the problem that gave rise to doubt no longer arises. Ochs thus found in Peirce a model of inquiry as what Nicholas Adams has labeled *reparative reasoning*,[25] reasoning whose goal is the amelioration of the problematic conditions that stimulated it, prototypically the problematic condition of suffering.[26]

As inquiry into rationality, the central concern of Peirce's philosophy is *logic*. It is a symptom of our artificially narrow late-modern conceptions of rationality that for many readers the word "logic" denotes only the formal analysis of deductive reasoning in the tradition of Aristotelian syllogistic. Although Peirce made significant contributions to modern symbolic logic, his conception of logic also includes the *empirical* study of actual reasoning practices and normative questions about the relation of thinking to its objects, what Kant called *transcendental* logic.[27] On Peirce's view, the logical intuitions that serve as sources for formal logic are not insights into eternal laws of thought, but rather symptoms of deep beliefs, embodied in practices, that certain rules of reasoning prove reliable, and their validity extends only to those contexts in which they continue to prove reliable in practice.

Peirce's mature view was that logic in its broadest sense is identical to what he called "semiotic," the theory of signs.[28] Peirce's sophisticated semiotic theory provided Ochs with a set of analytic tools capable of making intelligible the rationality of Jewish practices. Unfortunately, Peirce's use of the term "semiotic" is as likely to mislead contemporary readers as the term "logic,"

24. *CP* 5.375.

25. Adams, "Reparative Reasoning." Ochs adopts this terminology in Ochs, "Reparative Reasoning."

26. This formulation is due in part to John Dewey. In his *Logic*, Dewey defines inquiry as "the directed or controlled transformation of an indeterminate situation into a determinately unified one" (117). When an indeterminate situation is clarified in the course of inquiry, it becomes a "problematic situation" (105).

27. For Ochs, what Kant calls "transcendental" reasoning in the *Critique of Pure Reason* is a form of regressive reasoning that proceeds "from effect to possible cause" ("Reparative Reasoning," 195). Strictly speaking Kant distinguished the synthetic or "progressive" method of the first Critique, which constructs the possibility of human cognition out of its elements, from the analytic or "regressive" method he adopted in the *Prolegomena to Any Future Metaphysics*, which takes cognition as a fact and reasons backwards to its conditions (*CP* 4.277; see Kant, *Prolegomena*, 73). Ochs' interpretation follows Hermann Cohen, who, taking Kant's account of his method in the *Prolegomena* as his paradigm, argued that transcendental reasoning proceeds regressively from existing scientific or other cultural practices to principles that account for their validity (*Kants Theorie der Erfahrung*, 66–79).

28. *CP* 2.227–29.

and for analogous reasons. Contemporary notions of semiotics, especially in the humanities, tend to derive from Saussure's account of the sign as a cultural unit of meaning, a conventional and arbitrary equivalence between a signifier and a signified. The Saussurean sign is a social entity, where "social" functions as the logical contrary of "natural."[29] By contrast, Peirce's identification of semiotics with logic inherits the classical tradition of semiotics as a theory of *inference.* On this view the paradigmatic sign is not linguistic meaning but rather material inference: if P then Q.[30] This is why Ochs describes the objects of Peircean semiotics as "rules of reasoning":

> *Peirce's theory of signs offers a set of conventions for diagramming any patterns or rules of reasoning.* Consider, for example, his conventions for diagramming semantic reference or signification. The fundamental unit of reference is the sign: a *signifier* that displays its *object* (reference or meaning) only with respect to a particular *interpretant* (context of meaning, interpretive mindset, or system of deep-seated rules).[31]

It is one of Peirce's core insights that the sign is irreducibly triadic— that is, that inferential reasoning is a relation involving at least three irreducible terms: that from which some inference may be drawn (the "signifier"), that about which one infers (the "object"), and those habits or practices of reasoning by means of which this inference may be drawn and which are themselves affected in the process of reasoning (the "interpretant"). Unlike the Saussurean sign, these embodied habits of inference in relation to which signs operate are not "social" *in opposition to* "natural" because they emerge from the biological dimension of human life. Animals communicate and draw inferences, and these natural capacities are continuous with the sorts of inferential reasoning that function within human social practices like language and scientific inquiry.[32] Moreover, because these practices are formed diachronically through interaction with the empirical world, signs are not intrinsically arbitrary, though they may become arbitrary in limit cases when they lose their capacity for self-correction. Peirce's semiotic

---

29. Saussure says that the association is "unmotivated, i.e. arbitrary in that [the signifier] actually has no natural connection with the signified" (Saussure, *Course in General Linguistics*, 69).

30. See Eco, *Semiotics*, 14–45, esp. 39–45. For classical semiotics, see Manetti, *Theories of the Sign*.

31. Ochs, "Reparative Reasoning," 190–91.

32. As Dewey says, "Intellectual operations are foreshadowed in behavior of the biological kind, and the latter prepares the way for the former" (*Logic*, 43).

theory thus shows how a community's linguistic practices can embody relatively reliable rules of reasoning.

II. Beyond Common Sense

וְלֹא הַמִּדְרָשׁ הוּא הָעִקָּר, אֶלָּא הַמַּעֲשֶׂה.

The fundamental thing is not interpretation but action.
(Pirkei Avot 1:17)

While Peirce aimed primarily to correct modern philosophy in light of
the scientific method, his core insight that rationality is practical is not
new. William James famously called pragmatism "a new name for some
old ways of thinking," identifying Socrates and Aristotle as ancient fore-
runners.[33] Peirce himself framed the pragmatic maxim as commentary
on the words of the rabbi of Nazareth, calling it "an application of the
sole principle of logic which was recommended by Jesus; 'Ye may know
them by their fruits,'" and adding that "it is very intimately allied with
the ideas of the gospel."[34] Ochs takes Peirce's remark as an important clue
that pragmatism recapitulates the practical orientation of the scriptural
wisdom tradition that Jesus' aphorism so aptly summarizes.[35] Pragmatic
thinking also shapes the rabbinic wisdom tradition, as with Shimon ben
Gamaliel's aphorism above, in which we might hear another echo of the
pragmatic maxim: it is not interpretation (merely verbal clarification), but
action (lived practice), that gets to the root of a matter.

Ochs' thought deepens pragmatism by recalling it to its scriptural
roots. His *magnum opus—Peirce, Pragmatism and the Logic of Scripture—*is
a reparative account of Peirce's own intellectual development as a process of
pragmatic inquiry, culminating in Peirce's post-1905 reformulation of his
philosophy as a "critical common-sensism" that identifies indubitable rules
of reasoning in common sense beliefs implicit in everyday practices.[36] Ochs
frames his own "scriptural pragmatism" as commentary on Peirce's critical
common-sensism, clarifying (as Peirce does not) how common sense itself
may be repaired by God's Word through scripture during times of crisis.
Scriptural pragmatism is the form critical common-sensism takes in light
of scriptural communities' recurring experience of possibilities of healing

33. James, *Pragmatism*, 50.

34. *CP* 5.402 n.2. See also *CP* 5.464–6.

35. *PPLS*, 323–25. Cf. *PPLS*, 9, where Ochs draws a parallel between pragmatic
writing and wisdom literature.

36. *CP* 5.439–52.

and repair that transcend human capacities. It is, we might say, an account of how human wisdom can be healed by divine wisdom.

1. Critical Common-Sensism

Peirce calls his late pragmatism "critical common-sensism" to identify an affinity between his response to Cartesian skepticism and that of the Scottish common sense philosophers. Provoked by the massive social and intellectual upheavals of early modern Europe, Descartes argued that modern philosophy must begin anew by adopting a method of systematically doubting every belief in order to discover secure first principles that cannot be doubted. He thought he had discovered such principles in beliefs that are clear and distinct to the individual thinker (the *cogito*). According to Ochs, however, by failing to analyze the contextual conditions that gave rise to his doubt, Descartes misinterpreted his doubt as a universal problem afflicting human beings in general. As a result, Descartes sought to resolve his doubt by identifying clear conditions grounding all human knowing. By taking the generality and clarity of the theoretical sciences as the paradigm of philosophical repair, Descartes sought his foundational principles in concepts whose truth is purportedly guaranteed by their clarity and distinctness for any rational mind. Ochs argues that this foundationalist strategy fails to resolve adequately the real doubts that animate its inquiry, generating instead either dogmatic philosophical systems that tacitly place obstacles in the course of inquiry or skeptical misologies that abandon confidence in rational inquiry altogether.

Common sensists like Thomas Reid sought to repair Cartesian philosophy by grounding knowledge in first principles "common to philosophers and to the vulgar."[37] These principles would be instinctive beliefs given by nature along with our other faculties,[38] rather than principles—like Locke's simple ideas or Leibniz's principle of contradiction—whose supposed self-evidence is clear only to philosophers.[39] By attempting to ground all human knowledge in a set of universally evident beliefs, Scottish common sensism undoubtedly reiterated Cartesian foundationalism; but in its insistence that the philosopher's doubt must be answered by

---

37. Reid, *Essays*, 16.

38. See *CP* 5.439ff.

39. For example, Reid includes principles like "the existence of everything of which I am conscious" (*Essays*, 328) and "that we have some degree of power over our actions" (*Essays*, 334).

appeal to principles implicit in everyday practice and ordinary language, it anticipated a core insight of pragmatism.

Since the philosopher may find her community's common-sense rules operative within ordinary linguistic practices, a characteristic tendency of common sensism is to approach language as a potential source of rationality rather than as mere subjective opinion or social convention. There is a logic to our living linguistic practices, a Socratic intuition that pragmatists share with Wittgenstein and the ordinary language philosophers. Part of the common sense philosopher's task is thus explicative, or in Ochs' language, diagrammatic. She must introduce context-specific clarity to deep rules of common sense in order to correct particular philosophical problems. Peirce's pragmatic maxim exemplifies this process. Aphorisms like "the proof is in the pudding" or "by their fruits ye shall know them" express a common sense belief with a great deal of vagueness. Peirce's various formulations of the pragmatic maxim explicate this belief by introducing further clarity relevant to the particular failures of modern philosophy.

Ochs argues that one reason modern philosophers have struggled to extricate themselves from Descartes' mode of thinking is the difficulty involved in understanding how a tradition of inquiry can correct its own deepest norms and commitments. It seems that one must "both affirm and criticize his own method of reasoning,"[40] and it is difficult to see how this is possible without asserting (as Descartes did) that some of one's existing normative commitments are beyond the possibility of rational criticism. Peirce resolved this problem by arguing that the deepest corrective principles to which we appeal are different in kind from the rules of reasoning they correct. The rules of reasoning that govern everyday life are frequently used but very liable to error. Peirce called these "B-reasonings." When a B-reasoning fails, stimulating a doubt, we do not correct it by appeal to a rule of the same order. Rather, we appeal to rules embodying deeper convictions that are rarely useful, but highly reliable when applicable. Peirce called these deeper principles "A-reasonings." The activity of self-correction may then be understood as the use of a deeper A-reasoning to correct some errant B-reasoning.

As Ochs points out, the notion of reasonings of different depths can be iterated: a deeper corrective rule may itself be in need of correction, and so on. In iterating Peirce's model, Ochs transforms his distinction between B- and A- reasonings into a distinction between what we might call *finite* and *infinite* reasonings. A finite (B-) reasoning is one that "diagrams and corrects

40. *PPLS*, 259.

another such B-reasoning."[41] Such reasoning is stimulated by a problem in another reasoning, of which it provides some map or analysis (a "diagram") and recommends an action or habit change to alleviate the problem (a "correction"). These reasonings are finite because they are stimulated by a finite class of problems whose resolution is the criterion of its success and which come to an end when the problem that stimulated them is resolved. Because B-reasonings are corrected by other B-reasonings, they can be organized hierarchically in an ordered series of corrective reasonings of increasing depth. The intuitive reasonings we use to solve problems that arise in everyday life are finite (B-) reasonings in this sense, but so are the reasonings that guide doctors and engineers, medical researchers, and physicists.

By combining this hierarchical model of reparative rationality with Peirce's architectonic classification of the sciences[42] and Dewey's pragmatic analysis of social institutions,[43] Ochs arrives at an account of reparative reasoning as a social activity occurring within hierarchically ordered institutions of repair.

> We might conceive of social institutions as if they were progressively ordered to serve the relative ends of repairing suffering, then of repairing the repair of suffering, and so on. Say we start with the *Lebenswelt*, or the world of everyday practices that includes not only doing this or that but also repairing how one does this or that. A doorknob won't open, so I oil it. Then I scratch myself, so I put on a Band-Aid.[44]

When finite rules of reasoning like "if you scratch yourself, apply a Band-Aid" prove insufficient—if the wound is too deep, for example—then we may seek repair through what Ochs calls "practical arts" practiced in "service institutions" like hospitals, mechanics, and churches, which operationalize higher-order rules of repair. These institutions in turn may lack the capacity to resolve our problem—the doctors may not know how to cure an ailment, the priest may find herself at a loss for words. In these cases, we may develop higher-order practices to repair the repairers, which Ochs calls "theoretical sciences" or "reparative sciences," such as those practiced in research institutions like the modern academy. But these institutions may themselves fail to address the problems of the

---

41. *PPLS*, 263.

42. *PPLS*, 264, where Ochs refers to Peirce's "A Detailed Classification of the Sciences" (*CP* 1.203–83).

43. Ochs, *Another Reformation*, 11. Ochs may have in mind texts like Dewey, *Reconstruction*, 187–216; and Dewey, *Liberalism*.

44. Ochs, *Another Reformation*, 11. See the longer treatment in *PPLS*, 263–68.

practical sciences they serve. It is the task of the philosopher to analyze and repair ("diagram-and-correct") theoretical sciences.[45]

We may think of Cartesian doubt as a symptom of a crisis threatening the philosopher's ability to perform her reparative function. Ochs suggests that Descartes suffered from an *infinite doubt*—doubt not about a particular finite rule of reasoning (that might be repaired by another, deeper but still finite rule of reasoning), but rather about an entire infinite series of B-reasonings. Infinite doubt is, for Ochs, a philosophical performance of the logic appropriate to historical moments when one's world comes crashing down and nothing seems intelligible. Despite his critique of Descartes, Ochs does not reject the validity of infinite doubt; indeed, he can say that, "like Descartes, pragmatic logicians are motivated by infinite doubt."[46] But pragmatists reinterpret this doubt as a symptom of a deep problem that arises in a particular context rather than as a universal problem facing human beings as such. Descartes' problem is that by correcting his doubt by appealing to clear and distinct (hence, finite) principles, he makes a kind of category error, "failing to note that the doubt one has about any particular B-reasoning must be of a different kind than the doubt one might have of all B-reasonings."[47] By treating philosophical reasoning as grounded in finite principles, whether on the model of practical or theoretical sciences, modern philosophers tend, like Descartes, to apply finite rules appropriate for repairing a specific problem as though they were relevant to every problem.

For the pragmatist, however, an infinite doubt requires an infinite reasoning to repair it, a reasoning capable of repairing an entire problematic chain of corrective reasonings. Ochs identifies these infinite reasonings with Peirce's A-reasonings.[48] Infinite reasonings avoid the Cartesian tendency towards either dogmatic arbitrariness or skeptical misology because they differ in two important ways from Descartes' first principles. First, Cartesian first principles are supposed to be self-evident, and hence immune to any possible doubt. Pragmatic infinite reasonings are, by contrast, indubitable beliefs in the more modest sense that one cannot bring oneself to doubt them in one's actual conduct. They are immune not to any possible doubt but to any *actual* doubt. As Ochs comments,

> The difference lies in the etiology of the two sets of indubitables and, thus, in their empirical import. A priorists [such as Cartesian foundationalists] arrive at their acritical beliefs by tracing a

45. *PPLS*, 267.

46. *PPLS*, 266.

47. *PPLS*, 263.

48. *PPLS*, 263.

series of *imagined* doubts to a finite limit. . . . Pragmaticists [i.e. critical common sensists], on the other hand, would arrive at their indubitables by tracing a series of *actual* doubts to a finite limit. . . . This difference is revealed only in *practice*: indubitable beliefs are successfully tested and refined against everyday experience; a priori beliefs show themselves, in the long run, to be empirically untestable.[49]

In this respect, the logical difference between a Cartesian and a pragmatist emerges only diachronically. Viewed synchronically, the beliefs of a critical common-sensist share the same hierarchical structure and indubitable basis as a foundationalist system. But while the Cartesian understands her first principles as self-evident to any human being, the indubitable beliefs of a pragmatist are formed through a temporal process of corrective reasoning—for Peirce, not only a socio-historical process but also a biological evolutionary one—and they may in principle be called into question in the future. Pragmatic ultimate commitments prove themselves indubitable practically, by their history of reliably resolving actual doubts and emerging unscathed from criticism.

Second, indubitable beliefs are *irremediably vague*. An irremediably vague belief is one that guides action, yet whose consequences for action in particular cases cannot be fully determined prior to the occasions in which action is required.[50] Infinite reasonings must be vague in this sense, Ochs argues, because they make reference to an infinite series that cannot be determined fully by some finite rule. One must avoid clarifying irremediably vague beliefs prematurely, since doing so would amount to making rash prejudgments about cases without adequate reason. Ochs follows Peirce in arguing that one of the most egregious errors of modern philosophy has been to neglect vagueness as a distinct logical mode alongside individuality and generality and then to regard nonvagueness (clarity and distinctness) as a sign of truth. Indeed, the opposite is more nearly the case. Because the consequences of a clear idea are more precisely determined, it is far more fallible and dubitable than a vague idea. This is why clarifying the implications of a hypothesis is an important step in submitting it to empirical verification. A vague idea is harder to disprove precisely because it determines less.

Indubitability and irremediable vagueness are also characteristic features of our deepest common sense beliefs in contrast to claims generated through more precise technical discourses. This is why the pragmatic philosopher

49. *PPLS*, 170.
50. *PPLS*, 47–48.

performs her most radical reparative task not by drawing on clear principles evident to philosophers, but rather by appealing to deep rules of common sense implicit in everyday practice—rules such as the pragmatic maxim itself. By doing so, the pragmatic philosopher returns the sciences to the problems of everyday life that stimulated their inquiry in the first place.

2. Scriptural Pragmatism

For the common-sense pragmatist, there is always already some rule implicit in a community's everyday practices that may be brought to bear for the repair of some philosophical problem; it is simply a matter of unearthing it. This reparative appeal to common sense may take the form of a relatively confident reappropriation of deep resources already present within a particular tradition; but it may also take increasingly radical forms.[51] Through mathematics, the science of the possible that, according to Peirce, "posits hypotheses, and traces out their consequences,"[52] human beings explore the internal possibilities of common sense in a controlled and systematic way, often hitting upon hitherto neglected concepts and relations. Through playful or anarchic practices like art, poetry, or musement, human beings open their minds to generative wells of creative possibility immanent in the created order. Such practices may even take on a "religious" character, but in Ochs' framework they remain within the bounds of a kind of natural theology or immanent Logos philosophy, and hence within the broadest sphere of possibilities available to common-sense philosophers.

The need for a specifically *scriptural* pragmatism arises for those who believe that communities may face situations so traumatic they challenge even their most fundamental beliefs, so catastrophic that no rule of common sense, no traditional wisdom, and no insight of human rationality, however radical, provides an adequate response. In these situations, Ochs says,

> the world itself may be brought into question. The world of experience is served by a finite set of common-sense beliefs, and

---

51. In *Peirce, Pragmatism, and the Logic of Scripture*, the practice Peirce calls "Musement" exemplifies for Ochs the most radical appeal to common sense, generating "three part dialogues among mathematical imagination . . . logical criticism . . . and elemental habits of common sense . . ." (*PPLS*, 318–19). Later, speaking with reference to Plato's Allegory of the Cave, Ochs refers to common-sense philosophers as potential "'seers' (muses and visionaries)" (*PPLS*, 322). In *Another Reformation*, by contrast, Ochs operates with a somewhat narrower conception of common sense, so that he can say that philosophers adopt practices like "mathematics, art, and prophecy" when common sense fails them (Ochs, *Another Reformation*, 12).

52. *CP* 1.240.

> there are terrible occasions when this world breaks down and
> common sense is confounded.[53]

For modern Jews, the Shoah is a civilizational crisis of this magnitude. The
tragedy of the Shoah is not only the unspeakable destruction of innocent
human life but also its challenge to the intelligibility of Jewish tradition.
As for most Jewish thinkers of his generation, the Shoah casts a dark and
heavy shadow over Ochs' thought. Ochs' response is to seek communal
restoration in the God of Israel, a source of repair deeper than common
sense (though one to which Jewish faith acquired through millennia of
experience bears witness). "There is more than *this* world, however," Ochs
insists; "for scriptural pragmatists, there are resources *out* of this world for
correcting the inadequacies *of* this world."[54]

Scriptural pragmatists are common sense philosophers—not only
Jews, but also Christians, Muslims, and others—who believe that such
radical crises may occur and that divine help may come through a certain
kind of appeal to scripture. This reparative use of scripture differs from its
function during what we might call "ordinary times," when a community
remains relatively confident in the adequacy of its common sense as embodied in its traditions, doctrines, and linguistic practices. The scriptures
are, of course, always integral to the life of scriptural communities as objects of study, scripts for prayer, or guides for action. But during ordinary
times, a scriptural community interprets its scriptures in tradition-bound
ways that accord with its common sense commitments. Members of such
communities tend to experience the meanings of their most important
texts as plain or obvious, but this intuitive sense of scripture's clarity reflects their implicit confidence in the general reliability of the communal
linguistic rules by which they interpret scripture.

For just this reason, however, scripture cannot deliver new reparative rules directly, through its plain sense. "The Bible is *not*," Ochs says,
"a source of alternative common sense. . . . The Bible's plain sense guides
everyday practice only when it reinforces common sense (however much
that common sense has been reshaped by previous biblical legislations)."[55]
To appeal directly to the scriptures in what we might call "extraordinary
times" of crisis is to reproduce Descartes' error of assuming that ultimate
reparative rules should be both indubitable and clear. This characteristically
modern strategy ends up foreclosing the more radical kinds of repair that

53. *PPLS*, 319.
54. *PPLS*, 319.
55. *PPLS*, 320.

are needful in just those circumstances, reiterating rather than repairing the community's broken linguistic practices.

An infinite rule of repair that could correct a community's deepest common-sense rules of reasoning must come not by way of the plain sense of scripture but rather by the *disruption* of its plain meaning. In times of crisis, language fails; the community comes to doubt not only that it knows what to say on this or that occasion, but also the adequacy of its deepest, hitherto indubitable commitments. Scripture's sense for such communities becomes troubled. And just as the "maculate" text Ezra corrected was a symbol of the wounds of the post-exilic Jewish community, so the troubled sense of scripture is a mirror of the breakdown in a community's language and a symptom of its sufferings. Paradoxically, however, it is just this experience of alienation from scripture's plain meaning that manifests the community's need to return to scripture. While it is logically possible to conclude that the scriptures have exhausted their usefulness, the scriptural pragmatist continues to read in faith that the scriptures may yet again deliver life:

> . . . as the process of reading continues, the very text that gave rise to the discomfort also gives rise to an unexpected sense that, while as yet inapparent, a solution is already available. . . . The reader is moved by an odd sense that repairing this discomfort will require finding the right repair-person ("redeemer") as much as it will require conceiving the right repair.[56]

In a manner specific to each crisis, the divine Word delivers new reparative rules to the troubled community. In keeping with the reparative logic outlined above, only an infinite rule (an A-reasoning) could repair the infinite doubt that afflicts a community in times of crisis. Such a rule, we have seen, must be indubitable (able to bring doubt to an end) but also highly vague about its determinate meaning in particular contexts. In practice, while as an *indubitable* word scriptural communities may be sure of having received something beyond their own rational capacities, as a *vague* word it remains the fallible work of finite human beings to clarify its full meaning—its practical implications in particular contexts. The divine Word really speaks, but not apart from human interpreters.

Change is, of course, implicit in the notion of repair. The infinite process of repair in times of crisis might be compared to conversion, or to a Kuhnian paradigm shift.[57] It is salutary to recall how different was ancient Israelite religion from the Judaism that emerged after the Babylonian exile. While one

56. *PPLS*, 319.

57. As Ochs says, "Within the academic disciplines, these failings are analogous to the epistemological crises that stimulate what Thomas Kuhn labeled scientific 'paradigm shifts'" (Ochs, *Another Reformation*, 12).

can say that scriptural pragmatism is continuous with the common sense norms of the rabbinic tradition itself, which preserves the memory of these reparative encounters with God, there are no guarantees that a tradition after a crisis will retain its identity according to standards that seemed decisive prior to the crisis. Divine repair is, as Ochs said in his 2015 Cambridge lectures, a radical transformation that can lead to "the reappearance of the community in another form,"[58] an event akin to death and resurrection, to the Spirit bringing life to a valley of dry bones.

III. Practices of Wisdom

דְּרָכֶיהָ דַרְכֵי-נֹעַם וְכָל-נְתִיבוֹתֶיהָ שָׁלוֹם.

> Her ways are ways of pleasantness, and all her paths are peace.
> (Prov 3:17)

The meaning of Ochs' pragmatism is inseparable from practice. It is not that pragmatism has practical *applications*, a term which implies (unpragmatically) that thinking proceeds from theory to practice. Rather, for the pragmatist even the conceptual content of pragmatism remains vague apart from the practices in which it is concretized. For this reason, an account of Ochs' pragmatism must also be an account of the practices and institutions he has labored to bring into being.

Wisdom leads to life, as already adumbrated in the book of Proverbs: individual life experienced as *pleasure* and communal life experienced as *peace*. It is fitting that Ochs is most identified with the practices of Textual Reasoning and Scriptural Reasoning, in which the joy of studying scripture together overflow into unexpected friendships across difference (peace in microcosm). Scriptural Reasoning in particular, which uniquely exemplifies the distinctive logic of scriptural pragmatism, becomes the prototype for Ochs' other practical interventions, such as the Scripture, Interpretation, and Practice program at the University of Virginia and his Hearth to Hearth peacebuilding work. These practices exhibit the inextricable link between the pursuit of wisdom and ethical life, between Torah study and acts of loving-kindness (*gemilut hesadim*), that lies at the heart of Ochs' philosophical vision.

---

58. Ochs, "Lecture Handout 4."

1. Textual Reasoning and Scriptural Reasoning

Textual Reasoning (TR) emerged in the 1980s from conversations among Jewish philosophers disappointed by the failure of modern Western philosophy to provide principles of inquiry capable of addressing the pressing concerns of living Jewish communities.[59] These philosophers developed a novel practice of Jewish text study rooted in the Jewish textual tradition itself which they aspired to activate as a source of communal repair. Textual Reasoning brought text scholars familiar with rabbinic reading practices together with Jewish philosophers skilled in illuminating logics of reading and reasoning.

Throughout the 1990s, Textual Reasoners joined together in an online chat forum to study rabbinic texts and discuss critical issues affecting Jewish communities. In his own account of these often charged exchanges, Ochs has noted how frequently they motivated participants to exercise and display their own rational commitments and identify rules of reasoning shared with others in order to facilitate communal problem-solving. In an essay entitled, "Scripture and Text," Ochs explains that

> TR practices emerge out of modest-sized fellowships of rabbinic text study and of scriptural text study. . . . TR neither eschews its capacity to frame a *ratio* . . . nor presumes that its first principles . . . are self-evident, self-justified, or of universal import. The minimal requirements for such principles are that they emerge out of disciplined readings of rabbinic and scriptural sources that are applicable to the project at hand, and that they are refined as needed in the process of inquiry.[60]

More often than not, Ochs observed, identification of shared rules emerged in the course of conversational appeals to rabbinic texts such that Textual Reasoning conversations could provide limited evidence of the pragmatic benefit of intra-Judaic communal text study.

Textual Reasoning gave birth to Scriptural Reasoning (SR) as early Textual Reasoners developed friendships with Christian and Muslim scholars and began to experiment with reading scripture together. If any single practice exemplifies Ochs' recourse to scriptural wisdom as a source of life, it is surely this practice of Scriptural Reasoning.[61] According to Ochs,

59. See Ochs, "Behind the Mechitsa." For other accounts of TR, see the other essays in the same issue of the *Journal of Textual Reasoning* and the essays in Ochs and Levene, *Textual Reasonings*.

60. Ochs, "Scripture and Text," 197.

61. Many scholars have offered theoretical accounts of SR. See Pecknold and Ford, *Promise*; Adams, *Habermas*, 234–55; Higton and Muers, *Text in Play*; and the essays by

> Beginning in 1994, a group of scholars of Islam, Judaism, and Christianity joined together to discover a way to conduct dialogue across the borders of these three Abrahamic scriptural traditions. Our goal was not to generate a theory of dialogue and then apply the theory to form a new practice, but to experiment with many practices of study until we discovered the best method for "studying across difference." Our theory of SR would then emerge from out of our descriptions and analyses of SR practice. We met for five years of biannual study until we discovered and refined the best method, which we called "Scriptural Reasoning" (SR).[62]

Over time Ochs has come to distinguish what he calls "Formational SR" from a wider network of SR practices that would apply SR's reparative rationality in various institutional contexts.[63] For the most part, this network remains hypothetical, a proposal about how the SR community should develop in the future. We focus here on Formational SR because it resources these other SR practices and exemplifies their underlying logic.

Formational SR is the familiar practice of interfaith text study,

> symbolized by study around a small table, with three or more chairs, one small selection from each of the three Abrahamic scriptural canons, and three or more persons of any age eager to enter into a conversational fellowship with one another and, as it were, with these three text selections.[64]

While one might certainly call SR a practice of "interreligious dialogue,"[65] Ochs tends to resist the inference that its primary purpose is "interreligious understanding or peacebuilding."[66] There are at least two reasons for this. First, Ochs tends to understand SR's basic reparative function as primarily a *logical* repair of modern academic practices. The "original purpose" of its founders, he says, was a desire to repair "inadequate academic methods for teaching scripture and scripturally-based religions."[67] Second, while the

---

Mark Randall James, Randi Rashkover, and Daniel Weiss in *Journal of Scriptural Reasoning* 16, no. 1 (June 2017). See now Ochs, *Religion without Violence*, which appeared too late for us to make use of here.

62. Ochs, "Introduction to Scriptural Reasoning," 16–22.

63. Ochs, "Re-socializing Scholars," 210–18.

64. Ochs, "Re-socializing Scholars," 207.

65. Ochs discusses SR as a practice of inter-religious dialogue in Ochs, "Possibilities and Limits," 488–515.

66. Ochs, "Re-socializing Scholars," 205.

67. Ochs, "Re-socializing Scholars," 205.

pursuit of peace and understanding may motivate people to participate in SR, they are not *internal* norms of SR as a practice. That is, one need not intend to seek peace in order to participate in SR. Rather, Ochs frames SR as a way of inviting people to share their affection for their scriptures by studying in the rabbinic spirit of study *l'shma*, "for its own sake" or "for God's sake." SR is akin to what Peirce calls Musement, "a lively exercise of one's powers [that] . . . has no rules except this very law of liberty."[68] This is not the spirit in which we actually repair things, though it is the spirit in which we imagine possibilities that might later be useful for reparative purposes.

There is risk involved in studying *l'shma* because of what Scott Appleby calls "the ambivalence of the sacred."[69] The same sacredness and life that rewards *l'shma* study can also be the cause of absolutism and violence when a community feels under threat. Scripture is *powerful*: "Is not my word like fire, says the Lord?" (Jer 23:29). The same fire that warms and gives life can also kill and destroy. Ochs discerns that the impulse to guard the sacredness of scripture, even violently, is often an index of the community's *love* of their sacred scriptures as a primal source of divine life.[70] Rather than unleashing the destroying fire of scriptural passion, SR is a practice of offering a measure of scripture's warmth to others.

Sharing this affection for scripture may have a contagious effect, as the warmth displayed by one participant may tempt another to reveal warmth of her own. The result is often "unexpected friendships across the borders of religious traditions."[71] In this way, interreligious friendship is another possible outcome of SR practice. This in turn often leads to a third kind of outcome: the discovery of new meanings or insights.

> With inhibitions reduced by the friendships, participants often voice cognitive and affective responses that they would not usually share in such settings: responses to words and verse in their "own" scriptures as well as those of the others. The exchange of responses stimulates further responses, resulting . . . in insights and readings they had not previously considered.[72]

The result is not usually generalizations about "what Christians believe" or "the nature of Islam," let alone novel interpretations of a religious tradition as a whole. Rather, SR illuminates something much narrower: "mere words

---

68. *CP* 6.458.

69. Appleby, *Ambivalence of the Sacred*.

70. Ochs, "Possibilities and Limits," 489.

71. Ochs, "Re-socializing Scholars," 207.

72. Ochs, "Re-socializing Scholars," 207.

and verses"[73] of scripture, and the small handful of individual religious people with whom one is studying.

Over time, however, discovering new possibilities within one's own scriptures can effect a subtle cognitive shift in perception.

> Participants will usually affirm the beliefs they came in with. *They will not, however, define their belief as the only legitimate one in their religion.* They may still regard others who do not share their belief as somewhat weak and in need of teaching. But their attitude toward these others will lack the all- or-nothing judgments they may have brought to the SR study: that those who do not share their beliefs represent intolerable threats to their beliefs. We believe this to be the only change that is necessary to transform the conditions for violent disagreement (where A is true, B is false, and there are no other possible options) into conditions for nonviolent disagreement (where A is true and several other options are less true).[74]

Nonviolent disagreement remains real disagreement. To affirm truth by degrees (A is more true than B) is not equivalent to the sort of relativism ("all religions are true," "all religions are equally valid") that in its own way precludes genuine disagreement as much as the binary assumption that the truth of one's own position entails the falsity of everyone else's. Yet the sort of disagreement cultivated in SR is genuinely nonviolent because, as Ochs says, to affirm

> that scripture tolerates, say, two meanings of a crucial verse, and not only one, is already to soften the rage that such participants may feel toward those whose readings differ from theirs. In place of rage, such participants may adopt, for example, a superior and patronizing—but nonviolent—attitude toward these others as errant, but guilty only of a weaker reading of scripture rather than a reading that defies the very truth of things.[75]

The consequences of these discoveries can be paradoxical. On the one hand, SR is friendly to religious tradition and traditionalists. It does not impose a modernist liberal ethos on participants; it bears a family resemblance to traditional scripture study practices; and by not proposing new readings of the tradition *per se*, it seems to leave the traditions more or less untouched. On the other hand, if scripture is to deliver a corrective rule to a community's

---

73. Ochs, "Re-socializing Scholars," 207.
74. Ochs, "Possibilities and Limits," 494.
75. Ochs, "Possibilities and Limits," 496.

common sense in time of crisis, as Ochs hopes, it might take just this form: a new or strange interpretation, available in the scriptures but not consistent with what the community currently takes for granted. Such interpretations offered in a playful spirit need not directly challenge the tradition, but they may, if taken up as hypotheses, lead to change *in the long run*. Thus even when SR is directly practiced for its own sake, it may have an indirect repara- tive function.[76] This is one reason Ochs insists that SR's capacity to repair is "fully displayed only in social networks of Scriptural Reasoning and may be visible in Foundational Scriptural Reasoning only for those who have seen how it works across a whole network."[77]

2. Scripture, Interpretation, and Practice

One context in which the fruits of SR have been displayed is the community of scholars at the University of Virginia called the Scripture, Interpretation, and Practice (SIP) program. This graduate program, founded and directed by Ochs, represents his most concrete attempt to enact the reparative logic of SR institutionally in the modern academy. SIP takes seriously the fact that "scrip- tures are literatures that generate communities of religious practice: practices of study, of interpretation and reflection, of ritual, and of social life."[78]

The SIP program cultivates academic inquiry that does justice to both the common sense and scriptural dimensions of Ochs' pragmatism. It dis- plays its common sensism by inviting graduate students to seek the rational- ity of religious traditions in their embodied communal practices. They tend to approach religious texts primarily as snapshots of an ongoing communal conversation whose full significance only emerges in relation to their effects on the living process from which they are abstracted. SIP enacts scriptural pragmatism by inviting students to ask how the ongoing life of scriptural communities is in some sense generated by their scriptures. Whether they are offering empirical descriptions or normative interventions in a religious community, SIP students tend to understand scripture and its interpretation as integral parts of the scholarly task. Hence the three "pillars" of SIP: scrip- ture, interpretation, and practice. Through disciplines like ethnography and orality theory, they examine the lived *practices* of religious communities that embody their common sense. Through disciplines like hermeneutics,

76. This is a familiar paradox for those within scriptural religions, which often make the blessings of finite life consequent upon the pursuit of God for His own sake, without concern for those blessings. "Seek first the kingdom of God, and all these things will be added to you as well" (Matt 6:33).

77. Ochs, "Re-socializing Scholars," 207.

78. "Comparative Scripture, Interpretation, and Practice."

philosophy of language, and logic, they describe the operative rationality of those communities, especially as it takes the form of *interpretation*. Finally, through modern Biblical and Qur'anic scholarship guided by the example of traditional interpreters, they study *scripture* in its history of interpretation for the sake of its possible reparative potential.

Methodologically the SIP program might be called (to borrow an Ochsian phrase) "doubly dialogic."[79] It is dialogic first in its distinctive interdisciplinarity that attempts to set objectivist (or neutral) and subjectivist (or self-referential) modes of modern scholarship into a fruitful relation. Steven Fraade's rabbinic scholarship may serve as a prototype.[80] In Ochs' account of Fraade's work,

> His method is to find *within [rabbinic] texts* a mode of inquiry that, when reappropriated within the context of modern scholarship, would enable that scholarship to reclaim the dimension of textual meaning it had lost. His method is thus dialogic—in his terms, a "shuttling back and forth" between modern and ancient discourses in order to recover both the overlooked meaning of rabbinic literature *and* the appropriate method for disclosing it. He calls this the method of *commentary* and sets out both to *describe* rabbinic scriptural commentary *and* to *perform* his new variety of modern scholarly commentary.[81]

To understand the ongoing process of text study that transforms the rabbinic student and to which rabbinic texts bear witness, the modern scholar must approach these texts both as a historian examining "how rabbinic redactors integrated various traditions into running commentaries" and at the same time "as if they were its intended students, thereby achieving some understanding of its performative method and force."[82] To apprehend a performance in its performativity requires the scholar to reiterate this performance herself. SIP students tend to approach other texts in a similar way, seeking both to describe from outside and to participate from within the material they study.

SIP is dialogic in a second way as well: SIP students tend to participate in modes of interreligious dialogue analogous to Scriptural Reasoning. As in SR, SIP students are not required to "bracket" their individual religious

79. Ochs, *Return to Scripture*, 27.

80. We have not chosen Fraade at random. His work has had an especially substantial influence on SIP as mediated through one of his students, Elizabeth Shanks Alexander, who also teaches in the SIP program.

81. Ochs, *Return to Scripture*, 24.

82. Ochs, *Return to Scripture*, 26–27.

commitments, but nor do these commitments determine the results of inquiry *a priori*. Instead, students bring with them both the wounds of their communities and the deep common sense and scriptural wisdom from which reparative reasoning in scriptural traditions tends to emerge. The result is often like the playful thinking that takes place in SR, but now situated in the academy where it can be brought to bear with precision to address specific problems.

The SIP program does not signify a general critique of academic methods of inquiry. This kind of critique (a frequent "postmodern" move) would simply repeat the binaristic logic of modernity that needs repair. Conventional academic methods of study are often the appropriate methods to use, particularly with reference to communities whose rules are relatively untroubled. The danger lies in attempting to use these methods beyond their appropriate limits, or worse, with a self-understanding of these disciplines that denies in principle that such limits exist. Modern or postmodern scholars who are animated by deep civilizational crises but trained in academic disciplines sometimes try to use the language and logic of their disciplines to *directly* address the crisis that animates them. Such scholars confuse the clear urgency that animates their quest for repair with the conventional clarity of their academic discipline, and consequently, their language remains determined by a logic of suffering. Discourse capable of repairing deep problems must instead be vague— sufficiently determined by existing conventions to be intelligible, but sufficiently open and indeterminate as to make available a genuinely new possibility. These deepest sources of repair cannot correct everyday life directly, which would reduce them to fallible finite practices. Rather, they must operate indirectly by repairing *philosophical* and *academic* practices, redirecting them to their proper reparative task.

The SIP program is an attempt to train students *both* in the disciplines of the modern academy *and* in methods of pragmatic and scriptural inquiry for repairing academic practices if necessary. Even in times of peace cultivating pragmatic methods is important, if only to keep alive their memory for future occasions of crisis. But SIP students also tend to be animated by a sense that our present moment is one in which deep repairs are urgently needed in modern Jewish, Christian, and Muslim communities.

3. Hearth to Hearth

For Ochs the fruit of wisdom must ultimately be *peace,* the deep correspondence of the habits of individuals and their communities with the broader social and natural world. Years of experience practicing SR persuaded Ochs that shared scriptural study is "the behavior around which we could build a best practice of inter-Abrahamic peace."[83] In the past decade, Ochs has been involved in a number of experimental enterprises aimed at bringing the logic of Scriptural Reasoning to bear more directly on the problem of global interreligious violence.

In doing so, Ochs generalized his concept of scripture into that of a *hearth*, that which is for some tradition its deepest source of holiness. Like fire, the holy is ambivalent: like a flame burning in the hearth it may bring warmth and life, but like an inferno it may also burn and kill. *Hearth to Hearth* refers to modes of interreligious engagement that engage with the holy as a potential source of peace, rather than bracketing it out of fear of its potential for violence. Ochs partnered with the U.S. State Department during the Obama administration to train diplomats to engage with religious ideas and practices as potential sources of solutions to religious violence. He and other members of the Scriptural Reasoning community founded an organization called the Global Covenant of Religions that brings together religious leaders, scholars, and civic organizations who seek to reduce religious violence by drawing on resources within religious traditions themselves. His recently founded Global Initiative on Religion, Politics, and Conflict at the University of Virginia cultivates interdisciplinary research into the causes of and potential solutions to religious violence.[84]

As part of this University of Virginia initiative, under his leadership a team of scholars has begun to develop empirical methods for predicting occurrences of religious violence that can guide the interventions of peacemakers. Religious violence is the kind of "wicked" problem whose uniqueness and complexity make it ill-suited for ordinary methods of analysis.[85] In collaboration with scholars of religion and data scientists, Ochs' team has begun developing methods for predicting religious violence by analyzing changes in a community's linguistic practices. Many scholars have attempted to develop *semantic* tools for predicting religious violence by drawing inferences from the meanings of words. In a method like sentiment analysis, for example, researchers might assign positive or negative values to key words (such as "love" or "kill") and predict the behavior of a group by the frequency with which these words appear.

However, Ochs' team argues that when dealing with wicked problems like religious violence, a *pragmatic* method of analysis that attends to the

83. Ochs, "Possibilities and Limits," 494.

84. "UVA Research Initiative."

85. On wicked problems, see Rittel and Webber, "Dilemmas," 155–69.

various ways words are used is more predictive. In their method of Value Predicate Analysis, researchers identify words that express the predicates of value judgments, such as "love" or "hate." They then count the number of distinct ways core value terms are used within a given community. Rather than asking about the positive or negative *content* of the term, this method determines its *semantic range*, the number of distinct meanings a community assigns to a given value term. The semantic range can then be used to determine the *linguistic flexibility* of a community. Groups for which key value terms tend to have a low semantic range (only one or two meanings) display significant inflexibility. Groups for which key value terms have between three and six meanings display moderate linguistic flexibility. Groups for which key terms have seven or more display extreme linguistic flexibility, where interpretive freedom passes into license and anarchy.

Ochs' team has found that this performative analysis of linguistic flexibility is more predictive of a group's behavior than ordinary semantic analyses.

> Linguistic response to other groups is a measure of how a group's language use adjusts to a group's proximity to other groups of various kinds. Moderate linguistic flexibility corresponds to a group's moderate openness to intergroup communication, within the limits of what is deemed necessary to preserving group identity and purpose.[86]

By contrast, excessive linguistic flexibility or inflexibility signal different kinds of threats to communal life. Excessive flexibility signals the "anarchy of individual choice," auguring societal breakdown. Excessive inflexibility signals resistance to engagement with other groups or forms of engagement that are dangerous or predatory. These kinds of communities are especially prone to violence. Ochs' work suggests that communities with moderate flexibility are especially fruitful partners for peacebuilding efforts. This result holds irrespective of the meaning or valence of their value terms. All other things being equal, a group that frequently uses a "positive" word like "love," but does so in only one way, is more prone to violence than one that frequently uses a "negative" word like "hate" in four or five different ways. When a community's language becomes less flexible—if the number of distinct meanings of value predicates is reduced to one or two—this is a sign that religious violence has become more likely.

It is fitting that our exposition of Ochs' thought culminates here, in his efforts to enact the irenic logic of pragmatism by working for peace and justice. Ours is a historical moment marked by both misological skepticism

86. Ochs et al., "Value Predicate Analysis," 101 (italics original).

and a troubling increase in religious and other forms of violence. Within his lifetime, Ochs' pragmatic vision of rationality as wisdom that brings peace has perhaps never been more needful than it is today.

IV. Essays in This Volume

καὶ ἐδικαιώθη ἡ σοφία ἀπὸ πάντων τῶν τέκνων αὐτῆς.

Wisdom is justified by all her children. (Luke 7:35)

The essays included in this Festschrift are another display of the fruits borne by his thinking, in its capacity to generate thought in his colleagues and students. Most of these authors have been shaped not only by Ochs' writings but by friendship with Ochs himself and by participation in the communities of study and practice that he has spent his life cultivating.

The essays in part one, Logic and Philosophy, pay tribute to Ochs as a teacher of philosophy whose careful accounts of how people think speak directly to the communal needs of Jews and Christians. This section begins with Robert Gibbs' meditation on Ochs' work as a performance of the Mishnaic teaching, "make yourself a teacher, buy yourself a companion. Judge every person in the side of merit" (Pirkei Avot 1.5). Gibbs' reflection illuminates the particular lines of communal relation that emerge from Ochs' account of the sociality of judgment, lines that connect students to teachers, teachers to companions, and companions to moral guides. Each is needed to exercise the perpetual connection between learning and doing, study and practice, knowledge and virtue. Gibbs' essay is a fitting introduction to the whole volume because it identifies a common thread linking each of the essays that follows: the shared appreciation for Ochs as a companion and fellow laborer in the work of practical judgment and, above all, as a teacher who helps them "address [their] most compelling and difficult questions."

In his essay, "The Neglected Argument Against Nominalism," Nicholas Adams explains how his encounter with Ochs' reparative understanding of inquiry dramatically altered his participation in the Christian theological tradition. He learned from Ochs that thinking is at once inquiry, investigation, repair, and discovery. Unlike the razor sharp dismissal and dichotomization of claims characteristic of modern conceptions of "critique," Ochs' scriptural pragmatism taught Adams to identify and wisely discern the difference between claims that speak to urgent communal problems and those that do not. So understood, the work of critique feeds traditions of thought instead of polarizing them.

Like Nicholas Adams, Daniel Weiss also honors Ochs' pragmatic logic. In his essay, "Nonviolence without Conceptualism," Weiss examines how Ochs' work on John Howard Yoder shows that nonviolent conceptual content may nevertheless be *logically* violent. By investigating the relationship between rabbinic texts and an ethics of nonviolence, Weiss appeals to Ochs' pragmatism to caution against a crude and ultimately polemical conceptualism that itself does violence to the reflective possibilities implicit in the practical reason displayed in rabbinic texts.

In his essay, "Ochs, Wisdom, and the Logic of Vagueness," Mark Randall James uses Ochs' logic of vagueness to rebut the charge that Ochs' theological "post-liberalism" collapses into relativism. James shows that vagueness is a mode of indeterminacy whose full meaning depends on the outcome of inquiry, rather than the arbitrary application of communal conventions. Ochs' appreciation for a "logic of vagueness" enables us to understand how, for post-liberal theologians, communal religious claims can be accountable to the world.

Ochs' logic of vagueness not only short-circuits commonly held accusations of post-liberal relativism, however. As Jim Fodor explains in his essay, "Phronesis, Friendship, and SR," it also promotes a conception of inquiry as an exercise in the development of Aristotelian *phronesis* (practical wisdom) and friendship. If, as Fodor maintains, friendship is an outcome of practicing Scriptural Reasoning, it is one that emerges from the logic of vagueness, which requires scriptural reasoners to identify the communal contexts and needs of real persons to generate the judgments that promote their existential, material, and ethical well-being.

The essays in part one demonstrate how Ochs' scriptural pragmatism gives new life to age-old wisdom traditions that challenge modernity's abstract and narrow construal of the relationship between logic and communal ways of living. Doing so not only alters modern conceptions of inquiry, however. It also reconceptualizes the academy, the site within which inquiry transpires. As described above, Ochs has concretized a number of these connections in the development of the Scripture, Interpretation, and Practice program at the University of Virginia. In part two of the volume, Academy and Method, contributors honor the transformative effects of Ochs' reparative reasoning on the theory and practice of the modern Western academy.

Ochs' deep concern with repairing the divide between inquiry and common-sense problem-solving has resonated with many readers. In his essay, "Peter Ochs and the Purpose of Philosophy," Jacob Goodson illuminates the impact of Cartesianism on Ochs' description of the role of the philosopher in the academy. In particular, Goodson focuses on Ochs' writings from 1991–2001 which applaud the Cartesian concern to repair problems in one's received tradition, but also call for a recognition of the context-specific nature of the problems in need of repair and the value of an appeal to the logic and wisdom of scripture as a resource that enables the philosopher to appreciate the limits of her diagnostic and reparative efforts. In Goodson's estimation, Ochs' account not only provides a model for the role of the philosopher as scholar but informs Goodson's own understanding of the role of the philosopher as teacher as well.

If, however, Ochs' work reforms teaching and learning practices in the university classroom, it does so in large measure as a consequence of its intervention into academic methods of inquiry. In their contributions, Emily Filler, Rumee Ahmed, Basit Koshul, Laurie Zoloth, and Rachel Muers attest to the wide-range of scholarly areas affected by Ochs' reflections on academic method. In her essay, "Pragmatic Historiography," Emily Filler reflects upon Ochs' "pragmatic historiography," which recognizes the role that nonstrictly empirical factors play in the development of a thought-system. Contemporary Jewish philosophy in particular has much to gain from pragmatic historiography, as Filler demonstrates by applying it to scholarly accounts of Martin Buber's reading and translation of 1 Sam 15.

Similarly, Rumee Ahmed's essay, "Scriptural Reasoning and Islamic Studies," discusses reparative reasoning's value for resolving the Insider/ Outsider debate within Islamic studies. Ahmed also discusses how Ochs' attention to the context specificity of rules of reasoning has enriched his own scholarly efforts to examine genealogical developments in Islamic law.

In his piece, "Scripturally Inspired, Philosophically Sound: From the Personal to the Academic," Basit Koshul describes Ochs' role in the dramatic shift in his understanding of the work of Max Weber, typically considered the father of secularism. Even more important for Koshul is how in his person and in his teaching, Ochs helped Koshul overcome the binary between academic inquiry and faithful religious practice.

In her essay, "Reading Your Neighbor's Scripture: Peter Ochs and the Creation of Religious Community," Laurie Zoloth honors Ochs' reconceptualization and reconfiguration of the academy as a public space of neighborly conduct, embodied in the practice of Scriptural Reasoning. Scriptural Reasoning, she maintains, instills an ethics of exchange, existential concern, and peacemaking that alters the complacent sense of privilege and privacy often present across academic disciplines and institutions. For Zoloth, Scriptural Reasoning reminds us of the higher social purpose and responsibility scholars have to the public sphere we all inhabit.

Lastly, Rachel Muer's piece, "What Is the Real Problem?" highlights her appreciation for Ochs' reparative reasoning as a guide to a "therapeutic" approach to inquiry. Not only, in her estimation, does Ochs' work allow scholars and teachers to acknowledge points of individual and communal anxiety as justifiable origins for academic reflection and adjudication. It also instills in them a sense of moral responsibility and accountability to respond to these points of suffering as they manifest themselves in processes of knowledge production and acquisition.

Chief among the disciplines most affected by Ochs' work is contemporary theology. In part three, Theology, we include essays that detail the consequences of Ochs' pragmatism for contemporary theological work. The first three essays in this section celebrate Ochs' importance for Jewish theology. In his essay, "Theosemiosis and the Void: Kabbalistic Infinity through a Peircian Lens," Eliot Wolfson identifies similarities between the Kabbalistic account of the emanation of the universe from an original infinite nothing and Peirce's theosemiotic conception of the universe's emergence from pure possibility. The playful and prayerful practice of Musement that, for Peirce, awakens a living belief in God's reality, echoes, for Wolfson, the joyful eroticism with which the kabbalist speaks of the overflow of divine being.

Along similar lines, Steven Kepnes' piece, "Naming God," illustrates the connection between Ochs' semiotics and a negative Jewish theology. For Kepnes, appreciation for God's name as what Ochs calls a "genuine symbol" captures both the "unsayability" of God's nature and the ongoing hermeneutical conversations about God that this name inspires.

In his contribution, "Supersessionism, Zionism and Reparative Theology," Shaul Magid earmarks the positive consequences of Ochs' theological pragmatics for Jewish political theology. Magid argues that Ochs' pragmatism inspires a detailed and situational examination of the practical outcomes of particular forms of Zionist political theology that introduces a much-needed rational standard for evaluating long disputed ideological positions.

In their essays, Mike Higton, Tom Greggs, and Susannah Ticciati pay tribute to the value of Ochs' thought for their own work in Christian theology. In an essay entitled, "Lindbeck, Doctrine, and Reading," Mike Higton discusses the conceptual resemblance between George Lindbeck's postliberalism and Ochs' scriptural pragmatism. Ochs' interpretation of Lindbeck helps clarify Lindbeck's account of reading within and without the Christian tradition.

Tom Greggs' essay, "Never a Liberal to Be 'Post' It: (Re-)learning to Be a Better Evangelical with Peter Ochs," performs an encounter between Ochs' Scriptural Reasoning and the Reformation's doctrine of *sola scriptura*. Interpreted through the lens of his appreciation for Ochs' theological humility, Greggs concludes that *sola scriptura* is not an authorization for the individual to interpret God's Word alone, but rather an ecclesial doctrine that signals the ultimate strangeness of the Word of God and invites individuals to practice communal forms of scriptural reasoning.

Finally, Susannah Ticciati's essay, "Who Is Israel: Ochs, Barth and Romans 9–11" explores the value of Ochs' logic of vagueness for assessing Karl Barth's *Israellehre*. Ticciati explains that Ochs' work shows how Israel forgetfulness is first and foremost a scriptural forgetfulness, which can be remedied through a renewed Christian commitment to engaging with the Hebrew Scriptures. This central Ochsian insight challenges Karl Barth's over-determined account of Israel. Instead, Ticciati calls Christians to recognize the diversity and provisionality of accounts of what it means to identify with the biblical community of Israel.

We cannot imagine a more fitting conclusion to our volume than the tributes to friendship in the essays by Stanley Hauerwas and David Ford. Hauerwas' meditation on theology as humor aptly titled "How to Be Theologically Funny" celebrates the many years of laughter he has shared with Peter. As anyone who has had the privilege of befriending Peter knows, humor is a *lingua franca* that he most joyously uses to communicate across religious, cultural, economic, and ideological differences. If, as Hauerwas insists, theology is and even should be funny, this is because, as Ochs has long realized, knowing God is a fundamentally human task. The slippage between God's perfection and human error is funny, if and when the God before whom we slip is a loving God whose greatest effects appear in our efforts to be holy as he is holy—despite the comedy of errors that inevitably ensues.

In his essay, "Mutual Intensities; Abductive Attraction; God: Thinking with Peter Ochs," David Ford offers an elegant tribute to his nearly three decades of friendship with Peter and their shared connection to the late Daniel Hardy, David Ford's father-in-law and Peter's dear friend. Here Ford recounts the vibrant colored threads of these relationships and their emergence in Scriptural Reasoning, through times of prayer and in the ongoing labor and mystery of the theological imagination.

In our deepest gratitude for what he has taught us, for being our companion and aiding us in cultivating wise judgment, we offer these essays in honor of Peter Ochs and with the laughter and joy we hope to share with him for many years to come.

Bibliography

Adams, Nicholas. *Habermas and Theology*. New York: Cambridge University Press, 2006.

———. "Reparative Reasoning." *Modern Theology* 24, no. 3 (July 2008) 447–57.

Appleby, Scott. *The Ambivalence of the Sacred: Religion, Violence and Reconciliation.* Oxford: Rowan & Littlefield, 2000.

Cohen, Hermann. *Kants Theorie der Erfahrung.* 2nd ed. Berlin: Dümmler, 1885.

———. *Religion of Reason Out of the Sources of Judaism.* 2nd ed. Translated and Introduction by Simon Kaplan. Atlanta: Scholars, 1995.

"Comparative Scripture, Interpretation, and Practice." University of Virginia Department of Religious Studies. https://religiousstudies.as.virginia.edu/compar ative-scripture-interpretation-and-practice.

Dewey, John. *Liberalism and Social Action.* New York: G. B. Putnam's Sons, 1935.

———. *Logic: The Theory of Inquiry.* New York: Henry Holt and Co., 1938.

———. *Reconstruction in Philosophy.* New York: Henry Holt and Co., 1920.

Eco, Umberto. *Semiotics and the Philosophy of Language.* Bloomington: Indiana University Press, 1984.

Halivni, David Weiss. *The Book and the Sword: A Life of Learning in the Shadow of Destruction.* New York: Farrar, Strauss and Giroux, 1996.

———. *Breaking the Tablets: Jewish Theology After the Shoah.* Edited and Introduction by Peter Ochs. Lanham: Rowman & Littlefield, 2007.

———. *Peshat and Derash: Plain and Applied Meaning in Rabbinic Exegesis.* New York: Oxford University Press, 1991.

Higton, Mike, and Rachel Muers. *The Text in Play: Experiments in Reading Scripture.* Eugene, OR: Wipf and Stock, 2012.

James, William. *Pragmatism: A New Name for Some Old Ways of Thinking.* New York: Longmans, Green, and Co., 1907.

Kant, Immanuel. *Prolegomena to Any Future Metaphysics.* In *Theoretical Philosophy after 1781,* edited by Henry Allison and Peter Heath, translated by Gary Hatfield, et al. New York: Cambridge University Press, 2002.

Manetti, Giovanni. *Theories of the Sign in Classical Antiquity.* Translated by Christine Richardson. Bloomington: Indiana University Press, 1993.

Ochs, Peter. *Another Reformation: Postliberal Christianity and the Jews.* Grand Rapids: Baker Academic, 2011.

———. "Behind the Mechitsa: Reflections on the Rules of Textual Reasoning." *Journal of Textual Reasoning* 1, no. 1 (2002). http://jtr.shanti.virginia.edu/behind-the-mechitsa-reflections-on-the-rules-of-textual-reasoning/.

———. "The Bible's Wounded Authority." In *Engaging Biblical Authority: Perspectives on the Bible as Scripture,* edited by William P. Brown, 113–21. Louisville: Westminster John Knox, 2007.

———. "Editor's Introduction." In *Breaking the Tablets: Jewish Theology After the Shoah,* by David Weiss Halivni, edited and introduced by Peter Ochs, xii–xxix. Lanham: Rowman & Littlefield, 2007.

———. "An Introduction to Scriptural Reasoning." *Journal of Renmin University of China* 26, no. 5 (2012) 16–22.

———. "Lecture Handout 4: Language Beyond Language: Scriptural Interpretation as Reparative Reasoning." Academia.edu. https://www.academia.edu/11435054/Lecture_Handout_4_Language_beyond_Language_Scriptural_Interpretation_as_Reparative_Reasoning_Hermann_Cohen_.

———. *Peirce, Pragmatism and the Logic of Scripture.* Cambridge: Cambridge University Press, 1998.

————. "The Possibilities and Limits of Inter-religious Dialogue." In *The Oxford Handbook of Religion, Conflict, and Peacebuilding*, edited by Atalia Omer, R. Scott Appleby, and David Little, 488–515. New York: Oxford University Press, 2015.

————. "Rabbinic Semiotics." *American Journal of Semiotics* 10, no. 1/2 (1993) 35–65.

————. "Rabbinic Text Process Theology." *Journal of Jewish Thought and Philosophy* 1 (1991) 141–77.

————. *Religion without Violence: The Practice and Philosophy of Scriptural Reasoning*. Eugene, OR: Cascade, 2019.

————. "Reparative Reasoning: From Peirce's Pragmatism to Augustine's Scriptural Semiotic." *Modern Theology* 25, no. 2 (April 2009) 187–215.

————. "Re-socializing Scholars of Religious, Theological, and Theo-Philosophical Inquiry." *Modern Theology* 29, no. 4 (October 2013) 210–18.

————, ed. *The Return to Scripture in Christianity and Judaism: Essays in Postcritical Scriptural Interpretation*. Mahwah, NJ: Paulist, 1993.

————. "Scripture and Text." In *The Cambridge History of Jewish Philosophy: The Modern Era*, edited by Martin Kavka, Zachary Braiterman, and David Novak, 191–223. New York: Cambridge University Press, 2012.

————. "Talmudic Scholarship as Textual Reasoning: Halivni's Pragmatic Historiography." In *Textual Reasonings: Jewish Philosophy and Text Study at the End of the Twentieth Century*, edited by Peter Ochs and Nancy Levene, 120–43. Grand Rapids: Eerdmans, 2002.

————. "Torah, Language and Philosophy." *International Journal of Philosophy of Religion* 18, no. 3 (January 1985) 115–22.

————. *Understanding the Rabbinic Mind: Essays on the Hermeneutic of Max Kadushin*. South Florida Studies in the History of Judaism 14. Atlanta: Scholars, 1990.

————. "Wounded Word, Wounded Interpreter." In *Humanity at the Limit: The Impact of the Holocaust Experience on Jews and Christians*, edited by M. Signer, 148–60. Bloomington: Indiana University Press, 2000.

Ochs, Peter, and Nancy Levene, eds. *Textual Reasonings: Jewish Philosophy and Text Study at the End of the Twentieth Century*. Grand Rapids: Eerdmans, 2002.

Ochs, Peter, et al. "Value Predicate Analysis: A Language-Based Tool for Diagnosing Behavioral Tendencies of Religious or Value-Based Groups in Regions of Conflict." *Journal for the Scientific Study of Religion* 58, no. 1 (2019) 93–113.

Pecknold, C. C., and David Ford, eds. *The Promise of Scriptural Reasoning*. Oxford: Blackwell, 2006.

Peirce, Charles. *Collected Papers of Charles Peirce*. Edited by Charles Hartshorne, Paul Weiss, and A. W. Burks. Cambridge: Harvard University Press, 1935–58.

Reid, Thomas. *Essays on the Intellectual Powers of Man*. London: Charles Griffin and Co., 1865.

Rittel, Horst W. J., and Melvin M. Webber. "Dilemmas in a General Theory of Planning." *Policy Sciences* 4, no. 2 (June 1973) 155–69.

Rosenzweig, Franz. "The New Thinking." In *Franz Rosenzweig's "The New Thinking,"* edited and translated by Alan Udoff and Barbara E. Galli, 67–102. Syracuse: Syracuse University Press, 1999.

Saussure, Ferdinand de. *Course in General Linguistics*. Edited by Charles Bally and Albert Sechehaye. Translated by Wade Baskin. New York: Philosophical Library, 1959.

"UVA Research Initiative in Religion, Politics, and Culture." University of Virginia. rpc. virginia.edu.

Part One: **Logic and Philosophy**

1

A Mishnah for Ochs

—Robert Gibbs, University of Toronto

> Joshua ben Perachia and Nittai of Arbel received from them.
>
> Joshua ben Perachia said: Make yourself a teacher. Buy yourself a companion. Judge every person on the side of merit. (Avot I, 5)

THINKING, FOR PETER OCHS, is an intensely personal activity, or perhaps better, interpersonal. While one might assume that the work of thinking, reading, and writing was itself private or solitary, Ochs not only has lived to think with others, but has also practiced and refined and explored and analyzed how one does that activity. I hope others will speak to the pragmatic logic, and others still to the dialogues between traditions, but I wish to focus my reflection on a mishnaic text, for with it as a lens we can first see through it to much of Ochs' thinking, and then with only a modest twist, we can also see the lens itself and the use of that lens as a pragmaticist rabbinic reading, as the activity that Ochs argues he and we need to engage.

Make Yourself a Teacher

Scholars often create heroic figures to guide their work. Kant or Shakespeare or Austen become the hero—that person whose writings, if only read well, will reveal truth to our generation in a way that exceeds contemporary scholarship. The hero has answers to our most pressing questions, he (only occasionally, *she*) can address that question, even if the plain sense of the texts in question seem to add little on the topic. The hero is produced by a strong reading, and the strong reader is the scholar.

Ochs, however, goes through and past this relation, as he engages with others and generates with them a teacher for Ochs, and then also for us. So much of his writing is highly technical, even scholastic, because the careful layered readings of his teachers will yield the teacher that Ochs needs. The careful calibration of presentation and then re-presentation, of layers of reading that emerge directly from the text to be recast by further readings represents to his reader how a teacher is made. But in person, Ochs makes teachers by engaging and sitting and writing and rewriting texts with his teachers. It is not merely the midwifery of seeing something to press, or drawing out a teacher from what was said. Rather, it is a work of creation, of making. To make for yourself a teacher is to find in the teaching of the teacher a teaching for you—and so for Ochs, a teaching about logic and about theology.

We can set out with one of Ochs' earlier teachers: Max Kadushin.[1] Ochs studied with Kadushin at the Jewish Theological Seminary, and was able to transform Kadushin into someone who was not only skilled at reading and thinking with rabbinic texts, but whose own organicism could yield to a rabbinic pragmatism—the method that Ochs would champion through his career. No one else reading or studying Kadushin would have discerned this sort of pragmatism, but it also is important to note that Ochs did not impose or import the features and insights into Kadushin's teaching and writings. Instead, Ochs made him into a teacher for Ochs—still Kadushin, but able to address the most compelling and difficult questions for Ochs. Moreover, as a teacher for Ochs, he could also become a teacher for us in Ochs' writing about Kadushin. Such philosophical and theological hermeneutical virtue is the quality I choose to explore. Not a plain sense of the teacher's statements, but also not an arbitrary eisegesis of subjective views. Ochs' reading of Kadushin is nuanced and explicit: he indicates exactly where he is stretching the text, but it also is not arbitrary.

How do you make a teacher? With an amplifying and explicit reading of the teacher, but based also on true attention to the person and time spent with the person. This attention is even more evident in Ochs' work with David Weiss Halivni. Here years of sitting and learning from his teacher, close dialogue on matters theological and biographical created a new teaching. Halivni is recognized as a great scholar of the Talmud, compiling demanding scholarly readings of manuscripts and traditions of texts that themselves are vague and complex. With Ochs as interlocutor he developed

---

1. Ochs, *Understanding the Rabbinic Mind.*

his theological voice, in both *Revelation Restored*[2] and *Breaking the Tablets*.[3]
The main text in each case is unmistakably Halivni's, bringing a reflection
on Jewish tradition that is uniquely his, but both books also include writings
of introduction by Ochs. Those writings describe how Ochs makes Halivni
into his teacher, and by extension offers to let us make Halivni into our
teacher, either with the same content and style as Ochs does, or even to
make the effort and study and explore the texts in such a way that we can
make for ourselves another Halivni as teacher.

There is, however, no clearer case of this kind of making a teacher than
Ochs' extensive and compelling work on C. S. Peirce. While there are other
Peirce scholars who explore Peirce's philosophy of religion, and others who
engage in technical and rigorous readings of Peirce's writings, there is no
book and no reading that compares to Ochs' *Peirce, Pragmatism and the Logic of Scripture*.[4] It is beyond the scope of this short essay to explain or even to
sketch the shape of that book, and indeed, the contributions it makes to both
Peirce scholarship and contemporary theological reflection. What seems
most important here is that Peirce was not physically present—Ochs could
sit for hours with microfilms of manuscripts and various versions of essays,
but he could not sit in conversation with the living person. Here the illusion
of heroic reading is most tempting—a scholar can make of a great writer
the expert and font of wisdom for all things. But Ochs makes Peirce into his
teacher by layering readings of key texts, by letting the texts yield linked and
various insights, and also showing them to demonstrate the claims about
thinking that Ochs himself is enacting in his reading. When the book arrives
at a Peircean reading of twentieth-century theological reflection, it displays
not "what Peirce would have said," but what the student (Ochs) has made
of the teacher in order to read and to learn from others. Extending Peirce is
done explicitly, and reflectively, in a way consistent with not only what Ochs
has done in reading Peirce's texts, but also consistent with what he claims
about reading on the basis of those texts. In this context I am reminded of
Kierkegaard's Climacus ironically concluding in "The Moral" of *Philosophical Fragments*, "But to go beyond Socrates when one nevertheless says essentially the same as he, only not nearly as well—that, at least, is not Socratic."[5]
The extension of Peirce, and truly throughout Ochs' works, may be Peircean
and not Socratic, it may even be Kierkegaardian, but it also is rabbinic, for
Peirce is made to be a teacher for Ochs, and does indeed teach Ochs not only

2. Halivni, *Revelation Restored*.

3. Halivni, *Breaking the Tablets*.

4. Ochs, *Peirce, Pragmatism*.

5. Kierkegaard, *Philosophical Fragments*, 111.

how to read, how to read Peirce, and how to think, but also how to read and to think and to write about many others.

There is one last case for this essay, and it is much harder to parse. Ochs worked for years with Dan Hardy, and they thought together. In Dan's final months, Ochs accompanied him and together with Deborah Ford and David Ford, daughter and son-in-law of Dan, produced a unique book about Dan and pilgrimage.[6] Ochs helped make the book, and especially Part Two, where he spoke and edited and commented upon a text that is Hardy's. While there are many of us who are Ochs' companions, I hesitate to locate Hardy in our set—for Ochs' relation to Hardy is in many ways more that of student to teacher. Of course, that also means that Ochs makes Hardy into his teacher. The essay, "An Ecclesiology of Pilgrimage" draws on Hardy's own intellectual guide, Coleridge, and while Ochs is clearly engaged, the voice is the teacher's, Hardy. And here, in the latter days of his life, theology is not a mere consolation, but a real vocation and an opportunity to teach how to think.

(One aside seems requisite here. Ochs makes for his teachers sages who are drawn to express their own thinking in extremely difficult, technical idioms. Grasping what they are about, what they are claiming, even how they go about it, is difficult and often daunting. But this scholastic proclivity also is bound to the most important issues for humanity. These texts deal with life and death, with the suffering of innocents, with the struggle with God. Maybe we should not be surprised that addressing the deepest and hardest questions requires a rigor and an attention that embraces the thinking about vague and complex texts. And whether by providence or deliberate choice or the circumstances of proximity, Ochs made for himself teachers who were at home in truly complicated thinking, when simple, clear and distinct thinking would not do.)

Buy Yourself a Companion—

I am one of those companions, and most of the other authors in this volume are also companions. Joshua's insight is that a friend, a study partner, someone to eat with—such a person is acquired, not merely made or found. The contract of study depends on eliciting a commitment from the other person, and producing that commitment requires of us that we be willing to give up something, that we be even more eager and devoted than our companion might be, especially at first. Ochs has cultivated or acquired study partners through his career, and the dialogues that occur are marked

6. Hardy et al., *Wording a Radiance.*

by the work over a text. This is a deeply rabbinic practice of *havruta*. A teacher also teaches a text, and to make for yourself a teacher is to make someone into the one who can teach you how to read the text. But the companion serves a different relation to the text (not utterly separate but still different). The teacher teaches you with a text; the companion is your companion but both serve the text. And the text serves to keep the two companions apart and distinct. The text has the authority; each companion depends on the other to challenge and to struggle and to literally combust in the fire they draw from the text as embers.

Ochs is not the only companion of many of the circles of companions. We had read with others in *havruta*, in bible circles, in reading groups, and so on. His influence here is not to show us something unseen. But his influence was also to struggle with each of us over the texts, and to reopen old and new texts. In his company, we were free to pursue the questions and the tendencies, and even the passions, of our own. The texts set us free, and Ochs requires that of each of us, and indeed, to that end acquired us as partners. There is not a desire for simple consensus or agreement, but rather for performed disagreement, and for a free and full airing of different approaches to texts.

For me, this took root in Talmudic *havruta*, and even produced a joint authored piece on "Gold and Silver."[7] But it also produced the multi-voiced dialogic book *Reasoning After Revelation*, with Steven Kepnes and me.[8] The circles of company went in so many directions, from the dialogues of philosophers and rabbinics scholars that was *Textual Reasoning*, to the intense company with Christian theologians from Cambridge and from the US, to the intense company with Islamic partners that eventually produced the Society for Scriptural Reasoning, as well as extended dialogues with many others. It is not just that little of Ochs' writings would be possible without these companions; but rather, that his thinking itself lives in these various intellectually demanding dialogues. Perhaps the most important irony is that Ochs himself is drawn to a much more solitary reflection or even meditation—but the task of thinking leads him to these partners, to these companions. At every stage and in every place, Ochs sought to found the dialogue of study, the societies, institutions, practices, and also the reflection about this kind of study. And in so many cases, he demanded and then sustained that each companion exercise her own reasoning, experience her own freedom to exchange and debate, to contest and to be burned by the holy texts.

7. Ochs and Gibbs, "Gold and Silver."
8. Kepnes, et al., *Reasoning After Revelation*.

In the generation proceeding ours, the Academy of Jewish Philosophy provided a space for the dispersed scholars of Jewish Philosophy to meet and to debate. Annually and then semi-annually the circle met and grew and explored classic and contemporary Jewish philosophical texts. I can report that they were a group of people in which each was unique, even verging on the idiosyncratic. They always had texts to mind, whether rabbinic or Maimonides or Kant or others. But with Ochs, in our generation, the value of the texts as the place where the partners converged, where the friendship was forged, increased. Scholars, both secular and Jewish, are ever passionate about ideas and their friendships are fragile, often explosive. Ochs helped lead not only Jewish philosophers but many others to recognize that holding the text between us would allow us more freedom and divert the tensions away from the personality of the other person. He found ways to acquire many and diverse companions, and showed many of us that a holy text could sanctify the dialogue of two friends, could, indeed, create the friendship.

Judge Everyone on the Side of Merit

Even the rabbinic commentators could not quite face this text—they would comment by splitting the world into those who are known to be wicked and those who are righteous. Who can judge every human, even the wicked ones, from the side of merit? What would it mean to seek always and for each case to ascribe merit and goodness to the one before you? Like so much rabbinic advice, so much insight, this is not a simple Aristotelian choice to aim for the mean, or even the more basic claim to judge each on their own merits. This is a remedy, a repair of our moral prejudices, calling us to lean hard toward merit, away from blame and suspicion. I feel unable to explore this last piece by engaging in moral weighing—of Ochs, of his influence, nor least of all of myself.

But there is one series of practices that are characteristic of Ochs' thinking that do reflect this maxim indirectly —and we find this in the inter-religious study that he has developed and championed in his work. I am sure that other contributors will address the distinctive contributions Ochs has made to inter-religious dialogue and study. I will not rehearse here the story of the emergence of Scriptural Reasoning, and the 1000 Cities, Debru Emmet, and the Global Covenant. What I can add in the context of Joshua's text is that there is a form of judgement at work in these practices. Not only logical judgement but actually critical or moral or even spiritual judgement—and at its core is to regard other religions from the side of merit. Judgement is not a waiver that ignores failings; and it is not a veil of indifference. But what stands out in the various forms of this inter-religious thinking is the attention to what other people say about their own traditions. To collect people in a room for the discussion, and to stage it neither as reduction to consensus nor as a debating society where the goal is a victory over the other. To judge among equals, and to seek the merit in the others' practices and doctrines—this requires a profound shift in our practices. Much of this activity for Ochs has been to try to connect outside the university, to cultivate these practices and attitudes among the religious communities, and indeed, to recognize it as a global goal. But these efforts are directed, or so I see, to judging and seeking the merits of others. So much of Ochs' inter-religious work is developing the ability to judge, and reflecting on what makes a good judgement of the others' religions. There is the school for this, Scriptural Reasoning, where studying holy texts with companions of other traditions trains us in attending to other traditions of interpretation and learning how each judges, in order to learn to see from the side of merit. And there also is a more public theological work which articulates these judgements for a wider audience. Ochs has led in these various contexts, and has shown us much about the practice of so judging.

Perhaps no mode of thinking is more directly related to Ochs' work than the recourse to a rabbinic text on thinking to explain his thinking. That is, the rabbinic text, the three statements of Joshua ben Perachia, is a vague text, destined to its readers for interpretation. I have not focused on the classic commentators upon it, but instead have shown its flexibility as a lens through which to consider Ochs' thinking. The three activities—*make, acquire, judge*—do offer access to Ochs' practices, and one can easily ascribe influence to these value concepts in Ochs' own method and methodeutics. For me, and for you readers, this capacity of interpretation through a rabbinic text is key to recognizing both the practices Ochs employs, and also the theoretic account of how thinking reiteratively engages for each thinker the thinking of others.

Bibliography

Halivni, David Weiss. *Breaking the Tablets: Jewish Theology after the Shoah*. Edited and introduction by Peter Ochs. Lanham: Rowan & Littlefield, 2007.

———. *Revelation Restored: Divine Write and Critical Responses*. Boulder: Westview, 1997.

Hardy, Dan, et al. *Wording a Radiance: Parting Conversations on God and the Church*. London: SCM, 2010.

Kepnes, Steven, et al. *Reasoning After Revelation: Dialogues in Postmodern Jewish Philosophy*. Boulder: Westview, 1998.

Kierkegaard, Søren. *Philosophical Fragments.* Edited and translated Howard V. Hong and Edna H. Hong. Princeton: Princeton University Press, 1985.

Ochs, Peter. *Peirce, Pragmatism and the Logic of Scripture.* Cambridge: Cambridge University Press, 1998.

———, ed. *Understanding the Rabbinic Mind: Essays on the Hermeneutic of Max Kadushin.* Atlanta: Scholars, 1990.

Ochs, Peter, and Robert Gibbs. "Gold and Silver: Philosophical Talmud." In *Textual Reasonings,* edited by Peter Ochs and Nancy Levene, 90–102. London: SCM, 2002.

2 _____

The Neglected Argument against Nominalism

—NICHOLAS ADAMS, University of Birmingham

IN THE LATE 1990S, when many of my colleagues in Christian theology were exercised by the problem of nominalism, and especially those forms which reproduced the univocity of being, a quite different critique of nominalism appeared on the stage. Peter Ochs' study *Peirce, Pragmatism and the Logic of Scripture* (hereafter *PPLS*) changed the way I think. I do not mean that it added new knowledge to an existing store of knowledge, or that it corrected errant claims, although it certainly did that, too. Rather, it both added a new logic and corrected those logics that were operative for me at the time.

Ochs' study of Peirce is not a quick read. It builds its arguments patiently step by step, with detailed attention to Peirce's texts and even more detailed reconstructions of the implications of their arguments. The crucial observation by Ochs, which hooked me as a reader and which led incrementally to other insights, was this:

> Conceptualism is a name for the doctrine that follows when the realist critique of nominalism is distorted: that is, when realism is defined as a uniform line of argumentation contrary to nominalism, rather than as a means of repairing nominalist errors.[1]

This states in outline what those of us who have learned from Ochs now call "reparative reasoning." Instead of formulating the logic of critique as the one-step replacement of an errant line of reasoning by its opposite (here the

1. Ochs, *PPLS*, 62.

replacement of errant "nominalism" by true "realism"), it advances a two-step operation: first analyze an errant line of reasoning into as many constitutive parts as is relevant to the problem in hand; second attempt repair only of those parts that contribute to the errant reasoning, and leave others intact. In such an approach, "realism" exhibits many tendencies, some valid and others invalid; likewise "nominalism" exhibits valid and invalid tendencies. One does not decide *in toto* to embrace realism or nominalism, conceived as opposing totalities. Rather, one embraces (or perhaps ignores) those valid tendencies in either (or both) and seeks to repair invalid tendencies, in such cases where they cause problems (and thus stimulate what Peirce elsewhere calls "real doubts").

To one who had recently completed a doctorate and was somewhat preoccupied by the effects of univocity in the domains of time-and-space, method, the meaning of terms, metaphysical claims about substance, etc., and who was quite certain that "realism" was the answer, this alternative response was striking. It would be tempting to say with hindsight that the scales fell from my eyes, I saw the light, or whatever. But this was not the case. I, and several colleagues, were worried and intrigued by the possibility that realism and nominalism were not simple opposites, between which one might decide—like a martyr forced to choose whether to kiss the Bible or burn incense at the feet of the emperor's statue. What if they were entangled complexes requiring discernment and repair? Working through this set of puzzles did not happen for me all at once.

This journey into an alternative universe of tendencies rather than positions, and of texts rather than figures, received a significant boost shortly afterwards when discovering R. G. Collingwood's "logic of question and answer." Collingwood insists that to understand a statement requires one to understand the meaning of an utterance *and* to know the question to which that utterance is an answer. An account of "realism" and "nominalism" as totalities must be replaced by an account of realist and nominalist arguments; and those arguments must be understood not as rival positions in a world of warring ontologies, but as answers to particular questions. Realist claims might answer different questions from those answered in nominalist claims. Repairing errant reasonings in nominalism would require specifying what, exactly, was errant (and what not); and such specification would require identifying what questions were being asked. Learning Ochs' logical lessons from Peirce was greatly assisted by engagement with Collingwood's logic of question and answer.

One striking feature of Ochs' narrative was that Peirce himself was on this very journey from "conceptualism" to "pragmatism" and the reader was invited to join this pilgrimage and undergo a similar transformation.

When *PPLS* first came out I remember encouraging Christian theological readers, especially those who might be tempted to lose patience with the book, to skip directly to chapter 8, "Pragmatism Reread: From Common-Sense to the Logic of Scripture." There are perhaps still good reasons, in some circumstances, to take that shortcut. But if the goal is to undertake apprenticeship in the logic of repair, and to learn how to repair errant claims rather than choose between rival totalities (rival systems, for example), then one needs to work through the earlier chapters, including the one in which the short quotation above appears (chapter 3, "Problems in Peirce's Early Critique of Cartesianism").

Another striking feature of this narrative was that Peirce's own journey ended at a certain point, and Ochs pressed its logic forward towards new discoveries which Peirce very likely could not have imagined. This merits some rehearsal and explanation.

While the more theologically significant reasonings are displayed in the final chapter of *PPLS*, the heavy lifting begins—the intellectual engine is developed—much earlier, and especially in the chapter before: "Irremediable Vagueness in Peirce's Pragmaticist Writings." It is worth noticing, in passing, that while the first six chapters of the book (those that offer a plain-sense reading of Peirce's essays) take up about 150 pages, the final two chapters (those that offer a "deeper plain-sense reading" and a "rereading" of pragmatism) take up the same space and more (over 160 pages). The balance, and the attention demanded of the reader, is tilted significantly towards the final two long discussions.

Ochs offers a taxonomy of interpretation that is perhaps unfamiliar to theologians and was certainly unfamiliar to this one. This taxonomy includes "plain-sense reading," "corrective pragmatic reading," "deeper plain-sense reading," and "pragmatic reading." These ways of reading are distinguished by the kinds of reader who might find them persuasive as much as by the qualities they display. Who might accept them is as significant as what they claim.

Plain-sense reading is an interpretation offered in the expectation that a general reader would find it persuasive. It lays out what the text says and what it might plausibly be taken to mean for a general reader. If disputes break out as to whether a particular interpretation is correct, it is to be settled by appeal to the texts.

Corrective pragmatic reading is likewise an interpretation offered in the expectation that a general reader would find it persuasive. It identifies problems in what the text says, and makes corrections that might command the assent of the general reader. Disputes about whether the correction is valid are to be settled by appeal to the texts (if the interpretation is in question) or by appeal to common rules for identifying and repairing arguments (if the identification or the repair of the arguments is in question).

Deeper plain-sense interpretation is offered in the expectation that some readers will find it persuasive, but not others. There is, Ochs argues, "irremediable vagueness" to Peirce's pragmaticist writings (i.e. his later essays). This vagueness cannot be remedied by appeal to the texts: the reader must specify extra conditions, not present in the texts, in order for their arguments to be determinate enough to guide everyday action. The arguments in question are not errant so much as incomplete. Those extra conditions must be supplied from particular traditions of practice, and thus the persuasiveness of the ensuing interpretation will be limited to those who inhabit those traditions. To a vague claim one can ask, "Under what conditions would I assent to this?" If one supplies some conditions, and if under those conditions one would indeed assent, the question still arises, "But would I supply those conditions?" To those who would, the deeper plain-sense reading is persuasive. To those who would not, the reading is unpersuasive or even irrelevant.

Deeper plain-sense readings are offered to some readers, not the general reader. Deeper plain-sense readings require the supply of extra conditions not found in the text. And of course there may be multiple, and indeed mutually incompatible, extra conditions that could be supplied; this means that one deeper plain-sense reading might be persuasive to one set of readers, while another deeper plain-sense reading might be persuasive to a different set of readers. The crucial point is that to the question "under what conditions would I assent to this?" the answer is not, "under all conditions!" Likewise the answer to the question, "but would I supply those conditions?" is not, "you must supply those conditions!" There is a certain contingency and unavoidable local particularity to the provision of extra-textual conditions.

Pragmatic reading extends this operation to progressively smaller and smaller groups of readers. At the opening of the final chapter, "Pragmatism Reread," Ochs describes it this way:

> I have different kinds of claim to offer, and the different claims will speak to different communities and to more or less inclusive communities. So, if I address you now as "dear reader," it is because the way I hope you will read different parts of this chapter depends on who you are.[2]

---

2. Ochs, *PPLS*, 246.

The vagueness of certain arguments requires the addition of the conditions under which one would accept them. Those conditions are not supplied by the arguments themselves, nor by Peirce in his published writings. These arguments include Peirce's remarks about experimentalism, common sense, vagueness (i.e. Peirce's arguments about vagueness are themselves vague), graphs and the neglected argument for the existence of God. Ochs argues, in some detail, that each of these areas of inquiry includes argumentation that is vague, and this requires one to specify conditions under which they would be accepted.

The important quality of "vagueness" in Peirce's arguments is that they are not incorrect or faulty in some way, but rather that they are incomplete. They would be acceptable (to some readers) if one adds to them (e.g. specifying the conditions under which one might affirm them). One does not correct an incomplete argument. One provides what Ochs calls "further definition."[3]

The important quality of "further definition" in Ochs' arguments is that the reader must look to practices of everyday life to supply it. It is not a product of reason, to use an Enlightenment expression, but of particular habits of thinking and acting. To take an example that Ochs does not give, Aquinas' "five-ways" arguments are vague in the relevant sense.[4] They follow a chain of reasoning in a way that is persuasive for some readers (certain kinds of Christians) and not others (certain kinds of atheists). Aquinas is quite explicit that they require "further definition," in Ochs' sense, when he points to particular habits of speaking: "and this is what everyone names God." There is a clear reference here to everyday practices of "naming." There is a confusion in the "five ways," however, in that Aquinas says "everyone" (*omnes*). This could be taken as a universal and necessary claim about what any and every person must say, or it could be a more informal construction: "this is what everyone says; let me spell it out." The text permits both readings and any disagreement about it can be resolved only by agreeing what kind of thinker Aquinas was. And disagreements about what kind of thinker Aquinas was can only be resolved by ... etc. But the main illustrative point stands: to make sense of the reasonings in the "five ways" one needs to make reference to actual everyday practices of speech, of "naming." Without such reference there is no way to connect the chains of reasoning with the theological questions (about God's existence) that stimulate those chains.

Particular habits of thinking and acting may be shared very widely (among "pragmatic readers," a fairly large group in Ochs' account) or shared

3. Ochs, *PPLS*, 252.
4. *ST* I, q.2, a. 3.

by a much narrower constituency ("scriptural pragmatists," i.e. those for whom scriptural texts are authoritative). Practices of reasoning (especially doubting) rest on beliefs that are not called into question ("indubitable beliefs"). But different communities have different indubitable beliefs (the philosopher tries in vain to identify beliefs that no-one could doubt or, if any are discovered, they turn out to be trivial). Practices of reasoning are also guided by implicit rules. Such rules can be made explicit. But different communities have different rules. It is possible, in principle, that one might identify rules that no one could dispute (e.g. the law of noncontradiction), but again such rules would be trivial. (And to digress from Ochs' discussion for a moment, in this particular example, and following Collingwood, the law of noncontradiction can be said to be incomplete. The claims "x is A" and "x is not-A" only exclude each other if the meaning of "A" is identical *and* if the question to which "x is" is the answer is the same for each claim. To insist that the law of noncontradiction is incomplete is by no means to reject it, but it is to have some kind of dispute with its most common forms.)

There are two main points from which one might learn. The first is that any reference to particular habits of thinking and acting, in order to remedy the vagueness of certain claims, restricts the persuasiveness of the ensuing argument to those who share those habits. The second is that any claim that makes reference to particular habits of thinking and acting, and yet insists that any and all readers should find them persuasive, is errant. To diagnose incomplete arguments as errant is also itself errant.

A "logic of repair" can be specified with hindsight from Ochs' engagements with Peirce, and in such a logic two dimensions (among many others) can usefully be distilled. The first is the diagnosis of errant tendencies rather than errant totalities. This is a shift from accepting or rejecting positions to investigating braided arguments for particular errant strands. The second is the diagnosis of incomplete rather than errant arguments. This is a shift from correcting a mistake to supplying the (contingent and extra-argumentative) conditions under which one might assent to an argument.

Equipped with such a logic of repair, we can return to the question of nominalism. Applying Collingwood's logic of question and answer we might briefly wonder what the questions are to which "nominalism" and "realism" are kinds of answer. This has an historical dimension: we might ask what questions Scotus and Luther were asking, to which they gave "nominalist" answers. And, pursuing the method of attending to the logic of question and answer, we might wonder whether these questions were the same in each case, and to be open to the possibility that they might not be. It also has a more contemporary focus: why might young theologians in the early 1990s be exercised by nominalism? What questions were we asking at the time?

With an answer to this, I might be able to account for why Ochs' reparative approach was and remains so appealing.

It is probably best to face the bad news immediately. Nominalism is an equivocal term. That is, it is used to mean different things in different contexts. In addition, and not entirely separable from this observation, the questions whose answers include references to "nominalism" are not uniform either. However, claims about nominalism are typically stimulated by real doubts. The principal doubts relate to liturgical and doctrinal loci. Liturgically, and especially in relation to Eucharist, participatory language (both language about participation and accounts of language as itself participatory) is central to many understandings of divine and human action but certain philosophical positions threaten to render it unavailable or meaningless or both. Doctrinally, and especially in relation to Nicene and Chalcedonian formulations, the "oneness" of the Father's and the Son's substance is undermined; and the "sameness" of Christ's and our human nature is challenged. Nominalism here names the claim that universals (concepts like "substance" or "nature") are extrinsic to objects (beings like Christ and other humans). It also names the claim that objects are "real" but universals are not. Liturgical practices which stress our sharing in Christ's humanity, for example, become questionable if "humanity" is not real, whereas the particulars "Christ" and "us" are real. The connectivity of core theological terms like grace is attenuated if the reality of the connective universals (especially "nature") is denied. Likewise those forms of connective language such as analogy, which lie at the heart of poetic and dramatic forms of speech and whose force derives from universals, lose their claim on us and become mere *façons de parler*. In its most lurid form, nominalists insist we inhabit a universe of particulars, each unconnected to the next, intelligible only because of a univocally understood "being" with no hierarchies or contours.

In Ochs' terms we can readily diagnose rival totalities or competing positions. On one side we have "nominalism" which denies the reality of universals and which thus renders us strangers to God and to each other. On the other side we have "realism" which affirms our participation in divine love, our sharing in Christ's humanity and, through the Eucharist, our sharing in Christ's divinity, and indeed the connectedness of all beings through analogy. Faced with this stark opposition, the case for realism is overwhelming.

The reparative method commended by Ochs, which encourages the diagnosis of particular tendencies and the identification of incomplete arguments, offers some further (and more differentiated) possibilities. In the "either/or" version of rival totalities, one can discern a nominalist braid of various strands: an affirmation only of particular beings, an affirmation of being understood univocally, a denial of universals, a denial of participation, a denial of analogy, a denial of connection, a denial of the reality of Trinitarian unity or the unity of Christ's divinity with the Father's or of Christ's humanity with ours, a denial of liturgical meaningfulness.

To this diagnosis of tendencies (as opposed to the construction of a singular nominalist "position") one can apply the logic of question and answer. An affirmation or a denial is the answer to a question: but what questions are being asked here? At the very least: more than one. To the question, are universals real, one can readily identify a clear nominalist answer: no. To the question, is the unity of Father, Son and Spirit in the Trinity real, it is not at all obvious that the nominalist will answer "no." Indeed if one asks the complex question, can one deny the reality of universals like "substance" but affirm the reality of Christ "being of one substance with the Father," every nominalist theologian (most obviously including Luther) would answer "yes." There is a pressing need for further investigation in the light of such discoveries, including into the univocity of "reality" in the denied and affirmed clauses.

Ochs' logic of repair encourages discussion of this kind. The claim "one can deny the reality of universals like *ousia* but affirm the reality of Christ being of one substance with the Father" is not self-evidently errant. But it is very likely incomplete. One needs to specify the conditions under which one would assent to this denial and affirmation of such realities. This we can readily do. The denial and affirmation can be made consistently if the affirmation of the reality of the unity of substance does not depend on the reality of universals like substance. The contrary also holds. Under what conditions would one refuse this denial and affirmation of such realities? Under the condition that the affirmation of the reality of the unity of substance does indeed depend on the reality of universals like substance. Is a nominalist, simply by virtue of denying the reality of universals, thereby committed to holding a view about the dependence of divine unity on the reality of universals? No. And the same goes *mutatis mutandis* for the realist.

Disagreements between nominalists and realists turn out to be a matter of incomplete rather than errant claims, at least in part. The nominalist claims do not supply the conditions under which they might command assent or refusal. These must be added to them. But the conditions for assent or refusal are not themselves determined by one's nominalism or realism. They are a somewhat contingent matter, perhaps influenced by the styles of worship or church architecture to which one is accustomed.

Ochs diagnoses equivocation in Peirce's own use of "nominalism" in the latter's criticisms of nominalist thinking. Nominalism names two tendencies diagnosed by Peirce which may or may not accompany each other.

The first is a tendency towards overgeneralized doubt. The second is a denial of the reality of universals.

This is interesting for those who wish to understand Peirce because while the second tendency is what is typically meant by nominalism, the first tendency (that of overgeneralized doubt) is by far the more significant philosophical error for Peirce. Ochs persuasively argues that such equivocation obscures important lessons, and for this reason he commends the term "conceptualism" for the tendency towards overgeneralization, while reserving "nominalism" for the denial of the reality of universals.[5]

It is also interesting for those who have an interest in contemporary theology, because the tendency towards overgeneralized doubt (especially towards received doctrines) is by far the more serious problem today than the denial of the reality of universals (the answer to a question which many theologians today do not ask).

Peter Ochs' philosophical method, and in particular the logic of repair, transformed my thinking about nominalism. It did so not by reinforcing or undermining a realist position but by furnishing an intellectual engine in which the contest of totalities was itself called into question. It provided a tool with which to distinguish tendencies as contributing strands in any braided "position" or, to switch metaphors, to resolve the forces whose original effects appeared unidirectional.

It is a powerful piece of diagnostic technology which proved most useful to me when criticizing Jürgen Habermas' arguments about religion and, later on, when interpreting the apparently theological claims of GWF Hegel. Habermas could be characterized as offering incomplete arguments about communicative action. He famously commends a set of rules for nonviolent argumentation, but he fails to specify the conditions under which one would assent to them. In his work on "discourse ethics" he proposes that one must assent to them under all conditions in which everyday argumentation is undertaken: he claims there are "unavoidable presuppositions."[6] In later work, where religious traditions are more explicitly in the frame, he acknowledges the contingency of such affirmation. Habermas argues that religious actors must "translate" their tradition-specific languages into "generally accessible language"[7] or embrace "a public-discursive *appropriation* [*Aneignung*, his emphasis] of the particularistic semantic potentials locked up in particular languages."[8] Habermas offers incomplete arguments about the conditions for

5. Ochs, *PPLS*, 69.

6. Habermas, *Moral Consciousness*, 88–89.

7. Habermas, *Between Naturalism and Religion*, 131.

8. Habermas, *Between Naturalism and Religion*, 249.

argumentation; these must be supplemented by specifying the conditions under which one assents to them; Habermas offers such conditions and in later work suggests that these include "translation" and "appropriation" of religious particularities. It is, however, one of the lessons of Ochs' logic of repair that "pragmatic readings" which supplement incomplete arguments are drawn from and addressed to the contingent everyday practices of particular communities of readers. Habermas, however, offers his self-corrective readings (specifying the conditions for assenting to his formal rules) to the general reader, rather than to particular communities of readers. I did not grasp this fully, and did not articulate it clearly, at the time I was working on Habermas. Nonetheless, this insight drove the final chapter of my critique of Habermas, which discussed the practice of Scriptural Reasoning as an instance of argumentation, but one whose nonviolent rules are operative not because of "translation" or "appropriation" but because members of religious traditions learn each other's languages.[9] This account is unlikely to be plausible to those Ochs calls "the general reader": it anticipates assent will be confined to those who seek the deep reasonings of their traditions in scripture. What this meant for a critique of Habermas was that instead of a contest of totalities (e.g., Habermas versus Lyotard or Habermas versus Derrida) it became more a matter of diagnosing certain tendencies. These were principally matters of overgeneralization or incomplete arguments advanced by Habermas. The corresponding repair was to specify the conditions where overgeneralized claims might command assent, and to limit their application to those conditions, or to complete the arguments by specifying the communities (and their scriptural practices) for which certain habits of argumentation might be authoritative. I later did something similar for Hegel, identifying overgeneralized claims and restricting them to the domains in which they are valid, rather than treating his claims as errant.[10]

Today's younger generation of theologians is, it seems to me, open to logics of repair in a way my generation was perhaps rather slow. The contest of totalities may have been thrilling in the 1990s. In the age of Brexit and Trump its appeal has faded. The work of Peter Ochs has taught many of us how to reason differently. Our reparative reasoning is unthinkable without it.

Bibliography

Adams, Nicholas. *The Eclipse of Grace*. Malden, MA: Wiley-Blackwell, 2013.
———. *Habermas and Theology*. Cambridge: Cambridge University Press, 2006.

9. Adams, *Habermas and Theology*, 234–55, esp. 252.
10. Adams, *Eclipse of Grace*.

Habermas, Jürgen. *Between Naturalism and Religion*. Translated by Ciaran Cronin. Cambridge: Polity, 2008.

———. *Moral Consciousness and Communicative Action*. Translated by C. Lenhardt and S. Weber Nicholsen. Cambridge: Polity, 1990.

Ochs, Peter. *Peirce, Pragmatism and the Logic of Scripture* [*PPLS*]. Cambridge: Cambridge University Press, 1998.

3

Wanted: Nonviolence without Conceptualism

—DANIEL H. WEISS, University of Cambridge

ONE OF THE RECURRING themes of Peter Ochs' work has been the attempt to draw upon resources within existing religious traditions that can contribute to greater communication and understanding between religious traditions, and thus help to ameliorate the violent relations that too-often characterize inter-group dynamics today. His work in Scriptural Reasoning is a case in point, and in theorizing nonviolent forms of thought and communication, he has frequently pointed to the discourse and hermeneutics of classical rabbinic literature as representing an example of the type of nonbinary logic that can serve as an alternative to the violent binaries of much modern thought and philosophy.[1] In my own research, influenced by Ochs, I was likewise drawn to classical rabbinic hermeneutics. Alongside the interpretive stance displayed by those texts, however, I also developed a sense that the classical rabbinic tradition appeared to put forth an ethical-normative stance with regard to violence and bloodshed that stood sharply in contrast to the normal "ways of the nations" as they are manifested today.

In seeking to pursue this latter intuition, Ochs' work was crucial in helping to keep me aware that the attempt to draw an account of nonviolent ethical content out of historical texts—in this case, those of classical rabbinic literature—can itself be marked by a form of logical violence.

---

1. For Ochs' account of the contemporary philosophical and hermeneutic potential to be gained from engagement with classical rabbinic literature, see Ochs, *Peirce, Pragmatism,* esp. 290–316; and Ochs and Levene, *Textual Reasonings,* esp. 2–14.

Thus, for instance, John Howard Yoder had previously put forth an account of rabbinic Judaism that highlighted its anti-violence elements. In commenting on these elements, Yoder identified rabbinic Judaism with a principled "pacifism." From my own studies of rabbinic texts, it seemed to me like Yoder was onto something important, at least in his basic description of the rabbinic ethos and its underlying theological commitments. However, Ochs' writing (as well as conversations) pushed me toward a greater attunement to the dangers of conceptualism lurking in claims like those of Yoder. Ochs writes,

> Part of the postliberal critique of modern thought is that neither the things of the created world nor the messages of God's revealed Scripture are adequately "captured," represented, or defined by humanly constructed claims. "Conceptualism" refers to efforts of individual thinkers to bracket this critique and present their conceptual constructions as though they were reliable representations of God's creating and revealing Word.[2]

In this sense, it is possible for a human being to come up with a fully clear and consistent theory of "how things are" or "how humans ought to act." Indeed, there can be good intellectual warrants for striving—at least as a heuristic exploratory investigation—to construct such clear and consistent accounts. The danger lies in falsely projecting the clarity and consistency of one's constructed account *onto* the starting material that the account seeks to interpret. One may come up with a clear and consistent account of how things are in the created world—but one should be wary of assuming that one's fallible human account necessarily captures the full complexity of the created world. Likewise, after engaging the scriptural text, one may come up with a clear and consistent account of scripture's normative ethical message—but one should be wary of assuming that one's account captures the fullness and complexity of scripture's manifold communication.

Thus, Yoder's Anabaptist hermeneutic reads scripture and draws from it a strikingly clear and distinct normative message of "pacifism": for a Christian, violence is never a legitimate response to any ethical dilemma that one may face in the course of one's life. Ochs does not express explicit concerns about the conceptual "purity" of this stance with regard to the Christian community. His chief concern comes to expression when Yoder seeks also to attribute this clear stance of pacifism to the texts of classical rabbinic Judaism. In response to such attempted attributions, Ochs writes, "Neither true nor false, Yoder's notions of "universalism" and "messianic pacifism"

---

2. Ochs, *Another Reformation*, 159. For discussion of conceptualism in a more strictly philosophical context, see, e.g., Ochs, *Peirce, Pragmatism*, 69.

overgeneralize trends in rabbinic thinking that the rabbis refuse to define in clear and distinct ways. Yoder conceptualizes in a way that is strange to both biblical and rabbinic discourse."[3] Ochs is happy to admit that there are certain trends in rabbinic literature that express an opposition to violence. However, such trends do not represent the sole voice that speaks from the text, as there are simultaneously passages in rabbinic literature that uphold the religious legitimacy of certain acts of violence.

The rabbinic texts generally orient themselves towards interpretation of the Hebrew Bible. Within the laws and narratives of this text, there are elements of institutional violence that appear to have divine approval. The two main categories of such violence that stand out most prominently are war and the death penalty. For Yoder, engagement in these activities, with the bloodshed and killing that they entail, is categorically ruled out by a pacifist stance. Yet, classical rabbinic literature does not put forth a clear and categorical rejection of such activities. On the contrary, it devotes many pages of discussion to the details of how precisely war and the death penalty ought properly to be carried out. In the rabbinic presentation, such institutions of violence thus appear to retain an in-principle legal legitimacy.

For Ochs, accordingly, Yoder is able to attribute his desired pacifist stance to "rabbinic Judaism" only by neglecting key elements of the foundational texts of that tradition. In so doing, Yoder engages in a type of violence: in order to get rabbinic Judaism to fit with his own way of thinking and with his own clear and distinct conceptual construction, he distorts the discourse and content of the actual texts of rabbinic Judaism. This type of logical or procedural violence is, ironically, carried out in the name of an ethical stance of nonviolence. For Ochs, while physical and material violence and bloodshed represent real and pressing ills in the contemporary world, he strongly emphasizes that one should not slip into modes of conceptual or logical violence in one's intellectual attempt to establish relations of nonviolence. Rather, true steps towards nonviolence can be attained only by first disciplining one's inclination to treat one's own clear conceptual construction as fully capturing the reality one is seeking to

3. Ochs, *Another Reformation*, 159–60. See also Ochs' criticism of Yoder's problematic representation of rabbinic Judaism in "Editors' Introduction," 4: "The Rabbinic Judaism that remains the source for contemporary Judaisms is, however, neither anti- nor pro- pacifism and universalism. Contemporary Jewish thinkers should be troubled, in fact, by the conceptual purity of Yoder's 'isms' and by the way this conceptual purity leads him to divide the theological universe radically between what is purely pacifist and universalist and what is not. For theologians of post-Shoah Judaism, Yoder's purisms retain too much of the conceptualism that marked the colonialist philosophies of western civilization, even if they are offered beautifully and virtuously on behalf of God's gracious compassion for human suffering."

engage. By recognizing that reality may often be more "messy" and vague than one's clear constructions, one can gain a better ability to engage with the otherness of that reality in a less violent manner. Thus, in the case of rabbinic Judaism, a less conceptualizing approach would recognize that the rabbinic texts contain both "pro-violence" trends and "anti-violence" trends, and that one cannot draw a fully clear and distinct stance from this with regard to the question of violence.

For my own research, Ochs' critique of Yoder's *logic* represented a clear challenge to my initial sense that Yoder was honing in on something important with regard to the *content* of his account of rabbinic Judaism. If it is true that rabbinic texts contain both "pro-violence" and "anti-violence" tendencies, does that mean that these texts cannot function to present a radical challenge to contemporary violence? Is the only conclusion that one can draw from them something more wishy-washy, such as, "Rabbinic Judaism generally views violence as negative, but it also recognizes that sometimes it is tragically necessary in this ethically complex world of ours"? Or, is it possible that rabbinic texts may yet convey a more "radical" opposition to human violence, but in a manner that does *not* manifest the clear and distinct conceptual purity of Yoder's account? While I retained an intuition that this latter possibility was still plausible, Ochs' convincing criticism of Yoder's conceptualism led me to seek out a mode of thought that would be more in keeping with the dynamics of rabbinic discourse. The goal, ideally, should be to arrive at an account of nonviolence and classical rabbinic literature that does not merely extract or abstract out a "content" from the texts, corresponding to a certain ethical or theopolitical "stance"; rather, the account put forth must seek simultaneously to be attentive to the *form* and *logic* of rabbinic reasoning as displayed in the classical texts. I have described aspects of such an attempted account of rabbinic nonviolence in more detail and with more engagement with specific rabbinic texts elsewhere.[4] Here, I will here limit myself to a more concise version, with a particular focus on highlighting the ways in which my account is shaped by the desire to avoid "nonrabbinic" conceptualism.

One key trend in classical rabbinic literature is the notion that each individual human being, specifically in his or her fleshly and embodied life, instantiates the image of God (*tselem elohim*). This status places sharp restrictions on the legitimacy of causing the death of another human being, which is seen as an annulment of God's image—not merely an ethical failing, but a profoundly grave metaphysical rupture in the universe. By placing the

---

4. See, for example, Weiss, "John Howard Yoder"; Weiss, "Direct Divine Sanction"; and Weiss, "Just Peacemaking."

life of other human beings in a transcendent and "off-limits" status, classical rabbinic literature maintains that one should let oneself be killed rather than causing the death of another human being. In this sense, while remaining alive and preserving life are strong rabbinic values, in that being alive enables the physical carrying-out of God's commandments, it is better to let death occur than to cause the death of an innocent person. If the only way to save one's own life, or that of another person or persons, would be by causing the death of an innocent person, one's tragic duty is to let oneself or the other endangered persons die, rather than causing the death of the innocent person. In this line of thought, the prohibition on causing the death of another appears to approach an absolute and exceptionless norm.

The concept of the *rodef*, one who pursues another with intent to kill or rape, does not create any greater scope for causing the death of innocent persons. The rabbinic texts authorize and even obligate one to prevent the *rodef* from carrying out the criminal act, and even say that if the only way to prevent the *rodef* from killing or raping is to kill the *rodef*, such an act of killing *is* permissible. Yet, if the *rodef* could have been prevented by other means, then killing the *rodef* is impermissible. Thus, we are left with a situation that creates a space for justified killing, but one that remains exceedingly narrow. It is only in the immediate moment when the *rodef* is just about to carry out the criminal act that killing becomes possible, since prior to that moment, there is greater scope for other means of prevention, and thus killing would not be legitimate. Likewise, if stopping the *rodef* would involve causing the death of any innocent bystanders, one must refrain from stopping the *rodef*, since one not is authorized to cause the death of anyone other than a *rodef*. Thus, the only person who can be legitimately killed is the *rodef*, and this only in the moment of last resort. As such, the prohibition of taking human life remains strongly in place.

At this point, it should be noted that if the above trends were the only ones present in classical rabbinic literature, we would have a strong case for arguing for a rabbinic stance of radical nonviolence. Human life (apart from an otherwise-unstoppable *rodef*) belongs strictly to God, and human beings are simply not given the authority to cause death. Due to this restriction, one should be prepared to let oneself or others lose their life, if the only way to preserve such life is by causing the death of another person. Moreover, within this framework, war and the death penalty would appear to be prohibited actions, as both involve causing deaths that cannot be included under the category of the *rodef*. In the case of the death penalty, the criminal has already been subdued and captured, and no longer represents an imminent threat of killing or rape. Thus, the criminal's life is not open to being legitimately taken under the category of *rodef*. Likewise, war—particularly in the rabbinic conception, drawing upon biblical narratives—inevitably involves the death of innocent people, including men, women, and children. Such deaths, too, cannot be justified by the category of *rodef*. Thus, in rendering such forms of killing as illegitimate, the rabbinic framework would represent a profound challenge to the ethos of modern sovereign states, as the latter are predicated on the claim to be able to engage in war, as well as capital punishment. From this perspective, such activities would represent unauthorized judgments for annulment of the transcendent image of God, extending human judgment into areas beyond its proper finite scope.

Yet, it is notable that the rabbinic texts do *not* say "capital punishment is incompatible with God's commands to Israel" or "engagement in war is incompatible with God's commands to Israel." To attribute such claims to rabbinic literature would be to fall back into the error of overgeneralizing conceptualism. Alongside the stream of opposition to bloodshed, the rabbinic texts also contain streams in which state-level institutions of killing appear to be authorized. The biblical text presents descriptions of God's commands to the Israelites to carry out capital punishment and to engage in warfare, thus causing the deaths of individuals outside the rabbinic category of *rodef*. The rabbinic texts themselves, in viewing the biblical text as normative, thus appear to view themselves as obligated to incorporate such institutions into their own account of Israel's normative practices.[5] They view the notion of "image of God" as a biblically-derived normative concept, but they also view the notions of war and capital punishment as biblically-derived normative concepts. Thus, by hermeneutically incorporating the diverse streams of thought present in the biblical texts, their overall framework involves elements of normative nonviolence as well as elements of normative violence. With these categories both present, rabbinic discourse thus does not lend itself to any clear and distinct articulation of absolute nonviolence. There may indeed be a sharp prohibition on taking life in many or most contexts, but the elements of war and the death penalty appear to provide separate frameworks of action in which that sharp prohibition is mitigated, resulting in an overall "messier" or more vague orientation to bloodshed.

However, a closer examination of the rabbinic treatment of war and the death penalty reveals additional key categories that further reconfigure the broader picture. While human beings can in principle legitimately engage in such forms of institutional killing, the rabbinic texts seem to specify that such death-causing actions are legitimate only when explicitly authorized

5. For a related treatment of dynamics wherein classical rabbinic texts uphold biblical laws in principle, while simultaneously move away from enacting them in practice, see Halivni, "Can a Religious Law Be Immoral?"

by divine sanction in the immediate moment. Thus, when the Jerusalem Temple—serving as the locus for God's authorizing presence amongst the community of Israel—is standing, capital punishment can be legitimately carried out. However, if the Temple is destroyed and is not standing, capital punishment cannot be legitimately carried out, as God's authorizing presence is no longer present. Likewise, Israel can engage in warfare only when first authorized by an affirmative oracle of God's approval via the *urim* and *tumim*, or via a direct prophetic command. Without such direct divine approval, by contrast, Israel cannot legitimately engage in warfare. Notably, in addition to war and the death penalty, the institution of animal sacrifice appears to fall in the same basic category. Animal sacrifice is a clear part of the biblical framework of commandments, and the rabbinic texts uphold its full legitimacy and normativity. However, they simultaneously hold that the spilling of animal blood for sacrificial purposes can only take place in the Jerusalem Temple, when it is standing. Apart from that specific context, animal sacrifice is not an authorized action for Israel.

With regard to all three of these practices, rabbinic discourse does not condemn war, capital punishment, or animal sacrifice as inappropriate for Israel or as out of keeping with its normative duties. What it does do, however, is group all of them under the category of "requiring immediate and present divine authorization." While many other commandments can be carried out on the basis of "merely human" judgment, these commandments appear to require an additional level of explicitly-divine authorization. Thus, while these actions remain *conceptually* legitimate, their enactment requires an empirical *judgment* in the moment of decision: do I currently have the necessary divine authorization in my present situation? If the judgment is affirmative, then the action can potentially be carried out. However, if in the moment of decision the judgment is negative, then one must refrain from carrying out the action.

Here, we can see the difference between this approach and the "conceptual purity" characteristic of forms of pacifism like Yoder's. In the case of the latter, the question of "Can I carry out this act of war or capital punishment?" can be answered without needing to make any empirical judgments. The answer will be a clear "no" in *all* cases, based simply on the a priori conception of the illegitimacy of bloodshed, and so there is no need to assess the particular features of the current situation. In the rabbinic framework, by contrast, one cannot answer "yes" or "no" in an a priori fashion. Rather, the answer would be: it depends! In some cases, carrying out the act of war or capital punishment would be legitimate and just, but in other cases, carrying out such an act would represent an illegitimate and unjust form of bloodshed. There is thus no purely conceptual or abstract answer to the question as posed.

At the same time, it is notable that, in the rabbinic framework, the acts of bloodshed entailed in war and capital punishment cannot be justified by any humanly-perceived societal or political desires and concerns. Since annulment of the divine image is involved, only direct divine authorization can enable the actions to pass from illegitimate bloodshed to legitimate bloodshed. In addition, another key axiom of the rabbinic framework is that in the current era, with prophecy and the *urim* and *tumim* normatively held to have ceased, with the Temple destroyed, and with the messiah not yet having come, such divine authorization is *not* presently available. Thus, under these conditions, while the actions remain conceptually legitimate, the necessary empirical judgment will return a negative answer, and so the actions cannot be carried out in practice at present. In this case, with merely-human capacities at Israel's disposal, the forms of killing involved in warfare and capital punishment cannot be legitimately justified, and so a more radical stance of nonviolence, in which human life remains off-limits, appears to be the practical consequence. Again, however, this more "consistent" practical stance still cannot be captured by any abstract conceptual account, as the question of empirical considerations always remains a key element. Accordingly, it seems that this portrayal of the classical rabbinic orientation can succeed in fulfilling Ochs' call to "account for the generality of norms without appealing to the generality of concepts."[6]

The rabbinic approach also points to the possibility of constructing a practical ethical orientation that avoids assigning purity and absoluteness to humanly constructed claims. A conceptually pacifist stance effectively says: "I, as a human knower, am able to judge absolutely and in advance that bloodshed is always wrong." In this manner, by assigning an a priori absoluteness to one's ethical judgment, a person may run the risk of putting human knowledge on par with divine knowledge. By contrast, the rabbinic stance appears to leave room for a greater openness to different ethical possibilities, and to the notion that some actions may, in certain circumstances, be justified even when one is not able to perceive such justification from the perspective of one's current human judgment. Rather than saying, "Bloodshed is always wrong," the rabbinic stance instead says, "On the basis of my merely-human judgment, I cannot presently see a justification for such bloodshed, as it would represent an annulment of the image of God. However, I do not equate what I can currently perceive with absolute truth. I remain conceptually open to the possibility that God can command forms of bloodshed that

6. Ochs, *Another Reformation*, 68.

are not otherwise humanly-justifiable. So, I remain aware of the finitude of my judgment in that regard. Yet, at the same time, I do not perceive any present access to such specifically-divine judgments. I therefore also enact my awareness of my human finitude precisely by refraining from such acts of bloodshed, since to engage in such actions presently would lay claim to divine authorization that I do not currently possess."

In this way, while the pacifist stance refrains from bloodshed on the basis of a *claim* to functionally-divine knowledge and judgment, the rabbinic stance refrains from bloodshed on the basis of a human *lack of* divine knowledge and judgment. The rabbinic approach preserves God's freedom to act in ways not available to mere human beings, rather than insisting that God's commands must conform to the confines of finite human conceptual constructions. There is thus a *double movement* of "awareness of merely-human finitude": an awareness that the divine image of the living human individual properly lies beyond the calculations of finite human social-political judgments, so that the former must remain off-limits to the latter, and an awareness that God's more-than-human ability to authorize judgments over life and death lies beyond any clear and distinct conceptual constructions produced by finite human beings, so that one must consciously refrain from reducing the former to the latter. Only by upholding both movements can one avoid the arrogance of practical-ethical violence *and* the arrogance of logical-conceptual violence.

Moreover, the rabbinic stance not only remains open in theory to bloodshed being legitimately authorized by God, but it also remains open to the authorization of such actions in *any given moment*. That is to say, while up to this point God has not yet sent the messiah, and so such authorization has remained absent, God could conceivably send the messiah at any moment, and so one cannot rule out the possibility of renewed authorization with regard to any future moment. Thus, in response to the question, "Can I legitimately engage in such bloodshed in such-and-such future situation?", the rabbinic stance holds open the possibility that, indeed, such bloodshed might in principle be legitimate at that future point in time. To be sure, the rabbinic stance also holds that the messianic future will be an era of peace, in which war and capital punishment will no longer have an active role, but the point here is that the messianic orientation of a future restoration of divine authorization serves to prevent a *conceptual* closing-off of the question. In this manner, although such bloodshed has remained illegitimate up to this point in time (as the world still remains unredeemed at the present moment of the writing of this essay), the dimension of messianic temporality means that no clear and distinct answer can be given in abstract terms, thus serving as an added bulwark against temptations of conceptualism.

I have attempted to convey the ways in which Peter Ochs' critique of conceptualism, particularly with regard to the ethics of violence in biblical and rabbinic texts, has profoundly influenced the direction of my research. Without the goad of Ochs' critique, my initial intuition of a rabbinic opposition to bloodshed would likely have manifested itself in a much more conceptualist form. The attempt to retain elements of this intuition while also avoiding conceptualism led me to explore the key distinction between human judgment and divine authorization in rabbinic thought, and this latter dimension has in turn pointed the way to new possibilities for further philosophical as well as textual-historical research. While there may potentially be some conceptualist remnants still clinging to this account, it seems to me to hew more closely to biblical and rabbinic discourse and to have highlighted dimensions of rabbinic texts that had previously received a lesser degree of scholarly attention. As such, it hopefully represents at least a few initial steps along the road towards a more robust theological criticism of unjust bloodshed and towards a form of ethical-normative nonviolence without the logical violence of conceptualism.

Bibliography

Halivni, David Weiss. "Can a Religious Law Be Immoral?" In *Perspectives on Jews and Judaism: Essays in Honor of Wolfe Kelman*, edited by Arthur A. Chiel, 165–70. New York: Rabbinical Assembly, 1978.

Ochs, Peter. *Another Reformation: Postliberal Christianity and the Jews*. Grand Rapids: Baker Academic, 2011.

———. "Editors' Introduction." In *The Jewish-Christian Schism Revisited*, by John Howard Yoder, edited by Michael G. Cartwright and Peter Ochs. Grand Rapids: Eerdmans, 2003.

———. *Peirce, Pragmatism and the Logic of Scripture*. Cambridge: Cambridge University Press, 1998.

Ochs, Peter, and Nancy Levene, eds. *Textual Reasonings: Jewish Philosophy and Text Study at the End of the Twentieth Century*. Grand Rapids: Eerdmans, 2002.

Weiss, Daniel H. "Direct Divine Sanction, the Prohibition of Bloodshed, and the Individual as Image of God in Classical Rabbinic Literature." *Journal of the Society of Christian Ethics* 32.2 (2012) 23–38.

———. "John Howard Yoder, Classical Rabbinic Judaism, and the Renunciation of the Sword: A Reappraisal." *Journal of Scriptural Reasoning* 13.2 (November 2014).

———. "Just Peacemaking and Ethical Formation in Classical Rabbinic Literature." *The Conrad Grebel Review* 30.1 (Winter 2012) 76–95.

4

Ochs on Vagueness and Inquiry

—MARK RANDALL JAMES, Independent Scholar

RANDI RASHKOVER HAS SAID that "Peter Ochs' work offers the single most creative and generous recovery of the Jewish wisdom tradition for our time."[1] So it is a great privilege to be able to write about Peter Ochs from the perspective of one of his students, one of so many who have learned wisdom at his feet. My aim in this essay is to explicate a central but often misunderstood aspect of his work: his claim that scriptural pragmatism operates according to a logic of vagueness displayed in the classical sources of the Abrahamic religions. I do so by developing the suggestive link between Ochsian pragmatism and the Biblical wisdom tradition. In the introduction to his *Peirce, Pragmatism and the Logic of Scripture,* Ochs identifies an affinity between Peirce's writings and the wisdom literature in that both are characteristically *vague,* "deferring the activity of completing their definitions to some other occasion."[2] Although the Western tradition has often viewed vagueness as an intellectual vice, Ochs' work shows that by retaining openness to novelty and change, vagueness is the most appropriate mode for certain kinds of discourse, particularly that of one engaged in a process of inquiry. By displaying this connection between vagueness and inquiry, I also show how Ochs' logic of vagueness avoids the sort of relativism with which he and other postliberal theologians are often charged.

1. Rashkover, "Introducing the Work," 439. Similarly, for David Ford, Ochs exemplifies a post-Holocaust wisdom able to critically reimagine Jewish life in the face of devastating catastrophes, one element of which is the sort of "inter-faith wisdom" practiced in Scriptural Reasoning (*Christian Wisdom,* 145–48; 302–3).

2. Ochs, *PPLS,* 9.

Peirce on Vagueness

Peter Ochs argues that modern thinking characteristically neglects the logical function of vagueness by confusing it either with determinate individuality or with generality. Determinacy refers to the character of concrete individuals and context-specific actions. According to Charles Peirce, a subject is *determinate,* "in respect to any character which inheres in it or is . . . predicated of it, as well as in respect to the negative of such character."[3] Peirce then distinguishes vagueness from generality as two distinct species of indeterminacy, offering several related definitions of these terms. In what has been identified as his game-theoretic approach to logic,[4] he defines them in terms of the freedom each affords a person interpreting the meaning of a sign. A sign is *general* "in so far as it extends to the interpreter the privilege of carrying its determination further." He tends to use universally quantified propositions as examples: "Man is mortal," i.e. *all* men are mortal. He comments, "To the question, What man? the reply is that the proposition explicitly leaves it to you to apply its assertion to what man or men you will." By contrast, a sign is *vague* "in so far as it reserves further determination to be made in some other conceivable sign, or at least does not appoint the interpreter as its deputy in this office." He tends to use existentially quantified propositions as examples: "A man whom I could mention seems to be a little conceited," i.e. *some* man is conceited. He comments: "The *suggestion* here is that the man in view is the person addressed; but the utterer does not authorize such an interpretation or *any* other application of what she says. She can still say, if she likes, that she does *not* mean the person addressed."[5] In short, while a general sign affords its interpreter an arbitrary freedom in some domain, a vague sign limits the interpreter's freedom.

These game-theoretic definitions build upon Peirce's pragmatic maxim, his method of eliminating vagueness by determining the practical consequences of a concept. In a later work, he formulates the maxim in this way:

> To ascertain the meaning of an intellectual conception one should consider what practical consequences might result from the truth of that conception—and the sum of these consequences constitute the entire meaning of the conception.[6]

3. *CP* 5.447.

4. Cf. Brock, "Peirce's Anticipation."

5. *CP* 5.447. Presumably singular propositions involving deixis, such as "this is mortal," would exemplify a determinate judgment.

6. *CP* 5.9.

In terms of the pragmatic maxim, a general sign affords the interpreter an arbitrary freedom to further determine its meaning by making clear that some facts and consequences are irrelevant with respect to action, supposing the sign is true. If "man is mortal" is true, then each individual person will die, irrespective of her other characteristics. The truth of this sign leaves its interpreter free to apply the predicate "mortal" to any arbitrary human being. By contrast, a vague sign restricts the interpreter's freedom because even if it is true, a vague sign does not determine the consequences of its truth sufficiently for action in particular circumstances. "A man whom I could mention is conceited"—without further information, one cannot know *which* man the speaker has in view, and so one cannot fully adjust one's actions to the consequences of his being conceited. At most, one might cultivate a certain inquiring openness to the possibility of meeting this conceited man among the speaker's acquaintances, a vague habit of action appropriate to the sign's vagueness.

In the same passage, Peirce offers alternative definitions of generality and vagueness in terms of how their use relates to Aristotle's logical laws of the Excluded Middle (LEM) and of Non-Contradiction (LNC). Modern formal logicians often interpret these as laws governing relations between propositions, and hence as expressible in terms of a first-order propositional logic. On this view, LEM would state that a proposition p or its negation must be true (p ∨ ¬p), and hence that both cannot be false. Similarly, LNC would state that a proposition p and its negation cannot both be true (¬(p ∧ ¬p)). Peirce, by contrast, interprets these laws as governing the relation between predicates and subjects, and hence as requiring a second-order logic of predicates to express. On this view, LEM states that a predicate and its negation cannot both be false of the same subject (in the same respect). Likewise, LNC states that a predicate and its negation cannot both be true of the same subject (in the same respect).

Peirce argues that these laws are not universal logical laws, but rather define the grammar of determinacy. For a subject to be a determinate individual is to have its predicates clearly defined, and so signs identifying a determinate individual are those whose use is subject to both these laws. For example, LEM holds of an individual like *this* camel, since it must be either brown or not brown (in some respect). Similarly, LNC holds of *this* camel, since it cannot both be brown and not brown (in the same respect).

Because general and vague signs do not fully determine their object, however, their use is not fully governed by these laws. General signs are those that do not obey LEM, for a general predicate and its negation may both be *false* of the same subject. While LEM holds with respect to a determinate individual like *this camel*, it does not hold with respect to a general subject like "camel," that is, camels *in general* or *all camels*. After all, it may be false both that all camels are brown and that all camels are not brown, since it is possible that some camels are brown and some are not brown. By contrast, vague signs are those that do not obey LNC, for a predicate and its negation may both be *true* of the same subject. While LNC holds with respect to a determinate individual like *this* camel, it does not hold with respect to a vague subject like *some* camels. After all, it may be true both that *some* camel is brown and that *some* camel is not brown. For this reason, the truth of a vague sign does not in itself preclude contradictory clarifications of its meaning. Vague beliefs, Ochs says, "allow for contradictory propositions among their interpretants, until such time as the beliefs have been made fully determinate."[7]

Vagueness and Wisdom

To make these formal definitions intuitive and to diffuse some of the apparent oddity in denying the universality of LEM and LNC, let us follow up Ochs' suggestion that vagueness operates within the literature of the wisdom tradition, focusing on that prototypical wisdom genre: the proverb. A proverb is a short verbal formulation that expresses some piece of wisdom or counsel in a pithy form. By virtue of its brevity and a certain poetic crafting, a proverb facilitates memorization and ongoing use within the oral discourse of a community whose wisdom it encapsulates. These formal features also remind users that the wording of a proverb alone does not fully determine the wisdom it expresses: proverbs are characteristically *vague*. "A watched pot never boils"—but of course some do. Learning a proverb thus requires developing the wisdom to apply it in appropriate circumstances, circumstances which are not explicitly determined by the vague wording of the proverb.

In an illuminating passage, the biblical book of Proverbs juxtaposes a striking pair of proverbs:

Do not answer a fool according to his folly,

Or you will become like him.

Answer a fool according to his folly,

Or he will be wise in his own eyes. (Prov 26:4–5)

7. Ochs, *PPLS*, 181.

These proverbs violate LNC by giving contradictory advice—answer, and do not answer, a fool according to his folly.[8] Indeed, their juxtaposition in writing makes it all but impossible for a reader to ignore this contradiction, which would have been less overt if or when these proverbs circulated orally.[9] By juxtaposing them, the text not only invites readers to learn a few pieces of wisdom about dealing with fools but also provokes readers to learn about the *way* proverbs operate by coming to understand how both can be true despite their contradictory form. In this way, these proverbs teach a lesson in the logic of vagueness.

We can understand the logic governing their use in relation to two other features of these proverbs. First, since the application of proverbs depends on context-specific factors, the rules of action that they commend are not universal. Instead, they must be logically particular. This means that we may roughly explicate their logical force by adding an existential quantifier. The first proverb means that *some* fools should not be answered according to their folly. The other means that *some* fools should be so answered. Second, the wording of these proverbs does not give us enough information to reliably determine in advance which fools are which. Further wisdom is required to use these proverbs, namely, a wise capacity to make context-specific judgments about particular fools and the consequences of speaking to them.

To see this, consider the alternative: that these proverbs function as general signs determining a universal rule of action in advance. On this reading, we could explicate them by adding a universal quantifier: "answer *every* fool according to his folly." The truth of this sentence would grant the interpreter an arbitrary freedom to answer according to his folly whatever fool she encountered. This requires that the meaning of the predicate "fool" be sufficiently clear for an interpreter to reliably identify these instances. Moreover, on this reading LNC certainly would apply, since one cannot answer every fool according to his folly *and* not answer every fool according to his folly. Interpreted as general signs, these proverbs harden into an irreconcilable opposition, requiring one to choose one or the other. Surely the text juxtaposes these contradictory proverbs to foreclose just this interpretation.

Since Plato and Aristotle, Western philosophers—impressed by the form of geometrical reasoning—have often made the generality and clarity of a deductive system the ideal of scientific discourse. Descartes is an influential prototype of this tendency, attempting to ground all knowledge in truths that

8. The (vague) subject is "a fool" and the contradictory predicates characterize the action appropriate in relation to a fool: "is-to-be-answered-according-to-his-folly" or "is-not-to-be-answered-according-to-his-folly."

9. For a longer treatment of these issues, see the last chapter in my book, *Learning the Language of Scripture.*

appear clear and distinct to the thinking subject. One lure of foundationalist systems is that if only one's foundational premises could be established with certainty, it seems that one could construct a whole system of knowledge on this basis that likewise obtains universally and with certainty. Yet as skeptics ancient and modern have insisted, foundationalist systems over-promise. Their universal premises are never as certain as they claim to be, however rigorously and elegantly constructed the systems erected upon them might otherwise be. Indeed, the clarity and distinctness of foundationalist systems tends to mask the arbitrariness of their initial premises.

Vague propositions and beliefs offer a different sort of impervious-ness to doubt. Precisely because a vague proposition withholds judgment about the results of further inquiry, it is far more difficult to doubt than cor-responding singular or general propositions. Peirce called this "inductive certainty," giving as an example, "the sort of certainty we have that a perfect coin, pitched up often enough, will *sometime* turn up heads."[10] Notice the vagueness of this existentially quantified sentence: while he affirms that a coin will *sometime* turn up heads, he leaves indeterminate the particular occasions with respect to which this truth applies. Peirce's sentence is vague because its truth does not entail of an individual coin on an individual oc-casion that *this* time *this* coin will turn up heads. Rather, making that judg-ment depends on factors specific to the context of interpretation, in this case, the results of an actual coin flip. Yet one can be far more certain that *some* coin will turn up heads than one can be that *this* coin will turn heads (let alone that *every* coin will turn up heads).

Now suppose again that a proverb like "answer a fool according to his folly" were interpreted as a universal judgment: "every fool should be answered according to his folly." Because this judgment is universal, it is also fragile, overturned by a single case. For this universal judgment en-tails the truth of *every* possible singular judgment of the same form—"this fool should be answered according to his folly," and this fool, and so on. Assuming it expresses a general rule, one would need only to find a single fool who should not be answered according to his folly to falsify the prov-erb. (This vulnerability of universal rules to empirical falsification is why those who make universal judgments tend consciously or unconsciously to do so on *a priori* grounds.)

By contrast, if the proverb is interpreted as a vague (particular) judg-ment—"(at least) some fool should be answered according to his folly"—it commits one to very little, merely that "this fool should be answered ac-cording to his folly" will prove true on at least one occasion (or at any rate,

10. *CP* 6.474.

on some unspecified number of occasions). Since an existential judgment is equivalent to the negation of a universal, to falsify it, one would have to demonstrate a negative universal: no individual fool should be answered according to his folly. We all know how hard it is to prove a negative. Precisely because a vague proposition commits itself to less than its corresponding general, it is far more difficult to doubt.[11] "All the veritably indubitable beliefs are *vague*," said Peirce.[12] Proverbs deliver truths with just this sort of indubitability, crystalizing patterns of communal experience in a vague poetic form.

One of the deep insights of what Peirce called "critical common-sensism," as explicated by Ochs, is that while Descartes was not wrong to resolve his doubts by seeking indubitable principles, he sought these principles in the wrong place. While he sought indubitable beliefs in clear philosophical principles, he should rather have sought them in the vague practical principles of common sense. While Descartes' clear and distinct proposition *cogito, ergo sum* has, ironically, proved highly dubitable, a vague rule of action like, "sometimes it is best to answer a fool according to his folly, but sometimes it is not" is much harder to doubt. Yet despite its vagueness, it does have content, for its truth is incompatible with beliefs like "there is no such thing as foolishness" or "all fools should be answered in the same way." Vague beliefs can guide philosophical inquiry, not as a foundational premise from which a system can be deduced, but by holding philosophical claims accountable to everyday beliefs that we cannot help enacting in practice.

For Peirce, the pragmatic maxim itself formulates one such common sense belief, clarified (and thus rendered more dubitable) with reference to the particular problems of modern philosophy. English proverbs like "the proof is in the pudding" formulate this belief with a good deal more vagueness. We already observed that Peirce connects the pragmatic maxim to Jesus' saying, "by their fruits ye shall know them," which saying, in turn, aptly summarizes the pragmatic orientation of the Biblical wisdom tradition and its continuation in rabbinic wisdom texts like *Pirkei Avot*. As a maxim of common sense, the pragmatic maxim is a preliminary teaching that guides inquiry vaguely without determining its use in particular

---

11. In general, this is because universal propositions entail their corresponding individual propositions, and individual propositions entail their corresponding particular (vague) propositions, but not vice versa. If all x are P, then this x is P, and if this x is P, then some x is P; but it may be true that some x is P without it being true that this x is P, and likewise it may be true that this x is P without it being true that all x are P. Since vague sentences are true in more cases, they are less likely to be false, and hence easier to be sure about.

12. *CP* 5.505; cf. Ochs, *PPLS*, 180.

cases, and hence it requires something more to apply rightly, which the Biblical wisdom tradition calls "wisdom."

Vagueness and Inquiry

The meaning of a vague sign like a proverb is not determined by the sign itself, but nor is it simply a function of the decision of the individual or the conventions of her community. Reducing wisdom to either amounts to assigning individual or communal interpreters the arbitrary freedom of determination characteristic of generality rather than vagueness. As vague signs, by contrast, proverbs instead bind their interpreter to something that is neither the proverb *nor* her own decision and conventions—namely, the subject matter of the proverb itself. Acting on these proverbs wisely depends on one's ability to make empirical judgments about the likely consequences of speaking to fools in particular ways. This helps make sense of what Peter Ochs means when he says,

> To say that [a belief] is *vague* is to say that it refers to something particular (thus, that it is not merely nominal and does not allow the interpreter to do with it as he or she pleases) but that it has yet to identify this particular explicitly (and, thus, that it is not determinate and does not preclude further discussion and interpretation).[13]

A proverb refers to something particular—in this case, *fools and the consequences of answering them.* But it does not identify instances of this class explicitly, leaving it instead to readers to determine them. The truth of the proverb does not preclude ongoing discussion about exactly when and how it applies because its full meaning depends on facts about the situation in which it is enacted. But this does not entail that there is no right answer to questions about its meaning. This becomes clearer when the existential stakes involved in interpreting a proverb are higher: hitting upon a wise answer to a fool may be, after all, a matter of life and death. What Ochs means by the "discussion and interpretation" of a vague sign must involve, to a significant extent, *inquiry.*

In this light, we might then say that a vague sign is one that withholds or delays judgment about the results of further inquiry. This helps explain why vagueness has often been viewed with suspicion in the Western philosophical tradition. At best, vagueness is useful as a pedagogical

13. Ochs, *PPLS*, 181.

strategy for provoking inquiry.[14] At worst, vagueness is a fundamental abdication of intellectual responsibility. One thinks of the vagueness of an undergraduate essay that has not thought its idea through to the end; or the vagueness of a political slogan that sounds good only because it leaves unresolved the messy details of policy.

But vagueness is sometimes the most appropriate way of speaking because *the things about which we speak* are themselves vague. "The inherent vagueness of things is the subject matter of Peirce's pragmatism and his semiotics," Ochs says.[15] What does it mean that things are vague? The idea, I think, is that the determinate character of real things is not given all at once, but rather emerges over time and through relational processes. This is a metaphysical claim, which means that for Ochs, it cannot be established by *a priori* reasoning, but only by extrapolating abductively about the ultimate practical results of inquiry. Peirce and Ochs are realists in the sense that they posit no thing in itself lurking behind the results of inquiry. If in the long run the best possible predictive theory in some domain involves vagueness, then the object of inquiry is *really* vague. This sort of vagueness is a feature of the probabilistic models of phenomena that contemporary scientists use in a wide range of domains. Peirce pointed to the productive randomness that drives the evolution of species and the probabilistic laws governing the behavior of gasses. To this we might add the indeterminacy of quantum particles, the behavior of chaotic systems like the weather, or the dynamics of social groups. Probabilistic models are vague because they identify a pattern of events without fully determining the outcomes of individual experiments in advance, just as a proverb encapsulates a pattern of experience without fully determining action on any particular occasion.

To the extent that vagueness is a real feature of the universe, the most adequate habit of action in the world—what the Bible calls "wisdom"— cannot take the form of fixed general rules. The clarity that such rules introduce is premature. Acting in relation to vague things according to universal rules amounts to judging precipitously events that can be anticipated only probabilistically but not known determinately in advance. The most adequate forms of knowledge therefore cannot be merely icons or diagrams, but must be dynamic habits of action that include the capacity for

14. Some ancient readers of Plato distinguished between "dogmatic" dialogues, which teach their content clearly and directly, and "zetetic" dialogues, which teach indirectly to provoke inquiry (see, e.g. Diogenes Laertius, *Lives of Eminent Philosophers,* 3.49; Albinus, *Eisagoge,* chapter 3). Peter Ochs frequently embraces zetetic pedagogical strategies, sometimes setting up whole classes as experiments.

15. Ochs, "Continuity as Vagueness," 247.

responding and adjusting to the conditions in which action is demanded.[16] Habits and practices—unlike icons and general rules—unfold in time, in which they can wait for events, be interrupted by them, and importantly, change in response. Inquiry and the capacity for correction are *internal* to the meaning of those vague habits that, Ochs argues, are the most adequate form of knowledge to which we can attain.

Relativism

That inquiry is internal to our vague concepts can also help us understand what Ochs calls the "relativity but nonrelativism" of Christian and Jewish postliberalism.[17] Like other postliberals, Ochs has sometimes been interpreted as a kind of relativist. "Relativism" is itself a vague term. I use it here to refer to a family of reasoning practices implicit in phenomena as various as, say, my undergraduates' easygoing indifference towards questions of religious truth; the common assumption that argument about truth across religious boundaries is in principle fruitless; or the academic tendency to treat arguments about religious truth as reducible to aesthetic, political, or cultural questions. I assume that these practices display a common assumption, namely, that there is no nonarbitrary way for members of different religious traditions to adjudicate questions about truth. It is this belief that, in this context, I call "relativism."

From the outset it must be said that many features of Ochs' work are *prima facie* incompatible with the charge of relativism. There is the central place of Charles Peirce in his work, a hard-headed scientist whose central teaching was that concepts in general should be clarified the way scientists clarify their concepts. In his Scripture, Interpretation, and Practice program at the University of Virginia, Ochs has cultivated an environment that involves students from different religious traditions who have a lot of arguments with one another across traditional boundaries. Even Scriptural Reasoning invites people from different religious traditions not so much to share their equally valid interpretations as to offer readings *subject to criticism* from members of other traditions. Ochs insists on using those stern words "logic" and "reasoning," which imply that thinking is not arbitrary and may need to be corrected.

16. This is one reason that Ochs says things like "the ultimate interpretant of all our representations of the world [is] our habits of conduct in the world" (*PPLS*, 189).

17. Ochs, *Another Reformation*, 253. See David Lamberth's worry about Ochs' "restriction to particularity" ("Assessing Peter Ochs," 464–65) and Gary Slater's question whether Ochs "can allow for mediation between different faith traditions" (*Peirce*, 128–31).

The preceding discussion of vagueness, however, helps make intelligible how Ochs avoids relativism. The relativist's belief that certain claims are arbitrary is a probable indication that, for the relativist, those claims operate within a logic of generality rather than vagueness. We saw that a general sign determines some aspect of a predicate while leaving an arbitrary freedom to the interpreter to complete its determination. Modernist universalism applies this logic to religion by determining predicates of religion in general— universal truth claims, ethical principles, experiences—while leaving each historically-specific tradition an arbitrary freedom to further determine these predicates in their own way. So long as these particulars are consistent with the general predicate "religion," they are logically a matter of indifference. More extreme forms of relativism simply reduce to zero the universal content of religion, leaving only the particular definitions of a tradition, sub-tradition, or individual, each indifferent or "equally valid." Relativistic arbitrariness is the logical remainder of modernist universalism.

A vague sign, by contrast, does not afford an arbitrary freedom to an interpreter or even to a community. Rather, it restricts their freedom by referring to some partially determined real individual that conditions further determination of the vague sign. In assenting to the truth of a vague sign, one delays judgment in such a way that further inquiry is necessary for determinate action. Vagueness bears upon religious difference not least because, as we have seen, vague signs do not obey LNC. In Ochs' work, Christian supersessionism—the view that the church replaces Israel—exemplifies the problem, since this view assumes that God's ongoing faithfulness to Israel contradicts his faithfulness to the church. But terms like "Israel" and "the church" are vague, and their vagueness is a function of the vagueness of their objects, real communities whose determinate identities are still unfolding in time, in relation to the potential novelty of historical events and even divine action. To deny the real vagueness of these things, to forego waiting and inquiry by attempting to determine their full identity in advance, is to judge precipitously and therefore to risk believing something false because one believes more than one has reason to believe. In the language of the wisdom tradition, we might call this a kind of foolishness.

But to place claims about Israel and the church within a logic of vagueness does not require treating the truth about them as arbitrary or as matters of indifference. Communities acting in the spirit of Ochsian pragmatism and the wisdom tradition may be relatively confident when applying their wisdom locally, while being tentative when making judgments in relation to other contexts. But this is not the same as the relativistic claim that no argument or judgment is possible beyond the bounds of one's context or tradition. Ochs' *Another Reformation* is itself a philosophical intervention in Christian theology. Nor does it mean that all existing religious traditions will prove their fruitfulness in the long run. Indeed, running through Ochs' work is an awareness of the terrible possibility that, as he puts it in his Peirce book, some entire world of common sense might be called into question;[18] or in his Cambridge lectures, that the conventions of community, its living wisdom, might *die*. In the scriptures, this possibility requires the wisdom of the sages to give way to the wisdom of prophets, who speak of a divine source of healing that can raise the wisdom of a community from the dead, as Israel was raised from the valley of dry bones (Ezek 37). Although there is some continuity—in the individuals who survive, in the wisdom and practices they retained—this kind of resurrection can involve radical and unexpected change. How different the religion of the Talmud is from ancient Israelite religion! Ochs does not teach that every religious tradition is equally valid or equally vital. Instead, Ochs recognizes that the vagueness of a community's wisdom—especially its deep common sense and, for the Abrahamic traditions, the scriptures to which they turn especially in times of crisis—is a necessary condition for a community to adapt and to be resurrected—and thus to go on living and bearing fruit.

Bibliography

Brock, Jarrett. "Peirce's Anticipation of Game Theoretic Logic and Semantics." *Semiotics* (1980) 55–64.

Ford, David. *Christian Wisdom: Desiring God and Learning in Love.* Cambridge: Cambridge University Press, 2007.

Hilpinen, Risto. "On C. S. Peirce's Theory of the Proposition: Peirce as a Precursor of Game Theoretical Semantics." *The Monist* 65.2 (April 1982)182–88.

James, Mark Randall. *Learning the Language of Scripture: Origen, Wisdom, and Interpretation.* Brill, forthcoming.

Lamberth, David C. "Assessing Peter Ochs through *Peirce, Pragmatism and the Logic of Scripture*." *Modern Theology* 24.3 (2008) 459–67.

Ochs, Peter. *Another Reformation: Postliberal Christianity and the Jews.* Grand Rapids: Baker Academic, 2011.

———. "Continuity as Vagueness: The Mathematical Antecedents of Peirce's Semiotics." *Semiotica* 96.3/4 (1993) 231–55.

———. *Peirce, Pragmatism and the Logic of Scripture* [*PPLS*]. Cambridge: Cambridge University Press, 1998.

Rashkover, Randi. "Introducing the Work of Peter Ochs." *Modern Theology* 24.3 (July 2008) 439–45.

Slater, Gary. *C. S. Peirce and the Nested Continua Model of Religious Interpretation.* Oxford: Oxford University Press, 2015.

18. Ochs, *PPLS*, 319.

5

Phronesis, Friendship, and Scriptural Reasoning

—JIM FODOR, St. Bonaventure University

IN HIS TRIBUTE TO the work of David Ford, Peter Ochs speaks of their long-standing friendship: "David Ford has been my theological and theo-social dialogue partner for twenty years. Over a lifetime, I have enjoyed just a very few such partnerships, and in each I have experienced what Aristotle says of friendship—that we seek in the other what raises us up in ourselves."[1] Indeed, Ochs elaborates on how friendship, in a context of inter-Abrahamic study called Scriptural Reasoning, comes front and center for those participating in the "hospitality of the Word":

> In SR ["Scriptural Reasoning"], folks from different houses of worship gather round a few verses of sacred poetry (scripture) and share their astonishments or wonder or concepts or concerns that this word and that have arisen from some depths (or have not). After much conversation, the sharing of words often takes on the movement of a kind of reasoning that involves affect as well as cognition, that represents no one participant but somehow most or all, that opens wounds that open hearts, and that often takes on an energy and force and direction we call 'reparative.' In the process, more often than one would imagine, deep friendships are formed, across the table and across religious divides . . .[2]

1. Ochs, "What Kinds of Thinking?," 193.
2. Ochs, "Focus on Scriptural Reasoning," 143–44.

Other practitioners of Scriptural Reasoning have similarly commented on friendship's importance. Nicholas Adams, for instance, maintains that friendship is the "true ground" of Scriptural Reasoning. He contends that in contexts where the Abrahamic scriptures are read and interpreted together in small groups of Jews, Christians and Muslims, whenever one of the participants acknowledges the authority of the other tradition *for the other*, this is given as a gesture of friendship, not as "'rational assent' or an intellectual position vis-à-vis that tradition."[3] What makes Scriptural Reasoning "work" is not so much a formal set of rules of engagement agreed upon in advance by the participants, but friendship. Apart from a shared desire to study together scriptural texts, no other expectations are required—least of all the expectation that a final agreement can or must be reached or even that common ground can or must be identified. Adams captures this succinctly: "the most striking thing about the context of Scriptural Reasoning is not consensus but friendship."[4] Mike Higton appropriates the phrase "not consensus but friendship" as something of a defining motto for Scriptural Reasoning.[5] David Ford turns the phrase into a maxim: "*Let conversations around scripture be open to all people, religions, cultures, arts, disciplines, media and spheres of life. Let us read for the sake of friendship with all!*"[6]

This chorus of praise for friendship among scriptural reasoners warrants further examination. Parsing out a bit more carefully what exactly interreligious friendships of the sort nurtured by Scriptural Reasoning might entail will, I believe, take us some way toward appreciating more fully the contributions that Peter Ochs has made to Scriptural Reasoning as a leading scholar of Charles Sanders Peirce. I intend to highlight the ways in which Ochs' Peircean-inspired model of reparative, pragmatic reading reveals an important correlation between, on the one hand, a type of rationality Aristotle characterizes as *phronesis* (practical judgment or wisdom) and, on the other, the kind of abstractive Peircean logic of vagueness that Ochs offers as

3. Adams, *Habermas and Theology*, 243, 248. Adams not only offers insightful analysis and commentary on friendship's centrality to Scriptural Reasoning, he himself displays these very gestures of friendship in his response to Basit Koshul's and Steven Kepnes' readings of select passages from Surah 2 and Gen 16, 21, and 25 in Adams, "Beyond the Logics."

4. Adams, *Habermas and Theology*, 243.

5. Higton, "Editorial," 131 n. 3.

6. Ford, *Christian Wisdom*, 87. In a book-length study, *Uncommon Friendships*, William Young holds up to scrutiny the centrality of friendship to interreligious engagements, including practices like Scriptural Reasoning. Young examines friendship between important religious thinkers from different religious traditions: Franz Rosenzweig and Eugen Rosenstock-Huessy; Emmanuel Levinas and Maurice Blanchot; and Julia Kristeva and Catherine Clément.

a distinctive feature of Scriptural Reasoning. I have in mind especially the last chapter of Ochs' *Peirce, Pragmatism and the Logic of Scripture* where he addresses scriptural pragmatists and their concern to follow a scriptural rule of compassion. Compassion is best exemplified in the person of "the attentive reader" whose imagination has been shaped and transformed within a community of reader-disciples (*qua* friends). Scripture texts function as vague symbols that acquire clarity—i.e., display appropriate, context-sensitive meanings—only in their performative interpretations. Insofar as the scriptural rule of compassion/love ultimately teaches by way of its own performance, attentive readers are able to discern wisely a fitting interpretation of these texts that best speaks to the urgent cries of this world, here, at this time, and with respect to this particular group of people. Drawing on Peirce, Ochs' language of pragmatic discernment is redolent of Aristotle's *phronimos*, the wise person whose judgment "reflects what is beneficial, about the right thing, in the right way and at the right time."[7]

Peter Ochs' signature work, *Peirce, Pragmatism and the Logic of Scripture*, is dense and difficult. Part of what makes it so challenging is that it has diverse aims, it operates on several different levels, and it is written for various audiences. It offers, first, a genealogy of the developmental evolution of Peirce's philosophy;[8] second, it offers Ochs' own "way of pragmatically and thus correctively studying [Peirce's] performance";[9] and third, it aims to show how a pragmatic model of reparative reading has ramifications for several distinct communities of readers: "pragmatic readers," "commonsense pragmatists," "pragmatic logicians," "theosemioticians" and "scriptural pragmatists" of either a Christian or rabbinic variety.[10] Ochs' work is challenging because his thesis is itself a corrective reading, a pragmatic performance of the sort which does not so much admit of objective description as invite a self-involving performance of an appropriate reparative reading. The reparative reading need not be of Peirce, but, following Ochs' lead, of whatever specific philosophical and practical problems insinuate or impose themselves upon the everyday communal life of the reader.[11] In performing

---

7. Aristotle, NE1142b25–30.

8. Ochs reads "Peirce's writings on pragmatism as his corrective performance of pragmatism." Ochs, *Peirce, Pragmatism and the Logic of Scripture* (hereafter cited as *PPLS*), 5.

9. Ochs, *PPLS*, 5.

10. Ochs, *PPLS*, 246–47.

11. Because "reading cannot be done 'in general,' or 'for anyone,' but only for someone: for some community of readers," this means that "pragmatism can show itself to another thinker only in the way that thinker acquires the practice of corrective reading" (Ochs, *PPLS*, 5).

his own corrective reading of Peirce, Ochs offers several insights germane to the task at hand, which is to outline a fruitful analogy between Ochs' reparative pragmatic model of reading and Aristotle's understanding of *phronesis* as the defining moral and intellectual virtue of a life lived in the pursuit of the good, and ultimately the source of all goodness, God.

Ochs identifies a leading tendency of Peirce's philosophical maturation that moves him away from preoccupations with foundational system building to concerns about pragmatic intervention and healing—namely, a proclivity to deploy logical rigor compassionately in the service of repairing, or at least responding to, various kinds of intellectual suffering that afflicts modern philosophy.[12] Ochs discerns an overall progressive development, culminating in Peirce's post-1905 writings. In his latter philosophical writings Peirce kept running up against "a persistent vagueness" that called for another kind of clarification.[13] This provoked Peirce, in his shift from pragmatism to pragmaticism, to begin developing a logic of vagueness (a system of sign relations expressed in terms of a predicate calculus or set of existential graphs) that, in Ochs' judgment, bears a striking resemblance to the rabbinic model of interpretation. Indeed, placing Peirce's system of sign relations side by side with the ancient wisdom tradition of rabbinic Judaism throws important light on the present potential of Peirce's pragmaticism, especially for those who see themselves as scriptural pragmatists. Both Peirce's pragmaticism and the ancient wisdom traditions confront a similar challenge: how to interpret persistent or inveterately vague symbols. By continuously referring vague symbols back to their contexts of interpretation, these respective traditions of inquiry and discernment highlight the "irrevocable contextuality" of rational judgment.[14] Using a rabbinic analogue as a guide, Ochs advances a novel, highly generative way of searching after a pragmatic interpretation of Peirce's writings that not only does justice to Peirce's pragmatic tendencies but extends them accordingly to different communities of readers. There are, of course, similarities and differences between Peirce's pragmaticism and the rabbinic model of interpretation; each has strengths and weaknesses.

According to Talmudic and medieval Jewish exegetical practice, the "plain sense" reading of a text (*peshat*) is its meaning within a corpus of received texts deemed authoritative by a particular community. It is the meaning of the text that has been "passed down to us," at once familiar and normative. Although distinguishable from one another, the "plain sense"

12. Ochs, *PPLS*, 13.
13. Ochs, *PPLS*, 9.
14. Ochs, *PPLS*, 4.

reading of the text and the "interpreted sense" (*derash*) are nonetheless organically related, and thus inseparable. One cannot arrive at an "interpreted sense" reading of the text apart from the "plain sense" reading precisely because "the *derash* is itself performed within the grammatical, philological and semantic rules of the *peshat*."[15] For the rabbis it is not a question of *whether* to move from the "plain sense" to the "interpreted sense" but *when*. The rule indicating when to move to the *derash* is straightforward enough: whenever the text becomes disrupted, troubled or "burdensome." Signs of textual encumbrance are as manifold as they are recurrent, varying in form, scale, depth, centrality, and intensity. They range from, on the one end, noticing "some apparent contradiction (*stira*) or textual difficulty (*kashia*),"[16] perhaps in the regular rhythms of Torah study or daily prayers, to, on the other end, something as profoundly disorienting as reciting prayerfully a familiar scripture as a prisoner in exile. Furthermore, "because the plain sense in question is the plain sense of Scripture (Torah) as God's revealed word, the rabbis assume that the textual burden is merely apparent and that the nonburdensome meaning of a given passage will be disclosed through further 'searching out' (*derasha:* 'interpreted meaning,' or the result of 'searching out')." The Scripture, in other words, is marked by a superabundant plenitude of meaning because it is God's revealed word. As such, the "nonevident meaning of a burdensome passage" cannot in principle ever be discerned fully all at once but is "disclosed only through the indefinite give-and-take of past, present and future readings. Otherwise put, a particular interpretive meaning for a particular passage could be identified only for a particular reader in a particular context. New contexts of interpretation would disclose new aspects of meaning."[17]

In this light, facing the task of interpreting Scripture's inexhaustible riches generates not so much a sense of frustration and futility as it does feelings of joy and hope in the promise of what further goods might flow from the immense resourcefulness and abundant goodness of God's word. Ochs recasts this theological truth into a formal philosophical principle: interpretation is unending because Scripture consists of inveterately vague

15. Ochs, *PPLS*, 6. See also Halivni, *Peshat & Derash*, 82, who, in discussing Maimonides, remarks: "where the Rashbam quotes the dictum *ein mikra yotze middei peshuto* . . . he understood it to mean—and he is not alone in this—'No text should be deprived of being interpreted according to *peshat.*' Even when the *peshat* is not followed practically, one still has to study the text according to *peshat*. The theoretical value of *peshat* ought never to be ignored." For a more extensive discussion of the *peshat/derash* distinction, see Ochs, "Scripture and Text," 199–205.

16. Ochs, *PPLS*, 6.

17. Ochs, *PPLS*, 6.

symbols whose meanings remain indeterminate until further defined with respect to particular problematic contexts of interpretation. Interpreting these vague symbols is fruitful to the extent that it speaks to the concrete, immediate needs of the community to whom is offered in healing response to its needs. It is Ochs' contention that Peirce's pragmaticist writings—along with the rabbinic method of interpretation and other literatures of the great wisdom traditions—"defer the activity of completing their definitions or meanings to some other occasion: prototypically, this means the occasion of some community's reading them for some particular purpose."[18]

The pragmatic character of Ochs' reparative model of reading developed in *Peirce, Pragmatism and the Logic of Scripture* can be profitably compared to another "great wisdom" tradition alluded to but not explicitly named by Ochs: Aristotle's practical philosophy. The way that Ochs retrieves from his own rabbinic ancestry a hermeneutical rule about moving to *derash* whenever the plain sense reading (*peshat*) becomes problematic, which then becomes transposed into his corrective method for rereading Peirce's pragmatism, evinces several strong affinities with Aristotle's characterization of the good life as one guided by *phronesis* or practical wisdom. The kind of pragmatic thinking or method of reading/reasoning Ochs sees displayed in Peirce's pragmatism accords with the sort of ethical-political intelligence or rationality Aristotle describes as *phronesis*. *Phronesis* is for Aristotle a key concept signifying the excellence of practical judgment or wisdom characteristic of all well-formed, virtuous communities. This practical wisdom, moreover, shows itself in many ways, perhaps measured most reliably in the quality of friendships found among its adherents.

The aim of Aristotle's practical philosophy (ethics and politics) is to develop and improve individuals and communities together by cultivating excellences (virtues) in both. Apart from these virtues, the good life—a life of human flourishing (*eudaimonia*)—cannot be realized. A life lived in the pursuit of the good, then, is one lived in accordance with virtue. The acquisition and exercise of virtue, however, cannot be reduced to a matter of merely learning moral rules and following them, but rather entails a process of cultivating excellence in character, from which ensues fine and noble actions. Even for those of mature moral character, who have attained a settled disposition to act well, living virtuously presents an ongoing challenge. What guides persons and communities of good moral character, aiding them in negotiating life's vicissitudes and contingencies, is practical wisdom (*phronesis*)—the capacity to make wise decisions regarding which virtues are called for in particular circumstances. As Aristotle repeatedly insists, "it is

18. Ochs, *PPLS*, 9.

not possible to be good in the strict sense without practical wisdom"[19] because wisdom is the ability to pursue what is worthwhile in a way fitting to
a specific situation. One might say that "practical wisdom is less a capacity
to apply rules than an ability to see situations correctly."[20] Insight—at once
intellectual and moral—lies at the heart of *phronesis*.

Aristotle's practical philosophy—like Peirce's pragmatism and Ochs'
deployment of the *peshat/derash* rule of rabbinic hermeneutics as a method
for repairing Peirce's pragmatism—is both thoroughly intellectual and
eminently practical. Even in his most theoretical endeavors, Aristotle is profoundly practical. Put otherwise, Aristotle exhibits a nonbinary, all-encompassing way of thinking where the rational and ethical are simultaneously
and fully engaged because mutually defined and actualized. According to
Aristotle, *phronesis* is one of the "intellectual virtues" or "excellences of the
mind." Yet it is not only an intellectual virtue, but an ethical virtue as well.[21]
This means that one cannot be (intellectually) wise without also being (ethically) good.[22] The point is worth underscoring: while *phronesis* is included
in Aristotle's catalogue of distinct virtues—courage, temperance, generosity,
etc.—it is not just one virtue among others. Rather it is a necessary ingredi-
ent in all the others insofar as it supplies the necessary element of judgment.
Following Joseph Dunne, one might describe *phronesis* as playing a central,
albeit "eccentric," role in Aristotle's practical philosophy.

> [*Phronesis*] is eccentric first of all in not lying comfortably on
> either side of the division that Aristotle himself makes between
> "intellectual" and "ethical" virtues. It is officially designated an
> intellectual virtue, but its deep involvement with the other side
> of the divide is evident from the fact that not only is it required
> to complete each ethical virtue by providing the element of

19. Aristotle, *The Nicomachean Ethics* (trans. Ross), 158.

20. Aristotle, *Nicomachean Ethics*, "Introduction," by Roger Crisp, xxiv. *Phronesis*
seems to entail more than a matter of "seeing" the salient features in a situation that
calls for action; it also involves deliberation and reason. Joseph Dunne expresses the
point thus: "*Phronesis* then is at once a deliberative excellence (*euboulio*) and a disposition for perceiving, or having insight (*aisthesis*); it is deliberative in so far as it helps
one to mediate between more generic, habitual knowledge and the particularities of
any given action-situation, and it involves perceptiveness in so far as its apprehensions
are not deductively derived, but are freshly generated in response precisely to the particularity of this situation and the individual's involvement in it now" (Dunne, "Virtue,
Phronesis, and Learning," 53).

21. Aristotle, NE1140b25.

22. Aristotle, NE1144a36, 1178a16–19.

judgement indispensable to the concrete exercise of the latter, but conversely . . . ethical virtue is itself required for *phronesis*.[23]

In construing *phronesis* as an intellectual virtue, Aristotle describes it as an activity of the mind or intellect. Thinking (*dianoeisthai* or *noesis*) is, moreover, lingual. That is to say, thinking or reasoning consists in the (internal and external) use of language or reasoned speech (*logos*).[24] All the various intellectual virtues have—or rather are—*logos* in this sense and their proper deployment is precisely to use *logos* correctly to achieve the purposes or ends (*teloi*) of the respective virtues. What makes them virtuous is using them "correctly." Here *phronesis* is key. It coordinates the virtues in ways that enable them to work in concert toward an overarching telos that is the good of a whole or "complete" life—and it does so in a manner that distinguishes without dividing the intellectual from the moral excellences. Hence Aristotle is able to say that while the ethical virtues are concerned with the formation of character (*ethos*) and the intellectual virtues with the right use of reason (*logos*), the ethical virtues are not in themselves reasons or knowledge in the strict sense (*episteme*), but dispositions that are "converted"—according to the workings of practical wisdom (*phronesis*)—into right action and right emotion with the right reason.[25]

Phronesis serves as a kind of unifying or coordinating power to all the virtues. Part of that coordination involves a certain circularity or mutually implicative movement, whereby the intellectual and the moral virtues become increasingly clarified and integrated as they unfold through a kind of back-and-forth dialogical interplay. The example of courage helpfully illustrates this dialectically-clarifying movement.

> To know that . . . courage is a virtue is to possess a type of universal knowledge. . . . The real nerve of moral knowledge, however, is to know the latter in such a way that one knows what *counts as* courage in the variety of situations in which one finds oneself as an agent. . . . [Indeed, it is all too easy] to have "the theory without the experience" or to be a person who "knows the universal but does not know the universal included in this." In fact "included" is in many cases too firm a term because, in the process of moral experience, by being "applied" to particular situations universals are at the same time being refined and enriched: in coming to recognize what courage

---

23. Dunne, "Virtue, Phronesis, and Learning," 51.
24. See Aristotle NE1139a21–32, 1139b11–17.
25. Aristotle, NE1144b20–33.

requires here, I may be learning not only about this new situation but also about courage itself.[26]

Because the exercise of *phronesis* is unavoidably linguistic and communicative, this means that it will invariably come to expression within political
and ethical structures of one kind or another. A life lived in pursuit of the
good cannot be achieved alone nor is it possible for someone to possess in iso-
lation an intellectual or moral virtue. In order to pursue, and in some limited
sense realize, a life of human flourishing, certain types of social or political
arrangements, some more conducive than others, are necessary.

The *dialogical* and *communal* aspects of *phronesis* have an especially
important bearing on the practice of Scriptural Reasoning and on Ochs'
pragmatic, reparative model of reading. For Aristotle, the best forms of political life are those rooted in friendship.[27] Aristotle's emphasis on the fundamental importance of human sociality in pursuing a life of virtue, and on
friendship's significance and centrality to that enterprise, is echoed in Ochs'
own philosophical-rabbinic outlook. Ochs' remark quoted at the outset of
this essay is a case in point: "I have experienced [in my long partnership
with David Ford] what Aristotle says of friendship—that we seek in the
other what raises us up in ourselves."

Aristotle several times speaks of a friend as "another self."[28] While
Ochs' pragmatic philosophy resonates strongly with this Aristotelian sensibility, his own understanding of friendship—perhaps in part due to his
long apprenticeship with Peirce's pragmatic writings but also his long tenure with interfaith practices like Scriptural Reasoning—displays a peculiar
acuity both to the *proximity* and the *distance* entailed by the "other" in
Aristotle's "a friend is another self." The limitations of Aristotle's account
of friendship in particular and the moral life in general are well-known.
For Aristotle the virtues are universal in scope and based on human nature
as such. He shows little awareness of just how deeply grounded his views
are in a given historical period and community. That friendship is more or
less restricted to well-born, well-educated male citizens of the Greek city
state—and seems an unlikely prospect for men of other social rank, and
an even more remote possibility for women and children—exposes the
extent to which Aristotle's friendship is a "particular universal." Likewise,

26. Dunne, "Virtue, Phronesis, and Learning," 53–54.

27. To be sure, there are various species or degrees of friendship, for Aristotle. These
include friendships of utility, of pleasure, and of character. Whatever their intensity or
quality, "the particular kinds of friendship will correspond to particular kinds of community" (Aristotle, NE1160a29–31).

28. Aristotle, NE.

it does not seem to occur to Aristotle that a society of *phronimoi* (a friend-filled *polis*) should try to alleviate suffering or help their fellow humans no matter how removed from "their own" life they may seem to be. What from a present vantage appears limited and partial, even deeply flawed, should not however suggest that Aristotle's outlook ought to be dismissed as beyond repair. Any and all wisdom traditions of great antiquity are "correctable." Here an analogy might be appropriate.

Aristotle's reflections on courage above could equally well be applied to friendship—not only *within* a particular wisdom-faith tradition but *across* wisdom-faith traditions. Only as the concept friendship is "applied" to particular situations does it become refined and enriched. For in coming to recognize what friendship entails in a specific context it is possible to learn not only about the context but also about friendship itself. That is, as scriptural reasoners "apply" their individual understandings of friendship as best they know how—i.e., according to the habits, standards and rules acquired and practiced in their home tradition or sub-tradition—they are awakened to aspects of the immense richness of their own faith tradition that have been occluded, lost or forgotten. At the same time they are given some inkling of what this must also be for adherents of other traditions, equally rich in resources of friendship but susceptible to similar occlusions, losses and forgetfulness. The experience more often than not is as freshly exhilarating as it is disarming and unsettling, as deeply and hopefully alive as it is penitent and sobering. In an inter-faith context—an inhabitation of a liminal space where social context no longer dictates in any clear, straightforward way which concepts of and rules for practicing friendship ought to obtain (i.e., serve as normative)—the meaning of friendship is thrown up for reconsideration in ways that are unfathomable. For what friendship might mean in a Scriptural Reasoning setting is to be discerned only in the process of its actual performance: the give-and-take, the overtures and entreaties as well as the expectant and anticipated reciprocations of friendship. It is within the hermeneutical-dialogical-performative movements of a wisdom-guided practice that the *concept* of friendship unfolds, opening itself to mutual clarification and deepening, revision and supportive, critical correction.

The emergence of Scriptural Reasoning friendships does not advance or contribute toward some universal definition of friendship. The aim of Scriptural Reasoning is not to work out a satisfactory theory of friendship. For whatever conceptual elucidations of friendship are thereby achieved in Scriptural Reasoning apply, fittingly (i.e., according to *phronesis*), to *this place, at this time and with respect to these people*. One might say that Scriptural Reasoning is a quintessential practice of what is fitting in friendship. It is receiving and sharing in God's presence what is discerned to be the appropriate manna-sized portions of the Word needed for today, at this place, with respect to the felt sufferings voiced by this particular gathering of friends.

To have been drawn into the orbit of Peter Ochs' friendship I count a great blessing. Along with many others who have joined the ever-widening circles of Scriptural Reasoning, I have found the leading reparative and pragmatic tendencies of his work truly, deeply, and amicably hopeful. The central conviction animating Ochs' work, one might say, is that the scriptures are given for "the healing of the nations" (Ezek 47:12; Gen 2:10; Rev 22:2). Impelled by a *phronesis*-like rationality, Ochs' work enables one to see harbingers of hope within suffering itself, signs of elements already leading to its repair/healing. But it is also a guarded and in some sense chastened hope willing to submit to faith's discipline—a faith that acknowledges a proper human desire for rational understanding and analytic clarity, on the one hand, while also recognizing (and refusing), on the other, the seductive appeal of the Enlightenment desire for "a reason that would instruct and mend all humanity. That desire remains, but its fulfillment is projected onto the end of days and onto a Word that speaks nonclearly or locally."[29] An important corollary of Ochs' hopefulness is his nonfoundationalism.[30] Eschewing the false security of a universalist stance, Ochs seeks instead to live within the contingencies and indeterminacies of the everyday, content "to find reasonably precise ways of talking about imprecise things [among which are the ordinary practices of religion] without losing the meaning of the imprecision itself."[31] The work of interpretation is never finished precisely because scripture's signs are inveterately vague symbols. Moreover, the work of interpretation is not something to be carried out alone but always in the company of friends, the amplitude and extension of which reaches back indefinitely into ages past but also forward to include those yet to come, as well as encompassing those whose present company we are blessed to keep. To be enjoined by friends in the practice of Scriptural Reasoning is to

29. Ochs, "Another Enlightenment," 99.

30. A great advantage of Ochs' pragmatic, reparative model of reading is that it is generalizable and communicable without being universalist or foundationalist. Insofar as "vague symbols may be defined only with respect to particular contexts of interpretation," the "resulting definitions display . . . a species of indeterminacy that would enable interpreters to draw lessons from one context to another. This phenomenon is significant, since it discloses a way of generalizing the results of pragmatic inquiry without transgressing the limits of context-specific interpretation and, thus, without recourse to the universalisms (or 'foundationalisms') the pragmatists criticized" (Ochs, *PPLS*, 9).

31. Ochs, *PPLS*, 4.

participate in and enact—in modest but nonetheless genuine ways—God's work of redemption. It is to be drawn into the work of *tikkun ólam*.

Bibliography

Adams, Nicholas. "Beyond the Logics of Preservation and Burial: The Display of Distance and Proximity of Traditions in Scriptural Reasoning." *Iqbal Review* 46 (2005) 241–52.

———. *Habermas and Theology*. Cambridge: Cambridge University Press, 2006.

Aristotle. *Nicomachean Ethics*. Edited by Roger Crisp. Cambridge: Cambridge University Press, 2000.

———. *Nicomachean Ethics*. Translated by Terence Irwin. Indianapolis: Hackett, 1985.

———. *The Nicomachean Ethics*. Translated by David Ross. Oxford: Oxford University Press, 1998.

Dunne, Joseph. "Virtue, *Phronesis*, and Learning." In *Virtue Ethics and Moral Education*, edited by David Carr and J. W. Steutel, 51–65. London: Routledge, 1999.

Ford, David F. *Christian Wisdom: Desiring God and Learning in Love*. Cambridge: Cambridge University Press, 2007.

Halivni, David Weiss. *Peshat & Derash: Plain and Applied Meaning in Rabbinic Exegesis*. Oxford: Oxford University Press, 1991.

Higton, Mike. "Editorial: Scriptural Reasoning." *Conversations in Religion and Theology* 7.2 (2009) 129–33.

Ochs, Peter. "Another Enlightenment." In *How My Mind as Changed: Essays from the Christian Century*, edited by David Heim, 93–101. Eugene, OR: Cascade, 2012.

———. "Focus on Scriptural Reasoning." *Conversations in Religion and Theology* 7.2 (2009) 134–44.

———. *Peirce, Pragmatism and the Logic of Scripture*. Cambridge: Cambridge University Press, 1998.

———. "Scripture and Text." In *The Cambridge History of Jewish Philosophy: The Modern Era*, edited by Martin Kavka, Zachary Braiterman, and David Novak, 193–223. Cambridge: Cambridge University Press, 2012.

———. "What Kinds of Thinking Complement What Kinds of Societal Action?" In *The Vocation of Theology Today: A Festschrift for David Ford*, edited by Tom Greggs, Rachel Muers, and Simeon Zahl, 193–210. Eugene, OR: Cascade, 2013.

Young, William. *Uncommon Friendships: An Amicable History of Modern Religious Thought*. Eugene, OR: Cascade, 2009.

Part Two: **Academy and Method**

6

For and *Against* Cartesianism

Peter Ochs on the Purpose of Philosophy

—JACOB L. GOODSON, Southwestern College

THE MOST VALUABLE ASPECT of Peter Ochs' work for my own life and thinking concerns his reflections—and, sometimes, top-down proclamations—on academic philosophy and on the role the philosopher plays within the modern academy. Most of these reflections are found in his magnum opus entitled *Peirce, Pragmatism and the Logic of Scripture.*[1] As well, we find proclamations about academic philosophy and the role of the philosopher in an earlier essay entitled "Charles Sanders Peirce" (1993),[2] as well as a chapter in *The Blackwell Companion to Postmodern Theology* (2001).[3] After 2001,[4] Ochs tends to focus more on the academic discipline of Religious Studies—rather than philosophy—so my engagement with and interpretation of Ochs' thinking involves this very specific period of his publications: 1992–2001.[5]

---

1. Ochs, *Peirce, Pragmatism and the Logic of Scripture* (hereafter cited as *PPLS*).

2. Ochs, "Charles Sanders Peirce."

3. Ochs, "Renewal of Jewish Theology Today."

4. Exceptions are instances in *Another Reformation* where Ochs encourages philosophers to help Christian theologians avoid fallacies that lead to or result in Christian supersessionism.

5. I completed writing this chapter prior to publication of Ochs' newest book, *Religion without Violence*—which, I imagine, has further clues and guidance on the purpose of philosophy and the role of philosophers in the modern academy.

This chapter sets its course with the very modest goal of offering a genealogy of Peter Ochs' thinking concerning the purpose of philosophy and the role of the philosopher within the modern academy.

The genealogical findings of this chapter, perhaps surprisingly, involve a real struggle with the philosophical methods and positions of René Descartes—methods and positions that often get reduced to the philosophical label of Cartesianism. For Ochs, however, the matter is not so straightforward. In what follows, readers will find a back-and-forth—in terms of affirming and negating Descartes' philosophy, known as Cartesianism—by Ochs as he gives clues and guidance concerning the purpose of philosophy and the role of the philosopher in the modern academy.

Ochs on Ordinary Life, Postmodern Playfulness, and the Problem of Nominalism (1993)

In *The Blackwell Companion to Postmodern Theology*, contributors demonstrate how philosophers who seemingly are "modern"—actually offer models of "constructive postmodernism." Usually, postmodernism requires a wholesale rejection of Cartesianism; what we learn from Ochs, in particular, is that postmodernism might be better thought of as an open and real struggle with Descartes and Cartesianism.

In his chapter on Peirce, Ochs focuses on three aspects of Peirce's postmodern *method* as it serves as a model for philosophers today. Postmodern method : (1) receives the "gifts" offered to us found in everyday experiences and within ordinary life; (2) repairs problems that arise within ordinary life; and (3) relies on musement—the "free play" of the imagination—to help with problems in ordinary life. Additionally, Ochs offers several cautionary reminders against philosophical tendencies toward nominalism.

According to Ochs, Peirce can be considered "postmodern" because he offers a method for philosophical thinking that critiques and repairs methods found within modern philosophy. First, against the modern tendency to wage "war with the everyday," Peirce invites philosophers to consider the "gifts to be offered in the service of everyday life and everyday community."[6] Peirce makes the purpose of philosophy a consideration and exploration of everyday experiences and ordinary life. This does not mean, however, that in Ochs' estimation, Peirce idealizes the ordinary. As Ochs explains, "Without idealizing the everyday and without calling for any atavistic return to 'a time when,' he [Peirce] was a critic of the modern intellectual rather than

6. Ochs, "Charles Sanders Peirce," 46.

of ordinary life."[7] Making ordinary life part of the purpose of philosophy, for Peirce, entails neither an idealization nor a romanticization of ordinary life, but a critique and repair of the binary between intellectualism and the ordinary defended and developed within modern philosophy.[8]

Second, what does it mean to make ordinary life part of the purpose of philosophy? According to Ochs, Peirce turns "the business of philosophy" into an enterprise "to solve the problems that arise in everyday experience."[9] Ochs claims that this leads Peirce to the phenomenological tradition, within what we now call Continental philosophy, because "phenomenology sketches out the elemental qualities of everyday experiences."[10] Focusing on everyday experiences means that the purpose of philosophy becomes solving problems within ordinary life.

Third, what is it about philosophy that makes it capable of solving problems within ordinary life? Ochs claims that what underlies Peirce's phenomenology is the category of musement, and musement makes philosophy helpful for and within ordinary life. Defining musement as the "free play" of the imagination, Ochs writes,

> Given free play, the imagination gives uninhibited expression to the fundamental categories of expression . . . in the contemplation of which inquirers may construct norms for reforming our habits of action [within ordinary life]. . . . [Philosophy has] practical import . . . because it offers possibilities that might really be enacted within our contexts of action: possibilities of real habit-change, enabling us to comprehend the world as it now displays itself [rather than how modern philosophers think it *ought* to be displayed]. For Peirce, philosophy itself is the prototypical activity of constructively reimagining the fundamental norms of action.[11]

According to Ochs, Peirce strikes a balance between allowing everyday experiences to determine our thinking—instead of the modern tendency to over-intellectualize experience—and encouraging the "free play" of the imagination to address and solve problems found within ordinary life. This balance seems hard to accomplish because the move to the imagination might result in the same kind of intellectualizing that Peirce wants

7. Ochs, "Charles Sanders Peirce," 46–47.

8. For my own reflections on the strong connections between intellectualism and ordinary life, see *Strength of Mind*.

9. Ochs, "Charles Sanders Peirce," 65–66.

10. Ochs, "Charles Sanders Peirce," 66.

11. Ochs, "Charles Sanders Peirce," 72.

philosophy to avoid. Peirce thinks that if philosophers remain grounded in everyday experience and in ordinary life, however, then such a temptation will be avoided. Because it begins with ordinary life, Peirce's philosophy can be considered a correction or repair of modernity; because it encourages musement, Peirce's philosophy can be understood as a constructive version of postmodern playfulness.

Earlier, I suggested that Ochs sometimes makes top-down proclamations about academic philosophy. For example, throughout this essay, Ochs claims that philosophers should neither assume nor defend the modern position of nominalism. What are the problems of nominalism? In its rationalist manifestation, nominalism leads to an over-reliance on individual intuitions—which leads, at its worst, to tenacity and, at its best, to an *a priorism* unaccountable to other human thinkers.[12] Within philosophy, this version of nominalism has become synonymous with Cartesianism. In its empiricist manifestation, nominalism makes us think that individual sensations give us actual and reliable knowledge. Ochs says, "Peirce's critique of nominalism means that we do not *know* what we encounter merely by sensing it."[13] As a discipline, philosophy needs to move past nominalism.

Ochs' Appeal to American Pragmatists (1998)

Peter Ochs' scholarship focuses on the American philosopher Charles Sanders Peirce, and his research on Peirce's writings culminates in the scholarly book entitled *Peirce, Pragmatism and the Logic of Scripture.*[14] In *PPLS*, Ochs argues that Peirce's technical work in logic and the philosophy of science marks a return to Scripture (Old and New Testaments) within modern philosophy. Rene Descartes set modern philosophy on a course that rejected Scripture as a source for genuine knowledge, and instead trusted individual intuitions (Cartesianism) or individual sense impressions (empiricism). Peirce, Ochs argues, diagnoses the link between problematic features of modern philosophies and their neglect of Scripture. In order to correct Cartesianism and other problems within modern philosophy, Ochs argues that Peirce returns to Scripture as a source for different forms of knowledge.

Because of *PPLS*, Ochs is not popular among other Peirce scholars. Peirce scholars tend to downplay the religious and theological aspects of

12. See Peirce, "Fixation of Belief."

13. Ochs, "Charles Sanders Peirce," 70.

14. I have written much more (than I do here) on arguments found within Ochs' *PPLS*; see Goodson, *Narrative Theology*, chapter 5; Goodson and Stone, *Introducing Prophetic Pragmatism*, 35–38 and 129–31; Goodson, "'Ye Shall Know Them;'" and Goodson, *Introduction to Scriptural Reasoning.*

Peirce's work, and Ochs forces his readers to recognize how Scripture plays a necessary role within Peirce's philosophy.[15] To neglect the role of Scripture within Peirce's logic and philosophy of science is to perpetuate the problems within modern philosophy that Peirce, himself, addressed and oftentimes repaired and resolved. As such, Ochs rejects the forms of Cartesianism within academic philosophy that still encourage us to trust our individual intuitions over the logic and wisdom of Scripture.

In *PPLS*, Ochs writes to professional philosophers: "The philosopher's own suffering cannot . . . become the subject of philosophic concern."[16] What philosophers perceive as their own suffering, and the remedy/remedies for that suffering, cannot set norms for philosophical investigations. Rather he maintains that it is the suffering caused by problems within received traditions that ought to be "the subject of philosophic concern." In *PPLS*, therefore, Ochs reads Peirce's "The Fixation of Belief" as an account of how to fix or repair suffering rather than an analysis of how persons establish beliefs or convictions.[17] For Ochs, the role of the philosopher involves helping readers and students fix or repair the problematic aspects of their received traditions—especially those problematic aspects that have led to suffering at both communal and individual levels. Undoubtedly, when applied to pedagogical principles Ochs' view is tantamount to the notion that lectures in the philosophy classroom ought not advertise and work through the professor's own suffering but, rather should (a) offer insights for encouraging students to identify the parts of their received tradition that cause suffering and (b) provide tools and wisdom for those students to repair the problematic features of their received traditions that have led to suffering. This means that, although Peirce and Ochs are against Cartesianism in its prioritization of individual intuitions over the logic and wisdom of Scripture, Ochs is not against Cartesianism in the sense that the task of philosophy involves learning how to identify problems found within received traditions. While Ochs does not develop this point in *PPLS* (1998),[18] he explicitly defends it in 2001!

15. For further development of this claim, see Goodson, "Introduction."

16. Ochs, *PPLS*, 297.

17. Ochs is not the only Peirce scholar to read "The Fixation of Belief" in this way and to connect Peirce's pragmatism with the notion of repairing suffering; for instance, see Ejsing, *Theology of Anticipation*.

18. I arrived at it, inferentially, only by asserting that Ochs' reading of Peirce's "Fixation of Belief" is not the typical one where "fixation" means settling into one's beliefs and convictions.

Ochs' Defense and Explanation
of Academic Philosophy (2001)

Three years after the publication of *PPLS*, Ochs published "The Renewal of Jewish Theology Today: Under the Sign of Three" in *The Blackwell Companion to Postmodern Theology*. In his chapter, Ochs reflects upon three themes: Cartesianism, tradition, and the turn toward Scripture within philosophy.

Pragmatism does not simply allow one to reaffirm their "tradition."[19] Ochs writes that pragmatists, "*with* Descartes . . . recognize the failings of tradition *but also* . . . recognize that the modern project of reasoning itself takes flight out of the night of these failings."[20] According to Ochs, pragmatism adds to Descartes' reasoning

> the *memory* that this reason, [which] flies out of the night, is itself a messenger *only* of night . . . our means of seeing in bold relief just what has gone wrong in our religious and social traditions. This flight of reason is in this sense a prophetic complaint. But it is not itself the vehicle of redemption, a source of new light. It is the cry without which Israel in bondage could not be heard, the cry that goes up to God.[21]

Descartes' flight from tradition can be understood as "a prophetic complaint" but not the kind of prophecy that in itself leads to or seeks out redemption.

Pragmatism improves upon Cartesianism because of its desire for and openness toward redemption. In Ochs' words:

> If pragmatism is the logician's way of saying "know them by their fruit," this means both that prophecy's word is told only in the testing of its public consequences, and that reasoning is a vehicle of prophecy. Stated in Jewish terms, this means that what Descartes calls reason is prophetic, but only a prophecy of warning and condemnation. The fruit of such prophecy is

19. Another way to put it is this: "Tradition is complex. Tradition is complicated. Tradition is messy. . . . [We need] a less conservative, Romantic notion of tradition [and] one that includes the complications, complexities, and messiness of tradition in the concept of tradition itself. The distance one needs from this understanding of tradition is not a distance for the sake of distance but rather . . . a distance . . . encouraged by tradition through the practice of reflection. One does not overcome tradition in the practice of reflection, but one becomes more grounded in the[ir] tradition if the tradition is encouraging the kind of reflection that it ought to be encouraging" (Goodson, "What Is Reparative Reasoning?").

20. Ochs, "Renewal of Jewish Theology Today," 336.

21. Ochs, "Renewal of Jewish Theology Today," 336. I should note that Ochs' writing in this chapter represents some of his best, stylistically. I quote much from the essay because it reads so poetically!

redemption—or the lack of it. The question is, how to find the fruit? The pragmatic answer is: learn to read death, and understand its signs.[22]

The claims of prophetic reasoning must be tested by its "fruit," defined by Ochs in terms of "its public consequences."

Ochs outlines three ways for philosophers to "learn to read death, and understand its signs":

> (1) Realize that the mark of death is the individual reasoning that declares by its very individuation the death . . . of some specific, failed practices, failed bits of tradition and of social process. This mark is critical reasoning: the Western academy's defining tool. The method of critical reasoning is to thematize certain objects of inspection, which occupy the place, in the propositional logic of critical reasoning, of "subjects" about which certain predications are made. Each subject of this kind is a mark of something that has failed. . . .
>
> (2) Realize that every death of this kind is finite: the death of a creature. The reasoning that declares this death is itself finite: the finite mark of a finite death. Descartes errs only because he over-generalizes the failings of this or that aspect of his inherited tradition of inquiry (scholastic), as if he knew also of the potential failings of all of that tradition (all of scholasticism, or all of medieval Christianity). But there is no reason to doubt that some failing in Descartes' inheritance gave rise to his reasonings. Western academic reasoning is prophetic but finite.
>
> (3) Realize that, if this academic-philosophic reasoning is finite, then there must be more to say than what this reasoning has to say. If reasoning tells me what has failed, then more-than-reason alone will tell me what in my tradition, heritage, past, has not failed. . . . The Israelite prophets reject neither Israel itself, nor its divine law, nor its priesthood. They reject only the error and sin in all these.[23]

Before turning to a pragmatic interpretation of Scripture (Exod 3),[24] Ochs concludes his reflections on what his theological understanding of academic philosophy looks like:

> Philosophic [and] academic reasoning is comparably prophetic in the West. Whatever it assumes and continues of its cultural

22. Ochs, "Renewal of Jewish Theology Today," 337.
23. Ochs, "Renewal of Jewish Theology Today," 337–38.
24. See Ochs, "Renewal of Jewish Theology Today," 344–48.

> heritage is [neither] doubted nor negated . . . and is, therefore,
> affirmed by the very fact of its being left alone. Whatever is af-
> firmed in this way discloses the positive traces of the Redeemer
> in the academic's cultural heritage.[25]

Like Descartes and Cartesianism, philosophers and philosophy professors can share "complaint[s]" against tradition(s). Philosophers and
philosophy professors, however, should not remain closed off to the possibility of redemption while teaching different philosophical arguments
and theories—which relates to an argument made in the previous section:
philosophers and philosophy professors should provide tools and wisdom
(found in philosophical arguments and theories) for readers and students to
repair the problematic features of their received traditions.[26]

The "prophetic" aspect, which arises from the opportunity to teach
and write philosophy, comes about through connecting different philosophical arguments and theories with their possibility for redemption. Their
possibility for redemption occurs in the disclosure of "the positive traces
of [God] the Redeemer." These traces are located within Scripture—hence
Ochs' "return to Scripture" within philosophy.

Conclusion

In terms of how Ochs has shaped my own approach to philosophy in my ten
year professorial career, the primary lesson learned concerns how the history of philosophy goes from reparative moment to reparative moment—
which means (a) no single period of philosophy ought to be glamorized
or idealized over any other,[27] and (b) philosophy does not progress toward
some ideal stage of intellectualism but, rather, solves particular problems for
and within each and every generation.[28]

25. Ochs, "Renewal of Jewish Theology Today," 338.

26. See James, *Pragmatism*, for the fully developed thesis that philosophical arguments and theories can and ought to be used as instruments or tools.

27. For several years, John Milbank was Ochs' colleague at the University of Virginia. Milbank certainly glamorizes medieval Christian philosophical theology as the
period to which all philosophy ought to return. Ochs' Rabbinic Pragmatism differs
from Milbank's Radical Orthodoxy project exactly on this issue relating to the method
of reasoning and the temptation toward recovery.

28. Following the distinction made in the previous footnote: the nuance involved
in Ochs' thinking about these matters is that, on the surface, he seems to glamorize
American Pragmatism—especially Charles Sanders Peirce's philosophy—as the period
of philosophy that ought to be prioritized above all others. However, Ochs does not
present a glamorized or idealized version of Peirce's pragmatism other than describing
how Peirce's philosophy turns all of philosophy back to Scripture as a norm for "real

In summary, based upon the genealogy constructed in this chapter, we may conclude that on the one hand, Ochs is *for* Cartesianism in the sense that philosophy needs to critique received traditions of practice and thinking. On the other hand, Ochs is clearly critical of Cartesianism and in particular (1) the nominalist basis of individual intuitions, (2) the priority of rationality and intellectualism over ordinary life, and (3) the modern philosophical neglect of the logic and wisdom of Scripture. As a student of Ochs, I remain baffled by contemporary philosophy's continued rejection of Scripture as a given. By this I mean that philosophers no longer argue against the logic and wisdom of Scripture, but instead simply assume or assert that Scripture has no place within the study of philosophy, as if Scripture never had a place within the study of philosophy. Ochs continually reminds us that thinkers used to treat the logic and wisdom of Scripture as part of their role *as philosopher.*[29]

In conclusion, the purpose of academic philosophy involves prophetic complaints against received traditions. In this way, Cartesianism remains a model for academic philosophy even if in Ochs' view that model can and ought to be supplemented by the logic and wisdom perpetually offered by and within Scripture.[30]

Bibliography

Ejsing, Annette. *Theology of Anticipation: A Constructive Study of C. S. Peirce.* Eugene, OR: Pickwick, 2007.

Goodson. "Introduction." In *American Philosophers Read Scripture*, edited by Jacob L. Goodson, xiii–xxii. Lanham, MD: Lexington, 2020.

———. *An Introduction to Scriptural Reasoning.* Cascade Companion Series. Eugene, OR: Cascade, 2000.

———. *Narrative Theology and the Hermeneutical Virtues: Humility, Patience, Prudence.* Lanham, MD: Lexington, 2015.

———. *Strength of Mind.* Eugene, OR: Cascade, 2018.

———. "What Is Reparative Reasoning?" *Journal of Scriptural Reasoning* 10.2 (2011). http://jsr.shanti.virginia.edu/back-issues/volume-10-no-2-december-2011-public-debate-and-scriptural-reasoning/what-is-reparative-reasoning/.

---

generals." In this way, Peirce repairs the limitations found within modern philosophy without dismissing the helpful moments located within the arguments of modern philosophers. In what some might label a paradoxical move, Ochs claims that Peirce's philosophy gets philosophy back on track without calling for an overly simplistic recovery of or return to Peirce's work.

29. For more on this, see Goodson, "Introduction."

30. For how this works and what this means, see Goodson and Stone, *Introducing Prophetic Pragmatism*, 35–38, 129–31.

————. "'Ye Shall Know Them By Their Fruits': Ralph Waldo Emerson's Interpretation of Jesus' Logical Rule." In *American Philosophers Read Scripture*, edited by Jacob L. Goodson, 69–78. Lanham, MD: Lexington, 2020.

Goodson, Jacob L., and Brad Elliott Stone. *Introducing Prophetic Pragmatism: A Dialogue on Hope, the Philosophy of Race, and the Spiritual Blues*. Lanham, MD: Lexington, 2019.

James, William. *Pragmatism*. New York: Dover, 1995.

Ochs, Peter. *Another Reformation*. Grand Rapids: Eerdmans, 2011.

————. "Charles Sanders Peirce." In *Founders of Constructive Postmodern Philosophy*, edited by David Ray Griffin, 43–87. Albany: State University of New York Press, 1993.

————. *Peirce, Pragmatism and the Logic of Scripture*. New York: Cambridge University Press, 1998.

————. *Religion without Violence: The Philosophy and Practice of Scriptural Reasoning*. Eugene, OR: Cascade, 2019.

————. "The Renewal of Jewish Theology Today: Under the Sign of Three." In *The Blackwell Companion to Postmodern Theology*, edited by Graham Ward, 324–48. Malden, MA: Wiley-Blackwell, 2001.

Peirce, Charles Sanders. *The Essential Peirce: Selected Philosophical Writings, 1867–1893*. Bloomington: Indiana University Press, 1992.

————. *The Essential Peirce: Selected Philosophical Writings, 1893–1913*. Bloomington: Indiana University Press, 1998.

————. "The Fixation of Belief." *Popular Science Monthly* 12 (November 1877) 1–15. http://www.peirce.org/writings/p107.html.

Raposa, Michael. *Peirce's Philosophy of Religion*. Bloomington: Indiana University Press, 1989.

7

Making a Philosophical Problem Our Own

Peter Ochs' "Pragmatic Historiography"

—EMILY FILLER, Washington & Lee University

THIS ESSAY TURNS ON a phrase employed by Peter Ochs: "pragmatic historiography."[1] In this essay, I describe the way in which Ochs' exploration of this phrase serves both as a methodological gift and a serious challenge to contemporary Jewish philosophers and ethicists to address our work not only to a community of scholars, but to the communities whose needs have been identified by the philosophers who are our subjects. That is, while I will demonstrate a means by which Ochs' pragmatic invocation can expand our ability to reason philosophically and textually, this essay argues that the same approach, properly understood, should also make the same work much harder—by demanding that we attend to the needs of, among others, the extra-scholarly communities whose questions and concerns might be addressed by our scholarly work. Descriptively, therefore, my own work is indebted to Ochs' for providing language to characterize the instinct that we may find authorization to theorize beyond what the historical record can immediately provide. Below, I offer a case study of one attempt. But I understand Ochs' position here to have subtle prescriptive ethical and scholarly significance as well, which is to say that the pragmatic turn not only makes certain kinds of scholarship possible but also believes that scholarship to be *better* than it might have been. This essay is about the ways in which I have found this to be so.

1. Ochs, "Talmudic Scholarship," 120.

Ochs introduces the phrase "pragmatic historiography" in a generous and fascinating discussion of rabbinic historian David Weiss Halivni's
1997 English publication of *Revelation Restored: Divine Writ and Critical
Responses.*[2] Seeking to characterize Halivni's approach to rabbinic literature,
Ochs identifies two different kinds of inquiry in Halivni's work. The first is
historical reconstruction that might be understood as facilitated by conventional methodologies of historical scholarship. As Ochs puts it, it is work
that applies "the best scientific tools at our disposal to the documentary
evidence to disclose as much about the past as a discerning community
of scholars can recognize."[3] The second mode of inquiry, though, begins
when the scholar seeks to theorize beyond what the documentary evidence
at hand can definitively support. This "pragmatic historiography," as Ochs
terms it, is "historiography that begins where the plain-sense evidence
leaves off."[4] The task of Ochs' essay is to articulate how, by what warrant,
and to what ends such historiography may proceed.

Importantly, while Ochs' focus in his own essay is the work of one rabbinic historian, I assume here that his argument can, and should, be of use
to scholars in the humanities generally, regardless of their strict disciplinary
affiliation. I take it as axiomatic that all scholars are working within a realm
defined by attention to the historical record (whichever portion of that record
is of most use), and that therefore we are, in an important sense, all historians,
seeking to discern what claims we may legitimately make on an author or
text. Thus I also interpret Ochs' methodological claim as extending somewhat
beyond the disciplinary boundaries of history per se. In a broad idiom, I suggest that we might understand the claim as an application of his pragmatism
to the academic disciplines more broadly. In Ochs' terms, we might call those
claims "pragmatic" that both acknowledge the epistemological boundaries
of a given set of knowledge *and* seek to address the needs of a given community beyond what our strict disciplinary tools have provided. Ochs' use
of the phrases "plain sense" and "pragmatic" to describe these two modes of
argumentation further emphasize the expansive hermeneutical thrust of his
theory.[5] That is, while Halivni's distinctive scholarship has provided the occasion for Ochs' reasoning process, the terms as Ochs presents them are not
restricted to academic historical scholarship.

What Ochs terms pragmatic historiography should not be reduced to,
or dismissed as, mere "speculation." Rather, it is an approach with precise

2. Halivni, *Revelation Restored.*
3. Ochs, "Talmudic Scholarship," 121.
4. Ochs, "Talmudic Scholarship," 121.
5. Ochs, "Talmudic Scholarship," 123. Ochs himself places the phrases in quotes.

requirements, the first of which is that pragmatic historiography (or interpretation, or other related processes of reasoning) must not contradict the plain sense evidence with which the scholar is working; there is no leave to diverge from the historical record insofar as such a record exists. But when we reach the limitations of the historical record, the pragmatic historiographer may find that another set of tools is yet available to us. We have not necessarily reached the end of inquiry within the conventions of our academic disciplines. Rather, further questions may become part of the inquiry insofar as those questions are understood to emerge as the concerns and needs of a given community. As Ochs puts it, "The pragmatic historiographer asks the documentary evidence to answer questions about the past that we cannot answer incontrovertibly, *but which are consistent with the evidence and which a given community of enquirers demands that we must if we are to put our text scholarship to the ends for which we have produced it.*"[6] Ochs therefore assumes that the scholarly questions we have been pursuing may well contribute to conversations beyond those taking place within disciplinary boundaries.

In his description above, Ochs speaks in the descriptive present tense, and his theorization proceeds along these lines. The phrase "pragmatic historiography" is employed to describe what Ochs sees at least one historian—Halivni—having already done. Thus, on one level, we can understand Ochs' goal to be taxonomical, an exercise in properly categorizing the work of Halivni. Ochs does assert that this is his most "local" goal: to make the argument for the virtues of Halivni's scholarship against the critiques that he is either making historical claims that he cannot justify or making theological claims that depart from the historical record altogether.[7] In this reading, Ochs' pragmatism-inflected defense is both descriptive, and—in classical rabbinic terms—*bediavad*, in retrospect.

But Ochs' evaluation of Halivni suggests a responsibility as well. Ochs argues that Halivni's pragmatic turn should be understood as an attempt to, among other things, address a set of concerns in his own contemporary Jewish community struggling intellectually and spiritually. The pragmatic mode of inquiry, Ochs asserts, is "one that is motivated by the observation of crisis and suffering and performed as a means of repairing that crisis."[8] And this description, I suggest, makes a claim on other scholars as well: a claim that as Halivni has fashioned his argument to be attentive to the needs of a certain Jewish population, so too *should* other scholars take on

6. Ochs, "Talmudic Scholarship," 121; italics are original.
7. Ochs, "Talmudic Scholarship," 121.
8. Ochs, "Talmudic Scholarship," 131.

the responsibility of speaking not only to their disciplinary colleagues, but also to the wider Jewish world. There is, of course, no shortage of crises to which other scholars may attend.

A Troubling Text and a Precarious Solution: Martin Buber and 1 Sam 15

In what follows, I describe a problem of interpretation in modern Jewish philosophy—one with significant philosophical and ethical implications for contemporary Jews seeking to engage and be changed by their sacred texts, as well as for the smaller community of scholars of modern Jewish philosophy. In response to the limitations of what Ochs calls "plain-sense" historicism, I show that here as in rabbinic history, Ochs' pragmatic approach allows for more substantive and sustained interaction with the interpretive dilemma in question—by insisting that this interaction attend to the concerns of contemporary Jewish communities. The full implications of this turn I will discuss in the conclusion of this essay.

My text here is the famous, and famously bloody, chapter of 1 Sam 15, which gives an account of the downfall of King Saul as head of the Israelite monarchy under the disapproving eyes of the prophet Samuel. The chapter opens with Samuel giving Saul these instructions: "Thus said the Lord of Hosts: I am exacting the penalty for what Amalek did to Israel, for the assault he made upon them on the road, on their way up from Egypt. Now go, attack Amalek, and proscribe all that belongs to him. Spare no one, but kill alike men and women, infants and sucklings, oxen and sheep, camels and asses!"[9]

Saul, however, does not follow the Lord's instructions to the letter. Although he and his army do indeed rout the Amalekites, he fails to kill their leader, King Agag, as well as a number of choice livestock. First Samuel 15:8–9 clarifies that Saul "proscribed all the people, putting them to the sword; but Saul and the troops spared Agag and the best of the sheep, the oxen, the second-born, the lambs, and all else that was of value. They would not proscribe them; they proscribed only what was cheap and worthless."[10] As a result of Saul's disobedience, the prophet Samuel informs him that God has rejected him as king.

It is left for Samuel to deal with the captured King Agag as God has commanded—and as he is brought before Samuel, as the text says, "with

---

9. 1 Sam 15:2–3, JPS 1985. These verses make reference to Israel's previous dealings with the Amalekites as described in Exod 17.

10. 1 Sam 15:8–9, JPS 1985.

faltering steps," Agag says, "Ah, bitter death is at hand!"[11] Then, the text tells us matter-of-factly, "Samuel cut Agag down [*vayshasef*] before the Lord at Gilgal."[12]

In a short and rarely cited autobiographical fragment, this disturbing episode forms the basis of Martin Buber's reflections on the character of the biblical God and the existential difficulties of biblical translation. Buber introduces the subject by recounting a conversation with a traditionally observant Jew with whom he had previously been acquainted. When they happened to meet again, they fell into a discussion of the Bible—as Buber says, "not of peripheral questions but central ones, central questions of faith."[13] And in this conversation, Buber and his interlocutor came to speak of the brutal tale of Samuel and Saul, and Saul's punishment upon failing to destroy the Amalekite king. Referring to his childhood discovery of this story, Buber says, "I reported to my partner in dialogue how dreadful it had already been to me when I was a boy to read this as the message of God (and my heart compelled me to read it over again or at least to think about the fact that this stood written in the Bible). . . . I said to my partner: 'I have never been able to believe that this is a message from God. *I do not believe it.*'"[14] Buber's visceral reaction to this passage may be summed up in his rejection of the God depicted in this text: "Nothing can make me believe in a God who punishes Saul because he has not murdered his enemy. And yet even today I still cannot read the passage that tells this otherwise than with fear and trembling."[15]

In Buber's recollection, his pious conversation partner affirms Buber's own defiant rejection of the biblical text. He agrees that "Samuel has misunderstood God," and taken murderous action neither commanded nor sanctioned by the Divine.[16] Reflecting on this hermeneutical episode, Buber articulates, quite revealingly, what he believes has occurred in the

---

11. 1 Sam 15:32, JPS 1985. Note that this translation of Agag's words (*achen sar mar hamavet*) is contested. Martin Buber, in his reflections on this episode, translates Agag's last words as "Surely the bitterness of death is past," thus changing the sense of the phrase; in Buber's interpretation, Agag believes that the killing has ended, whereas, of course, Samuel is about to kill him. Both translations, however, preserve the emotional pain that the king appears to be experiencing as he approaches Samuel.

12. 1 Sam 15:32, JPS 1985. The verb describing Samuel's actions here is extremely rare and notably brutal; while "cutting down" might simply mean killing, the verb suggests a sustained hacking to pieces. See the note on this verb in Brown, Driver, and Briggs, *Hebrew and English Lexicon*, 8158a.

13. Buber, *Meetings*, 52.

14. Italics are my own.

15. Buber, *Meetings*, 54.

16. Buber, *Meetings*, 52.

observant Jew's refusal to affirm the divine mandate to kill Saul. He has, in Buber's terms, been forced to choose "between God and the Bible." What Buber witnessed was a kind of theological wrestling match with a definitive outcome: this man, "when he has to choose between God and the Bible, chooses God: the God in whom he believes, Him in whom he can believe."[17] As Buber tells it, when he confesses to the man that he cannot believe that God would command the prophet to such an action, the man's severity softens: "the angry countenance opposite me became transformed, as if a hand had passed over it soothing it. It lightened, cleared, was now turned toward me bright and clear. 'Well,' said the man with a positively gentle tender clarity, 'I think so too.'"[18]

Buber concludes with a reflection on the process of biblical translations—a process whose challenges are brought into sharp relief with texts such as these above. In the process of translating the Hebrew Bible anew, Buber (and his co-translator Franz Rosenzweig) frequently expressed that the new translation should shock or disorient the previous complacent biblical reader.[19] Theoretically, this translation process would be an opportunity to draw out the stark brutality of the text, and the uncompromising nature of God's judgments. But in this case, Buber's marked squeamishness about the plain sense reveals an acute theologically-inflected translation problem. Buber cannot guarantee that an unsuspecting reader of 1 Samuel will recognize that of which he, Buber, professes to be sure: that contrary to the seeming plain sense reading of the text, God did *not* order Samuel to slay the Amalekite king. Thus he concludes, "When I have to translate or interpret a biblical text, I do so with fear and trembling, in an inescapable tension between the word of God and the words of man."[20]

Establishing Scholarly Accountability

Buber's passionate refusal to accept the divine origin of Samuel's violent actions in 1 Samuel may generate quite a long series of questions for the reader—either of Buber or of the biblical text in question. As regards Buber's reaction to the text, we might ask what it is about this text in particular that has so wounded him. After all, this text is by no means the only, or necessarily most, violent or troubling in the Hebrew Bible, nor the only

17. Buber, *Meetings*, 52.

18. Buber, *Meetings*, 52.

19. Many of these reflections are compiled in a little edited volume, *Scripture and Translation*, now out of print. See Fox, *Scripture and Tradition*.

20. Buber, *Meetings*, 54.

one whose violence is (ostensibly) commanded by God. We might also inquire what is at stake for Buber in resisting the text's plain sense. Why is he so frightened by the possibility of a violent deity? Buber himself famously called for Jews to have a new "confrontation" with the Bible, and to revel in its raw and alien character, so different from the domesticated Lutheran Bible most familiar to secularized German Jews.[21] This text, it seems, should contribute nicely to jarring the complacent sensibilities of modern Jews—yet for Buber, its portrayal of a vengeful and violent God is intolerable, actually unbelievable. How, then, does Buber discern which biblical commands actually come from God and which are misunderstandings of the sort which he says has afflicted the prophet Samuel?

The biblical passage in question also generates numerous questions—literary, theological, ethical—of which we might consider but a few: why does King Saul fail to kill the Amalekite king or the choice livestock, as commanded? Why has God chosen this moment to strike back for the Amalekite attack on the Israelites long ago? Why is it important for the livestock to be murdered as well? Does Saul's act of disobedience here really warrant his deposition as king? What do we make of the ease with which Samuel commits the killing that Saul did not? And—since the question is not Buber's alone—what kind of God is this, who punishes his chosen sovereign for a rare act of nonviolence? Who is this God?

Few of these questions, however compelling they may be, are easily addressed with a conventional set of scholarly tools. The modern historian could at least attempt to situate Buber in a particular historical milieu which might account for his resistance to the text, though this would only address Buber's resistance in an indirect way (and the paucity of scholarship on Buber's biblical hermeneutics perhaps testifies to the scholarly limitations in this regard).[22] The biblical historian, meanwhile, might certainly situate the biblical passage within a set of text-historical considerations about the rise of the biblical monarchy and the role of prophets in this regime. But the source of Buber's resistance still will remain well out of reach, and the theological challenges posed by 1 Samuel even more so. All we have is Buber's one articulation of his conviction that "the God in whom [one] believes" and the God of the Bible sometimes diverge in ways that may cause the biblical reader great pain. A better understanding or evaluation of Buber's conviction here appears to be largely beyond the ability of historians to determine—to

21. See, for instance, Buber's essay "Man of Today."

22. Only recently have a few scholars taken up the question of Buber's biblical hermeneutics in particular, among which the most prominent are Kepnes, *Text as Thou*, and Claire Sufrin's unpublished dissertation, "Martin Buber's Biblical Hermeneutics."

say nothing of the content of his convictions, which generally lie outside the realm of historical speculation altogether.

But Buber's simple refusal to accept the plain sense reading of 1 Sam 15 is unlikely to satisfy many readers; Buber himself acknowledges the difficulty of the text even with the palliative interpretation he has provided: "even today I still cannot read the passage that tells this otherwise than with fear and trembling." Meanwhile, Buber's interpretive dilemma stands, and challenges anyone who seeks to affirm the sacrality of the Bible and the goodness of God.

Here, I suggest that to engage Buber on his terms, or to reflect philosophically on the interpretive dilemma he describes, invites us to expand our inquiry beyond what Buber's own writings or the tools of text-historicism can immediately provide. But in Ochs' pragmatic historiographical framework, another set of tools may be used. As Ochs puts it, this step is moving "to the level of speculative hypotheses that may not seem at all self-evident to the community of enquirers at large. The 'deeper' the reading, the less self-evident."[23] The method, descriptively speaking, is a conscious step beyond what can be gleaned from the historical record or easily verified by other scholars.

Lest Ochs' method here be misunderstood, the animating concern— that which "allows" us to persist in our questions beyond what the historical record can provide—is *not* simply our own intellectual curiosity (our scholarly "need to know"), but the needs of some community whose questions are not "merely" intellectual-historical but existential, theological, and ethical. Moreover, once we have pressed on beyond the sharp boundaries of historical inquiry, there is no clear way to determine in which direction our theorization should proceed. We could, hypothetically, go anywhere with little attention to the implications of our work or any means of determining the significance of our scholarship.

The "right" to reason pragmatically, therefore, is granted only to the degree that we are willing to envision an audience beyond our immediate academic community. Obviously, but also importantly, this is no arbitrary rule. Rather, as I understand Ochs' characterization, identifying the needs of a given community allows us to do two things: to identify the stakes of a given question for that community, and to make a set of arguments in line with its needs. These communal priorities, in Ochs' formulation, should provide the parameters of an expanded mode of inquiry, thereby disciplining scholars in our extra-historical theorization. The questions and concerns of a given community serve to direct our reflection and theorization.

23. Ochs, "Talmudic Scholarship," 128.

Here, in the case of Buber and the troubling text, Ochs' broad interpretive category, the pragmatic historiographical, can serve as an instructive case study. First of all, I suggest that Buber's striking refusal can itself be understood as a kind of a proto-pragmatism in the Ochsian sense. Buber's self-description of his reaction to the biblical passage evinces real pain. In Buber's description of his own "fear and trembling," as well as his initial confession of pain upon reading 1 Samuel, he reveals something of his own concerns and his concern for a community of other readers. For Ochs, this communal preoccupation is an important data point, not a factor despite which we take seriously a given argument. Ochs argues that this orientation "is the means through which the academic historian also serves the pragmatic needs of the contemporary Jewish community." In this vein, it is notable that when Buber speaks of his interpretive horror, it is also significant that his account involves not only his own reaction but that of a pious and traditionally observant Jewish man, one whom, as Buber says, "followed the religious tradition in all the details of his life-pattern."

The conversation that Buber recounts between himself and this man, and the care with which he describes his interlocutor's emotions, testify to his concern for broader communities: with his fraught reflections on the text, he maintains a focus on the spiritual needs of his dialogue partner and that man's milieu. But in Ochs' pragmatic register, Buber's concurrent unwillingness to rest easy in his own palliative conclusion is equally important. He has made a claim about the text that cannot be confirmed in the text's plain sense (though I suppose it is true that God never explicitly tells Samuel to carry out the killing that Saul has failed to achieve). Yet by insisting on "fear and trembling" when he sets out to translate or interpret the Bible, he also seeks to maintain the passage's historical and semantic integrity, acknowledging that his passionate refusal to believe it rests on perpetually shaky ground.

Ochs' formulation, therefore, may provide charitable and descriptive language for Buber's fraught attempt—in fact, such an attempt done correctly might only be fraught—to maintain both an enduring communal theological concern and a care for the historical and linguistic precision of good biblical interpretation and translation. But I understand Ochs' formulation to encompass a more explicitly constructive claim as well, about how contemporary academic scholarship in history, philosophy, textual interpretation, and the like may be done with another specific aim in mind: to, as Ochs concludes, "help repair the conditions of communal suffering that ultimately stimulate our enquiry."[24] Thus, Ochs' pragmatic account of Halivni's scholarship does

24. Ochs, "Talmudic Scholarship," 138.

not simply "allow" contemporary scholars to more subtly situate our historical subjects—but also challenges us to reconceive of the stakes of our own scholarship on these same subjects.

In this case, the process of pragmatic historiography as described by Ochs is the process by which we may—or perhaps *should*—make Buber's problem one that belongs not only to the historical record of twentieth-century Jewish thought, but also to contemporary communities who might share Buber's interpretive and theological concerns. Perhaps the most immediate community of readers is that broad community of biblical readers who find few easy answers to the Bible's frequent and often divinely commanded violence. What kind of God is the God of the Bible, and what does this mean for the religious communities for whom the Bible is a foundational and instructive sacred text? The stakes of Buber's question could be contemporary as well: should the Bible serve as an instructive political or ethical text for contemporary communities—and if so, how on earth can this be done? We do not need to look far to discover invocations of the text in contemporary American political life and theological discourse.

Of course, neither Martin Buber nor King Agag is required in order to echo these questions and engage them. But for the contemporary scholar, perhaps it is a quite compelling and generative way to do so. That is, given the fact of—in this case—Buber's anguished reflection on 1 Samuel, as well as the stark violence of the biblical text itself, the scholar who encounters these texts should hear Ochs' pragmatic challenge in addition to a body of more conventional scholarly queries. In naming and justifying the method, Ochs has, I suggest, already expanded from the descriptive—this is what at least one scholar is doing—to the prescriptive as well. Insofar as one can consider the ways in which a given community's concerns and questions might influence the trajectory of our theorization, perhaps one should. For Ochs, this is an essential means by which we "put our . . . scholarship to the ends for which we have produced it."[25] Which is to say that if we claim, as scholars in the humanities are wont to do, that our work has broad implications, this is one way to ensure that the claim has concrete meaning.

I understand Ochs' pragmatic historiography, therefore, to be as much a moral and ethical exhortation as a methodological defense (as well as, perhaps, an attempt to demonstrate again that these methods are not so very far apart as we might imagine). Such scholarship, in Ochs' terms, is not simply (contra the critiques of some scholars) methodologically acceptable, it is also ethically praiseworthy and powerful in its attention to the relationship between academic scholarship in the humanities and a community desperately in need of care, challenge, and inspiration.

25. Ochs, "Talmudic Scholarship," 121.

And although Ochs does not say this explicitly, I suggest—and suggest that this is implicit in his argument—that pragmatically informed scholarship may also be *better* scholarship. It may certainly be riskier scholarship, insofar as it self-consciously proceeds beyond the boundaries of the historical record and includes theorization that is by no means self-evident to readers familiar with the works under discussion. But it may also be, precisely for this reason, more interesting and evocative and generative scholarship, and this is no small thing. Because the work is more communally oriented and defined by communal concerns, it is also subject to a broader variety of critiques and considerations, and this too may render the work far more compelling than it might otherwise have been, as well as accountable to larger groups of contemporary readers.

Ochs' pragmatic historiography, therefore, is not merely that which allowed for a defense of Halivni's work, or that which has allowed me to press Buber and the Bible on questions not easily answered. It is also an invitation to scholars in the humanities to take more risks in the kinds of claims we are willing to make, while also being willing to acknowledge our own subjective position and our commitment to communities beyond the strictly academic. Such scholarship, Ochs implicitly suggests, may generate discourses both scholarly and extra-scholarly whose terms and stakes are far more compelling and possibly communally reparative than "safer" historical work may be. Such a methodological invitation may certainly be worth taking up.

Bibliography

Brown, Francis, R. Driver, and Charles Briggs. *A Hebrew and English Lexicon.* Peabody, MA: Hendrickson, 2004.

Buber, Martin. "The Man of Today and the Jewish Bible." In *On the Bible: Eighteen Studies*, edited by Nahum N. Glatzer. New York: Schocken, 1968.

———. *Meetings.* Edited by Maurice Friedman. LaSalle, IL: Open Court, 1973.

Fox, Everett, ed. *Scripture and Translation.* Bloomington: Indiana University Press, 1994.

Halivni, David Weiss. *Revelation Restored: Divine Writ and Critical Responses.* Boulder, CO: Westview, 1998.

Kepnes, Steven. *The Text as Thou.* Bloomington: Indiana University Press, 1992.

Ochs, Peter. "Talmudic Scholarship as Textual Reasoning: Halivni's Pragmatic Historiography." In *Textual Reasonings: Jewish Philosophy and Text Study at the End of the Twentieth Century*, edited by Peter Ochs and Nancy Levene, 120–43. Grand Rapids: Eerdmans, 2003.

Sufrin, Claire. "Martin Buber's Biblical Hermeneutics." PhD diss., Stanford University, 2008.

8

Scriptural Reasoning and Islamic Studies

—RUMEE AHMED, University of British Columbia

ABOUT TWENTY YEARS AGO, Peter Ochs, with the help of some friends
and colleagues, developed a vision for interreligious dialogue, known as
"Scriptural Reasoning," that has since been embraced by an international
network of scholars, statespersons, and practitioners.[1] Initially conceived
as a way of reading religious texts across different communities, Scriptural
Reasoning has since proved to have broad applications in several areas and
disciplines. That is no doubt because Scriptural Reasoning is based on the
idea that religious scriptures, at their core, command believers to respond to
the cry of the oppressed, care for those who are suffering, and repair what is
broken in the world,[2] commands that go well beyond merely sectarian and
academic concerns. Ochs hypothesized that scriptures contain an inherent
logic of repair, and that studying scriptures together would create relationships across religious boundaries that might otherwise seem insurmount-
able. Since its inception, Scriptural Reasoning has created relationships
in the most unlikely of places and amongst people who would otherwise
never speak to one another, suggesting that Scriptural Reasoning has the
ability to transcend many levels of difference and sectarianism, whether
religious or not. I have found that the practice of Scriptural Reasoning profoundly influences my own approach to Islamic law, and that it can repair
some of the divisions that pervade my field of Islamic Studies. The genius

1. For a brief history and current manifestations of Scriptural Reasoning, see Ochs,
"Re-socializing Scholars."

2. On the logic of repair in scriptures, especially in the Judaic and Christian traditions, see Ochs, *Peirce, Pragmatism*, 290–316.

of Scriptural Reasoning is that, in offering repair, it does not require individuals to all agree on a single conclusion. Rather, it allows individuals to come as they are, to find fellowship with those who might disagree, and to leave enriched, rather than in consensus. Ochs' vision offers repair without collapsing differences, and this is its greatest gift, applying just as well to Islamic Studies as it does to religious texts.

The ability for Scriptural Reasoning to bring people together in understanding while retaining difference comes out of Ochs' own reading of scriptural logic and medieval Jewish exegesis.[3] These texts suggest to him that scriptural logic transcends the simple binaries to which we are accustomed. Rather than promoting singularity and exclusivity, Ochs argues that scriptural texts embrace plural readings and ambiguity. This textual ambiguity allows scriptures to provide meaning to multiple audiences; it makes scriptures, in Umberto Eco's terms, "open" texts that admit various readings.[4] To reduce scriptures to any single reading—to make the text "closed"—is to violate the logic of scripture itself.

And yet, reduction seems to be standard operating procedure when it comes to reading scriptural texts. Both practitioners and scholars are obsessed with the question, "What does the text really say?", which is a question that assumes that the text has an ontological truth that must be exhumed in order to understand the text's inner meaning and message. This obsession leads us to read scriptural texts using a logic that Ochs calls "either-or"; that is, assuming that a reading is either true or it is false, either correct or incorrect. When readings are assumed to capture a text's ontological meaning, then readers believe that their preferred readings are right and all others are, as a matter of course, wrong. Ochs believes that applying the logic of "either-or" to scriptural texts results in exclusivist, "closed" readings that do not admit disagreement, ambiguity, or vagueness, in effect doing violence to the very logic of scripture itself. He laments the fact that so many scholars and practitioners read scriptures through a logic of "either-or," resulting in factionalism and division justified in the name of scripture.[5]

---

3. For a succinct exposition of Ochs' reading of scriptural and rabbinic logic as a compassionate response to suffering, see Ochs, "Compassionate Postmodernism," 74–79.

4. See especially Eco, *Open Work*.

5. Ochs, "Borowitz," 176. To those who would argue that scriptural sources lend themselves to binary readings, Ochs helpfully responds that "part of the modernist error is to have supposed that biblical and talmudic communal and text traditions were the source rather than the context of modernist suffering. To repair modernism in this way is to repair postmodern traditions of text and community . . ." (175). See this article also for a holistic exposition of Ochs' approach to scripture, especially 175–79.

According to Ochs, this obsession with "either-or" logic is thoroughly modern, with only rare parallels in the premodern period. Medieval exegetes, by contrast, regularly used a different, "both-and" logic, especially when it came to scripture. In this logic, two seemingly contradictory propositions can be reconciled, or might both be true at the same time in different ways, suggesting that they might not have been truly contradictory in the first place.[6] When modern interpreters misread "either-or" logic into scriptures and medieval commentaries, they end up missing the richness of the texts, and instead devolve into exclusivism. If, however, we approach scriptural texts and medieval commentaries assuming their "both-and" logic, then the texts become "open" to a host of possibilities, challenging the reader to move beyond simple binaries imposed by exclusivist readings.

As exciting as this might be, it is difficult to accept Ochs' theory because it threatens our deep-seated notions of truth itself. After all, how can two seemingly contradictory propositions both be true? To answer this, Ochs encourages us to think about the term "true" differently. Normally, we think of something as "true" or "false" based on whether a statement corresponds to some fact in reality. But it is quite possible for us to think of truth not as ontology ("does it exist?"), but as a result of practice ("does it work?"). In this way of thinking, we are less interested in the facticity of a scriptural reading than we are in its pragmatic effect. If a reading "works" in a certain time, in a certain context, for certain people, then it can be said to be "true" for them.[7] But that truth is only relative to the time, place, and people for which it works.[8] A different, seemingly contradictory reading might work just as well for another group, and would be "true" for them. The strength of an open text is that it can speak truth to multiple audiences, in that they can interpret propositions to "work" for their time and place.

Here, Ochs finds common cause with early American pragmatists, especially C.S. Peirce, who advocated a theory of pragmatism in which the truth of a proposition is judged by its effect.[9] The truth of the statement, "please pass the salt" is not in some ontological reality in which "passing" and "salt" either exist or do not, but in the effect in which the

6. Ochs states that "rabbinic reading . . . is not interrupted . . . by contradictions, but is, rather, displayed by way of them." Ochs, "Scriptural Logic," 66.

7. Ochs, "Pragmatic Conditions," 135.

8. According to Ochs, "Truth is the response traditional knowledge offers to particular crises of knowledge. Immanent in the tradition, it does not make itself known until behavioral failures signal the need for previously revealed truths to be modified." Ochs, "Scriptural Pragmatism," 135.

9. For more on Peirce and pragmaticism as it relates to Scriptural Reasoning, see Ochs, "Reparative Reasoning," 189–92.

addressee passes the salt to the speaker.[10] The falsity of the proposition might similarly be established if no salt is passed, or if it is passed in a way not intended by the speaker. Evaluating truth, then, has less to do with ontology—whether a thing actually exists—and more to do with relationality; pragmatic notions of truth are concerned mainly with how a proposition effects a relation between the speaker and the addressee. Truth is thereby judged by its ability to forge and destroy relations, and in this "both-and" logic in which two statements can be *both* different *and* true, truth is only interesting insofar as it can strengthen existing relationships, and repair broken ones.[11] This attention to repair is at the heart of scriptural logic for Ochs, and paying attention to the logic of repair has implications not only for our readings of texts, but for our relationships with one another. His insight into how scriptural texts work in the context of relationships has far reaching consequences that can move us beyond simple binaries that serve to divide, and into a "both-and" logic that can connect.

Central to Ochs' theory is the notion that the logic of repair does not manifest itself through solitary reflection alone. For one, a researcher cannot know if a reading "works" unless she sees its effects within a community of interpreters.[12] But more significantly, repair does not depend on finding some ontologically true reading of a text. Rather, it is found in the coming together of two otherwise disparate points of view, without compromising either. Repair does not require people with different viewpoints to agree to one belief; that would be coercive, and would follow the logic of "either-or." To truly bring about repair, participants in a conversation are brought together through a shared practice that allows them to retain their positionality in its fullness. They are *both* separate *and* connected.

Maintaining tension between separation and connection reflects, for Ochs, the logic of scripture and medieval commentaries, and of repair. The practice of Scriptural Reasoning (SR) is his bid to actualize that logic through a shared practice in interreligious dialogue. In SR, members of various faith traditions maintain their distinctive identities and commitments, but achieve fellowship through shared study. It is a remarkable demonstration of

10. Peirce and Ochs regularly cite the biblical maxim, "And you shall know them by their fruits" to remind the reader of the primacy of pragmatism.

11. Ochs demonstrates how Peircean pramaticism aims to bring about repair, and can even serve as a source of repair in debates amongst pragmatists themselves in "Sentiment of Pragmatism."

12. For Ochs, focusing on the scripture is not about studying the words that compose a scriptural text, but to "participate in some relationship that is already ongoing among that composition and some community/tradition of interpreter/practitioners and the Author of that composition as a whole." "Returning to Scripture," 449.

reparative reasoning, and it is made all the more remarkable by the obvious differences in the makeup of the participants. Jews, Christians, and Muslims—and more recently members of other faiths—come to the study-table with their identities intact, and leave the table with their identities intact; but during the practice, they forge relationships with one another that repair divisions that might otherwise seem inevitable.

Islamic Studies and the Insider-Outsider Debate

The promise of Scriptural Reasoning is that it might bring repair in situations that appear intractable. In my field of Islamic Studies, there is such a debate—mirroring debates in other realms of Religious Studies—that threatens to further divide the field. Specifically, I am referring to what is known as the "Insider-Outsider" debate. For many years, the academic study of Islam was dominated by white, secular-humanist, male scholars who argued that religious conviction and personal piety compromises academic objectivity. This was thought to be especially true for Muslims, whose religion apparently demands unquestioning obedience and blind faith. Unlike their Jewish and Christian counterparts who are somewhat capable of self-criticism, religious Muslims were presumed unable to study the religion of Islam "objectively," for they cannot fully engage in dispassionate and disinterested critical inquiry. The normative "Outsider" to Islam, then, was uniquely positioned for the objective study of the religion, just as the normative "Insider" was uniquely suited for subjective, confessional expressions of the faith.

As Muslim academics began to enter the field, many of them countered that, in fact, believers are the only ones who can truly understand and explain Islam. Fazlur Rahman, for example, likened the Insider perspective to that of a toothache sufferer: she can explain the pain and the experience in exquisite detail, but if you've never had a toothache, you will never really understand what it is.[13] The pain is always out of reach for the Outsider, and it is cognizable in its entirety only by the Insider. In this sense, Insiders have a decided advantage over Outsiders; they can study their faith dispassionately as an academic exercise, but then shed that dispassion to compare their "objective" study to their subjective, personal experience, and then describe the points of disjoint and intersection. Insiders have the ability to be both subject and object at the same time, a privilege denied to all Outsiders.

13. Rahman, "Approaches to Islam," 191.

Today, the debate has gained a level of theoretical sophistication, but the general thrust is the same.[14] Insiders are said to lack the ability to apply critical theory to Islamic Studies; the proof is that they have, by and large, failed to adopt many of the theories preferred by Outsiders. Outsiders are chided for failing to appreciate that Insiders have a unique and profound set of perspectives that they bring to Islamic Studies; just because an Insider might disagree with the theoretical approaches used by Outsiders does not mean that she cannot apply one if so desired. Insider bias is said to be dangerous to objective academic inquiry. Outsider failure to appreciate the complexity of the Islamic tradition is blamed for disastrous Western domestic and foreign policies related to Muslims. And so on and so forth; the debate will continue for the foreseeable future, because, as Peter Ochs noted, a binary logic in which one side claims exclusive access to ontological truth and/or method ensures that divisions will persist.

· The method of SR, however, promises to subvert this debate by redefining the terms that traditionally divide. In the practice of SR, participants are not primarily identified as either Insiders or Outsiders. Rather, participants are at once *both* insiders *and* outsiders. Each participant might have a unique perspective on the text/issue/tradition under study, but none have access to ontological truth, whatever their personal background or biases. Truth-claims are exposed as reflections of personal beliefs that might or might not be shared by others. This shifts the focus away from the theoretical tools and background knowledge that one brings to the study and toward the individual persons reading together, complete with their complex personal histories, beliefs, and practices. These individuals, in the context of shared text-study, resist categorization and reduction to any single identity; in SR one quickly finds that simple identity markers like "Insider," "Outsider," "Muslim," "Christian," "Jew," fail to capture the multifaceted personalities, perspectives, and beliefs of participants. A Muslim might espouse a reading of Christian texts that might be characterized as stereotypically Jewish; an Insider might feel like an Outsider to a morally outrageous text from her own tradition; an Outsider might feel ownership over a text to which an Insider might be indifferent.[15] That is not to say that participants move from one

14. For the latest incarnation of this debate, see the special issue of the *Bulletin for the Study of Religion* 43.4 (2014) in response to articles posted by Omid Safi and Aaron Hughes on jadaliyya.com.

15. Here, Ochs cleverly makes use of Peirce's identification of inductions as habits of belief, and Peirce's view that, in Ochs' words, "habits (as beliefs) are interpretants of habits (as objects)." Ochs, "Pragmatic Method," 282. Ochs extends Peirce's insight to argue that habits can be communicated through example and repetition, such that participants in Scriptural Reasoning might find that "by teaching their practice of dialogue, they thereby taught modest forms of habit-change in the way each of their communities

identity to another, but that identities themselves are complex, and the markers that we use to categorize people do not capture the richness with which they study texts and interact with others.

Just as it makes little sense to pinpoint one "true" identity marker for participants in SR study, so too does it make little sense to look for the one, true reading of the texts under study. Whether Insider or Outsider, participants will disagree with one another on the correct reading of a text, and no one reading can trump another. "Truth," in fact, shifts its location entirely; instead of being found in the text, truth is only found when a reading does something for the group of readers. When a reading spurs dialogue and understanding, then it can be considered "true," not because it is ontologically correct, but because it builds relationships amongst participants. When a reading of a text brings together individuals without requiring them to shed their deepest held presuppositions and convictions, then it is a fruitful—one might say "true"—reading for them, modeling the repair inherent in the "both-and" logic of scripture.

All of this to say that in SR there is an open invitation—or, perhaps, an unavoidable need—to shed the pretension of disinterested observation. More than merely an interesting thought-experiment, SR uncovers what is latent in all academic inquiry: no one is truly a disinterested observer, no one is privileged by dint of identity, and everyone makes relational arguments through truth-claims. SR forces us to confront the fact that our truth-claims are just that: claims that we make with the intention of challenging others to either agree or engage in debate. Understood in this way, truth-claims fulfill their unstated mandate when fruitful debate enriches all participants, and fails, or is "false," when it brings about divisions and mistrust.

The Insider-Outsider debate in Islamic Studies has much to learn from SR, as the debate has become only more furious in recent years. Scholars have taken to academic and public fora to denounce those whom they perceive as the opposition. Often, this is in the form of *ad hominem* attacks, castigating not only colleagues' academic rigor, but portraying them as insincere, disingenuous, and self-interested. The rancor ends up limiting academic discourse by forcing academics into one or another camp. Some of these academics see it as their duty to promote members of their tribe, and to denigrate others, all of which stifles new and creative thought that might challenge the lines between normative "Insiders" and "Outsiders." SR reminds us, however, that these divisions are of our own creation. Certainly, the supposed contentions between "Insiders" and

could conceivably relate to others. One of these changes was to recognize some of the ways in which habit-changes in one community might influence habit-changes in other communities." Ochs, "Reparative Reasoning," 197–98.

"Outsiders" in Islamic Studies are not as fraught as those between members of different Abrahamic faiths.

More importantly, SR suggests that there is a different way to do scholarship that overcomes tired, simplistic binaries. This would bring together the best tools of supposed "Insiders" and "Outsiders," thus being informed by both, but reducible to neither. SR has deeply influenced my own reading of Islamic law in a way that, I believe, cannot be reduced to that of an "Insider" or "Outsider." Instead, SR and pragmatism suggest to me a third way of approaching Islamic legal texts that gives us new insights into both how Islamic legal texts function, and how we can approach them as scholars.

Islamic Law

This third way requires viewing those involved in the production of Islamic law as complex individuals, rather than as mere objects of study. Many of us who study medieval Islamic legal texts are busy debating what Islamic law is and how Muslims received it. There is good reason for this focus: understanding what Islamic law is might help us understand how medieval legal texts were intended, and understanding Muslim reception of law can help us understand how law functioned in medieval Muslim societies. On the basis of this approach, some argue that Islamic law is an all-encompassing system that binds Muslims to certain conceptions of right and wrong. In this way of thinking, Islamic legal texts are manuals according to which Muslims and Muslim societies ordered themselves. Others counter that Islamic law was but one way to lead an ethical life, meant to function alongside other sciences to encourage moral behavior. In that view, Islamic legal texts are theoretical suggestions for ways to live good lives; legal texts were never binding commandments on Muslims, but rather helpful guides that pointed the way to morality.

Both of the above views put Islamic law and Muslims in a binary relationship of subject-object; law either has a direct impact on Muslim lives, or Muslims choose Islamic laws that might lead them to a good life. The pragmatist approach that Ochs models through SR, however, points out that there is a third factor in the articulation and reception of Islamic legal texts in medieval Muslim society: the author who interpreted Islamic law through his texts for a Muslim reader. The author was the mediating factor between Muslims and the legal texts, which should lead us to wonder, who was this author? What complex of relations did he work within to produce a text of Islamic law? Why did he bother writing it, and what did he expect from his readers? These questions are, of course, impossible to answer, but focusing our attention on them complicates our understanding of Islamic law in a way that breaks down binary relationships and instead offers a reparative way for us to engage with Islamic legal texts. To understand how, we will need to appreciate Ochs' use of Peircean semiotics to explain pragmatism and its influence on SR.

Peirce, in developing his semiotic system, was responding to the dominant semiotic theories of his time, which posited a binary relationship between signs and their signified, and between subjects and objects. Peirce argued instead that there is a third mediating element, the interpreter, that is always present in any semiotic relationship, and that there is never any unmediated, direct relationship between a sign and its signified. Instead, an interpreter uses signs to posit a relationship between that sign and some object. The interpreter does not make up these signs on her own; rather, signs are employed by a community of interpreters, who use them in order to make sense of a world of objects that would otherwise be incomprehensible. Each member of the community has her own relationship to the world of signs, and understands each sign in her own, unique way. However, her understanding of the sign must be somewhat analogous to others' understanding, otherwise she would be unable to communicate meaning through her sign.

The interpreter is thus in a relationship with the object through the sign, and that sign is itself in a relationship with the community of interpreters. The interpreter therefore never has complete mastery over the sign, the sign never truly captures the object, and the object never discloses itself completely to the interpreter. This world of indeterminateness, ambiguity, and vagueness would threaten to throw us all into an irremediable relativism, if it were not for pragmatism. The fact that one can never know the object, or have complete mastery over a system of signs is not a problem, because truth is found neither in the object nor the sign. Instead, truth is found in the ability for a relation that an interpreter posits between signs and object to provide meaning for a community of interpreters.

To put pragmatism and semiotics together: when anyone is interpreting a text, they are actually making an argument about the text that can never be ontologically validated. However, they can nevertheless work within a community of interpreters to provide meaning. This search for meaning is at the heart of the interpretive enterprise, in whatever field of inquiry, and it is what makes interpretation, argumentation, and proposition worthwhile. When Ochs shifts our focus from ontology to practice, what he is doing is placing our attention on the fundamental human endeavor of finding meaning in a world of ambiguity.

In a pragmatist paradigm, the search for meaning is more than simply a description of how language and texts function: it is a description of how we as humans make sense of the world. The quest for meaning is central to the human project of growth; it is not confined to monasteries and psychiatrists' couches, nor is it absent from academic inquiry. Ochs points out that academic inquiry is not really about texts, or events, or even ideas. In the end, it is about the people who write those texts finding and providing meaning for and within a community of interpreters.[16] In fact, meaning is the ultimate goal of most all inquiry, academic or not. Like participants around an SR table, every academic is searching for and providing meaning when they find meaning lacking. What we are doing is trying to fix a problem of broken meaning, and to repair it through our writings. As Jung observed,

> Meaninglessness inhibits fullness of life and is therefore equivalent to illness. Meaning makes a great many things endurable—perhaps everything.[17]

Meaning-making is the fundamental intellectual project of humankind, and academics are, whether explicitly or not, devoted to this project. We are all looking for and making meaning in our work, and the meaning that we project onto our work says a great deal about who we are as individuals and what we think about our larger world. Regardless of whether our concepts of self and world are accurate, the meanings that we ascribe to them create sets of relations that aim to repair what we see to be broken in the world. Meaning is found in the strength and quality of the relations our arguments foster, challenge, or break.

It is here that Ochs' work and the project of Scriptural Reasoning have most profoundly influenced my own work on Islamic Law. Islamic legal texts are, centrally, neither about Islamic law nor about the Muslims who apply it. An Islamic legal text is like any other text; written by a person who is trying to convey a meaningful message to repair something that is broken. Too often, in our theoretical abstractions on the proper way to read a text, we lose sight of the people behind the text. This, for me, is SR's greatest gift. We all have our ideological presumptions that we bring to text-study, but SR exposes the fact that we are all individuals trying to make meaning out of that which we hold most dear. Islamic legal texts should be read in such a light; not as a pedantic set of rules and regulations that lives outside history, but as a source of repair.

The problem is, Islamic legal texts make it hard to see them as a source of repair. In fact, they seem like impersonal and tedious lists of rules. When reading an Islamic legal text, one is confronted with thousands of dictates,

16. Ochs, "Scriptural Logic," 67.

17. Jung, *Memories, Dreams, Reflections*, 340.

encompassing everything from washroom etiquette to rules of war. Peppered throughout are historical references that catalog disagreements and precedents for legal positions. It's a bit like reading the tax code, if the tax code also included comparisons with other tax codes, a list of historical emendations, and the occasional admonition about the importance of paying taxes. But whereas it is easy to understand why someone would refer to the tax code—one has to pay tax, of course—it is less clear why anyone would read a book of Islamic law. Especially in the medieval period, when laws were not applied equally and exhaustively in the way we think of state law today. They were instead ad hoc applications that sometimes referenced Islamic legal texts, but usually did not. When political leaders wanted to pursue a certain policy, they rarely asked legal scholars for their opinions, and almost never read legal texts. When judges made rulings, they sometimes referenced legal texts, but often they did not. So why would anyone bother reading these texts, if they had no real practical application?

Here, Outsiders and Insiders alike have offered different answers that reflect different pre-commitments and assumptions about Islam, Muslims, and law. These answers are in tension with one another; some arguing that medieval Islamic legal texts were reference books, and others arguing that they were salvific texts that Muslims read to go to paradise, and yet others saying that they were helpful guidebooks for anyone who was so interested. But Ochs prompts us to change the question from "why would anyone read a book of law?" to "why would anyone write a book of law?" The texts in question were written by people who, presumably, were trying to reach some audience, or address something that was not being addressed. No one simply writes something or makes statements for their own sake, with no ulterior motive. Someone who, for example, went around making declarative statements out of context, like, "the car is red," would be considered crazy. However, if there were some precipitating question, like "Is the car red?" or "What color is the car?", then the declarative statement would make a lot more sense. It would be an answer to a question, something that aims to mitigate ambiguity, provide guidance, and offer repair. The declarative sentence, it turns out, only makes sense as a proposition, something more akin to, "in answer to your concern, I believe that the car in question is red."

We tend to read Islamic legal scholars as saying in their legal texts, "Islamic law on this issue is x," but they might actually have been saying, "in response to your concern, I believe that Islamic law on this issue is x." When we approach Islamic legal texts assuming that the authors were trying to engage with a community of interpreters through a series of propositional statements about law,[18] a whole different set of questions comes to the fore. These include: "What problem were they responding to?"; "Whose concerns were they addressing?"; and "How did their books offer repair, especially given that the legal scholars rarely had political power?" These questions humanize the authors of legal texts, and they are questions with which both Insiders and Outsiders can engage, but to which neither have exclusive answers. One might hypothesize that the repair that they offered was primarily a theological one, repairing the rift between God and creation,[19] or that the repair is philosophical, or that it was meant to repair the administration of law by describing a legal ideal to which society should be aspiring from a removed position. It is impossible to know the intentions of an historical person or the texts that they wrote—whether you are an Insider or an Outsider is irrelevant—the only things that you can bring to the table are your unique analytical tools, embodied experiences, and preconceptions. Every new set of tools and preconceptions can help shed light on the historical person, none is "better" or "worse," all have the potential to further enlighten, and none have privileged access to the truth.

When we engage in such a shared study in which the particularities of conversation partners shed light on the subject without agreeing on the conclusions reached—when we are *both* in fellowship *and* in disagreement—then we begin to appreciate the complexity and the humanity of those we study, whether we study historical persons or contemporaneous groups. That is because the same thing is true for Muslims today as it was for Muslims in the past: their receptions of Islamic law are highly personal, informed by their individual personalities, and responding to discrete sets of problems to which Islamic laws might be seen as a source of repair. And just as we cannot have access to historical persons, we can never truly know how different contemporary Muslims interpret Islamic law. We are always engaging in a world of signs in which there is radical separation between the sign, the object, and the interpreter. No one, then, can speak definitively

18. In the context of rabbinic Talmudic interpretation, Ochs cites Halivni as arguing that the term *peshat*, or plain-sense, "does not mean 'literal' or 'authoritative,'" but rather, "the 'context' of a phrase or verse," as in the meaning of the root *psht*, as "extension or continuation." "From *Peshat* to *Derash*," 285. As a contextualizing interpretation, Ochs finds that rabbinic commentaries are necessarily propositional, and should not be read as authoritative or authoritarian. A similar reading works well with medieval Islamic legal works, and helps to explain why jurists wrote texts, how they argued within them, and what they hoped to accomplish.

19. This is close to how Ochs reads rabbinic discourse, through Max Kadushin, in that for the rabbis "the pragmatic meaning of God's names is disclosed only in the way a community socializes its members in the rules of conduct which are attributes of those names." Ochs, "Charles Peirce's Unpragmatic Christianity," 71.

about Islam or Muslims; neither "Insiders" nor "Outsiders." But the tools that each brings to the study of Islam and Muslims can help uncover how Islamic law works—or does not work—to bring about repair in different contexts. This can only be done through sustained dialogue, in which academic works treat their subjects—whether in the form of persons or texts—as conversation partners rather than as objects of study.

Adopting an SR-approach to Islamic law can thereby offer repair to the academic study of Islamic law, and promises to overcome multiple binaries. It values embodied experience and text-study, "Insiders" and "Outsiders," academics and nonacademics, to provide thick descriptions of Islamic law as it functions in the lives of Muslims past and present. These descriptions are necessarily varied, as each scholar brings to the conversation her own background and unique insights. Individually, these descriptions are incomplete, but they strengthen one another through their particular offerings for repair.

Peter Ochs surely designed Scriptural Reasoning for loftier goals than bringing repair to the academic study of Islamic law, but the benefits that an SR-approach provides to Islamic law is a testament to its potential to bring about repair in many and varied contexts. While SR has historically brought disparate parties together in shared study, I believe that we have just scratched the surface of SR's potential for bringing about new, reparative ways of approaching Islamic Studies.

Bibliography

Eco, Umberto. *The Open Work*. Translated by Anna Concogni. Cambridge: Harvard University Press, 1989.

Jung, Carl. *Memories, Dreams, Reflections*. New York: Vintage, 1963.

Ochs, Peter. "Borowitz and the Postmodern Renewal of Theology." *CrossCurrents* 43.2 (1993) 164–83.

———. "Charles Peirce's Unpragmatic Christianity: A Rabbinic Appraisal." *American Journal of Theology and Philosophy* 9.1/2 (1988) 41–74.

———. "Compassionate Postmodernism: An Introduction to Postmodern Jewish Philosophy." *The European Legacy: Toward New Paradigms* 2.1 (1997) 74–79.

———. "From *Peshat* to *Derash* and Back Again: Talmud for the Modern Religious Jew." *Judaism* 46.3 (1997) 271–92.

———. *Peirce, Pragmatism and the Logic of Scripture*. Cambridge: Cambridge University Press, 1998.

———. "Pragmatic Conditions for Jewish-Christian Theological Dialogue." *Modern Theology* 9.2 (1993) 123–40.

———. "A Pragmatic Method of Reading Confused Philosophic Texts: The Case of Peirce's 'Illustrations.'" *Transactions of the Charles S. Peirce Society* 25.3 (1989) 251–91.

————. "Re-socializing Scholars of Religious, Theological, and Theo-Philosophical Inquiry." *Modern Theology* 29.4 (2013) 201–15.

————. "Reparative Reasoning: From Peirce's Pragmatism to Augustine's Scriptural Semiotic." *Modern Theology* 25.2 (2009) 187–215.

————. "Returning to Scripture: Trends in Postcritical Interpretation." *CrossCurrents* 44.4 (1994–95) 437–52.

————. "Scriptural Logic: Diagrams for a Postcritical Metaphysics." *Modern Theology* 11.1 (1995) 65–92.

————. "Scriptural Pragmatism: Jewish Philosophy's Concept of Truth." *International Philosophical Quarterly* 26.2 (1986) 131–35.

————. "The Sentiment of Pragmatism: From the Pragmatic Maxim to a Pragmatic Faith." *The Monist* 75.4 (1992) 551–68.

Rahman, Fazlur. "Approaches to Islam in Religious Studies: Review Essay." In *Approaches to Islam in Religious Studies*, edited by Richard C. Martin, 189–202. Tucson: University of Arizona Press, 1985.

9

Scripturally Inspired, Philosophically Sound

From the Personal to the Academic

—BASIT BILAL KOSHUL, Lahore University
of Management Sciences

THE EDITORS HAVE ASKED us to answer the question: "What aspect of Peter Ochs' work led you to make discoveries in your work that would otherwise be impossible?" Replying to this question provides an opportunity for both the pleasant task of acknowledgement and gratitude as well as the difficult task of self-reflection. While the influence of Professor Ochs on my work has been direct and deep, I have not taken the time to consciously reflect on its character and contours—the question by the editors provides the opportunity. In the broadest terms, my doctoral studies focused on Islamic philosophic theology and the philosophy of science, while I studied under Professor Ochs, first at Drew University and then at the University of Virginia (1996–2002). In the following pages I will describe how Professor Ochs' reading of Charles Sanders Peirce and his foundational work in the field have shaped the direction and character of my work in these areas.

Before I begin to describe Professor Ochs' intellectual influence, I have to describe his personal influence. To leave out effects of personal influence in an account of intellectual influence would be a most un-Ochsian move. Even though my first encounter with Professor Ochs took place almost twenty years ago (in Sept. 1996), my recollections of it remain vivid and vibrant even today. It was the first day of a course titled "From Phenomenology to Scripture." I arrived a little early and watched my classmates gradually enter the room, one by one. The teacher was among the last to join—upon entering he did what I had seen professors do countless times before: he took his seat at the front of the class and put his backpack on the desk. But what he did after that was something that I had never seen before: before uttering a single word, he reached into his backpack, pulled out a *kippa*, and placed it on his head. The single, smooth motion with which he did so signified that this was his normal routine. Now that the *kippa* was on his head and as he was reaching into his backpack for lecture material, I noticed him moving his lips in a way that clearly indicated he was saying a prayer. He did all of this before he spoke a single word to the class.

At that time I knew hardly anything about Judaism. But based on my general knowledge of religion and Islamic practice I inferred that the teacher was treating the act he was about to engage in (the act of teaching) as an act of worship. All indications were that before beginning his formal lecture, the teacher had very consciously performed a small ritual and said a short prayer. In all of my experience in a classroom setting—one BA, one MA, and just one paper short of a second MA (from Hartford Seminary)—I had never witnessed such a display of religiosity. I was puzzled; for the first time I saw a school/college teacher treat the act of teaching as a sacrament. Yet by the end of the very first lecture two things were clear. Firstly, the religious commitment of the teacher did not take anything away from his teaching—it in fact deepened it. Secondly, the act itself was as philosophically sound as it was religiously inspired.

This encounter forced me to rethink my attitude toward university studies. My previous experience in the college/university had led me to conclude that as long as I remained in academia there would always be conflict between my religious commitments and the demands of the academy. Consequently, I had entered the PhD program at Drew University with a very specific intent—go through the motions, complete the requirements, attain the degree, and then get down to doing "real" work. The "real" work at that time meant sociopolitical "activism." Very consciously I pursued the PhD for no other reason than the goal of having the letters "PhD" attached to my name for the purpose of legitimizing a preexisting activist agenda. This first encounter with Professor Ochs in the classroom was the beginning of a process during which I was forced to rethink (and then revise) my attitude toward the academy. I had come across a living example of something that I thought was not possible—an individual who successfully integrates his religious commitment with his academic pursuits without compromising the integrity of either!

When I first encountered this novel phenomenon I was not sure if it was the result of the peculiarity of the individual or perhaps some unique characteristics of Judaism that allowed him to bring religious belief and academic inquiry into a mutually enriching relationship. While the peculiarity of the individual and particularity of his religious traditions were critically important factors in the integration, by the end of the semester I learned that this integration could be replicated in other individuals belonging to other faiths—by means of something called "Scriptural Reasoning" (SR). The SR sessions that were organized by Professor Ochs during the course of the semester familiarized me with the theory and practice of Scriptural Reasoning. These sessions proved to be the first and most efficient means by which I came to understand Professor Ochs' pedagogy and scholarship—an understanding that proved to be of lasting significance for me. I am quite sure that if I had not encountered Scriptural Reasoning through Professor Ochs, I would not have stayed in the academy/university after the completion of my doctoral studies.

While my recollections of the first conversation I had with Professor Ochs outside of the classroom are not as vivid as my recollections of the first time I saw him, there is one sentence from that conversation that is etched in my memory: "Secular modernity and religious fundamentalism are two sides of the same coin." This sentence went against everything that I had learned both in the university and in my Muslim religious circles. In the university the rise of religious fundamentalism was seen as a quest to "turn the clock back" and return to the "old time religion" of a bygone era—trampling the ideals, norms, and achievements of secular modernity underfoot in the process. On the other side, almost all the Muslim thinkers I had come across painted secular modernity as the product of godless, Western civilization which was totally antithetical to Islamic teaching and from which Muslims had to protect themselves. Any attempt to accommodate, engage, or interact with modernity meant moving away from "authentic" and "pure" Islam. While they were in shrill disagreement about almost every other issue, the self-understanding and self-definition of both the typical university professor and the typical religious thinker hinged on the exact same point—a Manichean distinction between secular modernity and religious fundamentalism. When I began my doctoral studies, I had also embraced this dominant narrative about the (inverse) relationship between religion and modernity (and taken the side of religious fundamentalists). Yet I clearly recall that when I heard Professor Ochs say, "Secular modernity and religious fundamentalism are two sides of the same coin," I felt an inexplicable, intuitive attraction to this idea that was clearly challenging my own preexisting habits of thought. Professor Ochs went on to say something about "Cartesian anxiety," "binary logic," "nominalism," and a bunch of other terms (all of which meant nothing to me at that time). But I gradually came to learn about the meaning and significance of these terms as Professor Ochs introduced me to the work of Charles Peirce. As I became more fluent in these terms and used them to look at work being done in the sociology of religion, it became clear that secular modernity and religious fundamentalism were indeed two sides of the same coin; a mutually reinforcing dichotomy. Beginning with my first encounter and my first conversation with Professor Ochs and continuing through all the encounters and conversations since, I have seen the empirical evidence to confirm the following words of the Qur'an:

> All of them are not alike: Among the People of the Book is a group that stands (for what is just and right); they recite the verses of Allah throughout the night and they prostrate themselves in adoration. They believe in Allah and the Last Day; they enjoin what is right, and forbid what is wrong; and they hasten (in the doing of) good works: They are in the ranks of the righteous. Of the good that they do, nothing will be rejected; for Allah very well knows those who are God-conscious. (3:113–15)

In hindsight, it is now easy to see, both for me and the reader, how my intellectual and ethical formation was molded by the lessons and conversations I had with Professor Ochs. The first time I saw him (before I had spoken a word to him) I learned that two things which appear to be totally unrelated to each other (i.e., personal religiosity and academic inquiry) can be brought into a deep, intimate, and mutually enriching relationship. The first sustained conversation that I had with Professor Ochs taught me that those two things that appear to be deeply antagonistic (i.e., religious fundamentalism and secular modernity) can actually share the same roots. Abstracting from these two lessons, it is also the case that these very lessons are also two sides of the same coin. The former is the practical effect of a theoretical insight, the latter is a novel theoretical insight gained by deep, reflective study. Thus, the combined effects of learning the practice of Scriptural Reasoning and the ideas of Charles Peirce led me to radically revise my conception of a believer's place in the university/academy and my understanding of the relationship between religion and modernity.

After just one year of studying with Professor Ochs I already had a deep sense of indebtedness toward him. This was because the practice of SR and the study of Peirce had helped me to perceive three things clearly: 1) The grave mistakes I was making in my understanding of religion and modernity; 2) the valuable resources that lay outside my religious tradition (both in other religions and the secular university); and 3) the uniquely valuable contribution that my religious tradition could make in recognizing the value and worth of those resources. I was so inspired and enthused with this newfound knowledge that I started to discuss them with a missionary zeal among my Muslim friends. The immediate result of this was that a meeting was arranged where Professor Ochs met a group of five or six Muslim graduate students and young professionals for an evening study session, followed by dinner. Keeping in line with the practice of SR, the study session centered around a particular text—in this case Muhammad Iqbal's *The Reconstruction of Religious Thought in Islam*. Here was the setting: a Jewish professor (who placed a *kippa* on his head before opening the book), teaching at a United Methodist university, sitting with a bunch of Muslims, and discussing one of the seminal texts in modern Muslim thought. At the end of the sessions, as I was seeing him off, Professor Ochs gave me a copy of his recently published book *Peirce, Pragmatism and the Logic of Scripture*. He wrote the following message on the inside cover: "Basit, With a prayer that these exercises serve our communities' overlapping work today in America. Shalom . . . Peter." For me this message is the best summation of the logos and ethos that Professor Ochs embodies: Scriptural communities, not Cartesian egos; practical exercises, not abstract formulas; intentional prayer, not conceptual best wishes.

Thus far I have described the origins of my personal relationship with Professor Ochs. Now I will describe the "intellectual influence" that this relationship has engendered in more precise terms—or describe how my own work "could not do all that it does without" the work of Professor Ochs. In this respect, the influence of Professor Ochs has been direct and deep in three different areas: 1) Weber Studies, 2) Philosophy of Science, and 3) Islamic Studies. With the benefit of hindsight, I can now see that on each of these counts, I merely repeated in my own field what Professor Ochs had done in *Peirce, Pragmatism and the Logic of Scripture*. I will detail each of these points below in turn.

In his aforementioned work Professor Ochs notes that he seeks to address three different (but interrelated) issues. First, it tackles the issue of "the one Peirce and the many Peirces."[1] This point deals with the debate among Peirce scholars about the different readings of Peirce: Is there one Peirce? Are there two different (and conflicting) Peirces? Are there more than two Peirces? One finds a similar debate among Weber scholars: Are there one, two, or more than two Webers? For my part I narrowed the question down: Is Weber a sociologist? Is he a methodologist? Is Weber a child of the Enlightenment? Is he the resigned neo-Kantian of "iron cage" fame? Finally, is he a dead, white, male who has nothing of importance to say to us today?

---

1. Ochs, *Peirce, Pragmatism*, 15.

Or is he a voice of wisdom and insight from the past who directly speaks to us—only if we are willing to listen?

In tackling these questions, I followed Professor Ochs' lead in the way he dealt with Peirce:

> I read the problem in Peirce's early writings as signs of contra-dictions between two logically contrary leading tendencies. I read the unproblematic aspects of those early writings as tokens of another leading tendency that will eventually guide his cor-recting those tendencies and generating the relatively unprob-lematic essays of his later, pragmaticist period. There are thus three Peirces, if one adds up the two contrary tendencies and the one corrective tendency.[2]

My own reading of Weber followed this pattern. I began with identifying "two logically contrary . . . tendencies" in his work—an Enlightenment reading of his sociology of culture vs. a "beyond" the Enlightenment read-ing of his methodology. The former causes a yawning abyss to open up be-tween religion and science while the latter lays bare the intimate proximity between the two. Then paying careful attention to the text look for a third tendency that could serve as "tokens . . . that will eventually guide" the cor-rection and repair of the two conflicting tendencies. I found these tokens in Weber's methodology of the social sciences. A critical aspect of his meth-odology is turning the subject vs. object and fact vs. value dichotomies into subject-interpreter-object and fact-meaning-value relationships. Looking at the evidence that he presents for making this move, I argue that a third "corrective tendency" is implicit in Weber's work and this tendency opens up the possibility of "disenchanting disenchantment."

The second area where I have been influenced by Professor Ochs is the philosophy of science. The manner in which I have been influenced mirrors the second part of *Peirce, Pragmatism and the Logic of Scripture* in which he gives an account of Peirce's "mature pragmaticism."[3] After spending the first six chapters of his book bringing together the two contradictory tendencies in Peirce, Professor Ochs presents his own account of "Peirce as pragmatist and semiotician" in chapters 7–8—following the cues from his teachers (John E. Smith and Rulon Wells). Similarly, after dedicating one PhD dissertation to showing that Weber's work contains the potential to "disenchant disenchant-ment," I turned my attention to showing that a "philosophy of science" is im-plicit in his work. The most attractive feature of this Weberian "philosophy of science" is that it bridges the divide between the *Naturwissenschaften* and the

2. Ochs, *Peirce, Pragmatism*, 16.
3. Ochs, *Peirce, Pragmatism*, 16.

Geisteswissenschaften (or the hard and soft sciences). I could not have even theoretically contemplated this hypothesis (to say nothing of actually putting it down on paper) without the tools and methods I learned from Professor Ochs. A brief summary is as follows.

In one of his earliest methodological essays Weber argues that the difference between the hard and soft sciences "does *not* concern differences in the concept of causality, the significance of concept formation, or the kind of conceptual apparatus employed."[4] This observation itself suggests that a relational conception of science is implicit in Weber's methodology. He offers this hypothesis in the midst of the heated debate of the late-nineteenth, early-twentieth century *Methodenstreit* in German academic circles. This "battle of the methods" revolved around the relevance and applicability of the methods of the hard sciences in the study of social and cultural phenomena.

Because he is not a trained philosopher, Weber does not have the precise tools to articulate his ideas clearly. Consequently, his relational vision of science remains obscure. And it is here that I turn to Peirce—the Peirce that Professor Ochs taught me. Based on a close reading of Weber's text, I show that a phenomenology, logic, and semiotics are implicit in Weber's methodological writings and translate them into Peircean terms. Because Peirce explicitly offers his philosophy of science as a critique of the divide between the humanistic and natural sciences (as well as the divide between religion and science), my translation of Weber's methodology into Peircean terms has a double effect. Firstly, it clarifies Weber's insights into the methodology of scientific inquiry and shows that there is a deep and intimate relationship between the hard and soft sciences. Secondly, because Peirce's philosophy of religion is underpinned by the same phenomenology, logic, and semiotics that underpin his philosophy of science, we can begin to appreciate the fact that Weber's sociology of culture makes an important contribution to bridging the divide between religion and science. Read through the lens of Peirce's pragmatism, Weber's work not only helps us to better understand disenchantment as the fate of our times but also offers uniquely valuable resources to reach for cultural horizons that lie beyond it.

The last part of Professor Ochs' book on Peirce and pragmatism looks at Peirce "as theosemiotician and hermeneut."[5] This part closes by arguing that there is deep affinity between Peirce's hermeneutics and the method of reflection of the Talmudic sages. Stated a bit more boldly, the Talmudic sages had been embodying-enacting the principles of Peircean

4. Weber, *Roscher and Knies,* 186.
5. Ochs, *Peirce, Pragmatism,* 17.

hermeneutics millennia before these principles were actually formalized. If this hypothesis is correct then "wherever pragmatism has a voice, scriptural logic has a voice."[6] This is as remarkable a possibility for pragmatism and philosophy as it is for scripture and religion. It opens avenues of exchange between the two poles that have been progressively narrowing for the past four centuries—to the point of being practically closed at the beginning of the twentieth century. Professor Ochs offers this hypothesis not from some absolute, universalist perspective but rather from a very particular, specific standpoint. This standpoint comes in the form of bringing Michael Raposa's exposition of Peirce's pragmatism into conversation with scriptural logic as described by Max Kadushin.

During the course of my Weber and then Weber-Peirce studies I was quite conscious of the fact that this was preparation for first understanding and then (hopefully) building on Muhammad Iqbal's project of "reconstructing religious thought in Islam." As I turned my attention in this direction, the Ochsian influence has been maybe even more direct and deep than previously. Mirroring the move made by Professor Ochs in bringing together Raposa's exposition of Peirce and Kadushin's description of scriptural logic, my work in Islamic philosophic theology begins with bringing Muhammad Iqbal's treatment of scriptural logic into conversation with Professor Ochs' exposition of Peirce's pragmatism. Iqbal's *The Reconstruction of Religious Thought in Islam* is among the most seminal (and dense) texts in modern Islamic thought. It is my considered judgment that the relationship of logic, ethics, and esthetics in Peirce's pragmatism (as exposited by Professor Ochs) offers the best tools and most efficient approach to unpack Iqbal's text. At one level this is not surprising given the role of *ayah* (sign) in Iqbal's thought and the place of semiotics in Peirce's philosophy. I have begun to put pen to paper and an Iqbal-Peirce manuscript is beginning to emerge.

The implications of the opening up of Iqbal's text using Peirce's pragmatism are far-reaching. Firstly, it will show that Peirce's pragmatism and Iqbal's *falsafa-e-khudi* (philosophy of self) repair, complement, and confirm each other. Secondly, in light of this mutually enriching relationship between the two thinkers and the central place of the Qur'an in Iqbal's philosophy, the claim that "wherever pragmatism has a voice, scriptural logic has a voice"[7] will be strengthened. Thirdly, because Iqbal and Peirce are deeply rooted in the Islamic and Western philosophical traditions respectively the deep affinity between these two individuals points toward unexplored

6. Ochs, *Peirce, Pragmatism*, 325.
7. Ochs, *Peirce, Pragmatism*, 325.

avenues of dialogue between the two traditions/communities in which they are rooted (i.e., Islam and the West).

While I continued to work on my own Iqbal-Peirce project (complementing my Weber-Peirce project), I have started to introduce Peirce's work to students in Pakistan. The most immediate group of these students have been the students at the Lahore University of Management Sciences (LUMS). I have been teaching a course titled "Muhammad Iqbal and Charles Peirce" almost every year for the past five or six years. The result has been that as of 2015, four LUMS graduates are enrolled in the PhD program in religious studies at the University of Virginia. In addition, two other students from Lahore have gone for post-doctoral studies under Professor Ochs at the University of Virginia—Ahmad Bilal Awan and Junaid Akhtar. (Both of them are now assistant professors and have incorporated Peirce into their teaching—the former in the area of Urdu literature, the latter in the area of computer science.)

Outside of LUMS another group of students that has received Peirce's work enthusiastically are individuals who have approached Iqbal through the work of Muhammad Rafiuddin (d. 1967). Most of these students have a science and engineering background. A number of them have intuited the deep affinity between Iqbal (as presented by Rafiuddin) and Peirce (as presented by me). Some of them have been so taken by this affinity that they have switched their areas of study and enrolled in graduate programs in the social sciences and humanities so that they are better equipped to understand and explore this affinity. A sub-group of these students have studied medicine—with a few of them having reached the stage of residency in psychiatry. A few of these students (having seen of the effectiveness of Peirce in clarifying Weber) have decided to use the work of Peirce to bring clarity and depth to the work of Viktor Frankl. My educated guess is that the hermeneutical, theosemiotic reading of Peirce has deep affinity with Frankl's logotherapy.

As interesting and exciting as this developing interest in Peirce is on the part of university students in Pakistan, it is not nearly as intriguing as the possibility of Peirce being studied by *madrassah* students. I have been in touch with a group of these students for the past eighteen months or so and a sustained and substantive conversation has emerged. Thus far language has been the biggest hurdle in exploring this possibility—on this side, my Urdu is weak, on the other side, their English is weak. In spite of this hurdle there is eagerness on both sides to take the conversation further. Both parties have signified this eagerness in their own way. On this side, I have found a most able translator in the person of Asim Bakhshi. He has translated six of Peirce's papers and Charles Knight's introduction to

Peirce into Urdu. We hope to publish this manuscript in the near future. On the other side, a number of the *madrassah* students are working on their English and have enrolled in university degree programs. What will happen when individuals with a traditional *madrassah* training engage with Peirce's theosemiotics and hermeneutics? I don't know—only the future will tell. What will happen when the doctoral students at the University of Virginia sit with the *madrassah* students who have become versed in Peirce and the both of them sit with the university students who have integrated Peirce into their work? Even more so, I don't know. What I do know is that I could not have played the role that I have played in this course of events if, nearly twenty years ago, I had not come across someone who treated the act of teaching as an act of worship and did so based on reasoning that was religiously inspired and philosophy sound.

Bibliography

Ochs, Peter. *Peirce, Pragmatism and the Logic of Scripture*. Cambridge: Cambridge University Press. 1998.

Weber, Max. *Roscher and Knies: The Logical Problem of Historical Economics*. Translated by Guy Oakes. New York: Free Press, 1975.

10

Reading Your Neighbor's Scripture

Peter Ochs and the Creation of Religious Community

—LAURIE ZOLOTH, University of Chicago

Introduction

THE PRACTICE OF READING is a practice of becoming, of individual persons becoming "Readers of Scripture" and, within the academy, of students becoming scholars. And yet this act, this ontology, is fundamentally a public event, a public theology. In communities of particularity, Jewish, Muslim, and Christian, readers hold distinctive, traditional power and inhabit a particular place within these communities, and this sort of authoritative ontology reinforces social relationships and collective narratives that create and sustain. To be one who publicly reads Torah or who chants the Quran, implies a mastery of a particular language, it is to have a sort of possession of text that is then regularly given over, aloud, into public spaces. And this, I argue here, can be said to happen in the communities called Scriptural Reasoning, called into existence in large part because of a collaboration led by Peter Ochs, whose work we celebrate.

What then, does it mean to be a reader of the Scripture of another? Here is a paradox and, for a moral philosopher, quite an interesting one. One's Scripture is given within reception communities who understand the words as sacred, given by God to a special messenger, carefully recorded and kept, different than ordinary speech, and claiming a special place for the community in question, as God's chosen. The words are self-referential in that they ask and answer: who is chosen, who are God's own? The one in whose voice you hear this, however, in Scriptural Reasoning communities, may not be the voice of the one addressed—in fact, when a Jews reads the Quran, or a Muslim the New Testament, one is reading as an object, not subject of the text. The other is a reader who lives in proximity, a neighbor who has come over, as it were, to the public part in front of your house, to both overhear one's neighbor's reading and to participate in it, to offer response, to inquire after traditional meanings and challenge them. One reads one's own most precious speech in public, in front of the other, one reads the most precious speech of the other, and of the third. One leaves one's insider home of scriptural interpretive certainty, to listen and finally to offer the interpretation of the outsider, all of which shapes the self who listens and returns to communities of scholarship and practice.

Peter Ochs' genius was to imagine this act, and in so doing, both recreate the possibility of a traditionally coherent theological philosophy, and to create a community across particulars of discipline and tradition. He is not an ethicist, but this work of reading my neighbor's scripture is a genuine act of ethics, for it is, of course, the act of peace. This short reflection will raise the question of how such communities can be—and have been—created within academic settings.

For the last two decades, I have been a participant in Scriptural Reasoning. Before we turn to theory, let me pause to bless. What does that mean? I read Torah many times a week, three times a week liturgically, in communities of prayer, and more as a scholar and a teacher. But here are the differences—I don't read alone; I read and remember the comments of my neighbors, and I have watched my neighbors read their texts with me, so when I read the Quran or New Testament, I am not alone there either. I am with my neighbors.

In considering neighbors, a key category of scripture, in narratives that think in specific ways about place, land, and tribe, I turned to a recent book, *Good Neighbors: The Democracy of Everyday Life in America*, by political theorist Nancy Rosenblum. Attention to the neighbor is of particular interest, when, as Rosenblum says, the normal forms of democratic states can seem inadequate, and even broken, when democracy needs repair. In these moments, democracy is improvised, local, collectively pragmatic, and the focus on the neighbor operates, she notes, as "democracy's saving remnant." In times of crisis, storm and war, the loss of citizenship norms, all call on us to create new forms. One cannot abandon one's neighbors, and the substrate of democracy, its material form, embodied moral identity, can be considered as the quotidian necessity of societies. In America, in our frontiers, in the colonies come to worship, neighbors were the first station of the democratic ethics, and they are the last, a "bulwark against its disappearance rooted deeper even than a public culture of rights," she notes. It is

> a compass for maintaining our democratic bearings when orga-nized aspects of social and political life have lost their integrity or simply do not make sense to us. When public life is unjust, or beyond our capacity to influence, or so unappealing as to provoke retreat—when the mind is at the end of its tether with government and politics and with our fellow citizens, or when mindlessness rules, the democracy of everyday life is a heady remainder. Not a substitute for political democracy and or com-pensation for political disaster, but a saving remnant.[1]

There are three aspects of the phenomenology of good neighbors, she ar-gues. First, there is reciprocity, next there is "speaking out," meaning the ca-pacity for rebuke of one's neighbor, and finally, there is recognition, a sense of mutual tolerance she calls "live and let live."

Still, what happens when we apply this more general category of the neighbor to our own lives in the academy? We live, as scholars, in a neigh-borhood of others we did not exactly choose when we moved in here in the academy. Who knew, for example, that we would have to share the place with all those computer people and the business school? If you have trained in theology or religion, you have trained side by side with others in the academy who are committed to a life in relationship to a religious narrative, one that is sharply distinctive, even if that relationship is quite abstracted. But if you are a scholar of religious thought, you understand that the readers of your scripture have always lived side by side with others, our communities next to one another, with deep internal homes and complex familial obligations to which we must attend, but that we live on the streets of a city or town and always have, with others who we can see care about their God and what their God has left them to read and to study. To be a Jew or a Muslim has always been to live amidst Christians. It is no different now.

But this is a tribute to Peter Ochs, so let us understand that we live not just in any neighborhood, we live in Peter's. It is Peter Ochs who is the mayor of this town, so to speak, the one who, sometimes by the power of his own friendship, manages the introductions and organizes the ward captains. He is interested in how contemporary theology works, across religious tradi-tions, and he writes,

> I focus . . . on contemporary theologians with whom I have personal contact and can engage in sustained dialogue. I do

---

1. Rosenblum, *Good Neighbors*, 248.

this because I consider theology a dimension of immediate religious, social, and intellectual life. While theological inquiry must be informed by the long life of a traditions' commendation on revealed scripture, its criteria for participation in that life belongs to the time of a theologian's flesh and blood life on this earth, within the concrete movement and ruptures of lived salvation history . . . most of us live out lives under the influence of and in dialogue within a circle of many others and that these influences and dialogues are manifested not only in articulable worlds, but also through the less discrete ways that we act with one another and in the world. . . . My words, too are not only "my own." . . . Face to face inquiry of this kind tends to lead as well, to communal inquiry.[2]

In this face-to-face phenomenon, we can recognize elements of Rosenblum's understanding of the neighbor. In particular, to be a scriptural neighbor means to exercise three forms of theological practice: exchange, blood, peace.

Exchange

We read, first of all, as people who exchange things: gifts, words, tools, surprises. Let me explain.

There is an avuncular midrashic story about how to be a neighbor. Rabbi Simeon and Rabbi Judah are discussing a story that I first heard as "stone soup" and perhaps you know it too, about a reluctant set of neighbors who each give one item to a beggar to make a meal. The rabbis then turn from this tale to other quotidian relationships of relative power and need, tenant /landlord, loser/finder, and neighbor/ neighbor. Rabbi Aha describes the way a neighbor needs to act:

R. Aha said: There is a woman who is clever at borrowing, and there is a woman who is not clever at borrowing. There is a woman clever at borrowing: She goes to her neighbor, and though the door is open, she knocks at it, and says, "Peace unto you. How do you do? How is your husband? How are your children? Is it convenient for me to come in?" The neighbor says: "Come in, what do you require?" The visitor says, "Have you such-and-such a utensil that you can give me?" The neighbor answers: "Yes."—The woman not clever at borrowing goes to a neighbor, and though the door is closed, she opens it, and

2. Ochs, *Another Reformation*, 19.

says to her, "Have you such-and-such a utensil?" The neighbor answers, "No."[3]

Let us spend a moment understanding this story. A good neighbor is a person who asks permission to enter, even if the door is open, and her first word is "peace." She first speaks as a questioner: may I interrupt? Here, the speech is about the other: how are you, within your family, may I be with you? And then, and only then, after being placed in peace and family and time, she asks for a tool that she needs—it is not even an important tool, not a hammer or a weapon, it is a "so and so" a nameless kitchen utensil, the slotted spoon, perhaps? The cloth for cheese? We do not even need to know, because the point is that the gift is already given, the appearance, you, the word, the wish for peace, the opening and asking for your story.

The bad neighbor opens the door without questions (even the question, May I enter?), does not begin in peace, and begins with her need, a statement: gimme. Having given nothing, the answer is no.

Nancy Rosenblum writes about the exchange that neighborliness requires. "Reciprocity is a fundamental principle of morality and sociability in every domain. . . . Among neighbors, reciprocity holds sway . . . unadorned reciprocity, direct, face to face, and open ended is our foothold. It is a core element of the democracy of everyday life, the regulative ideal of the good neighbor."[4]

So we are led to reflect on how we read the neighbor's scripture, are we good neighbors. What are we exchanging? It is not story for a spoon, it is what then? In part, what we exchange happens on two levels, according to Ochs. First, we read one another's texts of scripture for their plain meaning, like people encountering them for the first time. I watch my neighbor read a text I love and in which I believe, or one that makes me miserable, and in which I believe, and I must see it in a new way, his gift to me, this newness. I read her text and I encounter it, it comes to my hand, to my voice and I speak it, and I encounter her Moses, or her Abraham, and it is both familiar and strange. My interpretation is new to her, it is me, handing over the tools I have, ones that are ordinary to me, but used in her house, may be new. And the physicality of the practice is a part of this, just as the midrash notes—sitting at a table, the texts between us, the capacity for interruption, the doing of the work over several days that have now grown into two decades. We have lived in this neighborhood for a long time, we are committed to living here a long time to come.

3. Leviticus Rabbah 5.8, quoted in Bialik and Ravnitzky, *Book of Legends*, 524.
4. Rosenblum, *Good Neighbors*, 71–72.

Blood

> GEMARA. Our Rabbis taught: whence do we know that he who pursues after his neighbour to slay him must be saved [from sin] at the cost of his own life? From the verse, Thou shalt not stand by the blood of thy neighbour (Lev. 19:16). But does it come to teach this? Is it not employed for the following [Baraitha] that has been taught: Whence do we know that if a man sees his fellow drowning, mauled by beasts, or attacked by robbers, he is bound to save him? From the verse, Thou shalt not stand by the blood of thy neighbor!—That in truth is so.[5]

But the discourse of neighbors is not only the rules of housekeeping. There are serious duties attendant to being a neighbor. You must not stand by the blood of your neighbor. Here is the verse:

> 15. You shall do no unrighteousness in judgment; you shall not respect the person of the poor, nor honor the person of the mighty; but in righteousness shall you judge your neighbor.

> 16. You shall not go up and down as a slanderer among your people; nor shall you stand idly against the blood of your neighbor; I am the Lord.[6]

The enterprise of neighborliness needs justice and judgement, without regard to their status, but with attention to their tragedy. There is blood everywhere in the Torah, it cries out from the ground. To be a neighbor is to be the one on the scene, the first responder, says Rosenblum, and the awareness of the stakes of this are a part of the phenomena of scriptural reading. We are responsible for our neighbor so profoundly, it notes in the Talmudic passage, that we are responsible to prevent his deadly sin, his shedding of the blood of another. We are responsible, too, if the neighbor is in trouble, it is always your business. How radical a demand! Being bound to save, getting between your neighbor, the guy across the hall, the Christian, and wild beasts? Saving a person from robbers? This should mean—it does mean—that the air is resonant with this tension in every place of reading—I will defend you, in all your difference, from the bear and the tenure committee, the taking on of your sin. Notice that the text allows you to kill the neighbor to prevent him from killing or raping an innocent person, "saved from sin at the cost of his own life."

5. B. Sanhedrin 73b (Soncino).
6. Lev 19:15–16.

That there is blood in these texts, death and danger in these texts, and that there is the promise to defend here, is what rescues the practice from a sort of sweet banality that can creep into so many interreligious discourses. If we read with neighbors, we take on the sort of relationship that is different from both scholarship on the one hand, or citizenship on the other. It is more intimate—they live *right next door*, and you can hear them fight and make love, but they are not your family. Your text is not theirs, theirs is not yours, not even when we share Moses or Mary. But yet, insists the law that emerges out of the text, you cannot live in a world where your neighbor sins violently, or one in which she is a victim, his blood is your concern, it should drive you into action.

Peace

And the action is critically important, for, as Peter Ochs says, the world is at war.

In a world at war, what does it mean then to love, and in particular, to "Love the neighbor as yourself"? For Ochs, in practice, much of the point of SR is to make peace. Here is the text in the Hebrew Bible:

> 17. You shall not hate your brother in your heart; you shall reason with your neighbor, and not allow sin on his account.

> 18. You shall not avenge, nor bear any grudge against the children of your people, but you shall love your neighbor as yourself; I am the Lord.[7]

Here is a text that anticipates our practice: you shall reason with your neighbor, for there is a logic in the Law, and reasoning is the way to avoid sin, and perhaps there is a larger reason beyond the cycle of sin and vengeance, of generational hatred, and it is this love, in which the reciprocity of the self-to-other is somehow possible, for you love yourself, in all your messiness, and thus you must love your neighbor, impossibly, as if she was you. It is a grand moment in Torah. And here is my conundrum. Seeking out this principle, loving the neighbor as yourself, in the Talmudic commentary turns out to be a disconcerting search, for the rabbinic understanding, the use of that as a proof text, is about execution (blood again), about seeking for your neighbor an easy death. There is a discussion about the number of faggots to be stacked in the burning pyre, methods of killing, and again and again (fifteen times) an explanation that the meaning

7. Lev. 19:17–18.

of this resonant text to love your neighbor as yourself, is that you should provide the quickest death for your neighbor. One can only speculate on the condition of exile that led to this despair. There is only one text in the midrashic commentary that is redeeming. Here it is:

> Ben 'Azzai said: THIS IS THE BOOK OF THE DESCENDANTS OF ADAM is a great principle of the Torah. R. Akiba said: But thou shalt love thy neighbor as thyself (Lev 19:18) is even a greater principle. Hence you must not say, Since I have been put to shame, let my neighbor be put to shame. R. Tanhuma said: If you do so, know whom you put to shame, [for] In the likeness of God made He him (Gen 2:4).[8]

This is a dense piece of theology. "The Book of the Descendants of Adam" may refer to one of the lost, mentioned in the non-mentioning books that show up in Hebrew Scripture, or it may refer to the long, rather boring list of names in Gen 2:4, and if this is the case, Ben Azzai (himself a person known only by his kinship role, son of Azzai), is making a claim about the importance of each and every being and that this is the "great principle" of the Torah. But Akiba disagrees, and says that loving your neighbor as yourself is the Great Principle of the Torah, and then Tanhuma makes the theological alchemy: your neighbor bears the likeness of God, and that is who you love. And this is the Great Principle.

But if you, my neighbor, are a Scriptural Reader, you know this already, because if you are a Christian, you know this verse, Mark 12:28–31 (NIV):

> 28 One of the teachers of the law came and heard them debating. Noticing that Jesus had given them a good answer, he asked him, "Of all the commandments, which is the most important?" 29 "The most important one," answered Jesus, "is this: 'Hear, O Israel: The Lord our God, the Lord is one. 30 Love the Lord your God with all your heart and with all your soul and with all your mind and with all your strength.' 31 The second is this: 'Love your neighbor as yourself.' There is no commandment greater than these."

Or Matthew 22:34–40 (NIV):

> 34 Hearing that Jesus had silenced the Sadducees, the Pharisees got together. 35 One of them, an expert in the law, tested him with this question: 36 "Teacher, which is the greatest commandment in the Law?" 37 Jesus replied: "'Love the Lord your God with all your heart and with all your soul and with all your

8. Genesis Rabbah XXIV, 7 (Soncino).

mind.' 38 This is the first and greatest commandment. 39 And the second is like it: 'Love your neighbor as yourself.' 40 All the Law and the Prophets hang on these two commandments."

And if you read the Qur'an you know Surah 4:36 (trans. Shakir):

> And serve Allah and do not associate anything with Him and be good to the parents and to the near of kin and the orphans and the needy and the neighbor of (your) kin and the alien neighbor, and the companion in a journey and the wayfarer and those whom your right hands possess; surely Allah does not love him who is proud, boastful . . .

In my neighbor's scripture is the interpretation of my own. And if this is possible, then peace may be as well, or at least recognition that the language we heard as language of God, theology, has a structure we can hear in our neighbor's voice. Of course, it is moments like reading this during which SR is at it richest, for as Ochs reminds us, then one can say: me too, I know this story, for suddenly we know, or we can imagine, that the trace of the conversation held in the room of the Beit Midrash, is recounted in the New Testament, resonant in the Qur'an, and overheard, now, by us, sitting in a room in 2016.

The phenomena of the life into which we are thrown, into the encounter that we choose, the face to face inquiry that becomes communal, as we think about exchange, blood, and peace, these elements that have shaped our talk. Over the past twenty years, since Peter Ochs understood that the outworking of peace might take place in the communities we call the academy, there have been many times when I was struck by the pure phenomena of the act of reading and hearing my neighbor speak. It is such a simple and such a rare thing, but it took a determination to create a practice, and for this I am extraordinary grateful for Peter's pragmatic leadership, his life work in tangible form.

Bibliography

Bialik, Hayim Nahman, and Yehoshua Hana Ravnitzky. *The Book of Legends: Sefer Ha-Aggadah; Legends from the Talmud and Midrash*. Translated by William G. Braude. Introduction by David Stern. New York: Schocken, 1992.

Ochs, Peter. *Another Reformation: Postliberal Christianity and the Jews*. Grand Rapids: Baker Academic, 2011.

Rosenblum, Nancy. *Good Neighbors: The Democracy of Everyday Life in America*. Princeton: Princeton University Press, 2016.

11

"What Is the Real Problem?"

Peter Ochs as Teacher of Responsible Reading

—RACHEL MUERS, University of Leeds, UK

Introduction: Peirce, Pragmatism and Problems with Reading

PETER OCHS' *PEIRCE, PRAGMATISM and the Logic of Scripture* was a transformative book in many ways. Its shaping influence on the practice and theory of Scriptural Reasoning is well known, and discussed elsewhere in this volume. Reading *Peirce, Pragmatism and the Logic of Scripture* as a graduate student engaged in Scriptural Reasoning certainly helped me to make more sense of that process. It also, however, helped me to make more sense of my own academic reading experiences—and consequently, to form many of my assumptions about what is important in scholarly work. In this essay, I explore how Ochs' therapeutic approach to scholarship enables key connections and reconnections within the modern academy—most notably, the reconnection of texts with the real problems, the embodied and historical situations of suffering, to which they point.

Here is the reading experience of which I needed (and still need) to make sense, and for which Peter Ochs' work provided valuable tools.

> I'm halfway through reading an article, and something is wrong with it. I know something's wrong with it, because my lower back is hurting. This is a comfortable chair and I'm sitting properly; the back pain is not related to my posture, it's related to the article. I'm used to the pain—it's the one I get when I'm

in a conversation or a meeting that isn't going well. It tells me there's unresolved tension in the dialogical space—somewhere between me and the article and the article's author. I'll carry on reading, the tension will get worse, and if I'm lucky I'll eventually spot what the problem is; I'll remember that things went wrong at about page six, and I'll look back and be able to identify the slippage in the argument, the example that doesn't quite show what it's supposed to show, the concept that's bearing more load than it's really able to bear.

Sometimes, though, I won't work it out. As I learn later, it might be that this article actually arises from a long-running debate that took a wrong turning a few years ago. More often the problem is that the author's afraid of something or hurt by something or angry with something, and sparring with shadows because of a conflict somewhere else that writing can't resolve. Equally often, of course, the problem is that the article pushed some of my buttons, uncovered an assumption I didn't want to look at closely, drew attention to something I've been trying to ignore.[1]

But all I have to show for it at the moment is the dull ache in my lower back, after reading an article that's apparently watertight.

As far as I can tell, there is no academic context in which this reading experience makes any sense. Maybe it's just me. It sounds worryingly like some sort of waffly feminine intuition—even when I write it down, even now.

Here is how I try to start thinking about it: they say academic work is like a conversation; but doesn't it matter that in real face-to-face conversations we pick up much of what we need to know before the other person's said a word? I think about Martin Buber's famous "visit from an unknown young man," in which as Buber reflected later he answered all the questions put to him but "omitted to guess the questions that [the other man] did not put."[2] I imagine Buber sitting there listening and speaking, all the time faintly aware that something was wrong; a dull niggling ache he chose to ignore. I think about the advice I was given about dealing with difficult interpersonal situations, advice that is maybe no longer fashionable in psychology but has in practice worked well for me: attend first to emotions, then to needs, and then, if necessary, to facts.

1. I usually spot it when the problem is that the article is telling me I do not or should not exist. Muers, "Feminist Theology."

2. Buber, *Between Man and Man*, 16.

I wonder what it would take to enable us occasionally to be serious about reading, serious enough to attend to what's actually going on. What would let us ask questions like: what motivates you? What troubles you? Where is the energy behind this work? With Simone Weil—"What are you going through?"[3] And with H. Richard Niebuhr—"What is going on here?"[4]

And then I come across a book by a philosopher who is serious enough about reading to ask that kind of question, to ask what the real problem is—and to ask it of Descartes, of all people. This could change a lot of things. And if nothing else, it encourages me not to ignore the niggling pain, but to work out how to read it.

Thinking about Peter Ochs' work, and participating in Scriptural Reasoning and similar academic experiments closely related to his work, has made a difference to the way I teach and think about reading—in theology and in biblical interpretation. Very important, in this, is his central insight into how the assumptions of modernity—in particular, assumptions about an ideal, unbiased, and decontextualized "real" or "original" meaning—might shape and misshape my own and my students' reading practices. Even more important, however, is the therapy Ochs offers for reading practices that are thus distorted.

Dyadic Anxieties of Reading

Ochs demonstrates, in his Peircean account of "Cartesian" doubt, how dyadic performances of the relationship between texts and meanings—this text means simply this, clearly and distinctly, always and everywhere —exert a powerful force in situations of uncertainty and anxiety. They provide a kind of response to lived suffering, disturbance, and discomfort, by offering fixed points in a shifting world; focusing on what can be known, clearly and distinctly, keeps various imponderables at bay. As Ochs goes on to show, however, the costs of this kind of response to suffering are considerable—and the first and most obvious cost is continuing anxiety, the niggling pain at the back of the mind whenever readings fail to meet the impossible requirements of clarity and fixity. I observe anxious readers in many areas of the contemporary academic enterprise—readers not merely accidentally anxious, but trained into anxiety. We might think about—students trained to be anxious about getting the right answer; academics trained to be

3. Weil, *Waiting for God*, 115.
4. Niebuhr, *Responsible Self*, 17.

anxious about pleasing student consumers (another dyadic relationship); and a wider public trained to be anxious about obfuscatory language or any attempt to make things complicated, on whose thinking the work of the academy is expected to have some "impact" (to use the terminology that UK academics currently most love to hate).

The anxiety of the dyadic reader finds voice in my introductory first-year class, as we discuss the challenges of reading texts in different genres. There are nods and murmurs of agreement all round when someone says that it is not only difficult, but also frustrating and dispiriting, to work with a text that does not present a single clear argument: "if it doesn't tell you ex-actly what it's saying, you don't know whether you agree with it or not." The students in that class, my experience suggests, have probably been trained to write essays in a standard "dyadic" form—a form that is not in itself prob-lematic, as a pedagogical stage and in the high school context, provided that the students can now find ways beyond its limitations. Given the question "Is x the case?", the essay goes: reasons to think x is the case; reasons to think x is not the case; and in a concluding paragraph, "my own opinion," coming down on one side of the question or the other. The students prob-ably also know this as the basic format of a debate on a news programmed, one speaker "for" and one speaker "against" a well-defined proposition; two options, you decide. Two and only two sides to every story: religion or athe-ism, reason or faith, us or them.

This is the starting point from which I am trying to teach students, and myself, to work with texts—starting with the texts in all their complex-ity, rather than with the "issues" extracted from the texts. In this context I go back to Ochs' work and the habits of mind it forms, firstly, for a way to move us past the anxiety lurking behind binary logics of interpreta-tion—the anxiety that once we allow alternatives to "this or not-this," "true or false," the clear and distinct argument, we will have no basis on which to make decisions or judgements. I find that simply raising the idea of a triad in interpretation, and asking questions about the third term, the interpretant, can feel, and be experienced as, surprisingly subversive and unsettling. I ask: if this is the right interpretation, for whom and in what situation is it the right interpretation? If this text says something new or puzzling "to us," who are "we"?

At this point, even a text that looks (and is) clear ceases to be simple. It opens up the text to open-ended processes of reasoning and interpre-tation that can still, at every stage of the process, be fully reasonable. It threatens to bring about a new level of critical thinking —critical thinking that increases rigor by refusing to compromise on complexity. The first challenge, which is difficult enough, is to accept that this is an acceptable, intellectually responsible, approach to reading.

More to the point, though, asking the question about the third term puts questions on the table that are usually left off it—or rather, questions that students (to stay with the university context for the moment) tend to assume are illegitimate in good academic work. It allows me to pay attention to the niggling pain in my back. Simply by asking "for whom and with respect to what does this interpretation work?"—and, even more basically, "for whom and why is this problem with the text a real problem?"—the reader or critic is forced to acknowledge and engage with her own locatedness, her own motivations and needs and passion, at the same time as she acknowledges and engages with the locatedness of another reader. She is not (I have to explain) allowed to give up at this point and say, "it's all relative" or "everyone has their own opinion so there's no point in arguing about it" or "anything goes." Once she has entered the relational space of reading, she is drawn in to questions that require more complex judgements—why and how and for whom and to what extent does this make sense? In this way she learns something about a different kind of intellectual responsibility—responsibility, not only to an extended intellectual community, but also to the particular other encountered through the text, calling for a response.

One of Peter Ochs' distinctive contributions to the re-formation of reading practices, seen particularly in *Peirce, Pragmatism and the Logic of Scripture*, comes in his attention to suffering, and his framing of interpretation as response to suffering. Ochs, in his Peircean reading of Peirce and his use of this reading to interpret wider dynamics in modern reading practices, pushes us to ask in regard to any text what the real problem is that motivates its project of enquiry. Taking his cue from Peirce's dismissal of Cartesian "paper doubts," Ochs commits himself not to dismissing the Cartesian project of enquiry but rather to the diagnosis and repair of the real suffering that motivates it.[5] Intellectual responsibility for Ochs is not, then, the general commitment to give an accurate and fair representation of the other; it includes the more specific commitment to understand, and to engage with practical compassion, the suffering that motivates a text or an interpretation.

"With Passion and Compassion":
Reading and the Response to Suffering

There are all sorts of reasons why the question about real suffering is unlikely to make sense to the groups of modern readers-in-training with whom we

5. On "paper doubts" see Ochs, *Peirce, Pragmatism*, 168.

work in university settings. Mostly, the questions they are accustomed to answering are the very epitome of "paper doubts." Plenty of essays are based around the doubts that an exam paper forces students to entertain about statements that they might otherwise have found entirely obvious or unproblematic. Even when the questions thus raised are the symptoms of real problems, we have been taught to leave other people's problems well alone, at least in academia. Or rather, we have been taught to dissociate from any real suffering that might underlie the doubts that have once been committed to paper—to focus on the paper and leave the realities alone.

It is difficult to find much material, in theology or anywhere else, that helps students to engage with the ethics of reading.[6] It is even difficult to find accounts of the responsible use of an author's context and biography—examples of how to understand the text and the body together. The default position of modern readers-in-training is, if anything, to treat attention to the author's life and attention to the text as mutually exclusive; the former explains away the latter, excuses us from having to think about it. "He is biased and unreliable," my students say, "because he is writing for this particular audience in this particular context"; "we cannot make sense of these [biblical] laws today," they say, "because people back then believed and did all sorts of crazy things." Thinking about the disincentives to take seriously the real problem (which is embodied and located) rather than the "paper doubts" (which can float free of context), I notice how, increasingly, the verbal conflicts of the blogosphere and the twittersphere and various other online fora remove words and claims from their contexts and from their authors. The "placeless" debates—in which I, also, find myself taking part—systematically disable attention to underlying problems or to the ways in which certain forms of arguments or reasoning exacerbate suffering. I notice how easy it is, once ideas are separated from complex historical bodies, for everything to fall apart. And then I notice the painstaking therapeutic work that Peter Ochs does to put things back together again—in the trickiest of cases, Descartes.

Feminist theologians and philosophers, among other feminist theorists, have been at the forefront of uncovering, analyzing, and critiquing certain prevalent intellectual binaries within the modern academy and of tracing their pernicious real-world effects. As Tina Beattie, Grace Jantzen, and numerous others have demonstrated at length, the disembodiment of the reasoning

---

6. Although, in the field of Christian theology, several of the pieces in the recently published collection in Higton and Fodor, *Routledge Companion to the Practice of Theology* are focused on what might broadly be called the ethics of academic practice. See for example Adams, "Arguing as a Theological Practice." See also Jacobs, *Theology of Reading.*

mind—and the exclusion of "passion" from rationality—is not merely an impoverishment of philosophical or theological thought.[7] It is at least an act of irresponsibility, and perhaps more fundamentally an act of violence—a refusal to acknowledge or respond to the passionate/impassioned/suffering body, which thus becomes complicit in the perpetuation of suffering. Seen from this perspective, attention to the embodiment and the "locatedness" of authors, readers, and reasoners is not an optional extra, an interesting gloss to be added on once we have done the hard academic work. It is a basic prior commitment, a modality of interpretation and of theological work. We can and should decide to reason "with passion and compassion" (to quote Mercy Amba Oduyoye and Virginia Fabella), to look for the possibility of "rational passion" (to quote Pamela Sue Anderson)—for the sake both of truthfulness and of effective action toward healing and repair.[8]

In fact, in feminist theology and philosophy as with Ochs' reading of Peircean pragmatism, the very idea of separating truthfulness and "effective action" rapidly stops making sense when we adopt a stance of intellectual responsibility that recognizes embodiment and asks about real suffering. What does it mean, after all, for academic work to be undertaken responsibly? Beyond rule-focused (and still important) accounts of the ethics of academic work—the responsible use of academic sources, the ethical treatment of personal data of all kinds—Peter Ochs' work draws attention to the prior movement of responsibility, the movement to respond to a cry (particularly, for Ochs, the cry of suffering—and paradigmatically, the cry of the oppressed Israelites in Egypt).[9] It is at least questionable whether someone who hears a cry and does not respond to it—or does not even think about how to respond to it—can really be said to have understood it.[10]

7. I am picking up here on common features in the diagnoses offered by Beattie, *Theology after Postmodernity*, and Jantzen, *Foundations of Violence*—commonalities despite very significant philosophical and theological differences in the accompanying constructive projects.

8. Fabella and Oduyoye, *With Passion and Compassion*; Anderson, *Feminist Philosophy of Religion*, 22–23.

9. See Ochs, *Peirce, Pragmatism*, 304–5. David F. Ford's work on theology and "hearing cries," in dialogue with Ochs and many others, extends the scope of the "cry" considerably beyond the "sign of suffering"—to cries of joy, praise, astonishment, and so forth. See for example Ford, *Christian Wisdom*, 14–45 and passim. I still find it helpful for many purposes, especially as a way into thinking about responsible reading, to retain Ochs' particular focus on suffering—while agreeing, as will become apparent, that it is important to expand the account of theological and indeed wider academic practice beyond the therapeutic/reparative.

10. I have suggested elsewhere, in relation to studying "difficult" texts and traditions, that there are at least some texts concerning which a reader who has no emotional response to them cannot really be said to have understood them; and that this

My point is not that doing academic work is the exact equivalent of social or political activism, such that people who do the one would be automatically excused the rather messier work of the other; nor that intellectuals should at a certain point stop thinking in order to act, or to make sure that their work is making the right sort of "impact" on the world beyond the academy. My point is, firstly, that academic work in general, and reading or interpretation in particular, always embodies ethical and political commitments; and, secondly, that there is no reason to assume that good interpretation is separable either from felt responses or from judgements about action. Peter Ochs' own wider project with Scriptural Reasoning, involving repeated crossings-over between academic and other spaces, taking the same basic modes of reading and attention into many different contexts, is itself an indication of how intellectual responsibility "crosses over" into other forms of social and political responsibility.

Attention to feminist critiques of theology and philosophy suggests that with the "re-embodiment" of reason will come new awareness of the asymmetries of power and vulnerability that shape all our practices of reasoning. One of the challenges that Ochs' call to intellectual responsibility puts to me, as a teacher and writer in contexts shaped by modernity's fears and anxieties, concerns the responsible use of power. I have suggested that it is extremely important for readers in academic contexts to re-embody their reading and reasoning, to acknowledge texts as signs of real suffering (and of the possibility of repair, in the world and not just in the text). I am, however, also obliged to recognize that "re-embodying" reading carries different risks for different people. Not every reader has or can have the emotional, social, and intellectual resources to engage in therapeutic work—to reinterpret a text's traces of violence as cries for help, to bring the suffering in her own life and context explicitly into the interpretive exercise, to place trust in authors and fellow readers. Moreover, there may be other responsible ways to think about reading.

In the spirit of re-contextualizing and re-embodying reasoning, it can be important to find ways of engaging with texts—and their gaps, silences and exclusions—that do not assume the weight of responsibility that a therapist carries. So, for example, faced with the exclusion of embodiment—and in particular of sexual difference and the female body—from the canon of

---

does not apply only to those texts written to elicit a certain kind of emotional response. Muers, "Reading Questionable Traditions," 253. Another good place from which to start thinking about the relationship between cry and response would be the—embodied, compassionate, *and* rational—maternal response to an infant's cry; on which see Soskice, *Kindness of God*, 7–34.

philosophy, Luce Irigaray chose to "have a fling" with the philosophers.[11] Her writing, while still a response to weighty "real problems" that motivate philosophical work, is playful and provocative, drawing attention gently to the vulnerability of the interlocutor without seeking to make herself invulnerable—and deliberately refusing to propose "solutions" other than the continuation of the conversation (or the fling).

Looking beyond the "Real Problem":
Reading In the Spirit

Strange as it may seem, the reference to Irigaray's "fling with the philosophers" points to the need to say something more about the theological basis for all of these claims about reading, responsibility, and embodiment. The response to distorted modes of reading is not just about the heroic reader/ reasoner taking responsibility for fixing all the anxieties and suffering of the past and present—but it is still about hoping for a different future, catching glimpses of new forms of mutual flourishing, refusing to be limited only to the questions already asked or the things already made clear. Indeed, while it might be tempting to read Ochs' work—particularly through "pragmatism"—as the basis simply for an activist ethic, its heart is in theology rather than (only) in ethics. The primary response to the cry of the oppressed Israelites—Ochs' paradigm case—comes from God; the creative and free human responses that follow, "follow after" God's response. They are truthful interpretations, responsible readings of the situation, not because they fix everything but because they engage in and respond to God's ongoing response—which is itself characterized by "passion and compassion," and also by promises that exceed any perceived lack or need. Truthful reading, we might say, can be faithful to embodiment and to history, to the sufferings and desires of people who read and reason, because (and just as) God is faithful to bodies and histories and suffering and desire.

This is, however, a difficult claim to make. Suspicious readers—like, for example, quite a few feminist critics of feminist theology—might suspect that this amounts to another way to absorb embodiment and difference back into a theological master-narrative. In the end, the suspicious reader says, theologians will want to come out with only one right answer, and to suppress any remaining inconvenient facts in the interests of cosmic harmony; by appealing to divine truth, even truth framed as response, we risk losing sight of the "real problem," the niggling pain in the back of the mind.

11. Irigaray, *This Sex Which Is Not One*, 150.

As a Christian feminist theologian, I am repeatedly made aware of this risk of too-hasty harmonization—which is not to say that I am particularly good at averting it. Peter Ochs' work, once again, read in the context of the ethical and political critiques of Christian theology as it has been practiced and enacted, points toward a possible theological response. As I read Ochs, his work points to a theological account of how theology, and in particular the interpretation of texts and traditions, is done. God "with" God's people—in the history of suffering and desiring and reading and reasoning—is not present as an ahistorical set of clear and distinct truths (a "right answer" that we know perfectly well all along) but rather as living truth, calling forth and enabling response, generating surprising new possibilities that are entirely consistent with who God is. The obvious way to talk about this from within my context is in terms of pneumatology. Reading "in the spirit" of re-contextualizing and re-embodying reading is reading in the Spirit—hoping to be guided into truth.

The promise of "reading in the Spirit," within the academy as anywhere else—and not only in explicitly theological contexts—is a kind of freedom beyond the anxiety-provoking freedom of "anything goes." It includes the freedom not to fix things—to acknowledge what the real problem is and to leave it open. It also, perhaps most importantly, includes the freedom to enjoy reading and reasoning—to take a step back from the anxieties of well-defined tasks that must be completed, and to respond with delight as well as with compassion to the texts and the people we encounter. And, as anyone who has studied with Peter Ochs will know, reading practices in which there was no place for laughter would be a highly irresponsible reading of his work.

Bibliography

Adams, Nicholas. "Arguing as a Theological Practice." In *Routledge Companion to the Practice of Theology*, edited by Mike Higton and Jim Fodor, 43–60. London: Routledge, 2015.

Anderson, Pamela Sue. *A Feminist Philosophy of Religion.* Oxford: Oxford University Press, 1998.

Beattie, Tina. *Theology After Postmodernity: Divining the Void.* Oxford: Oxford University Press, 2015.

Buber, Martin. *Between Man and Man.* Translated by Ronald Gregor Smith. 1947. Reprint, Routledge Classics. London: Routledge, 2002.

Fabella, Virginia, and Mercy Amba Oduyoye, eds. *With Passion and Compassion: Third World Women Doing Theology.* 2nd ed. Maryknoll, NY: Orbis, 1989.

Ford, David F. *Christian Wisdom: Desiring God and Learning in Love.* Cambridge: Cambridge University Press, 2007.

Irigaray, Luce. *This Sex Which Is Not One*. Translated by Catherine Porter with Carolyn Burke. Ithaca: Cornell University Press, 1985.

Jacobs, Alan. *A Theology of Reading: The Hermeneutics of Love*. Boulder, CO: Westview, 2001.

Jantzen, Grace M. *Foundations of Violence*. London: Routledge, 2004.

Muers, Rachel. "Feminist Theology as Practice of the Future." *Feminist Theology* 16 (2007) 110–27.

———. "Reading Questionable Traditions." In *Routledge Companion to the Practice of Theology*, edited by Mike Higton and Jim Fodor, 252–64. London: Routledge, 2015.

Niebuhr, H. Richard. *The Responsible Self*. 1963. Reprint, Lousiville: Westminster John Knox, 1999.

Ochs, Peter. *Peirce, Pragmatism and the Logic of Scripture*. Cambridge: Cambridge University Press, 1998.

Soskice, Janet Martin. *The Kindness of God: Metaphor, Gender and Religious Language*. Oxford: Oxford University Press, 2007.

Weil, Simone. *Waiting for God*. Translated by Emma Crauford. New York: Capricorn, 1959.

Part Three: **Theology**

12

Theosemiosis and the Void of Being

Kabbalistic Infinity through a Peircean Lens

—ELLIOT R. WOLFSON, University of California, Santa Barbara

> Breaking grains of sand more and more will only make the sand more broken. It will not weld the grains into unbroken continuity.
>
> —C. S. PEIRCE

ANY ATTEMPT TO REIFY a phenomenon as multifaceted as the kabbalah by identifying an essential core is dubious and runs the risk of the Whiteheadian fallacy of misplaced concreteness, obfuscating the intricacy of the concrete by a presumed abstraction that proffers a false sense of the whole. In Peircean terms, if we ignore the interdependence of all things, and consider each thing for itself, then general terms would correspond to no object; if, however, we accept that any particular thing is dependent on what lies beyond its immediate limits, then we discern that the perpetually abiding totality of that thing's true being—the generic—must be appraised constantly from the viewpoint of the changeable, transitory, and evanescent.[1] This criterion can be applied to the kabbalah: if we are to speak of an essence, then it can be ascertained only from the vantagepoint of the inessential. Any appeal to fixed meaning must be adduced from the fluctuating

---

1. Peirce, "Nominalism versus Realism," 153–54. See below, n. 62. On Peirce's rejection of the Kantian notion of things-in-themselves, see Rosensohn, *Phenomenology of Charles S. Peirce*, 16.

nature of historical contingencies; the variation of the invariable facilitates the continuity of the discontinuity.

On this score, it is legitimate to say that an enduring attraction for kabbalists has been the challenge to penetrate the impenetrable secret of infinity, to untangle the intractable knot of the mystery of the eternal beginning issuing from the nihilating nonground of the origin beyond conceptual and linguistic demarcation.[2] This generalization is justifiable not only because it is made on the basis of painstaking textual analysis across the span of many decades, but because it is pliable enough to comprise an endless array of variables. The larger hermeneutical assumption here is my conviction that the conservative and the innovative impulses at play in kabbalistic sources—and, I would argue, in human thinking more broadly—are not to be set in diametric opposition.[3] It is thus eminently defensible to assert that much energy has been expended on the part of kabbalists in deciphering the indecipherable materialization of the immaterial oneness of the indiscriminate being into the plethora of discriminate beings that constitute the nature of reality. From the very early stages of the history of kabbalah, one can detect an inordinate emphasis placed on the emanation from or coeternality with *Ein Sof* of the absolute nothingness (*ayin hagamur*), the first of the ten emanations (*sefirot*), commonly denominated as *Keter*, the crown, and identified variously as the incomprehensible thought (*maḥashavah*) or as the incalculable will (*raṣon*).[4, 5]

Insofar as the cosmological speculation of kabbalists has been fixated on the imponderable transition from infinity to finitude—the disclosure of the nondifferentiated nothingness of *Ein Sof* in the differentiated nothingness of *Keter*, and the further manifestation of the latter in the somethingness of *Ḥokhmah*, the divine wisdom, the indivisible point whence the line of equally indivisible points of zero-dimensionality extends[6]—we might even say the imaginal endeavor to penetrate this obdurate spot of impenetrability, the place that is no place, according to the memorable

2. Wolfson, "Nihilating Nonground," 31–45. I have taken the liberty to repeat here some of my argument from that study.

3. The paradoxical identification of novelty and repetition, innovation and conservation, is reiterated in many of my publications. See Wolfson, *Language,* 89–94, 116–17; Wolfson, *Alef, Mem, Tau,* 55–61; Wolfson, "Mythopoeic Imagination," 233–38; Wolfson, *Open Secret,* 22–24; Wolfson, "Anonymous Chapters," 152–54, 159–72.

4. Scholem, *Major Trends,* 207–9, 214–16; Scholem, *Origins of the Kabbalah,* 265–70; Scholem, *Kabbalah,* 88–96; Tishby, *Wisdom of the Zohar,* 229–55; Valabregue-Perry, *Concealed and Revealed;* Valabregue-Perry, "Concept of Infinity," 405–30.

5. Matt, "Ayin," 121–59.

6. Regarding this paradox of geometric points, see Huemer, *Approaching Infinity,* 18–20.

formulation in one zoharic passage,[7] is the central nerve that animates kabbalistic *poiēsis*. The latter term denotes the nexus of language, imagination, and world-making indicative of an ontic sensibility whereby things of the world are envisioned as word-images infused with the vibrancy of the visual verbalization of the verbal visualization.[8]

As Marc Alain Ouaknin has put it, the poetics of kabbalah can be understood primarily as an *opening onto infinity*.[9] This understanding brings to mind the Peircean *theosemiotic*, which is predicated, according to Michael Raposa, on viewing the universe as "God's great poem, a living inferential metaboly of symbols."[10] We could aptly apply to the kabbalists Raposa's insight that Peirce's theosemiotic is a complex theological method that starts with an interpretative reading of signs, and then proceeds with an elucidation of that gesture, culminating in its utilization and crystallization into a rule for living. Analogously, the ruminations of the masters of Jewish esoteric lore are, first and foremost, a hermeneutical act of interpretation predicated on the postulate that every entity in the chain of being is an expression of the inexpressible and therefore a sign to be decoded,[11] or as Gershom Scholem put it, seen kabbalistically, nature is nothing but a shadow of the name.[12]

The kabbalistic worldview has affinity with the conflation of the idealist and realist perspectives on the relation between matter and mind in Peirce's thought, in part due to the influence of Schelling's *Naturphilosophie*.[13] What is especially relevant is the contention that nature is "the essential medium through which the sacred reveals itself,"[14] the domain in which freedom and

7. Zohar 1:161b (Tosefta). The precise wording is *ha-hu atar law atar*, "that place is no place." See Wolfson, *Language*, 233–34.

8. Wolfson, *Language*, 25–26.

9. Ouaknin, *Mysteries of the Kabbalah*, 97–98.

10. Raposa, *Peirce's Philosophy of Religion*, 144. See Raposa, "Brief History of Theosemiotic." Raposa's taxonomy serves as the basis for the perspective enunciated by Peter Ochs, "Theosemiotics and Pragmatism," and later expanded in Ochs, *Peirce, Pragmatism*. My application of the theosemiotic to kabbalistic hermeneutics builds on Ochs' suggestion that Peircean pragmatism produces a scriptural logic whose goal is to repair broken lives and heal societal suffering.

11. Scholem, "Name of God," 165–66, 185–86; Scholem, *Origins of the Kabbalah*, 448.

12. Biale, "Gershom Scholem's," 81–82.

13. On the realist and idealist dimensions of Peirce's thought, see the analysis in Anderson, "Realism and Idealism," 185–92; Hausman, *Charles S. Peirce's Evolutionary Philosophy*, 140–93. See also Colapietro, "Ground of Semiosis," 129–40.

14. Matthews, *Schelling's Organic Form*, 7. Compare ibid., 19: "Exploding the linear causality of the mathematical categories, the multivalent causality of nature as a

necessity, in emulation of the divine,[15] are integrated into a unified account "in which the noumenal and the phenomenal intertwine in an organic, and thus chaotic, evolving cycle of self-differentiation."[16] Interestingly, Peirce explicitly acknowledged his indebtedness to the spiritualization of nature and the naturalization of spirit that may be elicited from Schelling:

> I have begun by showing that *tychism* must give birth to an evolutionary cosmology, in which all the regularities of nature and of mind are regarded as products of growth, and to a Schelling-fashioned idealism which holds matter to be mere specialized and partially deadened mind. I may mention, for the benefit of those who are curious in studying mental biographies, that I was born and reared in the neighborhood of Concord—I mean in Cambridge—at the time when Emerson, Hedge, and their friends were disseminating the ideas that they had caught from Schelling, and Schelling from Plotinus, from Boehm, of from God knows what minds stricken with the monstrous mysticism of the East.[17]

In the continuation of this passage, Peirce denies having been contracted by the virus of "Concord transcendentalism," but he admits that "it was probable that some cultured bacilli, some benignant form of the disease was implanted in my soul, unawares, and that now, after long incubation, it comes to the surface, modified by mathematical conceptions and by training in physical investigations."[18]

In a more candid moment, Peirce confessed in a letter to William James on January 28, 1894, that his views regarding the relationship of the inorganic and the organic "were probably influenced by Schelling,—by all stages of Schelling, but especially by the *Philosophie de Natur*. I consider Schelling as enormous; and one thing I admire about him is his freedom from the trammels of system, and his holding himself uncommitted to any

dynamic whole provides Schelling with an understanding of life, as absolute self-action, as the schema of freedom." See also Grant, *Philosophies of Nature*, 1–25; Mules, *With Nature*, 49–103; Sallis, *Return of Nature*, 22, 28–43. For a brief summary and background of Schelling's position, see Faivre, *Access to Western Esotericism*, 82–83.

15. Schelling, *Der Weltalter*, 209. For an English rendering, see Schelling, *Ages of the World*, 5. On the reconciliation of necessity and possibility in Peirce's idea of the vagueness of divine omnipotence, see Leahy, *Beyond Sovereignty*, 48–49.

16. Matthews, *Schelling's Organic Form*, 7.

17. Peirce, "Law of Mind," in *CP* 6.102. On Peirce and German Idealism, see Niemoczynski, *Charles Sanders Peirce*, 57–59. Peirce's relationship to the later Schelling is discussed by Ejsing, *Theology of Anticipation*, 59–73. Particularly noteworthy is the analysis of nature's sacred depths in Peirce, Schelling, and Heidegger offered by Niemoczynski, *Charles Sanders Peirce*, 109–48.

18. Peirce, "Law of Mind," *CP* 6.102.

previous utterance. In that, he is like a scientific man. If you were to call my philosophy Schellingism transformed in the light of modern physics, I should not take it hard."[19] Significantly, although evidently not appreciated by Peirce, Schelling's views on this subject likely betray as well the impact of Lurianic cosmology.[20] I shall return to this topic below. At this juncture, what needs to be emphasized is that the linguistic essence of reality is the axiological foundation for what is conventionally called in scholarship kabbalistic theurgy but which I would rename, in the spirit of Peirce, as semeiotic pragmatism.[21] The change in nomenclature is justified by the fact that, according to the kabbalists, the primary purpose of righteous action is to unify the letters of the Tetragrammaton, the name that comprises all the letters of the Hebrew alphabet—the *Ursprache* that, in medieval parlance, is the hylic matter through which all existents are constellated or, in a more contemporary idiom, the genome of being—and the principal danger of transgression is that the unity is torn asunder. The kabbalists surely would assent to Peirce's observation that "the universe is a vast representamen, a great symbol of God's purpose, working out its conclusions in living realities. Now every symbol must have, organically attached to it, its Indices of Reactions and its Icons of Qualities; and such part as these reactions and these qualities

19. Perry, *Thought and Character*, 415–16, cited in Matthews, *Schelling's Organic Form*, xi and 225 n. 2. On Schelling's critique of system, see Matthews, op. cit., xi–xii. Concerning the question of the legitimacy of positing a Peircean system, see Rosensohn, *Phenomenology*, 3–8. See also Short, "Peirce and the Incommensurability," 119–31, and the analysis of the structure of objectivity in Short, *Peirce's Theory of Signs*, 317–47. See also Nadin, "Logic of Vagueness," 154–66.

20. Franks, "Peirce's 'Schelling-Fashioned Idealism,'" 733–34, 745–51. Franks argues that when Peirce acknowledged in "The Law of Mind" the influence of "the monstrous mysticism of the East" (see reference above, n. 17), it alludes to the Lurianic kabbalah, which was disseminated to European philosophers through translations into Latin published in the mid-seventeenth century. Franks admits he has found no direct reference to the kabbalah in Peirce but he does cite (p. 745 n. 24) a passage from an address given in 1853 by his father, Benjamin, to the American Association for the Advancement of Science, wherein the kabbalah is invoked explicitly in support of the idea that there is an all-pervading language in nature that speaks to the human mind. This essay complements the study of Franks, although my emphasis is on elucidating some kabbalistic ideas utilizing Peirce rather than suggesting that Peirce was influenced, directly or indirectly, by the kabbalah. On the relationship of Schelling and the kabbalah, see references cited in Wolfson, *Heidegger and Kabbalah*, 18–19 n. 40.

21. Here I acknowledge my indebtedness to the attempt of Ochs, *Peirce, Pragmatism*, 290–305, to articulate a semeiotics of rabbinic pragmatism based on a restatement of the organic thinking explicated by Max Kadushin in light of a Peircean pragmaticism. My application of Peirce's hermeneutics to kabbalistic texts does not coincide with Ochs' strategy to establish a reparative semiosis of communal life, but it has been inspired by the *Sprachdenken* between us that began many years ago.

play in an argument that they, of course, play in the universe—that Universe being precisely an argument."[22]

The ideational foundation of the theosemiotic praxis is the concerted effort to explain the beginning that comes forth from the beginninglessness of the primordial nothing. This is the conceptual posture whence we can extrapolate the dialetheic paradox[23] that every being is a manifestation of the nonmanifest manifest in its nonmanifestation. The ascetic-quietistic underpinning of kabbalistic piety is grounded in this meontological orientation: attunement to the nothingness of being uncovers the inestimable value of the being of nothingness that is the cosmos. Expressed in a different terminological register, the ethos of the kabbalists—the demand to redeem the world theopolitically by liberating the sparks of light entrapped in the shards of darkness, or in its more radical formulation, to transpose the darkness into light—is sustained by the paradoxical presumption that the trace of infinity is tangibly present in the concatenation of the worlds from which it is intangibly absent, that nature is the place wherein the placelessness of the void is concomitantly placed and unplaced,[24] that the manifold reveals the face of the mystery of the one it conceals, that the projection of being must always be gauged from the standpoint of the nonbeing of the withdrawal of being—the more impervious the visible, the more transparent the invisible, the more hidden the exposed, the more exposed the hidden.

My hypothesis, simply stated, is that the kabbalistic symbolism can be beneficially translated into the evolutionary logic articulated by Peirce and the trichotomous structure that informed his philosophic architectonic.[25]

22. Peirce, "Reality of Thirdness," CP 5.119. Peirce, "On a New List of Categories," CP 1.564: "A representation is that character of a thing by virtue of which, for the production of a certain mental effect, it may stand in place of another thing. The thing having this character I term a *representamen*, the mental effect, or thought, its *interpretant*, the thing for which stands, its *object*" (emphasis in original). On the sign, semiosis, and the representamen, see Deledalle, *Charles S. Peirce's Philosophy of Signs*, 37–53.

23. The logic of dialetheism entails the repudiation of the law of noncontradiction based on the belief that the identification of opposites in the identity of their opposition yields a genuine and irresolvable contradiction; that is, the truth of a statement that presumes the paradoxical form α and $\neg\alpha$, which translates into the disjunctive syllogism if it is the case that α, then it is not the case that α, is a direct reproach of the more prevalent logic that for every statement either α or $\neg\alpha$ is true but both cannot be true at the same time and in the same relation. My embrace of dialetheism is indebted to the analysis of Priest, *Beyond the Limits*; Priest, *In Contradiction*. The logical and epistemological repercussions of dialetheism are explored critically in the studies included in Priest, Beall, and Armour-Garb, *Law of Non-Contradiction*.

24. My formulation here is indebted to the discussion of nature as the place of nonplace in Mules, *With Nature*, 39–40.

25. Rosensohn, *Phenomenology*, 8–17, 69–75; Fisch, "Peirce's Triadic Logic,"

Reflecting on the origin of the universe in an essay written in 1898, Peirce maintained that to account for this matter in a logical and scientific manner, we must suppose "an initial condition in which the whole universe was nonexistent, and therefore a state of absolute nothing."[26] However, this state before the universe existed is not a "pure abstract being," but rather a "state of just nothing at all, not even a state of emptiness, for even emptiness is something."[27] Elaborating the point, he writes,

> We start, then, with nothing, pure zero. But this is not the nothing of negation. For *not* means *other than*, and *other* is merely a synonym of the ordinal numeral *second*. As such it implies a first; while the present pure zero is prior to every first. The nothing of negation is the nothing of death, which comes *second* to, or after, everything. But this pure zero is the nothing of not having been born. . . . It is the germinal nothing, in which the whole universe is involved or foreshadowed. As such, it is absolutely undefined and unlimited possibility—boundless possibility. There is no compulsion and no law. It is boundless freedom.[28]

Translated kabbalistically, the two forms of nothing, the pure zero and the nothing of negation, correspond respectively to *Ein Sof* and *Keter*. The former is the origin, the germinal nothing in which the universe is foreshadowed, the "womb of indeterminacy,"[29] inchoate in its limitless potential[30] and boundless in its lawless freedom; by contrast, the beginning is the

---

171–83; Spinks, *Peirce and Triadomania*; Parker, *Continuity of Peirce's Thought*, 112–22. The Peircean phenomenological categories are critically evaluated by Leahy, *Foundation*, 282–86, 455–62; Leahy, *Faith and Philosophy*, 131–41; Leahy, *Beyond Sovereignty*, 90–93, 255–56, 294–95.

26. Peirce, "Objective Logic," *CP* 6.215.

27. Peirce, "Objective Logic," *CP* 6.215.

28. Peirce, "Objective Logic," *CP* 6.217 (emphasis in original). See Sheriff, *Charles Peirce's Guess at the Riddle*, 4. On the Peircean reflections on zeroness, see also Spinks, *Peirce and Triadomania*, 23–26.

29. Peirce, "Guess at the Riddle," *Writings* 6.209.

30. Here it is apposite to mention the following passage in the lecture Peirce, "Seven Systems of Metaphysics," 180: "The doctrine of Aristotle is distinguished from substantially all modern philosophy by its recognition of at least two grades of being. That is, besides actual reactive existence, Aristotle recognizes a germinal being, an *esse in potentia* or I like to call it an *esse in futuro*. In places Aristotle has glimpses of a distinction between ἐνέργεια and ἐντελέχεια." As the editors remark, Peirce, *Essential Peirce*, 522 n. 4, "Peirce originally inserted 'except perhaps Schelling's & mine' after 'modern philosophy'; he then apparently changed his mind, crossed out the insertion, and added instead the word 'substantially' earlier in the sentence." Even though Peirce crossed out the words "except perhaps Schelling's & mine," it is suggestive that, at first, he did consider that his thought was identical to Schelling in upholding Aristotle's distinction

flash discharged by the "principle of firstness," which, in turn, occasions the "principle of habit," or "secondedness,"[31] by which being begins to be differentiated from nonbeing. The beginning is thus the second that is first insofar as the origin is prior to every first. As a consequence of the coming forth of the nothing of negation from the pure zero—the movement within the immovable, the provocation of the novel repetition of the eternal beginning[32]—time emerges as the time before time, what Peirce refers to as the brute compulsion[33] confabulated as the logical sequence to depict the state of things before time was temporally organized.[34] In his own words, "Though time would not yet have been, this second flash was in some sense after the first because resulting from it. Then there would come other successions ever more and more closely connected, the habits and the tendency to take them ever strengthening themselves, until the events would have been bound together into something like a continuous flow."[35]

The view of temporality implicit in this comment resonates with the conception of the temporal order that shaped kabbalistic thinking—designated by the rabbinic locution *seder zemannim*—which precedes the computable ebb and flow of time.[36] The sempiternal nature of time presumed by the kabbalists is to be contrasted with the notion of timeless eternity, traceable to Parmenides and reinforced in Neoplatonic sources: the delimitation of the eternal as that which distends without beginning or end and is therefore devoid of the tensiveness of temporal elasticity.[37] The kabbalistic understanding of time that precedes time rests on the more paradoxical supposition that eternity is archetypically timelike in its capacity for

---

between actuality (ἐνέργεια) and potentiality (δύναμις), and the association of the latter with the temporal coordinate of the future. It seems reasonable to relate this comment to Peirce's idea of the germinal nothing, which, like the kabbalistic *Ein Sof*, comports the entelechic realization of the *esse in potentia*.

31. Peirce, "Guess at the Riddle," *Writings* 6.209.

32. With regard to the matter of the eternal beginning, one can detect the influence of Schelling. See Mules, *With Nature*, 61–62.

33. Peirce, "Issues of Pragmatism," *CP* 5.463.

34. Peirce, "Objective Logic," *CP* 6.147. Compare Peirce, "Neglected Argument for the Reality of God," *CP* 6.490: "A disembodied spirit, or pure mind, has its being out of time, since all that it is destined to think is fully in its being at any and every previous time. But in endless time it is destined to think all that it is capable of thinking."

35. Peirce, "Guess at the Riddle," *Writings* 6.209. On the continuity of time, see Parker, *Continuity*, 110–12. For an analysis of time in the various stages in the development of Peirce's philosophy, see as well Helm, "Nature and Modes of Time," 178–88.

36. Wolfson, *Alef*, 62, 73, 77–79, 84, 86–88, 109–11, 115, 216 n. 108, 220 n. 151, 222 n. 180.

37. Manchester, *Syntax of Time*, 107–8.

unremitting metamorphosis and that, inversely, time is paradigmatically eternal in its ability to sustain a vacillating stability.[38] Cast in Heideggerian terms, time, like the shadowy nature of the dream, is marked by the appearing of the nonapparent, that is, the appearing of what is withheld from appearing, the presencing of what prevails as absent, not because it is a presence that is not present—the nonbeing measured according to the metrics of being—but because it is present as nonpresent, the nonbeing that belongs to being as disclosed in the opening through the language of the human being.[39] In its oneiric fleetingness, time upholds the paradox that presencing is always concomitantly absencing,[40] indeed, a presencing that perseveres in the absencing of absencing, a disappearing of the appearance that withdraws in the appearing of its disappearance. Phenomenologically, the dream is the domain of the nonreal that is situated between the no-longer-real and the not-yet-real, and as a result, the line separating facticity and fictionality is conspicuously blurred.[41] Within the parameters of the spacetime apposite to the dream, the nonreal becomes the possible of what is actually real, and hence possibility is to be construed not merely as pure nonbeing, but rather as the state that oscillates between the being

38. Manchester, *Syntax of Time*, 108.

39. Heidegger, *Hölderlin's Hymn "Remembrance,"* 97; Heidegger, *Hölderlins Hymne "Andenken,"* 114.

40. Heidegger, *Hölderlin's Hymn "Remembrance,"* 100; Heidegger, *Hölderlins Hymne "Andenken,"* 117.

41. Wolfson, *Dream Interpreted*, 46–57. Compare the comment of Charles S. Peirce in the 1868 essay "Questions Concerning Certain Faculties," 196: "In trying to give an account of a dream, every accurate person must often have felt that it was a hopeless undertaking to attempt to disentangle waking interpretations and fillings out from the fragmentary images of the dream itself. . . . A dream, as far as its own content goes, is exactly like an actual experience. . . . Besides, even when we wake up, we do not find that the dream differed from reality, except by certain marks, darkness and fragmentariness. Not unfrequently a dream is so vivid that the memory of it is mistaken for the memory of an actual occurrence" (emphasis in original). On the semiotics of dreams, with a special emphasis on Peirce, see Spinks, *Semiosis*, 155–75. See also Merrell, *Peirce, Signs, and Meaning,* 209–29. Peirce's narrowing the epistemic gap between dreams and waking consciousness is connected to the supremacy he accords to the imagination. For instance, see the formulation in the 1893 essay "Mind and Matter," in *CP* 6.286: "Indeed, the whole business of ratiocination, and all that makes us intellectual beings, is performed in imagination. Vigorous men are wont to hold mere imagination in contempt; and in that they would be quite right if there were such a thing. . . . Mere imagination would indeed be mere trifling; only no imagination is mere" (emphasis in original). The great achievements of humankind, according to Peirce, are based on imaginary flights—or, in his precise language, the building of castles in the air—and the subsequent replication of them on the solid ground of practical reality. On the primary role accorded the imagination in the production of habits that mold human behavior, see Peirce, "Survey of Pragmatism," *CP* 5.479.

of nonbeing and the nonbeing of being.[42] The dream is thus illustrative of Peirce's larger claim regarding the phaneroscopy—in some measure reminiscent of the Husserlian *epochē* and the suspension of the ontological presuppositions of the natural attitude concerning the status of that which is manifest—as "the description of the *phaneron*; and by the *phaneron* I mean the collective total of all that is in any way or in any sense present to the mind, regardless of whether it corresponds to any real thing or not. . . . It will be plain from what has been said that phaneroscopy has nothing at all to do with the question of how far the *phanerons* it studies correspond to any realities. It religiously abstains from all speculation as to any relations between its categories and physiological facts, cerebral or other. . . . It simply scrutinizes the direct appearances, and endeavors to combine minute accuracy with the broadest possible generalization."[43]

Utilizing Peirce's signature conception of the triadic categories of reasoning,[44] to which he refers in one place as the ubiquitous elements of the universal phenomenon,[45] we can say that from the prospect of the firstness of the origin, the temporality that applies to the secondness of the beginning is centered in the moment—the present instant of infinitesimal duration[46]—that retrieves the existential actuality of the past as the necessary

42. Heidegger, *Hölderlin's Hymn "Remembrance,"* 100; Heidegger, *Hölderlins Hymne "Andenken,"* 117–18. Compare Heidegger, *Elucidations of Hölderlin's Poetry*, 62; Heidegger, *Erläuterungen zu Hölderlins Dichtung*, 45. See the discussion of the correlation of time and the imagination, based on the description of the latter as simultaneously being and nonbeing, in Wolfson, "Retroactive Not Yet," 27–30.

43. Peirce, "Phaneron," *CP* 1.284, 287. On Peirce's phaneroscopy, see Parker, *Continuity*, 104–6; Short, *Peirce's Theory of Signs*, 60–90.

44. See Peirce, "Architecture of Theories," *CP* 6.32: "First is the conception of being or existing independent of anything else. Second is the conception of being relative to, the conception of reaction with, something else. Third is the conception of mediation, whereby a first and second are brought into relation. . . . The origin of things, considered not as leading to anything, but in itself, contains the idea of First, the end of things that of Second, the process mediating between them that of Third. . . . Chance is First, Law is Second, the tendency to take habits is Third. Mind is First, Matter is Second, Evolution is Third." The triad of firstness, secondedness, and thirdness was originally demarcated by Peirce as the categories of quality, relation, and representation—the second term eventually changed to reaction, and the third term to mediation. See Peirce, "Detached Ideas on Vitally Important Topics," in *CP* 4.3. For an extensive discussion of the Peircean categories and phenomenology, see Hausman, *Charles S. Peirce's Evolutionary Philosophy*, 94–139. Other pertinent references to the Peircean triad are mentioned above, n. 25. On Peirce's triune God and the Christian Trinity, see Deledalle, *Charles S. Peirce's Philosophy of Signs*, 170–80.

45. Peirce, "Three Kinds of Goodness," *CP* 5.120.

46. Peirce, "Law of Mind," *CP* 6.126, p. 99. See Parker, *Continuity*, 75–101. On infinitesimals, infinity, and infinitizing, see Niemoczynski, *Charles Sanders Peirce*, 53–56.

contingency of the future,[47] the habitual element of thirdness mediated perpetually between the chance of what was and the law of what is to come. In a similar vein, kabbalists seek to demarcate the midpoint between the nothingness of the eternal origin of time and the somethingness of the temporal beginning of eternity, what Azriel of Gerona called the "now in proximity to the creation of the world" (*attah mi-qarov li-veri'at ha-olam*).[48] To the extent that the determinate beingness of the nothing of negation is contained in the absolute nothingness of the indeterminate zeroness, the second should be considered as primordial as the first, but the primordiality of the secondary is to be distinguished from the primordiality of its source in the same manner that the light of a primary candle is to be differentiated from the light of all the ancillary candles illumined subsequently from it. We may infer, therefore, that the manifestation of the sefirotic emanations as discrete entities—literally, according to Azriel's language, in the "division of their being" (*be-ḥilluq hawayyatam*)—does not imply that there is any innovation (*ḥiddush*) on the part of the infinite.[49] Even so, we can elicit from this kabbalist the view, shared by others, that the sefirotic gradations are not brought into being in time but they are nonetheless the enduring configurations that determine the contours of the evanescence of temporality. Ultimately, there is no answer to the question why did the emanation occur now and not before, since the *now*, when properly considered, is itself constituted by the delineation *from before*; that is, the moment can be commemorated only by the retention of the prehension of what has already never been, the retroactive not yet, the recurrence of the wholly dissimilar in which there is no time intervening between the first that is last and the last that is first.

The nullity of the nonrelative character of the monad yields the dyadic correlativity of the commencement, which engenders, in turn, the polyadic relationality that complements the abstractions of the zero and the nothing of negation; the third as correlate between the self and other secures the fact that the numerical passage from many to one will preclude the absorption of many into one.[50] The synthesis of the singular consciousness of the first and the dual consciousness of the second is adjudicated in the plural consciousness of the third, the psychological tripartite that corresponds logically to the conceptions of quality, relation, and synthesis or mediation, and semiotically to the trichotomy of signs—the icon, index,

47. Peirce, "Issues of Pragmatism," *CP* 5.459.

48. Azriel of Gerona, *Be'ur Eser Sefirot*, 86.

49. Azriel of Gerona, *Be'ur Eser Sefirot*, 87.

50. Peirce, "On a New List of Categories," *CP* 5.556, 5.565. See Rosensohn, *Phenomenology*, 12–13, 53–54.

and symbol—through which the relationship between sign, signified, and mental cognition, is clarified.[51]

> The First is that which has its being or peculiarity within itself. The Second is that which is what it is by force of something else. The third is that which is as it is owing to other things between which it mediates. The First presents itself as original, immediate, fresh, unsubjected to anything that went before or stands behind, and is therefore spontaneous and free. . . . The Second, last, term, or end is found in such facts as Another, Relation, Force [not in the abstract, but as it presents itself to one who gets hit], Effect, Dependence, Occurrence, Reality, Upshot. . . . By the Third, I understand the medium which has its being or peculiarity in connecting the more absolute first and second. The end is second, the means third. A fork in the road is third, it supposes three ways.[52]

The first assumes the status of the second, indeed the potentiality of the first is determined from the actuality of the second, which entails the "nothing of not having been born," as opposed to the "nothing of death."

In an unfinished letter to his student, Christine Ladd-Franklin, drafted on August 29, 1891, Peirce described his cosmology as espousing the theory that

> the evolution of the world is *hyperbolic*, that is, proceeds from one state of things in the infinite past, to a different state of things in the infinite future. The state of things in the infinite past is chaos, *tohu bohu*, the nothingness of which consists in the total absence of regularity. The state of things in the infinite future is death, the nothingness of which consists in the complete triumph of law and absence of spontaneity. Between these, we have on *our* side a state of things in which there is some absolute spontaneity counter to all law, and some degree of conformity to law, which is constantly on the increase owing to the growth of *habit*. . . . As to the part of time on the further

51. Peirce, "One, Two, Three," *Writings* 5.242–47. In that context, the third is not identified explicitly as a symbol but it is obvious that this is the appropriate classification from the characterization of it as "the general name or description which signifies its object by means of an association of ideas or habitual connection between the name and the character signified" (243). See the parenthetical gloss in the version of this study appended to Peirce's "Guess at the Riddle," *CP* 1.369. For a fuller analysis of the trichotomy of icon, index, and symbol, see Spinks, *Peirce and Triadomania*, 60–74. On thirdness and the sign relation, see Hookway, *Peirce*, 121–27.

52. Peirce, "One, Two, Three," *Writings* 5.299–300. Peirce's notion of generality, and the link between thirdness and continuity, is discussed by Hookway, *Peirce*, 172–80.

side of eternity which leads back to the infinite future to the infinite past, it evidently proceeds by contraries.[53]

As Peirce put it elsewhere, if we presume that "real existence," or "thing-ness," consists of regularities, we may infer that the "primeval chaos in which there was no regularity was mere nothing, from a physical aspect. Yet it was not a blank zero; for there was an intensity of consciousness there in comparison with which all that we ever feel is but as the struggling of a molecule or two to throw off a little of the force of law to an endless and innumerable diversity of chance utterly unlimited."[54] Geometrically, the primal chaos exhibits the quality of unlimited chance, the double absolute of probability; that is, the probability that "ranges from an unattainable absolute certainty *against* a proposition to an equally unattainable absolute certainty *for* it. A line, according to ordinary notions . . . is a linear quantity where the two points at infinity coincide."[55]

The coincidence of the two points at infinity is classified as the binary of being and nothing, the dyadic language that has dominated metaphysical speculation from antiquity. The proper assessment of this truism requires, according to Peirce, that at the outset we reject the Hegelian presumption that "Being is the abstraction belonging in common and exclusively to the objects of the concrete term, whose extension is unlimited or all-embracing, and whose comprehension is null," and that Nothing also is "an abstract term = nothingness; for otherwise to say that Being is Nothing, is like saying that humanity is non-man, and does not imply at all that Being is in any opposition with itself, since it would only say 'Das Sein is nicht Seiendes,' not 'Sein ist nicht Sein.'"[56] In a manner that curiously anticipates Heidegger's insistence on the ontological difference between being and beings, Peirce suggests that the seemingly paradoxical premise that being is nothing does not imply that being is not being but only that being is not a being. Nothing, on this account, would be the abstract term corresponding to the concrete term that is the logical contradictory of the concrete term that corresponds to being. In the 1890 "Lecture on Logic and Philosophy," Peirce offers his critique of Hegel's identification of being and nothing in terms of the image that Jacob saw in the dream at Bethel, the ladder resting on earth and stretching to heaven (Gen 28:12):

53. The text is cited in Peirce, *Writings*, 8.386–87 n. 111.3–5 (emphasis in original). On the nexus of law and thirdness, see Potter, *Charles S. Peirce*, 87–109.

54. Peirce, "Man's Glassy Essence," *Writings*, 8.181.

55. Peirce, "Architecture of Theories," *CP* 6.27 (emphasis in original).

56. Peirce, "Nominalism versus Realism," *Writings* 2.145. See Fisch, "Hegel and Peirce," 261–82.

It follows that our Jacob's ladder properly speaking has no definite top or bottom; above it is lost in the clouds of heaven, below
in the smoke of the pit. . . . Nevertheless, when we examine not
the relations of the objects named but the relations of the names
themselves as shown in Jacob's ladder, we are easily led to the
conception of a name whose logical comprehension shall be
null, and its extension unlimited, and this name is Being. We
are also led to the conception of a name whose extension shall
be null & its comprehension unlimited, & this name is Nothing. For we may predicate whatever we like of nothing and
there will be no falsity in the proposition. Thus we attain a pair
of clear metaphysical ideas of a most abstract nature. Being &
Nothing are not mere Reality & Figment. For even a figment is
something, and therefore comes under the head of being. But
the pure metaphysical being and nothing are conceptions which
have little place in our ordinary thoughts. What I wish to call
attention to is the very clear apprehension we obtain of these
notions when we consider them as representing the fictitious
extremes of the logical Jacob's ladder. For instance Hegel as you
know that tries to make out that Being is Nothing & nothing being. And how? Why he says Being is a purely empty conception.
That is true in this sense that it is the conception of a conception
devoid of logical comprehension. But that does not make it at all
like Nothing which is only devoid of Extension & has unlimited
Comprehension. Hegel would therefore not have fallen into his
contradiction if he had made his metaphysical conceptions clear
by insisting on determining what the phenomena of logic are
which these conceptions represent.[57]

Upholding the law of contradiction against the Hegelian dialectic,
Peirce affirms that "there is nothing which is, which is also not. Therefore,
it follows that *what is*, and *what is not*, are mutually exclusive and not
coëxtensive."[58] Insofar as beingness and nothingness are corresponding
abstractions devoid of determination, they are absolutely the same and
absolutely different—indeed, the same in virtue of their difference and
different in virtue of their sameness. Consequently, being is the analytic
equivalent to nothing—or the nought as Peirce prefers to name it—to the
extent that it is pure being in contradistinction to determined being, or,
expressed in German, *Daseyn* as opposed to *Seyn*, that is, existence or
extant being rather than being as such.[59] The nought, accordingly, is the

57. Peirce, "Lecture on Logic," *Writings* 4.8–9 (emphasis in original).
58. Peirce, "Nominalism versus Realism," *Writings* 2.145 (emphasis in original).
59. Peirce, "Nominalism versus Realism," *Writings* 2.146.

pure void to be distinguished from the nothing in the sense of no thing, the pure vacuity, the determination that is isolated from any substrate and therefore indeterminate.[60]

Analytic thought always "sunders the concrete, and never takes note of the link which binds"[61]—the singularity of being that can only be discerned from the interrelatedness of the multiplicity of all beings,[62] a particularity indexical of a universality that is always context-specific[63]—and thus, as a consequence of its dualizing proclivity, it arrives at the abstract simple, which leads one to consider the self-contradictory conundrum of the *genetic universal*: "To seize the pure simple in thought is to cancel it; for by seizing it in thought, we seize it as the negation of the determined, and by so doing we place it in opposition, and thereby determine it."[64] The turning point where analysis becomes synthesis relates to the pure simple, the ultimate abstraction that has two forms, pure affirmation and pure negation; the two coincide in the unconditional void in which there is no indistinct distinction and therefore no distinct indistinction. Expressed syllogistically, if difference is determination, and being has no determination, it follows that there is no differential mark that distinguishes being from nothing, and thus being is nothing.[65] It follows, therefore, that the perfect cosmology, according to Peirce, implies that all three universes—the number of universes that he thinks are ideationally possible—must be considered as "completely nil" to the extent that they are "necessary results of a state of utter nothingness. We cannot ourselves conceive of such a state of nility; but we can easily conceive that there should be a mind that could conceive

60. Peirce, "Nominalism versus Realism," *Writings* 2.146–47.

61. Peirce, "Nominalism versus Realism," *Writings* 2.147.

62. See the passage referred to above in n. 1. The view of Peirce can be profitably compared to Rosenzweig, *Star of Redemption*, 144–45 (*Der Stern der Erlösung*, 147–48) "The world is made of things; in spite of the unity of its concrete reality, it does not constitute a single object but a multiplicity of objects, precisely things. The thing does not possess stability as long as it is there quite alone. It is conscious of its singularity [*Einzelheit*], of its individuality [*Individualität*], only in the multiplicity of things. The thing can be shown only in connection [*Zusammenhang*] with other things; it is determined by its spatial relationship with other things, within such a connection. Furthermore, as specific thing, it has no essence of its own, it does not exist in itself, it exists only in its relationships. The essence it has is not within it, but in the relationship it keeps according to its genus; it is behind its determination, and not in it that it must seek its essentiality [*Wesentlichkeit*], its universality [*Allgemeinheit*]." For a more extensive discussion of interconnectivity and the system of philosophy in Rosenzweig, see Wolfson, *Giving beyond the Gift*, 39–41.

63. Ochs, *Peirce, Pragmatism*, 299.

64. Peirce, "Nominalism versus Realism," *Writings* 2.147.

65. Peirce, "Nominalism versus Realism," *Writings* 2.150.

it, since, after all, no contradiction can be involved in mere nonexistence."[66] A similar logic can be ascribed to the kabbalistic symbol of *Ein Sof*, which is outside the economy of the ontotheological binary inasmuch as it is the unconditional void that is simultaneously pure affirmation and pure negation. The self-determination of the indeterminate is such that it affirms itself to the degree that it negates itself and negates itself to the degree that it affirms itself. In the infinitivity of the absolute zero, all things are interconnected to the extent that the indefinite suchness of their nonbeing is the definite emptiness of their being. The meontology avowed by kabbalists comparably posits that, inasmuch as the source of everything is the utter nothingness of the infinite, finite existence is completely nil. We can speak, therefore, of naturalizing transcendence[67] in both Peircean and kabbalistic cosmology as long as it is understood that the transcendent is present in the world to the degree that it is absent from the world; indeed, the transcendent is present precisely as that which is absent.

But how do kabbalists understand the shift from absolute zero to the nothing of negation? In Peircean terms, what One of the boldest mythopoeic doctrines to explain this process can be found in the teachings promulgated in the late-sixteenth and early-seventeenth centuries by Israel Saruq[68] about the jouissance (*sha'ashu'a*) associated with the initial withdrawal or constriction (*ṣimṣum*) of the light of infinity.[69] As with many things kabbalistic, the choice of terminology reverberates with many layers of philological-textual sedimentation. In this particular case, the utilization of the term *sha'ashu'a* to depict God's relation to the Torah prior to the creation of the world is found in older rabbinic sources, based on the description of Wisdom in Proverbs (8:30) and echoed in Psalms (119:77, 92, 143).[70] The Saruqian materials also reflect the connotation of this term in

---

66. Peirce, "Neglected Argument," *CP* 6.490.

67. Niemoczynski, *Charles Sanders Peirce*, 1–34, esp. 26–28.

68. In scholarly literature, there is debate whether Saruq was a genuine disciple of Luria, an independent and perhaps less authentic interpreter of Lurianic doctrine, part of an independent circle of kabbalists in Safed that evolved alongside Luria's school, or perhaps someone who transformed Cordoverian themes in a Lurianic key. For some representative studies, see Wolfson, *Heidegger and Kabbalah*, 124 n. 32.

69. For my previous analysis of this motif, see Wolfson, *Circle in the Square*, 69–72, 189–92 nn. 174–80; Wolfson, *Language*, 271–87; Wolfson, *Alef*, 131–36; Wolfson, *Heidegger and Kabbalah*, 98–104. The motif of quivering in both Lurianic kabbalah and Heideggerian thought may be profitably compared to the state of trembling (*durchzittern*) in Hegel to mark the tension of the interiorization of alterity when the subject feels like an "other" in relation to itself. See Malabou, *Future of Hegel*, 32.

70. Bere'shit Rabba, 1:1, 8:1; b.Shabbat 89a.

the writings of previous kabbalists,[71] including especially the zoharic compilation, where it is connected most frequently to the theme of God taking delight with the souls of the righteous in the Garden of Eden,[72] and Moses Cordovero (1522–70), where it connotes, *inter alia*, the infinite's contemplation of its own essence, which is beyond human comprehension,[73] the first stirrings of the divine will to be garbed in the sefirotic gradations.[74] The erotic element amplified in the Lurianic sources is latent in some of the passages in Cordovero's voluminous corpus.[75]

An audacious articulation of this myth is found in an anonymous Lurianic text that begins with the startling assertion, "Before all the emanation *Ein Sof* was alone bemusing himself" (*qodem kol ha-aṣilut hayah ha-ein sof levado mishta'ashe'a be-aṣmuto*).[76] From the continuation, which describes the emergence of the letter *yod*—a cipher for the seminal point of divine wisdom—from the infinite, we can deduce that this text is a commentary on the notoriously difficult zoharic passage linked to the first verse of Genesis, "In the beginning of the decree of the king, the hardened spark engraved an engraving in the supernal luster" (*be-reish hurmenuta de-malka galif gelufei bi-ṭehiru illa'ah boṣina de-qardinuta*).[77] I render the term *sha'ashu'a* as *bemusement*—understood in an antiquated sense as to gaze meditatively or to ruminate and not in the more conventional connotation to be puzzled or to be bewildered[78]—to capture in a Lacanian fashion the dual connotation

71. See, for instance, Wolfson, *Language*, pp. 277–78, where I analyze the motif of *sha'ashu'a* in the Bahir.

72. See Zohar 1:178b, 245b; 2:173b, 217b, 255a; 3:193a.

73. See the Cordoverian texts cited in Wolfson, *Heidegger and Kabbalah*, 124 n. 37.

74. See primary and secondary sources cited in Wolfson, *Heidegger and Kabbalah*, 124 n. 38.

75. Wolfson, *Heidegger and Kabbalah*, 124–25 n. 39.

76. MSS Oxford, Bodleian Library 1783, fol. 48a and 1784, fol. 58a. For a list of other manuscript witnesses of this text, see Meroz, "Redemption in the Lurianic Teaching," 93. See, in particular, the reading preserved in MS Oxford-Bodleian 1741, fol. 128a: "When it arose in the will of the emanator to produce the letters, at first he was alone, delighting in himself." The text is published on the basis of MS New York, Columbia University X893 M6862 in Meroz, "Early Lurianic Compositions," 327–30 (Hebrew). The relevant passage appears on p. 327.

77. Zohar 1:15a. See Meroz, "Redemption," 111–12. It is noteworthy that Saruq's *Derush ha-Malbush* is presented as an explication of this zoharic passage. See Saruq, *Derush ha Malbush we-ha-Ṣimṣum*, 7. Concerning the zoharic symbol of the *boṣina de-qardinuta*, see the comments and reference to other sources in Wolfson, *Language*, 137, 321, 487 n. 198, 571–72 n. 200; and the more recent discussion in Necker, "Hans Blumenberg's Metaphorology," 194–98.

78. On musement in Peircean thought, see Raposa, *Peirce's Philosophy of Religion*, 117–41; Ochs, *Peirce, Pragmatism*, 228–29, 241–45, 250–51, 282–83, 288–89; White, *Hidden God*, 165–85.

of jouissance as erotic rhapsody and noetic bliss.[79] Hence, when I translate
the idiom of these texts as the infinite bemusing itself, what I have in mind
is an ecstatic amusement that is of a contemplative nature. The rapturous
nature of the kabbalistic *sha'ashu'a* is simultaneously cerebral and somatic.
The theme of the demiurgic playfulness of the stimulation on the part of
Ein Sof is highlighted by Saruq:

> You must know that prior to everything, the blessed holy One
> bemused himself [*mishta'ashe'a be-asmo*], that is, he was joyous
> and he took delight.... And from the quivering [*ni'anu'a*] of the
> spark the Torah was created.... Know that the quivering that
> arose from the bemusement consisted of ten quiverings, cor-
> responding to the *yod*, and they are the ten letters whence every
> tenfold derives.[80] When the blessed holy One was being amused
> prior to the [existence of the worlds of] emanation, creation,
> formation, and doing, and before everything, the blessed One
> filled all the worlds, that is, [he was] the place wherein it was
> appropriate for all the worlds to be created, he made a garment
> [*levush*] from the light of his essence, which is the Torah.[81]

It lies beyond the scope of this chapter to delve into the complexity of
the kabbalistic motif, but suffice it to note an interesting conceptual parallel
that can be found in the Peircean idea of the pure play of musement. In the
essay "A Neglected Argument for the Reality of God" (1908), Peirce utilizes
this motif to account for the meditative-experiential basis for belief in the
infinitely incomprehensible God:

> But let religious meditation be allowed to grow up spontane-
> ously out of Pure Play without any breach of continuity; and the
> Muser will retain the perfect candor proper to Musement. If one

79. Wolfson, *Language*, 278–79. Given the fact that kabbalists uniformly accepted
the Galenic idea that the semen originates in the brain, it stands to reason that self-
contemplation and auto-sexual arousal should be deemed two sides of the same coin.

80. It appears that the reference is to the ten sefirot that emerge from or correspond
to the ten letters of the name YHWH when written out in full in one of the following
three ways with the respective sums of 45, 63, and 72: *yw"d h"a wa"w h"a; yw"d h"y wa"w
h"y; yw"d h"y wy"w h"y*. The fourth permutation of YHWH, which has a sum of 52,
consists of nine letters: *yw"d h"h w"w h"h*. Another possible explanation is that the four
letters of YHWH can be written as a sequence of ten letters: *yod, yod heh, yod heh waw,
yod heh waw heh*. See Eliashiv, *Leshem Shevo we-Ahlamah*, 126. On the derivation of
the four different permutations from the letters of the name YHWH, which are set in
the garment, see Saruq, *Derush ha-Malbush*, 14.

81. Saruq, *Limmudei Asilut*, 3a. Compare the version in Delmedigo, *Ta'alumot
Hokhmah*, 77b, and the introduction to the commentary on *Sifra di-Seni'uta* in Saruq,
Limmudei Asilut, 34c-d.

who had determined to make trial of Musement as a favorite recreation were to ask me for advice, I should reply as follows: The dawn and the gloaming most invite one to Musement; but I have found no watch of the nychthemeron that has not its own advantages for the pursuit. . . . There is no kind of reasoning that I should wish to discourage in Musement; and I should lament to find anybody confining it to a method of such moderate fertility as logical analysis. Only, the Player should bear in mind that the higher weapons in the arsenal of thought are not playthings, but edge-tools. In any mere Play they can be used by way of exercise alone; while logical analysis can be put to its full efficiency in Musement. . . . But however that may be, in the Pure Play of Musement the idea of God's Reality will be sure sooner or later to be found an attractive fancy, which the Muser will develop in various ways. The more he ponders it, the more it will find response in every part of his mind, for its beauty, for its supplying an ideal of life, and for its thoroughly satisfactory explanation of his whole threefold environment.[82]

Prima facie, the obvious discrepancy between Peirce and the kabbalists must be noted: the focus of the former's remarks about musement is chiefly restricted to the psychological plane, describing the nature of meditation on the divine reality, whereas the latter is theosophic in orientation, deploying the motif of musement to depict the autoerotic/noetic activity of the infinite in the initial stage of the emanation. There is justification, however, to draw this parallel based on the alleged influence of German idealism on Peirce's description of the originary state of the self-becoming of the void of being.[83] More important than tracing the trajectory of this history of ideas is recognizing that, for both Peirce and the kabbalists, the dichotomy of mind and matter is challenged by the assumption that matter is a specialization of mind and that mind partakes of the nature of matter. Hence, it is be a mistake to conceive of the psychical and the physical aspects of matter as two categorically disparate aspects. The distinction rather is a matter of perspective: when a thing is viewed from the outside, it appears as matter; when it is viewed from the inside, it appears as consciousness. Peirce goes so far as to argue that mechanical laws are, in truth, acquired habits of the mind derived from the generalization inferred from the spreading of feelings.[84] That the laws of physics are, in the final analysis, expressive of a network of feelings attests to the fact that the materiality of things is constituted by the

82. Peirce, "Neglected Argument," CP 6.458–65.
83. Savan, "Peirce and Idealism."
84. Peirce, "Man's Glassy Essence," 181.

stream of mentation. Based on this surmise regarding the commingling of the physical and the psychical, Peirce insists, as I noted above, that even the nothingness of the primeval chaos is not a blank zero, since it exhibits an intensity of consciousness.[85]

Needless to say, kabbalists would not have used the precise language of Peirce, but the supposition that they conceived of *Ein Sof* as a field of consciousness, albeit a consciousness that exceeds the horizon of human consciousness, is hardly anachronistic. Moreover, in consonance with Peirce, the kabbalists did not view mind and body as autonomous substances but rather as heteronomous perspectives of one substance. And here again it is apposite to summon the semeiotic predisposition: kabbalists concur wholeheartedly with Peirce's view that God, humankind, and the universe are signs.[86] For the masters of Jewish esoteric lore, the somatic is transformed by this semeiotic conception: the substance of the body—divine, human, and cosmic—is constituted by the Hebrews letters, which are comprised within the Tetragrammaton.[87] Hence, the contemplative envisioning at the heart of the kabbalistic lifeworld—specularizing what defies specularization, ascribing an image to the imageless, beholding the icon of the invisible—is based on the transubstantiation of the physical body into the linguistic body. Not to understand the central role accorded this metamorphosis is to miss the phenomenological core of the kabbalah as a meditational discipline meant to foster an *embodied spirituality*,[88] a state of mindfulness whereby spirit mirrors body mirrored in spirit. The primeval chaos of the infinite is characterized equally as boundless consciousness and as unlimited protoplasm, and thus it comports the quality of chance that surpasses the bonds of law and the strictures of habit, the illimitable will that wills nothing but the nothing of its own willfulness.

85. Peirce, "Man's Glassy Essence," 181. The fuller text is cited above, on p. 175.

86. Spinks, *Peirce and Triadomania*, 202.

87. I have discussed this understanding of imaginal embodiment in many of my studies. For a relatively succinct summary, see Wolfson, "Bifurcating the Androgyne," 88–95; and see Wolfson, "Asceticism," 172–73.

88. Hecker, *Mystical Bodies*, 181. The intent of this taxonomy is made clear with respect to the particular topic of food in Hecker, *Mystical Bodies*, 3: "The kabbalah views food as something other than physiologically sustaining, and it idealizes foods as providing a key to sundering the boundaries between the spiritual and the material, bringing that which is on high to the realm of the mundane and that which is brought forth from the ground to the realm of the ethereal."

Bibliography

Anderson, Douglas R. "Realism and Idealism in Peirce's Cosmogony." *International Philosophical Quarterly* 32 (1992) 185–92.

Azriel of Gerona. *Be'ur Eser Sefirot*. In *Ma'yan Moshe*, edited by Moshe Schatz. Jerusalem, 2011.

Bere'shit Rabba, edited by Julius Theodor and Chanoch Albeck. Jerusalem: Wahrmann, 1965.

Biale, David. "Gershom Scholem's Ten Unhistorical Aphorisms on Kabbalah: Text and Commentary." *Modern Judaism* 5 (1985) 67–93.

Colapietro, Vincent M. "The Ground of Semiosis: An Implied Theory of Perspectival Realism?" In *Peirce's Doctrine of Signs: Theory, Applications, and Connections*, edited by Vincent M. Colapietro and Thomas M. Olshewsky. Berlin: Mouton de Gruyter, 1996.

Deledalle, Gérard. *Charles S. Peirce's Philosophy of Signs: Essays in Comparative Semiotics*. Bloomington: Indiana University Press, 2000.

Delmedigo, Joseph Solomon. *Ta'alumot Ḥokhmah*. Basle, 1629.

Ejsing, Anette. *Theology of Anticipation: A Constructive Study of C. S. Peirce*. Eugene, OR: Pickwick, 2007.

Eliashiv, Solomon ben Ḥayyim. *Leshem Shevo we-Aḥlamah: Haqdamot u-She'arim*. Jerusalem: Aaron Barzanai, 2006.

Faivre, Antoine. *Access to Western Esotericism*. Albany: State University of New York Press, 1994.

Fisch, Max H. "Peirce's Triadic Logic." In *Peirce, Semeiotic, and Pragmatism: Essays by Max H. Fisch*, edited by Kenneth Laine Ketner and Christian J. W. Kloesel, 171–83. Bloomington: Indiana University Press, 1986.

Franks, Paul. "Peirce's 'Schelling-Fashioned Idealism' and 'The Monstrous Mysticism of the East.'" *British Journal for the History of Philosophy* 23 (2015) 732–55.

Grant, Iain Hamilton. *Philosophies of Nature after Schelling*. London: Continuum, 2006.

Hausman, Carl R. *Charles S. Peirce's Evolutionary Philosophy*. Cambridge: Cambridge University Press, 1993.

Hecker, Joel. *Mystical Bodies, Mystical Meals: Eating and Embodiment in Medieval Kabbalah*. Detroit: Wayne State University Press, 2005.

Heidegger, Martin. *Elucidations of Hölderlin's Poetry*. Translated by Keith Hoeller. Amherst, NY: Humanity, 2000.

———. *Erläuterungen zu Hölderlins Dichtung* [GA 4]. Frankfurt am Main: Vittorio Klostermann, 1996.

———. *Hölderlin's Hymn "Remembrance."* Translated by William McNeill and Julia Ireland. Bloomington: Indiana University Press, 2018.

———. *Hölderlins Hymne "Andenken"* [GA 52]. Frankfurt am Main: Vittorio Klostermann, 1992.

Helm, Bertrand P. "The Nature and Modes of Time." In *The Relevance of Charles Peirce*, edited by Eugene Freeman, 178–88. La Salle, IL: Monist Library of Philosophy, 1983.

Hookway, Christopher. *Peirce*. London: Routledge, 1985.

Huemer, Michel. *Approaching Infinity*. New York: Palgrave Macmillan, 2016.

Leahy, David G. *Beyond Sovereignty: A New Global Ethics and Morality*. Aurora, CO: Davies Group, 2010.

———. *Faith and Philosophy: The Historical Impact*. Burlington, VT: Ashgate, 2003.

————. *Foundation: Matter the Body Itself*. Albany: State University of New York Press, 1996.

Malabou, Catherine. *The Future of Hegel: Plasticity, Temporality, and Dialectic*. Translated by Lisabeth During. London: Routledge, 2005.

Manchester, Peter. *The Syntax of Time: The Phenomenology of Time in Greek Physics and Speculative Logic from Iamblichus to Anaximander*. Leiden: Brill, 2005.

Matt, Daniel C. "Ayin: The Concept of Nothingness in Jewish Mysticism." In *The Problem of Pure Consciousness: Mysticism and Philosophy*, edited by Robert K. C. Forman, 121–59. New York: Oxford University Press, 1990.

Matthews, Bruce. *Schelling's Organic Form of Philosophy: Life as the Schema of Freedom*. Albany: State University of New York Press, 2011.

Meroz, Ronit. "Redemption in the Lurianic Teaching." PhD diss., Hebrew University, Jerusalem, 1988 (Hebrew).

Merrell, Floyd. *Peirce, Signs, and Meaning*. Toronto: University of Toronto Press, 1997.

Mules, Warwick. *With Nature: Nature Philosophy as Poetics through Schelling, Heidegger, Benjamin and Nancy*. Bristol, UK: Intellect, 2014.

Nadin, Mihai. "The Logic of Vagueness and the Category of Synechism." In *The Relevance of Charles Peirce*, edited by Eugene Freeman, 154–66. La Salle, IL: Hegler Institute, 1983.

Necker, Gerold. "Hans Blumenberg's Metaphorology and the Historical Perspective of Mystical Terminology." *Jewish Studies Quarterly* 22 (2015) 184–203.

Niemoczynski, Leon J. *Charles Sanders Peirce and a Religious Metaphysics of Nature*. Lanham, MD: Rowman & Littlefield, 2011.

Ochs, Peter. *Peirce, Pragmatism and the Logic of Scripture*. Cambridge: Cambridge University Press, 1998.

————. "Theosemiotics and Pragmatism." *Journal of Religion* 72 (1992) 59–81.

Oron, Michal, and Amos Goldreich, eds. *Massu'ot: Studies in Kabbalistic Literature and Jewish Philosophy in Memory of Prof. Ephraim Gottlieb*. Jerusalem: Bialik Institute, 1994 (Hebrew).

Ouaknin, Marc-Alain. *Mysteries of the Kabbalah*. Translated by Josephine Bacon. New York: Abbeville, 2000.

Parker, Kelly A. *The Continuity of Peirce's Thought*. Nashville: Vanderbilt University Press, 1998.

Peirce, Charles S. *Collected Papers of Charles Sanders Peirce*. Edited by Charles Hartshorne, Paul Weiss, and A. W. Burks. 8 vols. Cambridge: Harvard University Press, 1931–58.

————. *The Essential Peirce: Selected Philosophical Writings*. Vol. 2, *1893–1913*. Edited by Nathan Houser and Christian Kloesel. Bloomington: Indiana University Press, 1998.

————. "Nominalism versus Realism." In *Writings of Charles S. Peirce: A Chronological Edition*, edited by the Peirce Edition Project, vol. 2. Bloomington: Indiana University Press, 1984.

————. "Questions Concerning Certain Faculties." Reprinted in *Writings of Charles S. Peirce*, edited by the Peirce Edition Project, vol. 2. Bloomington: Indiana University Press, 1984.

————. *Writings of Charles S. Peirce: A Chronological Edition*, Volume I–VIII. Edited by the Peirce Edition Project. Bloomington: Indiana University Press, 1984.

Perry, Ralph Barton. *The Thought and Character of William James, as Revealed in Unpublished Correspondence and Notes, Together with His Published Writings.* Vol. 2, *Philosophy and Psychology.* Boston: Little, Brown, 1935.

Potter, Vincent G. *Charles S. Peirce: On Norms & Ideals.* New York: Fordham University Press, 1997.

Priest, Graham, J. C. Beall, and Bradley Armour-Garb, eds. *The Law of Non-Contradiction: New Philosophical Essays.* Oxford: Oxford University Press, 2004.

Priest, Graham. *Beyond the Limits of Thought.* Oxford: Oxford University Press, 2002.

———. *In Contradiction: A Study of the Transconsistent.* 2nd ed. Oxford: Oxford University Press, 2006.

Raposa, Michael L. "A Brief History of Theosemiotic: From Scotus through Peirce and Beyond." In *The Varieties of Transcendence: Pragmatism and the Theory of Religion,* edited by Hermann Deuser et al., 142–57. New York: Fordham University Press, 2016.

———. *Peirce's Philosophy of Religion.* Bloomington: Indiana University Press, 1989.

Rosensohn, William L. *The Phenomenology of Charles S. Peirce.* Amsterdam: B. R. Grüner, 1974.

Rosenzweig, Franz. *Der Mensch und sein Werk: Gesammelte Schriften II. Der Stern der Erlösung.* The Hague: Martinus Nijhoff, 1976.

———. *The Star of Redemption.* Translated by Barbara E. Galli. Madison: University of Wisconsin Press, 2000.

Sallis, John. *The Return of Nature: On the Beyond of Sense.* Bloomington: Indiana University Press, 2016.

Saruq, Israel. *Derush ha Malbush we-ha-Ṣimṣum.* Edited by Matthias Safrin. Jerusalem: Matthias Safrin, 2001.

———. *Limmudei Aṣilut.* Munkács: Blayer & Kohn, 1897.

Savan, David. "Peirce and Idealism." In *Peirce and Contemporary Thought: Philosophical Inquiries,* edited by Kenneth Laine Ketner, 315–28. New York: Fordham University Press, 1995.

Schelling, Friedrich Wilhelm Joseph. *The Ages of the World (Fragment).* In *The Handwritten Remains, Third Version (c. 1815),* translated by Jason M. Wirth. Albany: State University of New York Press, 2000.

———. *Der Weltalter.* In *Sämmtliche Werke,* edited by Karl Friedrich August Schelling. Vol. 8. Stuttgart: Cotta, 1861.

Scholem, Gershom. *Kabbalah.* Jerusalem: Keter, 1976.

———. *Major Trends in Jewish Mysticism.* New York: Schocken, 1956.

———. "The Name of God and the Linguistic Theory of the Kabbala." *Diogenes* 79 (1972) 59–80 and *Diogenes* 80 (1972) 164–94.

———. *Origins of the Kabbalah.* Edited by R. J. Zwi Werblowsky. Translated by Allan Arkush. Princeton: Princeton University Press, 1987.

Sheriff, John K. *Charles Peirce's Guess at the Riddle: Grounds for Human Significance.* Bloomington: Indiana University Press, 1994.

Short, T. L. "Peirce and the Incommensurability of Theories." In *The Relevance of Charles Peirce,* edited by Eugene Freeman, 119–31. La Salle, IL: Hegler Institute, 1983,

———. *Peirce's Theory of Signs.* Cambridge: Cambridge University Press, 2007.

Spinks, C. W. *Peirce and Triadomania: A Walk in the Semiotic Wilderness.* Berlin: Mouton de Gruyter, 1991.

————. *Semiosis, Marginal Signs and Trickster: A Dagger of the Mind.* London: Macmillan, 1991.

Tishby, Isaiah. *The Wisdom of the Zohar: An Anthology of Texts.* Translated by David Goldstein. Oxford: Oxford University Press, 1989.

Valabregue-Perry, Sandra. *Concealed and Revealed: 'Ein Sof' in Theosophic Kabbalah.* Los Angeles: Cherub, 2010 (Hebrew).

————. "The Concept of Infinity (*Eyn-sof*) and the Rise of Theosophical Kabbalah." *Jewish Quarterly Review* 102 (2012) 405–30.

White, Ryan. *The Hidden God: Pragmatism and Posthuman in American Thought.* New York: Columbia University Press, 2015.

Wolfson, Elliot R. *Alef, Mem, Tau: Kabbalistic Musings on Time, Truth, and Death.* Berkeley: University of California Press, 2006.

————. "The Anonymous Chapters of the Elderly Master of Secret: New Evidence for the Early Activity of the Zoharic Circle." *Kabbalah: Journal for the Study of Jewish Mystical Texts* 18 (2009) 143–278.

————. "Asceticism, Mysticism, and Messianism: A Reappraisal of Schechter's Portrait of Sixteenth-Century Safed." *Jewish Quarterly Review* 109 (2016) 165–77.

————. "Bifurcating the Androgyne and Engendering Sin: A Zoharic Reading of Gen 1–3." In *Hidden Truths from Eden: Esoteric Readings of Genesis 1–3*, edited by Caroline Vander Stichele and Susanne Scholz, 88–95. Atlanta: SBL, 2014.

————. *Circle in the Square: Studies in the Use of Gender in Kabbalistic Symbolism.* Albany: State University of New York Press, 1995.

————. *A Dream Interpreted within a Dream: Oneiropoiesis and the Prism of Imagination.* New York: Zone, 2011.

————. *Giving beyond the Gift: Apophasis and Overcoming Theomania.* New York: Fordham University Press, 2014.

————. *Heidegger and Kabbalah: Hidden Gnosis and the Path of Poiēsis.* Bloomington: Indiana University Press, 2019.

————. *Language, Eros, Being: Kabbalistic Hermeneutics and Poetic Imagination.* New York: Fordham University Press, 2005.

————. "Mythopoeic Imagination and the Hermeneutic Bridging of Temporal Spacing: On Michael Fishbane's Biblical Myth and Rabbinic Mythmaking." *Jewish Quarterly Review* 96 (2006) 233–38.

————. "Nihilating Nonground and the Temporal Sway of Becoming." *Angelaki* 17 (2012) 31–45.

————. *Open Secret: Postmessianic Messianism and the Mystical Revision of Menaḥem Mendel Schneerson.* New York: Columbia University Press, 2009.

————. "Retroactive Not Yet: Linear Circularity and Kabbalistic Temporality." In *Time and Eternity in Jewish Mysticism: That Which Is Before and That Which Is After*, edited by Brian Ogren, 15–50. Leiden: Brill, 2015.

13

The Semiosis of God, or Naming God

—STEVEN D. KEPNES, Colgate University

> Let them praise the name, YHVH [LORD]: for His name alone
> is exalted; His glory [is] above the earth and heaven. (Ps 148:13)

IF GOD IS TO communicate with humans God must, as the Talmud says, "use human language."[1] But this language is a limited tool. For simple things it is pretty good. "Snow is white." "Please pass the pepper." "The boy ran to the tree." However, when we get to more abstract concepts, language is a little less clear. What, after all, is virtue, love, justice? Here, when the subject matter is more abstract, we need to talk about it; we need human speech where back and forth dialogue helps to clarify what is meant by the term. Peter Ochs likes to call signs that initiate dialogue like this, "genuine symbols." Symbols he sees, following Peirce, as higher semiotic forms that depend upon the resources of the entire language system to communicate meaning. And symbols put that system to use not only by exploiting all of its semantic and syntactic complexity but also through generating inter-human discourse and extended communal conversations.

But if we agree that the full symbolic function of language needs to be used to communicate abstract concepts, what about communicating God, the most abstract and indeed the least expressible reality? What about saying the unsayable? What about naming God? What is the semiosis of God?

---

1. I want to thank James Diamond for his "Naming an Unnamable God," (forthcoming) which I read after writing an early draft of this paper. Diamond's paper is comprehensive on biblical scholarship, traditional exegetical and philosophical discussions of the name of God.

One could say that providing names for God is one of the important tasks of scripture and that the semiosis of God is one of the preoccupations of the scriptural traditions of the West. In this essay, I will attempt a meditation on the problem of naming God with regard to the Hebrew Bible and Jewish tradition. I call this a meditation and not an argument or thesis-generating exercise, since the process of naming God, if done well, does not produce propositions or theses but, rather, starts a discussion, initiates a dialogue, and enters us into a conversation in a community. If there is an argument here, in this exercise, it is that naming God, precisely because God is unnamable, requires the most sophisticated usage of language that we humans have. Naming God not only requires the use of complex semantic and syntactic forms, but it also requires entering into multiple conversations, and these conversations are not only conversations of the moment but conversations on past conversations, conversations with interlocutors throughout the ages. And since naming God involves naming the unnamable, one of the most sophisticated tricks of scripture is to use the language of God against itself; so that the best name of God is the one that destroys itself in the very act of signifying. What we have then is semantically and syntactically confused signs when we properly attempt to name God. This means that like an ouroboros eating its tail, we end up with self-contradictory signs. And these signs then often generate negative theologies, silent theologies, theologies of no-thing.

You Shall Make No Graven Images

God himself warns of the dangers of bad vehicles of signification and faulty semiotics for him when he bans graven images in the Decalogue. Indeed, right after declaring that God is God, *Anoki YHVH Elohekha*, "I am YHVH your God," (Exod 20:2) he engages in a semiotic lesson: "You shall not make for yourself an idol, whether in the form of anything that is in the heaven above, or that is on earth beneath, or that is in the water under the earth" (Exod 20:4). An idol is too concrete a representation for God. As a concrete physical representation or "likeness" (*Temunah*) of God, the worshipper too easily comes to associate the idol with God Himself. To use Peircean terms, we might also say that the idol is an "icon," a sign that communicates its meaning by its particular material features, rather than a "symbol," like a word imbedded in a linguistic system. In linguistic systems the shapes of the letters and forms of the words bear little or no relation to the meaning that is generated. Meaning arises from the words in their relation to other words in the language together with actual communal use. Clearly the Bible prefers words, i.e., symbolic representations, rather than iconic representations, for God.

However, in giving preference to words rather than idols, the problem of how we refer to or how we name God is not fully solved. Indeed, giving God a name still has dangers, since we might come to think that God is fully comprehended or his essential nature given in his name. We might think this because, unlike our contemporary practice of giving names to persons, where the name does not tell us much about the person, biblical names are often seen as providing a key to a person's character and nature. "For as his name is, so is he" (1 Sam 25:25). We see this particularly with important figures like Adam, Eve, Abraham, Sarah, Isaac, Jacob/Israel. Thus, Adam means "red clay" or "earth man," Eve/Hava means "life," Abraham means "father of many," Sarah means "princess," Isaac means "he will laugh," Jacob means "crooked" or "heel," and Israel means "he strives with God." To give God a name, then, might suggest that his nature can be defined. Knowing someone's name also carries the sense of gaining some control over him/her, or being entitled to a kind of intimacy that humans are simply not worthy of having with God. Since God's act of naming and creating was simultaneous in the creation of light, "Let there be light!" the process of naming comes with a sense of ontological power. God gives Adam power when he asks him, "What will you call it" (Gen 2:19)? (And perhaps a more wise God in the Qur'an reserves this power for himself and then teaches Adam these names.) The New Testament acknowledges the creative power of names when John, commenting on Genesis says, "In the beginning was the word" (John 1:1).

My Name for All Generations

The *locus classicus* for the attempt to name God in the Bible comes to us in the encounter between Moses and God at the burning bush in Exodus 3. Thus, our reflection on naming God will begin with the way in which this encounter is narrated in the Bible. In beginning with this narrative, I will note that the act of naming God, or rather the self-naming of God by God, is embedded in a linguistic context, in a story, in a book, Exodus, (*Shmot*, in Hebrew, meaning "names") in a larger book, Torah or Pentateuch. So that God's name is not dropped from heaven, out of nothing, *ex nihilo*, rather, it is embedded in a linguistic system with a grammar, a vocabulary, a syntax, and a linguistic history. Unraveling and discerning the name of God requires an investigation of biblical Hebrew, its grammar and history, its linguistic processes. And because God's name is revealed in a narrative, it is given in the temporal and dramatic processes of the narrative. Furthermore, the name, once revealed, is a genuine linguistic symbol in the sense that it initiates a centuries-, indeed, millennia-old dialogue on the meaning of the name. And beyond this, it also initiates a series of poems, prayers, songs, and liturgies through which the uttering, or rather the prohibition against uttering the name is enacted.

Moses Receives the Name (Exod 3)

> 1 Now Moses was keeping the flock of Jethro his father-in-law, the priest of Midian; and he led the flock to the farthest end of the wilderness, and came to the mountain of God, unto Horeb. 2 And the angel of the LORD appeared unto him in a flame of fire out of the midst of a bush; and he looked, and, behold, the bush burned with fire, and the bush was not consumed. 3 And Moses said: "I will turn aside now, and see this great sight, why the bush is not burnt."

The story begins with Moses shepherding his flock at the edge of the desert coming to God's mountain, "Horeb," which will also be called "Sinai," at a latter point in Exodus. Therefore, we see that this important place has at least three names, Mountain of God, Horeb (from *Harava*, meaning "dryness," "wilderness") and Sinai (perhaps from the root "bush"). This is a typical stylistic move of the Bible where a number of names are given to the same place, person, or thing with each name varying and deepening meaning. It is also remarkable that one of the most important places, the place upon which God will reveal not only his name but the Torah, is located outside of the land of Israel in a far off place which Jewish tradition is ignorant of and happy to leave unknown. Much has been made of this by commentators,[2] but one obvious thing we can say is that the unnamable God will reveal Himself at an unknown place "at the farthest edge of the wilderness." So, if we want to be cute here we could say that the "no-God" will reveal Himself at "no-place."

It is not clear if Moses knows that this is Horeb beforehand, but as he comes close "the angel of the LORD appeared to him in a flame of fire out of the midst of a bush." Here, we already have a complex sign that is composed of three elements: an angel that appears in a flame, that is in a bush. What Moses sees is not clear from the description we have. Does he see the face

---

2. The *Mekilta* of Rabbi Ishmael tells us why the Torah was given in the wilderness and not in Israel. "The Torah was given in public in a place free to all. For if the Torah had been given in the land of Israel, the Israelites could have said to the gentiles, 'You have no share in it.' But it was given openly in the wilderness so that anyone wishing to accept it could come and do so." (*Mekilta* on Exod 19:2).

or image of an angel inside the flame? Does the flame take the shape of an angel? What shape or form did the angel take so that it was recognizable to Moses as an angel? This threefold image (which it must be said is not given to us as a real plastic image but in words that describe it), is certainly strange and out of the ordinary. But it is also extra-ordinary, for the bush is not consumed by the fire. Moses, however, is not put off or scared. Indeed, he makes the important decision to "turn aside and see this great sight."

The great sight of the bush that burns even though it is not consumed is one of the central biblical images for God in Jewish tradition. But it is important to note that it is not a simple image but a complex even self-contradictory one, since flames normally consume their fuel and require more and more fuel to last. Another way to put this is that the burning bush is a sign of God's defiance of natural laws or of his supernatural power. The image is also used to point to God's eternality—glowing endlessly without need of any outside energy or fuel. The threefold image manages to be an image of divinity that challenges the limits of normal physical forms and images. In this sense it escapes the ban on images that God will establish later at Sinai. The burning bush, as a number of commentators have pointed out, is a marker of revelation since when Moses returns to Horeb with the entire people of Israel after the Exodus, the entire mountain, not a single bush, will be set ablaze (Exod 19:18). The fire will also be compared to Torah itself. As Rabbi Ishmael in the *Mekilta* says, "Torah is fire, was given in the midst of fire and may be compared to fire" (on Exod 19:18). Moreover, the fire at the burning bush recalls light as first creation of God. And in the Psalms light is associated with God and his power of salvation. "The Lord is my light and my salvation—whom shall I fear?" (Ps 27:1). However, after Moses turns toward the great sight the appearance of the threefold image seems to fall away to be replaced by a voice alone, the voice, however, of God Himself.

> 4 And when the LORD saw that he turned aside to see, God called unto him out of the midst of the bush, and said: "Moses, Moses." And he said: "Here I am."

Since the three-fold image is replaced with direct speech when God Himself addresses Moses, the Torah may very well be suggesting that the image is a lower form of revelation of divinity. And maybe we can say that all the images of God we just mentioned, from flame, to fire, to light, to angels, are lower, mediate forms of expression of aspects of divinity. So the Torah itself seems to move from icons, to images, toward words and direct speech as the preferred or perhaps highest level in God's revelation of Himself to humans.

But what does God say here in this conversation with Moses? He calls out Moses' name, and he calls it twice. "Moses, Moses." This is one of the true wonders of monotheistic religion that the transcendent God of the universe will address the lowly human, and he will do so, not in general, but by name. As God calls Moses by name, there is also the assumption that Moses is known by God without prior introduction or conversation. God knows Moses even as he knows all humans. The address of God to Moses, "Moses, Moses," should make the reader remember the earlier address of God to Abraham, "Abraham, Abraham," at the Akedah, or the binding of Isaac in Genesis 22. And Moses, too, is connected to the great patriarch Abraham since Moses, also repeats Abraham's words, "*Hineini*."

What this does is to open the revelation of God's name in this narrative in Exodus to connections back to the revelations and identity of God back in Genesis. This makes the Abraham narratives another series of texts to provide context, images, and symbols, to understand the revelation of God in our narrative. Right here, with the use of similar locutions, "Moses, Moses," "Abraham, Abraham," followed by the same answer "*Heneini*," we have one of the clearest and most significant examples of the Bible's penchant for what Martin Buber called the use of the *Leitwort*, the key word pattern. Here, the Bible repeats a word to draw attention to a similarity and make us reflect on that similarity as a key to meaning. The point of the repetition of the *Leitworte* here would be that Moses and Abraham have both been called by God as special people, as prophets or leaders with a mission. And we might also point out that both Abraham and Moses are figures who had to leave their original parental homes to find themselves and their mission. Since Moses uses the same words of reply "here I am" that Abraham used, he, too, must be regarded as another Abraham. And like Abraham in saying "here I am" (Gen 22:11) Moses declares himself present, open, ready for action, for mission, for response to God's will. And God, in calling Moses by name also may be opening Himself to the query that will come from Moses to Him, "what is your name?"

However, before God responds with a mission or his name to Moses, he sets limits to the encounter. For as important to the meeting as it was for Moses to make the first move to recognize the signs of God and "turn aside" to approach closer to the bush, God now tells him, "Draw not closer; put off your shoes from off your feet, for the place where you stand is holy ground" (Exod 3:5).

This is truly interesting, for after getting Moses' attention with the fire that is not consumed and calling out to him using his personal name, God sets up a condition, establishes distance, draws a line, a line between Himself and Moses. This is the line that separates the profane from the sacred, the ordinary, *khol*, from the holy, *kadosh*, literally "that which is separate." What God does here at Horeb will be crucial to divine human relations here on out in the Bible and beyond in Judaism. For the distinction unholy/holy will not only be used to separate God and Moses, but God and Israel, Israel and other nations, and then with correlate terms *tameh* and *tahor*, impure/pure, an elaborate classification system will be established by the Levitical priests to divide up all reality. And this classification system will determine not only what Israel can sacrifice to God, but what foods can be eaten, when sexual relations can occur, what clothes can be worn, and a host of other ritual and liturgical matters determined so that Israel can become a "kingdom of priests and a holy nation" (Exod 19:6). Furthermore, when the dichotomy holy/unholy is augmented with the ethical terms good/evil, the moral mission of Israel to attend to the needs of the poor, the stranger, and the orphan and establish a just social order receives powerful emotional and theological justifications.

> 6 Moreover He said: "I am the God of thy father, the God of Abraham, the God of Isaac, and the God of Jacob."

As well as drawing Moses closer to God, however, the most significant result of the declaration "God of your father" is to pull Moses away from Pharaoh as his father and the Egyptians as his people. So this statement not only assures Moses of his identification with this people and not the Egyptians in whose house he grew up, but also establishes that God is not the God of Pharaoh and the Egyptian people. Of course, Moses will find out eventually that his God is also the God of the Egyptians and, indeed, the God of all people. But this revelation is part of the story which is about to unfold. However, the statement that God who reveals Himself to Moses is the selfsame God that revealed Himself to Abraham, is also a statement of the identity of God as a consistent, even eternal, identity that does not change over time. What this means for Moses is that the God he is being addressed by is the same God that addressed Abraham, Isaac, and Jacob. And I might add that what this means for the generations of the people Israel after Moses up until today, is that the God they and now we address is the same God. This statement is made in liturgy three times a day when God is addressed in the central Amidah prayer in the same formulation we have in Exodus. God of the fathers, God of Abraham, God of Isaac, God of Jacob. But at this point in the story Moses is overwhelmed and is overtaken with fear: "He hid his face for he was afraid to look on God" (Exod 3:6).

This makes sense since God Himself has warned Moses not to come too close. But if God was communicating by speech alone, what does it mean that Moses "was afraid to look on God"? Is God actually speaking out of the burning bush and therefore has Moses been looking at the fire all this time? This interpretation is supported by the warning, "do not come close for the place is holy ground." Since it refers to holy ground, perhaps the ground out of which the bush grew?

Here, I would say that as with the threefold image angel/flame/bush, which is impossible to render into a near and simple image, similarly the Torah text here is purposely offering a confused picture of what is going on in the encounter with Moses. Have we left the sphere of images and entered only a linguistic arena where God speaks without images? Or does the image of the angel/flame/bush remain with God speaking out of it? Note that Moses here is afraid not to hear, but to look (*l'habit*) upon God, suggesting that it is the seeing and not the hearing of God that is problematic.

But there are still a few more important things to be said about the distance that God has established between Himself and Moses and about Moses' reaction, his hiding his face in fear of God. First, the distance that God establishes between him and Moses on the high place of a mountain could be interpreted as a sign of the "transcendence" of God from humans. God's transcendence here signals that there is a new chapter, a new book, in which the relation with God will be different from what it was with the patriarchs and matriarchs in Genesis. Now, the divine human conversation will be less direct, less spontaneous, and perhaps even less intimate. In Exodus, we not only have distance between God and human, there is also more mediation, the mediation of language, the language of Torah, the word of instruction and law that replaces direct speech. Certainly, there is some continuity here and God makes that clear when he identifies Himself as the God of the fathers. God will still speak to and through special representatives of Israel, like the prophets. But as I suggested earlier, a series of social and religious structures and even institutions and a system for access to the holy is about to be established through which Israel will be allowed careful access to God.

Moses, himself, senses this. He senses the need for distance when he hides his own face from the face of God. With this hiding from God, Moses introduces a notion of *yirat Hashem* or "holy fear." This is suggested by the fire that glows so hot it can burn if you get too close, but it also entails a recognition of the ultimate power of God and respect for that power as well as for the majesty, glory, righteousness, judgment and mercy of God. Moses' "holy fear" of God establishes most importantly an attitude of reverence and care that becomes the hallmark of the religious emotion we associate with holy space and with God. Abraham Joshua Heschel once remarked that *yirat Hashem*, fear of God, is used in rabbinic tradition to say what we mean in English by the word, "religion." So Moses becomes in Judaism the epitome of the religious man.

9 "And now, behold, the cry of the children of Israel is come
unto Me; moreover I have seen the oppression wherewith the
Egyptians oppress them. 10 Come now therefore, and I will
send you unto Pharaoh, that you may bring forth My people
the children of Israel out of Egypt." 11 And Moses said unto
God: "Who am I, that I should go unto Pharaoh, and that I
should bring forth the children of Israel out of Egypt?" 12 And
He said: "Certainly I will be with you (*Ehyeh Imokh*); and this
shall be the sign unto you, that I have sent thee: when you
have brought forth the people out of Egypt, you shall serve
God upon this mountain."

In this wonderful exchange between God and Moses, God further
reveals Himself to Moses as one who hears the cry of Israel, the oppressed
slaves in servitude in Egypt. So here Moses, and we, as readers, learn that
God attends to the voice of slaves, the oppressed, the downtrodden, and the
powerless. We also learn that God is concerned with earthly matters and not
only heavenly ones, and that God attends to human history and politics.

These are all crucial theological themes that separate the God of Israel from the pagan Gods of the ancient Near East. In this exchange, Moses'
identity is also further developed from one who is part of the people of
the patriarchs, to one whom God is with, to one who has a divine calling
or mission. So when Moses asks, "Who am I that I should go to Pharaoh?"
God says, "Certainly I will be with you" and my very being with you "shall
be a sign to you" that it is I who "sent you, when you bring forth the people
out of Egypt." This is a complex knot of answers to Moses' question on his
personal identity, "Who am I?" so let us try to unravel them. What makes
God's answer difficult is that it is based on a promise of God's presence
to Moses that will only be fully realized in the future after the people are
brought forth from slavery. Moses is clearly seeking from God something
concrete, some kind of real assurance or sign now, at the moment of the
burning bush, that he will actually succeed in his mission. But God refuses
to give this assurance to him. Moreover God's proclamation, "I will be
with you [*Ehyeh Imokh*] and this will be the sign," suggests that a sign
from God to human can be an individual or group action, here the action
of redemption of people from slavery which is a historical act in the public
world of actions. So God attempts to give Moses this sign which is a kind
of promise of a future sign. Note that God uses the same expression *Ehyeh*,
in verse 12 that he will use in verse 14 as a way of answering Moses' question about His, God's, name.

13 Then Moses said to God, "If I come to the people of Israel and say to them, 'The God of your fathers has sent me to you,' and they ask me, 'What is his name?' what shall I say to them?"

Moses follows God's answer to him which is put in the future tense by asking his own question in the form of a future hypothetical. "OK, let's say I go to the people as you tell me to, and I tell them that the God of my fathers sent me, what will I say if they ask me for his name?" Of course this is strange since Moses cannot know that the people will ask this question so, indeed, it must really be Moses' question. Given the power of names in the Torah, Moses is truly asking a big question here. He is asking for the equivalent of the self-revelation of God. Moses' attempt again to God to reveal his name and also, perhaps, another attempt to get a concrete assurance from God that he will be successful in his mission to free the people. And then he receives this answer.

14 God said to Moses, *Ehyeh Asher Ehyeh* "I AM WHO I AM." [or I WILL BE WHO I WILL BE] And He said, "Say this to the people of Israel, *Ehyeh* 'I AM' [I WILL BE] has sent me. 15 God also said to Moses, "Say this to the people of Israel, 'The LORD, [YHVH] the God of your fathers, the God of Abraham, the God of Isaac, and the God of Jacob, has sent me to you.' This is my name forever, and thus I am to be remembered throughout all generations."

So Moses receives four answers, three verbal signs, *Ehyeh Asher Ehyeh*, *Ehyeh*, and *YHVH*. Each of these are related to the word for "being," *hayah*, given in different verbal and noun forms, none of which conforms to normal biblical Hebrew grammar and usage. In addition, Moses is given the fairly straightforward expression: "the God of your fathers, the God of Abraham, the God of Isaac, and the God of Jacob." Taken together, these names must have challenged Moses and continue to challenge readers through history unto today, to attempt to make sense of them. Certainly God's answer to Moses' inquiry into his name is nothing but confusing. Aside from the meaning of the nongrammatical words, which of the three is God's name? *Ehyeh Asher Ehyeh? Ehyeh?* Or YHVH?

YHVH does become the central name for God and is known as the *Shem Hameforash* (the distinctive name) or the Tetragrammaton. But the unclarity of the meaning of this name can be seen in the multiple attempts to define the word in the standard Brown, Driver, Briggs, *Hebrew and English Lexicon of the Old Testament*.

Many recent scholars explain YHVH as Hiphael of "*hayah*," "the one bringing into being," but Nes inclines to the Qal form "he who causes to fall," or "faller"—destroying foes (dubiously). But most take it as Qal of "*haveh*," "the one who is." The Lexicon then suggests that "*Ehyeh*" from verse 14 "is a compressed form of *Ehyeh Asher Ehyeh* which is then given in the nominal form "YHVH," "He who will be," or "I am who I am." . . . [or finally] "He who is essentially unnamable, inexplicable."[3]

How is that for a dictionary attempt to define a word?! If we want to give an example of lexical confusion, frustration, and failure, there is probably not a better example than the final attempt at definition which declares that the name is "inexplicable."

But if the lexicographers have been frustrated by the meaning of YHVH, rabbinic commentators and philosophers have found a fertile home for their speculations. Since God answers Moses' question, "What is your name?" with "*Ehyeh*"—"Thus, you shall say to the children of Israel, *Ehyeh* sent me to you"—some say that the personal name of God is *Ehyeh* and not YHVH. In his Targum Onkelos says that *Ehyeh* is God's name and *Ehyeh Asher Ehyeh* is the explanation of the name. However, the Bekhor Shor refutes this by pointing out that God refers to Himself throughout the Torah as YHVH and not *Ehyeh*.

In Midrash Rabbah, Rabbi Itzhak says that the meaning of *Ehyeh Asher Ehyeh* involves God's transcendence of time. God is saying "It is I who was, I who am now, and I who will be in the future" (Midrash Exodus Rabbah on Exod 3:14). Nachmanides brings this understanding to explain YHVH as a statement of God's presence in all temporal dimensions at once. "Since past and future are all present for the creator—for with him there is no time and with him there is no change—and none of his days have past, therefore he is called by all tenses in a single Name, YHVH (Nachmanides Commentary on Exod 3:14). Rashi, however, stresses as he usually does that the meaning of the three expressions is to be found in the immediate context of the text, i.e., as a response to worries about the plight of Israel in Egypt. Thus the name of God is less about who God is in his nature, and more about who God will be in relation to Israel. Therefore the meaning of the names *Ehyeh*, and *Ehyeh Asher Ehyeh*, are "I will be *with* you in this trouble now [slavery in Egypt] and in your future troubles as well" (Rashi on Exod 3:14).

However, since the three expressions do all employ the Hebrew root for "being," Jewish philosophers have used the names to find a source of insight into the ontological character of God. Thus they suggest meanings like: "The One who has never ceased nor will he ever cease to be (Saadiah Gaon)." "The Being who exists" and "whose existence is necessary and can never be nonexistent" (Rambam Guide I:63). And also, "The existent,

3. Brown, Driver, and Briggs, *Hebrew and English Lexicon*, 218.

unitary Being" (Gershonides). Here, God is given static and eternal Aristotelian meanings and the King James translation, "I am that I am," reflects this interpretation.

The discussion of the meaning of the three-word expression *Ehyeh Asher Ehyeh, I WILL BE WHO I WILL BE,* continues to generate further reflection in the modern period. And this ability to continue to generate interpretation is, in itself, a testimony to the semiotic power of the expression as a "genuine symbol." Thus, the modern Jewish thinker Martin Buber argues that *Ehyeh Asher Ehyeh* should not be translated with the abstract and static statement of "pure existence." Buber, instead, suggests that the translation needs to convey the dynamic sense of "happening, coming into being, being there, being present, being thus and thus; but not Being in an abstract sense"[4] The second and third words "*Asher Ehyeh*" should be translated "as I will be present." Therefore, Buber suggests, "I will be present as I will be present" as the best translation.[5] Buber argues that this translation fits the context of the narrative and the special plea of Moses. "YHVH, indeed, states He will always be present, but at any given moment as the one who he then, in that given moment, will be present. He, who promises his steady presence, His steady assistance, refuses to restrict Himself to definite forms of manifestation."[6]

In Buber's view, the brilliance of the personal name for God that is revealed to Moses is that it at once gives assurance of his presence in times of need, and also preserves for God the exact way and form in which his presence will appear. In his very name, God assures that he will remain unknown, unpredictable, and absolutely free. God remains in control of his presence; it cannot be conjured, evoked, or demanded by humans. So the name of God as *Ehyeh Asher Ehyeh* could be seen as the appropriate name of God for the philosophers, i.e., God as Being, God as eternal, but also as the God who enters history to address the suffering of his people. But still, even as God of history, he is neither under the control of history (he is eternal) nor is he under the control, epistemological or actual, of humans. For God will be present in history only in the manner he chooses to be.

What most Jewish commentators seem to agree on is that YHVH is a personal name that God gives alone to his people. Buber speaks of it as a kind of special name of endearment, an exalted form of "nickname" that only God and his people know. But perhaps a better way to put this is that the name, YHVH, is a sacred or holy name.

4. Buber "Burning Bush," 52.
5. Buber "Burning Bush," 52.
6. Buber "Burning Bush," 52.

The Name as Holy Index

After Moses receives the Tetragrammaton, YHVH, we see a process occurring in the Bible to deflect reflection on its meaning and build up the sense of the power and holiness that adheres to the name by virtue of its closeness to God. Through this process the name YHVH takes on a kind of deference and respect that is close to the respect given to God Himself. Therefore we hear in Psalms, "Let them praise the name, YHVH: for his name alone is exalted" (Ps 148:13). "O Lord, your name endures forever" (Ps 135:13). The name YHVH becomes holy in itself and, as holy, the same set of protections, safe-guards, and distancing maneuvers that apply to sacred objects like the arc or altar are applied to the utterance of the name. One of the most emphatic statements comes in the Decalogue where YHVH is protected or shielded from profane use by the commandment not to "take the name of the Lord your God in vain" (Exod 20).

Although throughout biblical literature there does seem to be some use of God's name, most notably as the first two letters YH, "yah," are added as endings to proper human names like Jeremi*yah*, Yeshi*yah*, Eli*yahu* or simply, in the use of the expression, Hallelu*yah*, "praise God," eventually the utterance of the name is restricted to the sanctuary (Sotah vii.6) and to the High Priests on the High Holidays. By the second century, YHVH is pronounced as "Adonai," meaning, "My Lord" or "My Lords" instead of "Yahweh" or something close to this. But as Adonai is repeatably used and thus, sometimes misused or abused, the tradition adds another layer of protection, another fence of security, to improper utterance of the expression Adonai, by the addition of still another designation for YHVH. This is the expression *Hashem*, or "The Name." This expression hides God's name YHVH with a simple indexical expression that really says nothing all of the meaning of YHVH. With this designation, God's special name can be referred to without saying anything close to it. With this designation the tongue is kept far from God's special name, just as Moses was asked to keep his distance from the holy ground on Horeb. And just as Moses is told to hide his face from sight of the face of God, the name, Hashem, hides the real personal holy name YHVH. The utterance of God's holy name is then hermetically sealed off and totally protected from improper or profane use.

On the one hand, with the substitution of Hashem for YHVH we can say that the semiosis of God culminates in a kind of semiotic defeat whereby the very act of naming God becoming a kind of mute pointing to a name that is not said. On the other hand the Bible, the commentary tradition, the philosophers, and then the mystics about whom we had said nothing, also preserve an extended and lively conversation about not only the name YHVH but also the alternative expressions *Ehyeh* and *Ehyeh Asher Ehyeh*. This extended conversation serves as a model for what Ochs has called a "genuine symbol," which shows the semiosis of God to be a kind of rich and hidden underground stream of theological discourse that has multiple branches that continue to be extended underneath the protection of the rule of holiness.

Bibliography

Brown, Francis, S. R. Driver, and C. A. Briggs. *Hebrew and English Lexicon of the Old Testament*. London: Oxford University Press, 1953.

Buber, Martin. "The Burning Bush." In *On the Bible*, by Martin Buber, edited by Nahum Glatzer, 44–62. New York: Schocken, 1982.

Diamond, James. "Naming an Unnamable God: Divine Being or Divine Becoming." (forthcoming).

14

Supersessionism, Zionism, and Reparative Theology

Peter Ochs and John Howard Yoder

—SHAUL MAGID, Dartmouth College

I

OVER THE COURSE OF his career, Peter Ochs has been a leading voice in a team of scholars who have been instrumental in reconceptualizing the reading of scripture in the wake of creating a new paradigm for inter-religious conversation founded on a postliberal perspective.[1]

Ochs' own philosophical and theological contribution to the larger project includes creating a logic for adherence to scriptural authority without succumbing to fundamentalism, creating conditions for deep engagement with various scriptural traditions through close readings of scriptures by Jews, Christians, and Muslims and thinking about the conditions required for such a reading that is both anti-foundationalist and still modern (Ochs uses the term "postliberal") that includes translating that professional theological enterprise into language that can be used by religious communities. Finally Ochs has developed a way of thinking through the structures of not *what* each tradition needs to sacrifice but *how* each tradition can do so without either succumbing to the foundationalist modern notion of questioning all tradition or questioning Reason itself as a catalyst

1. On postliberalism, see Lindbeck, *Nature of Doctrine.*

for understanding tradition.[2] The third way Ochs calls postliberalism, a notion that seeks to simultaneously push aside modernity's foundationalism, counter postmodernism's relativizing all truth, and avoid fundamentalism's limiting truth to one particular tradition or revelatory experience. On Ochs' reading postmodernism makes inter-religious dialogue largely superfluous while fundamentalism makes it blasphemous.

Ochs' most definitive study that encompasses the above objectives is *Another Reformation: Postliberal Christianity and the Jews*. In this volume Ochs takes a two-pronged approach to the argument as to why only postliberalism can enable Christianity to truly integrate Judaism into its theological vision. In short the argument suggests that the main impediment for Christianity in its engagement with Jews and Judaism is the doctrine of supersessionism, that is, the Christian belief that Christianity comes to replace Judaism. The idea of supersessionism is arguably so deeply rooted in Christianity that it cannot easily be excised, if excised at all. In his discussion of the Mennonite theologian John Howard Yoder's work, Michael Cartwright puts it this way, "I do not believe that it is possible for Christian theologians to escape the problem of Christian supersessionism. I do believe, however, that we do not have to succumb to despair in this matter."[3] Writing on Yoder, Zionism, and supersessionism, Alain Epp Weaver writes, "If one can be non-supersessionist while affirming traditional theological claims, then the burden of proof will be on revisionist theological positions."[4] Ochs, Cartwright, and Weaver each understand the centrality of supersessionism and yet each equally recognizes that genuine Jewish-Christian dialogue cannot take place until the erasure of Judaism implicit in supersessionism is somehow mitigated.

Below I critically examine Ochs' reading of one of the postliberal figures he treats in his book, John Howard Yoder. Yoder serves as a centerpiece of Ochs' argument precisely because he is presented as the exception that proves the rule. While Yoder appears squarely inside the postliberal orbit he also exhibits certain traits that Ochs prefers to call "non-non-supersessionist" tendencies, specifically regarding Judaism and Jewish nationalism as an, or perhaps the, quintessence of modern Judaism. Ochs argues that this "non-non-supersessionism" is a consequence of certain non- or even

2. By foundationalist Ochs refers to an idea originating in Aristotle and taking on new meaning in Descartes and later in Wittgenstein whereby everything in the past is subject to more direct disclosures of knowledge. Ochs views this as "modern" and claims it undermines traditional/religious claims of truth. See Ochs, *Another Reformation*, 155, 156.

3. Cartwright, "Afterward," 231.

4. Weaver, "Constantinianism, Zionism, Diaspora," page 9 in online version.

anti-postliberal tendencies in Yoder's thought. Ochs' point, as I understand it, is that when Yoder deviates from a postliberal perspective, his supersessionism returns, perhaps by accident but more likely by design.

Below I examine Ochs' claim about Yoder in three ways: first by considering Yoder's own view on this question; second, critically examining Ochs' reading of him; and finally, by offering three Jewish models that share aspects of Yoder's critique of Jewish nationalism that may shed light on the ways in which Yoder can be a useful tool in Ochs' desire to create what he calls a theology of reparation between Jews and Christians. My aim is to question whether Yoder's notion of diasporism and anti-Constantinianism, notions Yoder believes are essential components of pacifist religion (and the genius of both Christianity *and* Judaism), are unhelpful for the promulgation of Ochs' theology of reparation.

II

Ochs begins *Another Reformation* by setting the methodological agenda for his more detailed analysis in the body of the book. He notes at the outset that he does not offer a definitive definition of postliberalism because he believes its contours are fluid and expand and contract with each thinker he examines. But he does give us some rubrics.

Postliberalism refers to an activity of reformation directed at once to the church or synagogue and to the university (or, more broadly the speculum as a public order). For postliberalism, "reformation" implies both reaffirmation and correction. Like other movements of reform and revitalization, it seeks to criticize certain institutions from within—from deep within, that is, which means according to norms embedded within the practices and histories of those institutions, but not necessarily visible to contemporary practitioners and histories of those institutions. Postliberals often attempt, therefore, to reclaim what they consider prototypical sources and norms of the church or synagogue and of the university (or speculum) and to offer their criticisms from out of these sources and norms.[5]

For Ochs postliberalism is a reparative project, recognizing the suffering that premodern religion has wrought and also believing that the resources of the tradition itself contain the requisite elements to repair that damage if they are examined with the goal of relieving suffering.[6] Reason alone cannot serve that reparative purpose for Ochs because Reason alone would

5. Ochs, *Another Reformation*, 6.

6. See Ochs, *Another Reformation*, 14, for further definition of "suffering" and "repair."

undermine the very scriptural authority that was the cause of the suffering that requires reparation. The relational model of postliberalism is presented to counter the dyadic model ("any problematic situation [is] the consequence of some faulty behavior X, which is the logical contradictory of some correct behavior –X").[7] The relational model rejects the dichotomy (Ochs prefers dyadism) that sets precepts as irreconcilable; thus relation is not one community to another but also a relation of a community with the divine Word and to another community with the divine Word. The two divine Words are also in relation and not in contradiction to one another such that they can be used to relieve the very suffering that they caused in the past, that is, when they were viewed only in dyadic fashion.

Scripture is a central part of Ochs' postliberal conception of religion. In some way, it replaces Reason, which dominated the "Epoch of Assimilation" that sought a Religion of Reason as the solution to the problems revealed religions created. For Ochs, "Scripture is the prototype as well as the primary book of instruction in how to compose diagrams of repair, which [Charles] Peirce calls 'existential graphs.'"[8] Scripture does not refer to one specific scripture but rather those books (if we can call them "books") that put the reader in relation to the divine, not in the prophetic sense of "thus says God" but in a relational sense. Ochs suggests that "to study Torah is always to enter into a relationship with a living God, and it is only by way of that relation that Judaism has had the capacity to be resurrected and renewed after each of the Jewish people's major catastrophes."[9] This is not meant as a platitude; rather the reader of scripture "reasons" with it, talks to it as well as listens to and it thus also seeks reason from it, always in a reparative mode, always to alleviate suffering, always to bring Judaism back from the precipice each tragedy presents. The following is a succinct exemplar of this approach: "The mediators tended to insist that belief in the factual occurrences reported in the Bible, especially those connected with Jesus, was indispensable. At the same time they either said or hinted broadly that the religious meaning or truth communicated through these events must be understood by reference to a content of religion and morality broader than the Bible."[10]

Ochs concludes that the deepest work Christians must do to enable their theologies to cohere with this new spirit of engagement in a post-Vatican II

---

7. For a slightly different use of the term "dyadic logic," see Ochs, *Return to Scripture*, 13. There Ochs claims that "dyadic logic" is the assimilation of mediation "of a biblical text to its meaning or referent" (38).

8. Ochs, *Return to Scripture*, 15.

9. Cartwright and Ochs, "Editor's Introduction," 5.

10. Ochs, *Another Reformation*, 23.

world concerns supersessionism since supersessionism has historically been the most common way Christianity rejected, repudiated, or ignored Judaism. And it is precisely here where postliberalism enters as Ochs' solution to this dilemma: how can Christians maintain fealty to their scriptural traditions and not succumb to supersessionism? If the rejection of supersessionism requires an undermining of scriptural authority by historicizing scripture such that it becomes a fully human and thus a fallible, even unredeemable, document (the modern foundationalist approach according to Ochs) it has betrayed not only Christian scripture (and Jewish scripture as well) but the Christian (and Jewish) community. Below I will examine a little more closely one case in Ochs' book, John Howard Yoder, perhaps the most vexing case precisely because Yoder seems to break the rules by opting out of a fully non-supersessionist theology while remaining wed to a postliberal approach.

III

John Howard Yoder (1927–97) was a Mennonite theologian most celebrated for his theology of Christian pacifism. His Anabaptist approach that embodies a contemporary version of what is known as the Radical Reformation seeks to recover the apostolic Christianity of the Jesus movement. He is strongly anti-Constantinianism and opposes the politicization of religion writ large.[11] Yoder remarks, "There is no alternative but to painstakingly, feebly, repentantly, patiently, locally, disentangle Jesus from the Christ of Byzantium and of Torquemada."[12] As a believer in scripture as the carrier of the divine Word Yoder fits nicely into Ochs' postliberal model. In Ochs' *Another Reformation* Yoder serves as the lynchpin to Ochs' thesis that postliberalism logically produces a non-supersessionist Christianity. Yoder plays this role because while some of his work indeed exhibits a non-supersessionist approach, especially regarding his belief in the shared roots of both apostolic Christianity and early Judaism and his claim that Jesus and Paul never rejected Judaism (they only rejected a certain *form* of Judaism), Yoder's anti-Constantinianism, his belief in religious practice as the foundation of faith communities and his unrelenting pacifism, yields an anti-Zionism that Ochs calls a "non-non-supersessionism" because it amounts to the erasure of the nationalistic dimension of Judaism as representing anything authentic and worth saving. For Yoder, Zionism is nothing less than a Jewish Constantinianism and does the same damage to Judaism that Constantinianism does to Christianity.

11. For an overview of Yoder's work see Cartwright, "Radical Catholicity."
12. Yoder, "Disavowal of Constantine" in Yoder, *Royal Priesthood*, 255.

Before getting to Ochs' critique of Yoder I will briefly rehearse Yoder's basic position on these matters as stated most clearly in a series of essays published as *The Jewish-Christian Schism Revisited*, edited by Ochs and Michael Cartwright. In these essays Yoder sets out what he believes is the shared roots of Judaism and Christianity, albeit each one refracted through very particular lenses. Yoder's understanding of "Judaism" and "Christianity" is often quite idiosyncratic and those shared roots, as he understands them, are what brings him to a new kind of supersessionism Ochs calls non-non-supersessionism. Thus, for Yoder it is precisely what he thinks Judaism and Christianity share that results in his rejection of a dimension of Judaism that dominates our contemporary scene.

Yoder uses his discussion of the "Jewishness" of Jesus and the Jesus movement as a way of fortifying his vision of the "free church movement" as a "Jewish" vision.[13] His understanding of "Judaism" that he finds authentic is something that exists in a thin slice of history after the destruction of the Jerusalem Temple in 70 CE and before the redaction of the Mishna in the second century. That is, a Judaism that was still arguably in a liquid state of formation (the question of Jewish normativity at this time will become relevant for Yoder later on). It was a de-politicized Judaism thinking its way through its newly realized de-territorialized fate. It was a Judaism trying to negotiate its oftentimes universalistic prophetic heritage as a minority culture. It is precisely here in this relatively narrow historical corridor after the loss of political power and before the abandonment of what Yoder considers Judaism's great missionizing project and the development of what he determines is the ethnic enclavism of Rabbinic Judaism, which Yoder posits, is largely a response to Christianity. It is here where Judaism and Jesus meet and where the truth of each most forcefully shines through.

In short, the ostensible schism happened for Yoder when Christianity lost its way and succumbed to the lure of political power (Constantine) and Judaism responded to powerlessness by turning in on itself (Mishnaic Judaism). Yoder considers Rabbinic Judaism (the Judaism of law) to be the first stage of Judaism's "Christianization." This intentionally provocative claim requires some scrutiny. Yoder is not arguing that *halakha* (Jewish normative law) is a product of "Christianization." *Halakha* was arguably the wedge, or one wedge, that separated Judaism *from* Christianity.[14] And yet that is precisely Yoder's

13. The Free Church Movement exists in the US and Europe and consists of churches of various Protestant denominations that are devoted to a complete separation from established churches and government. Yoder's Mennonite free church is part of that larger movement.

14. See, for example, Sanders, *Paul, the Law*; Sanders, *Jesus and Judaism*; and Neusner, *Judaic Law*.

understanding of "Christianization." He posits that the period of the Mishna (second century) marked a period of Judaism turning in on itself and opting to largely abandon the prophetic gesture toward the world. This, he argues, was in large part a response to an emerging Christianity. Yoder envisions Mishnaic Judaism as a turn away from Judaism's original missionizing status (one can cull this from various prophetic passages). It is worth quoting Yoder at length here to capture the turns in his argument.

> We noted before that the Judaism of Jeremiah, of Hillel, of Jesus, and of Johanan ben Zakkai was a missionary faith. It then represented an adaptation to Christianity when the rabbis by the time of the Mishna abandoned their missionary openness, leaving the function to the messianic Jews (i.e. the Christians). . . . Only now, after the schism could it make sense to spell out the argument that Gentiles do not need Torah because they can make it into the age to come by keeping the rules of Noah. . . . In any case, Judaism after the schism turns out to be an ethnic enclave, less missionary than before, if not committed to a near rejection of the accession of Gentiles to members in their community. Thus the abandonment of the missionary vision and action is a kind of backhanded adjustment, not to the Gentile world in general, but to Christianity. *Non-missionary Judaism is a product of Christian history* [italics in text]. For Jews to be non-missionary means that they have been "Christianized": they have accepted a slot within a context where telling the Gentiles about the God of Abraham is a function that can be left to the Christians.[15]

It is not radical nor even contentious to notice that Mishnaic Judaism deviates in significant ways from at least some prophetic teachings while cohering to others (Yoder focuses particularly on Jer 29:4–7 and the message of exile as divine will).[16] The reason for such deviation remains open to scholarly speculation and the role Christianity played in rabbinic self-fashioning has become a contested issue among historians of ancient Israel.

Yoder moves in a different direction by claiming that formative Judaism, that is, Mishnaic Judaism and what it produces was formed in part as a response to Christianity not via Christianity as a Jewish heresy but through the notion that Christianity now fulfilled a missionary function that Jews, and Judaism, no longer needed to fulfill. While such a claim is likely not historical, it may indeed emerge in at least two instances later in Jewish history.

15. Yoder, "Jewishness of the Free Church Vision," in Yoder, *Jewish Christian-Schism Revisited*, 106.

16. See, for example, Yoder's essay on Stephen Zweig's poem, "See How They Go with Their Face to the Sun," in Yoder, *Jewish Christian-Schism Revisited*, esp. 183–87.

First, in Moses Maimonides' notion that perhaps Christianity and Islam (although both deviant from Judaism) exist in order to pave the way for the final Jewish redemption. Second, in Franz Rosenzweig's notion in his *Star of Redemption* that Christianity fulfills an outward function to expose the world to monotheism while Judaism necessarily exercises the inward function of protecting the Hebrew Bible's true monotheistic core.[17] Maimonides may be asking the question, "Why did God bring Christianity and Islam into existence in the first place if Judaism is the true religion?" while Rosenzweig, in early twentieth-century Germany, may be trying to posit how both Judaism and Christianity are necessary to one another and thus need to enable each other to continue to serve their divine purpose.

In any case, Yoder's understanding/conception of Rabbinic Judaism as a process of "Christianization" also, or precisely, implies that Rabbinic Judaism ("Judaism" as we know it) is younger than Christianity. In at least one place Yoder says this outright. "It will take some time and testing to get used to the awareness that Judaism as we now know it, i.e. Rabbinic Judaism, is younger than Christianity—and in part a reaction thereto—but this is an indispensable straightening out of our categories."[18]

But in the end Yoder is making a different claim than either Maimonides or Rosenzweig. He claims the Mishnaic move undermines Judaism's true greatness in its choice to promote an ethnic enclavism. We must remember that for Yoder, as an anti-Constantinian, "Christianizing" is a negative term in a very specific way: it does not mean *becoming* Christian but rather abandoning authentic Judaism as a *response* to Christianity. There are two further instantiations of Judaism's "Christianizing" in Yoder's thought. The first is modern progressive Judaism's "theological assimilation" to Christianity (a Christianity that he believes had already lost its way) or the acquiescence to pluralism as a religious identity. For brevity's sake let's call this Reform Judaism. In this sense Reform Judaism mistakenly became like a Christianity that wasn't truly Christian. Yet the

---

17. See Maimonides, *Mishneh Torah*, "Laws of Kings." The passage reads, "All these matters relating to Jesus of Nazareth and the Ishmaelite who came after him only served to clear the way for King Messiah, to prepare the whole world to worship one God with one accord. . . . Thus the messianic hope, the Torah, and the commandments have become familiar topics—topics of conversation [among the inhabitants] of the far isles and many people, uncircumcised of heart and flesh. They are discussing these matters and the commandments of the Torah." I used the translation of A. M. Hershman in *The Code of Maimonides*, xxiii–xxiv. Franz Rosenzweig makes a similar point as his main thesis in *The Star of Redemption*, albeit Rosenzweig gives far more credit to the theological merits of Christianity than Maimonides does.

18. Yoder "Judaism as a non-non-Christian Religion," in Yoder, *Jewish-Christian-Schism Revisited*, 154.

final form of Jewish "Christianization" for Yoder, and the one that is so problematic for Ochs, is Zionism or Jewish nationalism. The claim that Zionism is "Christianization" in some way strikes at the very core of the problem. In today's world, to deny Jewish nationalism its role, even its central role, in Jewish identity, more forcefully to view Zionism as the *problem*, amounts to a kind of supersessionism. Judaism without Jewish nationalism, without a commitment to the land, is today almost erased, superseded, as it were, from the centrality of land and an autonomous Jewish polity. Thus non-nationalist Judaism, one closer to Yoder's view, becomes the victim of another kind of inner-Jewish supersessionism.[19]

What exactly is Yoder's problem with Zionism? It is not what you might think. Yoder believes that Zionism is a form of Jewish Constantinianism and therefore that Zionism undermines the separation between church and political and military power that he believes is central to Jesus' (and thus the Jewish) contribution to the world. And he does believe that Zionism makes Jewish pacifism almost impossible.[20] But just as problematic for Yoder is the extent to which Zionism removes religion as a requirement of Jewish identity.

> The State of Israel models itself on western thinking. It defines Jews in such a way that most of them may be unbelieving or unobservant. . . . The State of Israel is a state but no longer a believing community. Once the state was created, the separateness of Jewishness as an ethnic body is no longer needed as a base for religion or vice versa. . . . Committed Judaism, i.e. a discernable people ready thoroughly and sacrificially to order their lives around their convictions as to the substance of the Torah, is a minority sect in Israel just as is Christianity, and just as they both are today in Western Europe.[21]

There are many ways one can explicate this passage. One is that Zionism replaces religion with peoplehood and thus undermines Judaism's central and most powerful message of fidelity to the one God. One illustrative example might be Golda Meir's comment to Hannah Arendt. "I want you to understand, as a socialist I do not believe in God, I believe in the Jewish people."[22]

---

19. On this see Magid, "Butler Trouble."

20. This is not completely true as there were and are Zionists who are pacifists. See, for example, Cohen, "Foremost Amongst the Divine Attributes."

21. Yoder, *Jewish Christian-Schism Revisited*, 107.

22. Hannah Arendt to Gershom Scholem, July 20, 1963, in *Hannah Arendt and Gershom Scholem: Correspondence*, 361. See, in the same volume, the letter of August 6, 1963.

The notion of belief in a "people" as a substitute for "belief in God" is not uncommon in certain secular Zionist circles. The politicization of religion and thus reification of peoplehood in some forms of Zionist thought and the extent to which "people" replaces God, for Yoder, significantly undermine the very contribution Judaism makes to human civilization and erase the very reason he views it as the backbone of his "free church movement." One could surely contest this claim by citing the deeply religious nature of some streams of Zionism, especially in our contemporary world. But this too would bother Yoder as the very foundation of religious Zionism envisions God as party to the politicalization of Judaism, even, or in some cases, precisely, through military means.[23] Yoder thus has two basic problems with Zionism: first its notion of landedness, that is, that Judaism, or Jewishness, is fulfilled only, or primarily, by settling the land; and second the way that Jewish nationalism in complex ways inserts ethnic identity as a companion, at times a replacement, at other times, a fulfillment, for religion. Thus for Yoder Zionism is the final stage of the "Christianization" of Judaism in that the state, like Christendom, is no longer a "believing community" because its members are defined by fully secular means.

The final dimension of Yoder's thoughts on Judaism that require brief mention before turning to Ochs' critique is the notion of exile, or diaspora, as blessing rather than curse, something Yoder gleans from Jeremiah 29:4–7. This is tied to Yoder's argument that Judaism is originally a missionizing religion and also his critique of Jewish nationalism in that in exile Jews can better disseminate the true message of God's word it carries. The Talmudic dictum that "Israel was only exiled so that it could make converts"[24] is one way to articulate Yoder's view, although for Yoder exile is not a temporary state but a permanent one, in fact, it is the state that embodies the very truth of Judaism and makes it a stellar exemplar of his "free church movement." For him, Zionism undermined Judaism the way Constantinianism undermined Christianity.[25]

---

23. An example of this would be the work of R. Zvi Yehuda Kook. See Held, "What Zvi Yehuda Kook Wrought?" On Yoder and the messianism of religious Zionism see Yoder, "Jewishness of the Free Church," in Yoder, *Jewish-Christian Schism Revisited*, 112.

24. B. Talmud Pesahim 87b.

25. See Ochs, *Another Reformation*, 151. On this see Weaver, "Further Footnotes," 44.

IV

Ochs' chapter "The Limits of Postliberalism," in *Another Reformation*, is on one reading a critical reading of Yoder's theological critique of Zionism as introducing a non-non-supersessionism to an otherwise postliberal Christian theology. We must remember that for Yoder, Zionism is not damaging as a political movement as much as a theological deviation from Judaism's "Jeremianic" trajectory that he cherishes as one of its great theological innovations of human history. What Ochs means by a non-non-supersessionism is that Yoder does not fit into any of the common categories of supersessions enough to call him a supersessionist. For heuristic purposes I suggest using Kendall Soulen's three types of supersessionism and adding a fourth suggested by George Lindbeck. Soulen distinguishes between economic supersessionism, punitive supersessionism, and structural supersessionism. The first refers to "the ultimate obsolescence of carnal Israel [as] an essential feature of God's one overarching economy of redemption of the world." The second suggests "God abrogates God's covenant with Israel on account of Israel's rejection of Christ." The third suggests the exclusion of Israel as inhabiting the "standard canonical narrative," of how scripture is read.[26] Lindbeck adds another dimension he calls the erasure of the Jews, not necessarily the rejection of the Jews in classical supersessionism, but simply not considering them as part of the Christian vision of the world. None of these categories would apply to Yoder. In fact, not only does Yoder not want to excise Jews or Judaism from his theological vision; he wants to use Judaism (perhaps an exilic pre-rabbinic Judaism) as the very basis of Christianity's true theological vision. So perhaps we can rename Yoder's non-non-supersessionism as unintended supersessionism.

Yoder bases his reparation of the schism between Judaism and Christianity on the notion that Jesus never really rejected Judaism because there was no normative Judaism in Jesus' time to reject. Rather, he rejected one form of Judaism in favor of another. Explaining Yoder's position Ochs writes, "Neither Jesus nor Paul, nor the apostolic communities rejected normative Judaism. . . . If there was no such thing as normative Judaism no one could have univocally rejected it or be rejected by it. . . . What Jesus himself proposed to his listeners was nothing other than what he claimed as the normative vision of a restored and clarified Judaism, namely, the proper interpretation of the Jewish scriptures and tradition for this present, in light of the New Age which he heralded."[27]

---

26. Soulen, *God of Israel*, 29, 30. Cf. Weaver, "Constantinianism," 8.
27. Ochs, *Another Reformation*, 141.

Ochs lists four examples of Yoder's "modernist" and non-postliberal stance that he claims results in a non-non-supersessionist position: (1) Judaism is exilic; (2) Judaism is not a landed religion; (3) Judaism is non-violent; (4) and Judaism is missionizing. Ochs' main concern seems to be Yoder's claim that exclusive authentic Judaism is the Judaism of exile, and that exile is not merely a waystation for messiah, but the very completion of the messianic task. Both Ochs and Michael Cartwright claim Yoder overstates the case for exile made by Jeremiah as the *sine qua non* of Judaism and understates, even erases, the intrinsic tie rabbinic Judaism has to the land of Israel. Ochs, as opposed to Cartwright, focuses on the non-postliberalism these moves represent.[28]

On one level, it is hard to contest their criticisms. Historically, literarily, and theologically speaking Yoder's exclusionary vision is limiting. Ochs writes, "Yoder's exclusive choice for an exclusively exilic Judaism shares the same logic as the Maccabees' and Zealots' choice for an exclusively nonexilic Judaism of land and national power."[29] This is an interesting sentence for what it does *not* say. What it does *not* say is that the exclusively nonexilic Judaism is precisely what mainstream Zionism proffers (to say nothing of religious Zionism), illustrated by its foundational principle of "rejection of the diaspora."[30] In considering only ancient ideologies and not the ones that may have informed Yoder's theological critique Ochs has arguably concealed from his reader the very instantiation of Yoder's critical concern. I argue that this context is a crucial part of Yoder's assessment. In fact, in his list of postliberal criteria, Ochs writes that postliberalism must express and meet the needs and crises of a particular time and history.

Setting this aside for the moment Yoder is not blind to Ochs' critique. He writes,

> We cannot *not* be selective; we can ask that the selectivity should contribute to reciprocal recognition, finding in the other what one needs, for the sake of one's own integrity, to esteem. . . . I make no apology for reading the vast melee of the Jewish experience in such a way that Yochanan is more representative than Menachem, Abraham Joshua Heschel than Ben Gurion, Arnold Wolf than Meir Kahane, Anne Frank than Golda Meir. What goes on here is not that I am co-opting Jews to enlist them in my cause. It is that I am finding a story, which

28. Ochs, *Another Reformation*, 146.
29. Ochs, *Another Reformation*, 152.
30. See Schweid, "Rejection of the Diaspora." More recently see Eisen, "Zionism."

MAGID—SUPERSESSIONISM, ZIONISM, AND REPARATIVE THEOLOGY   213

is really there, coming all the way down from Abraham, that
has the grace to adopt me.[31]

If I read him correctly here, Yoder argues that making a case, or claim, of a lost message, or jewel, buried in the mire of history is not necessarily to exclude the multivocality of a tradition but instead to choose particular lenses through which to see them. Yoder is not denying the existence of other narratives, for example the so-called Zionist narrative that stretches from Bar Kokhba to Bar Giora to Zev Jabotinsky. One could read him to suggest, however, that *that* story does not serve the reparative purposes he seeks, not between Jews and Christians and not internal to Judaism itself. In fact, I would assume he considers *that* story simply a continuation of the schism precisely the way militant Christian evangelicalism is a continuation of the schism. If we bind ourselves to a reparative theology that is part of the postliberal position, wouldn't that create the possibility that certain forms of Judaism or Christianity might need to take precedence in favor of others that would serve that reparative purpose?

Ochs seems attuned to this. Yet he claims that Yoder's anti-Zionism is dyadic, thus not reparative, and not consistent with postliberal sentiments.[32] His reasoning is four-fold (of which I will mention three elements). First, Yoder argues against any "normative" Judaism and then claims that rabbinic Judaism is a fall from what Judaism *ought* to be. Second, because Judaism indeed flourished in exile, it is exilic as a consequence of divine will and thus its un-exilic projection of Judaism through Zionism subverts its true nature. In Ochs' view this undermines the role of the land in exilic Jewish life and literature, viewing it as counter to Judaism's major contribution. Third, the move from "Judaism is nonviolent" to "Judaism is pacifist," and thus involving itself with land, statecraft, and military power is antithetical to Judaism's central mission.[33] This essentially makes Zionism impossible. Ochs considers this a kind of foundationalism in that "Jewish life in exile is a direct illustration of the meaning of Jesus' narrative. The problem is in the clarity and finality of this claim."[34] That is, Yoder ignores accepted traditions in favor of "intuitive" alternatives.

31. Yoder, "Jewishness of the Free Church Vision," in Yoder, *Jewish-Christian Schism Revisited*, 115.

31. Yoder, "Jewishness of the Free Church Vision," in Yoder, *Jewish-Christian Schism Revisited*, 115.

32. For Ochs' definition of dyadic verses binary reasoning see Ochs, *Another Reformation*, 9, and Ochs, "Response."

33. Ochs, *Another Reformation*, 161, 162

34. Ochs, *Another Reformation*, 161. The fourth dyadic reasoning that speaks to Yoder's using scripture to get at "the essence of Judaism" is important but not germane to where I want to take Ochs' reading.

Rather than focusing on Yoder's ostensible silencing of these voices it would be more constructive to consider how Yoder's vision could contribute to our present climate regarding the limitations many of us experience when we dare to think outside the Zionist narrative that is now not only a part of the Jewish mosaic but arguably the very standard upon which it is defined.

What I mean to suggest is that today we are arguably not living in a postliberal Jewish world, but very much in a "dyadic" one that makes hegemonic claims of Jewish legitimacy. There is no doubt that the stories of the Davidic monarchy, and the scriptural books of Joshua, Ezra, and Nehemia tell a story quite different than Jeremiah 29. Yoder admits that as much as anyone. But it is legitimate to ask if these are the stories that need repeating today; are these the stories of reparation after the Holocaust? This is not to erase them as much as to "repair" them by rethinking categories of landedness that need not result in a hegemonic regime that exercises political power as it simultaneously makes a claim of Jewish legitimacy. "Negation of the Diaspora," a cornerstone of classical Zionism, is also a kind of supersessionism. In fact, taken literally it excludes almost half of the Jewish people and many Jewish ideologies that have flourished since the advent of modernity. Yoder addresses this problem by decoupling Judaism from Zionism in a way that would enable both to exist but disable the political theology that emerges when they become fused (this may arguably result in a post- and not an anti-Zionist perspective).[35]

V

As a way to offer a constructive critique of Ochs' reading of Yoder, I would like to briefly present three different positions that may help us understand how Yoder's theological critique of Zionism's political theology, even if we do not accept it, might help Jews come to terms with the challenges of political hegemony while recognizing Yoder's point about Jewish genius as he understands it. Even if Ochs is right that Yoder is not being postliberal in his critique of Zionism, we can still view him as contributing to a postliberal theology by creating a theology of reparation that seeks to relieve suffering. In the three cases below there is an attempt to decouple Zionism from Judaism which may be a way to salvage both while mitigating the negative dimensions each contributes to the other.

The first is the early to mid-twentieth century Canaanite movement led by Yonatan Ratosh; the second is Yoel Teitelbaum, the Hasidic grand rabbi of

---

35. See Boyarin and Boyarin, *Powers of Diaspora*, 53; and Weaver, *States of Exile*, 61. On Boyarin, see Weaver, "Further Footnotes."

Satmar who is responsible for the contemporary ultra-Orthodox anti-Zionist position; and the third is contemporary Jewish philosopher Steven Schwarzschild (who was also an important interlocutor of Yoder's).[36] In many ways, these constitute three failed experiments and have largely been either erased (the Canaanites), discredited (Satmar), or ignored (Schwarzschild). Yet all three address Yoder's concerns about the extent to which Zionism, as nationalism and landedness, has sullied what Judaism has to offer. Each in different ways uncouples Judaism from Zionism, in one case, to create a new Hebraic civilization (Canaanites), in another case to invalidate Zionism as a form of heresy (Satmar), and in the third case to make us think more carefully about the ways in which Jewish nationalism and militarism challenges a crucial part of the covenant (Schwarzschild).

In the early twentieth century Yonatan Rotosh and the Canaanites made the case that Zionism's success required it to be severed totally from Judaism.[37] The extent to which the Canaanites are Zionist at all depends on how one understands the term. They are certainly not the only ones who sought to decouple Zionism from Judaism, but they are perhaps the most radical and uncompromising.[38]

Avidly secular, the Canaanites believed that Zionism offered the possibility of a new autochthonous Hebrew civilization that would accompany (on some readings, replace) the older diasporic "Jewish" one. It would avoid the Jew-Gentile schism by making all inhabitants of the land of Israel, Jew or Gentile, citizens of a new Hebrew civilization. In this vision, Israel would not be a "Jewish" state but a Hebrew one. For the Canaanites (not unlike Yoder) Judaism was a product of the diaspora and it should remain so. Judaism may be needed for Jews to survive in *galut*. That is its origin and that is its place. The Canaanites thought the New Hebrew civilization could replace the old diasporic "Jewish" one but only if radical separation between Judaism and Zionism occurred. Otherwise Israel would simply turn into an ethnic enclave and the non-Jewish inhabitants who had been living there for generations would be excluded.[39]

36. Michael Cartwright treats Yoder and Schwarzschild's relation in his afterword to Yoder, *Jewish-Christian Schism Revisited*, 205–40.

37. The definitive study of the Canaanites in English is Diamond, *Homeland or Holy Land*. On this point see 49–76.

38. Diamond, *Homeland or Holy Land*, 9–23.

39. It is interesting that after the establishment of the state, some Canaanites like Ratosh became quite right wing while others became quite left wing. As Ron Kuzar notes, "[The Canaanites] exhibited an interesting blend of militarism and power politics toward the Arabs as an organized community on the one hand and a welcoming acceptance of them as individuals to be redeemed from medieval darkness on the other." See Kuzar, *Hebrew and Zionism*, 13.

In many ways, the Satmar position is structurally similar to the Canaanites that reaches the opposite conclusion. Teitelbaum viewed Zionism as the anti-Christ of the generation preceding messiah.[40] It was the final divine test Jews needed to withstand to merit redemption. For Teitelbaum, Judaism and Zionism are diametrically opposed and from his perspective any form of secular Judaism was false by definition. His real adversaries were not the secularists, but the religious nationalists who viewed Zionism as the fulfillment of Judaism and the ultra-Orthodox who succumbed to the seduction of Zionism, even if only for pragmatic reasons. Teitelbaum would have agreed with Yoder's use of Jeremiah 29 as the template of Jewish religiosity albeit not for the same reasons. For Teitelbaum exile is a divine decree not to be undone by any form of human agency. Ignoring or contesting that decree endangers the Jews by severing the covenantal protection awarded to them though the covenant.

Exile is not the place for Jews to disseminate their wisdom to the world but rather to create enclaves whereby they can maintain their traditions and wait for redemption.[41] Teitelbaum advocates a premillennial Judaism that seeks to cultivate a remnant of "true Jews" who live by their covenantal responsibilities and will ultimately merit redemption. Like Yoder, Teitelbaum also has strong pacifist tendencies, at least in terms of "forcing the end." While Teitelbaum and Yoder strongly differ on fundamental issues of theology, one place where they overlap is on the notion of faith in God and in God's covenant with Israel as the central tenet of Jewish life.

Here a brief examination of Steven Schwarzschild becomes relevant because it is perhaps the best place to view the overlap between Yoder and Teitelbaum. Schwarzschild was a long-time friend of Yoder and their communication on these matters illuminates much about both Yoder and Schwarzschild's theological positions. Schwarzschild was also one of the few modern Jewish thinkers who creatively used Teitelbaum's anti-Zionism in his theological work although he was in no way a follower. This comes through most clearly in his essay "On the Theology of Jewish Survival."[42]

In that essay Schwarzschild makes a distinction between what he calls the "ethical covenant" and the "metaphysical covenant."

> The ethical interpretation makes the religious, ethical, and historical honor of Israel the prerequisite of God's fulfillment of

40. See, for example, the Introduction to Teitelbaum, 'Al Ha-Geulah ve la Ha-Temurah, 1–27. Cf. Ravitzky, "Forcing the End"; Kaplan, "Rabbi Joel Teitelbaum"; and Sorotzkin, "Building the Earthly."

41. See Magid, "'America Is No Different.'"

42. See Schwarzschild, "On the Theology."

His part of the covenant; i.e. the preservation and advantage of the Jewish people: if they do not do their share He is relieved of His obligation and will let it lapse. The advantage of this view is obviously the responsibility which it places on the Jew and the ethical stimulus it thus constitutes. Its corollary disadvantage is equally obvious: it is entirely too anthropocentric. . . . The metaphysical view, then, represents the other part of the polarity. It speaks of the "eternal covenant": it assures mankind that as long as the rainbow will be in the sky so long—which is to say eternally—will humanity persist, and it assures Israel that its survival is coeval with God's existence.[43]

In some way, the very notion of Jewish nationalism (making the Jewish people, and not God the center of the covenantal axis) is a "secular" act in that it may remain wed to the "ethical covenant" (self-determination or the fulfillment of mitzvoth) but rejects the "metaphysical covenant" (God's promise to insure Jewish survival). The self-assertion of Jewish "survival" is founded in some way on two opposite poles: the fear of physical annihilation (the Holocaust) and the fear of assimilation. Thus, taking one's survival into one's own hands is understandable enough, especially given historical exigencies, but Schwarzschild asks us to consider the covenantal price of such a move when that effaces the metaphysical dimension. Since the ethical and metaphysical dimensions of the covenant exist in tandem and stand in dialectical relation to one another what happens when one is affirmed and one is marginalized, if not unwittingly denied?[44]

Schwarzschild applies this template to the reception of the Holocaust and to militant Zionism. Why, he asks, do we venerate those who "fought back" (the Warsaw ghetto uprising) and those who survived, but do not view those who perished as heroes but rather as victims about whom it is said, "who went like sheep to the slaughter"? Schwarzschild argues that this too easily translates to the militarism, the survivalism, of Zionism. And also, I would add, to the undermining of the metaphysical covenant.

Schwarzschild summarizes his position as follows:

What we have been saying is that the survival of the Jewish people is guaranteed by God—that we need not really concern ourselves with it—that to preoccupy oneself with it is a form of sickness, as health-faddists are invariably sick people—that to attribute our survival to human instrumentalities . . . inevitably

43. Schwarzschild, "On the Theology," 84, 85.

44. Here Meir Kahane's thinking is a good counter-point to Teitelbaum. See Magid, "Anti-Semitism as Colonialism."

218 PART THREE: THEOLOGY

leads to acts of *hubris, ga'avah,* which victimize other human beings and result in unending conflict and defeat—and that, on the contrary, the God who has brought us this far will also redeem His other promises to Israel. . . . In short, the Torah is our business, Israel's survival is God's.[45]

Schwarzschild certainly does not adopt Teitelbaum's political theology. But he *is* suggesting that Teitelbaum makes an important point for us to consider: how much of the covenant is erased through the adaptation of Zionism defined as the Jews being fully responsible for their own survival as the standard of Jewish legitimacy? Here I think Yoder makes a useful intervention, but to fully understand that one must see his work within its historical context.

I suggest that a robust Jewish theology emerges precisely when Schwarzschild's ethical and metaphysical covenantal postures act in relation, rather than opposition, to one another. Covenantal theology requires human action and divine promise. When human action functions without, or even against, divine promise, or when divine promise is defined by human action (God demands us to save ourselves) what easily results is a fetishization of power whereby human responsibility for the "other" is eclipsed by the obsession with the survival of the self. Yoder's understanding of the Jesus movement was that by uncoupling religion from the polis, religion (Christianity and Judaism) could assure that the polis would not succumb to theologizing its own muscularity, thus undermining precisely what it has to offer human civilization.

In any case, Ochs is certainly correct when he argues that "part of the postliberal critique of modern thought is that neither the things of the created world nor the messages of God's revealed Scripture are adequately 'captured,' represented, or defined in humanly constructed claims."[46] But this may be precisely Yoder's point viewed through the lens of Schwarzschild's ethical and metaphysical covenant. Jeremiah and Ezra live in dialectical tension, and they must, for the covenant to remain intact. Yoder is offering his vision "finding a story, which is really there, coming all the way down from Abraham . . ." Is it the only story? A postliberal would certainly say no. Whether Yoder would I do not know. But it is a story that today may be the victim and not the perpetrator of supersessionism.

45. Schwarzschild, "On the Theology," 96–98.
46. Ochs, *Another Reformation,* 159.

VI

If postliberal Judaism really wants to be a reparative theology in the twenty-first century, a theology born from the Holocaust but moving beyond it, it must address the reality in which it lives. Thus to extend Ochs' thinking I want to suggest that the twenty-first century presents us with another form of reparation—one that, perhaps ironically, presents certain challenges to the reparation of the twentieth century. While Zionism, and the Christian West's acceptance of Zionism, is part of a larger postliberal project of reparation that is in part about the alleviation of Jewish suffering living under the dominion of others during their long history, Zionism also *produces* the suffering of another people.[47] After the establishment of the state of Israel in 1948, and after 1967 when the state of Israel moved from being a democracy of all its citizens (flawed like every other democracy) to being overlords of another population, the partners of reparation may have shifted from Christians and Jews, to Palestinians and Jews. The movement of Christianity *toward* Judaism so elegantly articulated by Ochs, must also consider that Jews may find themselves on the other end of that equation. To deny that possibility indeed essentializes victimhood which makes the gift of political power not only superfluous but also unjust. Ochs indeed knows all this but I think it merits bringing it to the attention of his readers when considering his assessment of Yoder.

The Holocaust still remains a hovering dark cloud over the entire discussion. Whether or not we want to suggest a theological connection between the Holocaust and the establishment of the state of Israel, it is certainly legitimate to say that politically the Holocaust played a role in making Israel a reality.[48] And part of the reparation of the Holocaust, as Ochs notes, is the viability of Jewish sovereignty in the form of a Zionist nation-state.[49] But it is more complicated than that.

As we know, the land was never empty. The challenge of the new nation-state was the impact the founding of that state had on the Palestinian population who lived there, and the ways each side is now implicated in the narrative of the other. On this Edward Said wrote,

> Neither Palestinian nor Israeli history at this point is a thing in
> itself, without the other. . . . In doing so [seeing them as separate]

47. Here I think of Said's chapter "Zionism from the Standpoint of Its Victims," in Said, *Question of Palestine*, 56–114.

48. In terms of the Shoah and its theological implications, or lack thereof, in the state of Israel, see Novak, *Judaism and Zionism*, 225–49.

49. See Ochs, *Another Reformation*, 162.

we will necessarily come up against the basic irreconcilability
between the Zionist claim and Palestinian dispossession.[50]

The Jews now face a challenge, in part not of their own making, and in
part the result of precisely the reparation of a previous generation. That is,
a nation-state founded on the principle of Jewish (i.e., biblical) history, one
that, once enacted, has had a negative impact on another population, not
only by consequence but arguably also by design. This impact is certainly
not to the extent the Jews were victimized in the Holocaust, but it is a state
of dispossession nonetheless. On this Atalia Omer notes,

> The reading of the Tanakh (and the Holocaust), in socializing a
> particular historical Jewish Israeli consciousness, normalized and
> vindicated Jewish presence in Palestine. Therefore, it obscured
> the possibility of recognizing how the narratives of Palestinian
> displacement and uprootedness might challenge the perceptions
> of peace and justice as imagined within the Zionist vista.[51]

Yoder's anti-Constantinianism as the basis of his alleged anti-Zionism
may offer yet another alternative by suggesting that when the polis takes possession of religion, even, or perhaps precisely in a secularized form, it will
invariably corrupt the polis and that corruption will undermine religion's
greatness. This is as true of Judaism as it is of Christianity, or Islam. Ochs
may counter that because Yoder is an essentialist, his theory of non-non-
supersessionism cannot play a role in the new reparation paradigm. I am suggesting that viewing Yoder through Schwarzschild enables us to read Yoder
in a more generous, and perhaps less essentialist, way. Perhaps if Zionism
would become more openly uncoupled from Judaism,[52] if it wouldn't make its
politics the standard of Jewish theology and identity, it would enable Judaism
to remain closer to what Yoder thinks it originally was.

If we say that today's postliberal theology needs to respond to the
reparation of another state of inequality, ironically in part born from a
previous state of inequality, Yoder, along with others, may be useful tools
for a contemporary Jewish postliberal theological thinking on this point.
I will say in sum that Yoder's critique of Constantinianism, whether in
Christianity (Christendom) or in Judaism (Zionism) is a voice that needs
to be heard in a world where Constantine and Bar Kokhba's ghosts seem to

---

50. Said, "Method for Thinking," 193.

51. Omer, *When Peace Is Not Enough*, 41.

52. I do not mean the state should seek to erase religion. That may be one of liberal
politics' greatest failures, as Michael Waltzer notes in his *Paradox of Liberalism*. For a
sensitive analysis of Waltzer, see Mirsky, "Religious Fate."

be marching in step, perhaps preventing postliberal theology from more fully confronting the necessary healing in the twenty-first century. Ochs has shown us a path. The work continues.

Bibliography

Arendt, Hannah, and Gershom Scholem. *Hannah Arendt and Gershom Scholem: Correspondence* [Hebrew]. Israel: Bavel, 2014.

Boyarin, Jonathan, and Daniel Boyarin. *Powers of Diaspora: Two Essays on the Relevance of Jewish Culture.* Minneapolis: University of Minnesota Press, 2002.

Cartwright, Michael. "Afterword: 'If Abraham is Our Father . . .'" In *The Jewish-Christian Schism Revisited*, edited by Michael Cartwright and Peter Ochs, 217–77. Grand Rapids: Eerdmans, 2003.

———. "Radical Catholicity: The Witness of John Howard Yoder, 1927–1997." *The Christian Century* (Jan. 21, 1998) 44–46.

Cartwright, Michael, and Peter Ochs. "Editor's Introduction." In *The Jewish-Christian Schism Revisited*, edited by Michael Cartwright and Peter Ochs, 1–29. Grand Rapids: Eerdmans, 2003.

Cohen, Aryeh. "'The Foremost amongst the Divine Attributes Is to Hate the Vulgar Power of Violence': Aharon Shmuel Tamares and Recovering Nonviolence for Jewish Ethics." *Journal of Jewish Ethics* 1.2 (2016) 229–48.

Diamond, James. *Homeland or Holy Land.* Bloomington: Indiana University Press, 1986.

Eisen, Arnold. "Zionism, American Jewry, and the 'Negation of the Diaspora.'" In *Between Jewish Tradition and Modernity: Rethinking an Old Opposition; Essays in Honor of David Ellenson*, edited by Michael A. Meyer and David N. Myers, 175–91. Detroit: Wayne State University Press, 2014.

Held, Shai. "What Zvi Yehuda Kook Wrought? The Theopolitical Radicalization of Religious Zionism." In *Rethinking the Messianic Idea in Judaism*, edited by M. Morgan and S Weitzman, 229–56. Bloomington: Indiana University Press, 2015.

Kaplan, Zvi Jonathan. "Rabbi Joel Teitelbaum, Zionism, and Hungarian Ultra-Orthodoxy." *Modern Judaism* 24.2 (2004) 165–78.

Kuzar, Ron. *Hebrew and Zionism: A Discourse Analytic Cultural Study.* New York: Mouton de Gruyter, 2001.

Lindbeck, George. *The Nature of Doctrine: Religion and Theology in a Postliberal Age.* Philadelphia: Westminster, 1984.

Magid, Shaul. "'America Is No Different,' 'America Is Different'—Is There an American Jewish Fundamentalism? Part II: American Satmar." In *Fundamentalism: Perspectives on a Contested History*, edited by S. Wood and D. Watt, 70–91. Columbia: University of South Carolina Press, 2014.

———. "Anti-Semitism as Colonialism: Meir Kahane's 'Ethics of Violence.'" *The Journal of Jewish Ethics* 1.2 (2015) 198–226.

———. "Butler Trouble: Zionism, Excommunication and the Reception of Judith Butler's Work on Israel/Palestine." *Studies in American Jewish Literature* 33.2 (2014) 237–59.

Maimonides. *The Code of Maimonides: Book Fourteen: The Book of Judges.* Translated by A. M. Hershman. Yale Judaica Series 3. New Haven: Yale University Press, 1949.

Mirsky, Yehuda. "The Religious Fate of Secular Liberation." *The American Interest* 11.2 (2015) 11–17.

Neusner, Jacob. *Judaic Law from Jesus to the Mishna: A Systematic Reply to E. P. Sanders.* Tampa: University of South Florida, 1993.

Novak, David. *Judaism and Zionism: A New Theory.* Cambridge: Cambridge University Press, 2015.

Ochs, Peter. *Another Reformation: Postliberal Christianity and the Jews.* Grand Rapids: Baker Academic, 2011.

———. "Response: Reflections on Binarism." *Modern Theology* 24.3 (2008) 487–98.

———, ed. *The Return to Scripture in Christianity and Judaism: Essays in Postcritical Scriptural Interpretation.* Mahwah, NJ: Paulist, 1993.

Omer, Atalia. *When Peace Is Not Enough.* Chicago: University of Chicago Press, 2013.

Ravitzky, Aviezer. "Forcing the End: Radical Anti-Zionism." Translated by Jonathan Chipman. In *Messianism, Zionism, and Jewish Religious Radicalism*, 40–78. Chicago: University of Chicago Press, 1996.

Said, Edward. "A Method for Thinking about Just Peace." In *What Is a Just Peace?*, edited by Pierre Allan and Alexis Keller, 176–94. New York: Oxford, 2006.

———. *The Question of Palestine.* New York: Vintage, 1979.

Sanders, E. P. *Jesus and Judaism.* Minneapolis: Fortress, 1985.

———. *Paul, the Law, and the Jewish People.* Minneapolis: Fortress, 1983.

Schwarzschild, Steven. "On the Theology of Jewish Survival." In *The Pursuit of the Ideal*, 83–97. Albany: State University of New York Press, 1990.

Schweid, Eliezer. "The Rejection of the Diaspora in Zionist Thought: Two Approaches." In *Essential Papers on Zionism*, edited by J. Reinharz and A. Shapira, 133–60. New York: New York University Press, 1996.

Sorotzkin, David. "Building the Earthly and Destroying the Heavenly: The Satmar Rebbe and the Radical Orthodox School of Thought" [Hebrew]. In *The Land of Israel in Twentieth-Century Jewish Thought*, edited by A. Ravitzky, 133–67. Jerusalem: Ben Zvi Institute, 2004.

Soulen, Kendall. *The God of Israel and Christian Theology.* Minneapolis: Fortress, 1996.

Teitelbaum, Joel. *'Al Ha-Geulah ve la Ha-Temurah.* Brooklyn, 1967.

Waltzer, Michael. *Paradox of Liberalism: Secular Revolutions and Religious Counterrevolutions.* New Haven: Yale University Press, 2015.

Weaver, Alain Epp. "Constantinianism, Zionism, Diaspora: Towards a Political Theology of Exile and Return." *Mennonite Central Committee Occasional Papers* 28.

———. "Further Footnotes on Zionism, Yoder, and Boyarin." *Crosscurrents* 56.4 (2007) 41–51.

———. *States of Exile: Visions of Diaspora, Witness, and Return.* Waterloo, ON: Herald, 2008.

Yoder, John Howard. *The Jewish-Christian Schism Revisited.* Edited by Michael Cartwright and Peter Ochs. Grand Rapids: Eerdmans, 2003.

———. *The Royal Priesthood: Essays Ecclesiological and Ecumenical.* Grand Rapids: Eerdmans, 1994.

15 _____

Lindbeck, Doctrine, and Reading

—MIKE HIGTON, Durham University

Introduction

PETER OCHS GIVES GIFTS by digging deep. He delves into texts and questions, finds new ways of articulating them, and discovers the treasure they can yield for the conversations in which he is involved. In this piece, I will explore one of the most recent gifts I have received from him: his remarkable reading of George Lindbeck in *Another Reformation*.[1] As a Christian theologian working in a divided church, concerned about its witness to Christ in a post-Christendom world, and thinking about its relations to other faiths, Lindbeck's work is an obvious place to turn, but Peter's sharp spade has opened that work up for me like never before. What follows is an appreciation of Peter's reading: a presentation in my own terms of what, thanks to Peter, I see now in Lindbeck.

The Postliberal Proposal

Lindbeck's postliberal proposal is an act of construal (of Christianity, its scriptures, and its doctrines) with multiple layers.

- There is a *relational* level, on which Lindbeck asks who belongs together. His proposal is ecumenical (a construal of the whole Christian church as belonging together) but also a proposal about the relationship between Christians and Jews.

1. Ochs, *Another Reformation*, 35–62.

- There is a *hermeneutical* level, on which Lindbeck asks how these parties might read together, and how they will relate as readers of scripture: Christians as readers together of the New Testament and Old Testament, and Christians and Jews as readers together of the Old Testament/Hebrew Bible.

- There is a *doctrinal* level, on which Lindbeck asks what it means for Christians to have doctrines that limit and guide how they read together as followers of Jesus of Nazareth as Lord, and how they read as followers of this Jesus with Jews who are not.

- And there is a *theological* level, on which all this reading activity is underpinned by an apophatic pragmatism: an acknowledgment of the mystery of God's triune life, and an insistence that this God is spoken of more directly in the activity of God's followers than in the propositions of theologians or philosophers.[2]

At the hermeneutical level, a number of different patterns of reading are present in Lindbeck's proposal. Peter plausibly identifies these as "plain-sense reading," "formational/traditional reading," "reparative reading," and "reformational reading."[3] Plain sense reading is

> the eclectic use of philological, grammatical, rhetorical, narratological, and historical-critical inquiries, as well as reception theory, to augment traditional readings of the intratextual story line of the Old and New Testaments,

and formational reading is

> the ritualization of scriptural reading as a tradition-determined practice for the religious formation of individuals and the ecclesial formation of communities or groups.

These two together cover much of what Lindbeck says about narrative and figural reading, though the two pairs (plain and formational, narrative and figural) are not identical, since some aspects of Lindbeck's figural

---

. 2. This description of Lindbeck's proposal fits his later work, after *The Nature of Doctrine*. For the theological level (about which I shall say little in what follows), see Higton, "Reconstructing *The Nature of Doctrine*," 9–11. Lindbeck's focus on reading, and on relations with Judaism, only become fully clear in writings from 1987 onwards, such as "The Story-Shaped Church" (1987), "The Church" (1989), "Scripture, Consensus and Community" (1989), "Confession and Community" (1990), "Response to Michael Wyschogrod" (1995), "The Gospel's Uniqueness" (1997), his contributions to Frymer-Kensky et al (eds), *Christianity in Jewish Terms* (2000), and "The Church as Israel" (2003).

3. Ochs, *Another Reformation*, 57–59.

reading (figuration as a means for unifying the narrative of Old and New Testaments) are more plain than formational, and some aspects of his narrative reading (reading the Biblical narrative *as* the narrative of one's whole world) are more nearly formational than plain.[4]

Lindbeck speaks of a classic hermeneutical tradition that needs to be revived. In that tradition, the Bible is seen as

> a canonically and narrationally unified and internally glossed . . . whole centered on Jesus Christ, and telling the story of the dealings of the Triune God with his people and his world in ways which are typologically . . . applicable to the present.[5]

Christians are called to read their scriptures, Old and New testaments together, as presenting an overarching narrative of "God's dealings with the world and his people"[6]—the story of Israel and the church. Within that overarching narrative, the central place is given to the history-like, realistic narratives about Jesus of Nazareth, which render him as a particular, unsubstitutable character (that is, as the specific person he is, rather than as a cypher demanding to be decoded as a representative of some more general reality).[7]

Figural reading flows from this. Christians are called to the practice of "imaginatively inscribing the world in the biblical text and troping all that we are, do, and encounter in biblical terms."[8] Such reading is completed in Christian practice.

> To interpret the Bible is to use it to interpret other things. The strictly intratextual meaning of the cross, for example, is indefinite or vague (in Charles Peirce's sense of the term) until it is completed by such social-ritual-experimental enactments as taking up the cross, or bearing the cross, or being crucified with Christ so that we may rise with him.[9]

At the theological level of Lindbeck's postliberal proposal, then, Christian lives together are the primary form of speech about God; at the hermeneutical level they are the primary form of scriptural interpretation. Christian lives together are readings of Scripture that speak God's name. These pattern of scriptural reading are not imposed by the bare nature of the

4. See Lindbeck's writings mentioned above, and also "Spiritual Formation."
5. Lindbeck, "Scripture, Consensus, Community," 203.
6. Lindbeck, "Postcritical Canonical Interpretation," 29.
7. Lindbeck, "Story-Shaped Church," 164; Lindbeck, "Dulles on Method," 58–59.
8. Lindbeck, "Barth and Textuality," 371.
9. Lindbeck, "Atonement and the Hermeneutics," 151.

texts; it is, in the abstract, perfectly possible to read them otherwise, without contradiction. From the point of view of an outsider, Christian reading that takes this form will be an ethnographic fact: this is simply how these people read. From the point of view of a participant, however, it is possible to give a theological account of why this way of reading makes sense:

> The regula fidei which developed into the trinitarian and christo-
> logical affirmations of the early church was needed to make sure
> that the Bible is not read any old way . . . but as testimony to and
> from the creator God whose Word enfleshed is Jesus Christ.[10]

God is forming a people whose life together, as a reading of scripture, speaks God's triune name.

Lindbeck's postliberal proposal unabashedly involves a commitment to read within this tradition—indeed, he says that "the only rationally productive procedure . . . is to trust the tradition of which one is a part." That does not mean, however, that he advocates a static conservatism. That quotation continues,

> until anomalies arise, that is, until there is good evidence in terms
> of the criteria internal to the tradition that this or that strand in
> the web of belief which sustains the inquiry is untenable.[11]

It is in response to the arising of such anomalies that the other two patterns of reading that Peter identifies in Lindbeck's work come into play. In the first place, there is reparative reading. To inhabit a hermeneutical tradition in the way that Lindbeck advocates is to inhabit an ordered construal of the practices that constitute that inhabitation, by which some are seen as more and some as less central. When uncertainty or disagreement arises within practices construed as relatively peripheral, appeal to the rules embodied in deeper practices might be sufficient to resolve the issue.

To say that God is forming a people whose life together, as a reading of scripture, speaks God's triune name, does not provide a divine validation of the present form of the community's life. The community is being formed to speak of God only as it lives under a discipline of ongoing repair, and as a community dependent upon the ever-renewed gift of God's grace for any truthfulness that it displays. Reformational reading is the deepest form of such reparative reading. It is called for when the anomaly identified in present practices turns out to run deeply through the ongoing practice of repair

10. Lindbeck and Forde, "Confessional Subscription," 319.
11. Lidbeck, "Dulles on Method," 56.

itself, so as to make problematic the very process of rereading scripture for the sake of resolving problems. "This is a judgment," Peter says,

> that some entire series of reparative readings has failed . . . and that it is therefore time to introduce reforms in the deepest reparative dimensions of some ecclesial way of life: the elemental ways that some church, or aggregate of churches, practices its typological readings of Scripture.[12]

In such situations, doctrinal definition is called for: the development of a new rule, which determines how scripture can be read for the repair of the host of particular problems that were the presenting symptoms of this deep need for reformation.[13]

To an external observer, such a moment of doctrinal definition may well look like the arbitrary selection of one possible direction for development within an evolving tradition of reasoning. To a participant, it may instead be read in the light of a "confidence that the Holy Spirit guides the church into the truth."[14] The Spirit brings the church up against the scriptures again, to discover in disciplined attention to the text, and as an incoercible gift of God, something new about what is demanded of those who would read them as a narrationally unified whole centered on Jesus Christ, telling the story of the triune God's ways with his people and his world, in ways that are typologically applicable to the present.[15] Lindbeck's postliberal proposal therefore provides a way of construing Christian doctrine. The ur-doctrine—itself not so much a doctrine in the sense set out above, as an indication of the overall shape of the project within which doctrinal definitions arise—is "Jesus is Lord." Christian readers read Scripture as followers of Jesus, such that, as Peter says,

> The criterion guiding reform is the incarnate life of God in Jesus Christ, disclosed in the Gospel witness and as interpreted by way of the evolving history of church doctrine up through today.[16]

Doctrine guides the reading by which God is forming a people to speak the triune name truly. That is its nature and function, and any claims about

---

12. Ochs, *Another Reformation*, 59.

13. See my account of Lindbeck's "decision theory" of doctrinal development in Higton, "Reconstructing *The Nature of Doctrine*," 19–20.

14. Lindbeck, "Atonement and the Hermeneutics," 146.

15. See the quotation above in Lindbeck, "Scripture, Consensus, Community," 203.

16. Ochs, *Another Reformation*, 35.

the truth of doctrine, or about its relation to experience, must ultimately flow from this.[17]

The Church as Israel

Lindbeck's postliberal proposal, however, does not simply provide this construal of the nature of existing Christian doctrine. At its heart is advocacy for a new moment of doctrinal definition: an insistence that, in order to continue faithfully in this project of Christian reading in the present context, a new specification of the limits upon such reading is now demanded of the church. The doctrinal definition that Lindbeck advocates is at once christological and ecclesiological. The christological note is clear, for instance, when he thanks his colleague Hans Frei for making possible "the restoration of the christologically centered narrative sense of scripture to its traditional primacy" but goes on to gloss this by saying that the Gospel stories "unsubstitutably identify and characterize a particular person *as the summation of Israel's history* and as the unsurpassable and irreplaceable clue to who and what the God of Israel and the universe is."[18] Lindbeck's more common framing of the issue is, however, ecclesiological. Alongside Trinitarian and Christological doctrine, which offers an identity description of God and the incarnate savior, ecclesiological doctrine is needed that provides an identity description of the church in relation to Israel. Such description has been offered in multiple ways in Christian history, but in the present post-Holocaust situation it has become appallingly clear just how deathly some of those descriptions are when they function as rules for socially embodied reading of scripture. The church cannot but ask, in this situation, whether to continue reading faithfully, as followers of Jesus, now demands that a decision be made between these different possible ways of identifying the church. Lindbeck believes that such a decision certainly is needed: that the church must pronounce a new doctrinal prohibition against supersessionism. This claim has deep roots in Lindbeck's work. As far back as the 1960s, when looking for ways of making sense of the church's post-Christendom, diasporic situation, he had been attracted by the Second Vatican Council's emphasis on the church as the people of God, and the idea that "the church is the people of God in the same thoroughly concrete way that Israel is."[19] As his thought became

17. For Lindbeck's clarification of his ideas about truth, see Lindbeck, "Response to Bruce Marshall," and Lindbeck, "Reply to Avery Cardinal Dulles."

18. Lindbeck, "Story-Shaped Church," 161, 164, emphasis mine.

19. Lindbeck, "Ecclesiology and Roman Catholic Renewal," 194; cf. Lindbeck, "Protestant View," 249. See also my discussion of Lindbeck's catholic sectarianism in Higton, "Reconstructing *The Nature of Doctrine*," 11–12.

more explicitly scriptural and hermeneutical from the time of *The Nature of Doctrine* onwards, this morphed into an emphasis on "the messianic pilgrim people of God typologically shaped by Israel's story,"[20] and to the insistence that God, in gathering the church, is

> doing in this time between the times what he has done before: choosing and guiding a people to be a sign and witness in all that it is and does, whether obediently or disobediently, to who and what he is.[21]

It is impossible to explore this in any depth, however, without facing the question of the church's relationship to Israel—to Judaism before and after Christ. Lindbeck became convinced that two different patterns of reading have structured Christian life, and Christian practices of reparative reading. In both patterns, Christians appropriate the story of Israel because they follow a savior whom they believe to be the Messiah of Israel. In the first pattern, Christians regard themselves as sharing (rather than fulfilling) the story of Israel. Israel and the church are not related as type and antitype, but rather "the kingdom already present in Christ alone is the antitype, and both Israel and the church are types."[22] The creation of the church is "not the formation of a new people but the enlargement of the old."[23] Yes, in this pattern, the Jews are an unfaithful people—but so is the church. Yes, in this pattern, the church is the recipient of God's irrevocable promises, of God's Spirit, of God's gracious acceptance—but so are the Jews. Lindbeck tells the story, however, of the emergence of a second pattern in place of this first pattern. In this second pattern, the church is the antitype of Israel as type. Israel is faithless, the church faithful; Israel rejects grace, the church basks in it; Israel lacks the Spirit, the church is the community of the Spirit. And whatever the detailed story of the emergence of this construal, it has "monstrous offspring."[24] It entails the denial that, after the coming of Christ, Jews outside the church are the people of God; the church's *appropriation* of the story of Israel as God's people becomes *expropriation*. And it makes possible "the ecclesiological triumphalism of a *theologiae gloriae*"[25] in which (in more or less subtle forms) the church's purity is defined over against

---

20. Lindbeck, "The Church," 146.
21. Lindbeck, "The Church," 157.
22. Lindbeck, "The Church," 166.
23. Lindbeck, "The Church," 168.
24. Lindbeck, "Story-Shaped Church," 171; see also Lindbeck, "Church as Israel."
25. Lindbeck, "Ecumenical Directions," 120.

Israel's sinfulness. It also has hermeneutical consequences. Peter quotes an interview he conducted, in which Lindbeck said,

> Christian efforts to forget Israel and thus replace Israel's cov-
> enant are co-implicated in Christian efforts to read the Gospel
> narrative of Jesus Christ independently of reading the Old Tes-
> tament narrative of Israel, and such readings are the foundation
> of Christian efforts to read the Gospel narrative as [if] it were a
> collection of determine propositions or determinate rules of be-
> havior rather than as Scripture. The primary goal of postliberal
> reformation is to help the church recover its practice of reading
> the Gospel narrative as Scripture.[26]

The doctrinal decision advocated by Lindbeck is the rejection of this second, supersessionist pattern of reading, in favor of a version of the first, in which the church is read *as* Israel, alongside the Jews.

> Israel's Messiah, Jesus the Christ, has made it possible for gen-
> tiles while remaining gentiles to become citizens of the enlarged
> commonwealth of Israel (Eph 2:12). . . . [O]n this view the cho-
> sen people, the whole of Israel, includes non-Christian Jews as
> well as Gentile and Jewish Christians. Ultimately, however, in
> what for Judaism will be the First Coming and for Christianity
> the Second, the church and Israel will in extension coincide. . . .
> In short, Israel does not "rise to life in the church" (as Barth
> supersessionistically puts it), but rather the church of Jews
> and Gentiles exists as a transforming and serving movement
> within the messianically enlarged Israel in this time between
> the times. . . . One might say that the church . . . exists for Israel,
> not Israel for the church.[27]

Hermeneutically, this decision underwrites the whole hermeneutical framework described above, but with a particular spin. It supports a plain sense reading in which the narratives of Jesus of Nazareth are read *in rela-tion to the narratives of the people of God in the whole Bible*. It supports a formational reading in which the figural rereading of present experience in the narrative world of scripture is *a continuation of the rereading of Israel's history that takes place in Jesus*. As Peter says, in the light of the discov-ery that the gospel of Jesus Christ "is itself a practice of rereading the Old Testament narrative of the salvation history of Israel," Christians are called to the "perennial event of returning to the plain sense of Israel's story and

---

26. Ochs, *Another Reformation*, 48.

27. Lindbeck, "Response to Michael Wyschogrod," 206–7.

rediscovering every day what it now means in light of the Gospel narrative of Jesus Christ"[28] In Lindbeck's words,

> the worlds in which we live change. They need to be inscribed anew into the world of the text. It is only by constant reexplication, remediation, and reapplication that this can be done.[29]

Christian readers and Jewish readers can no longer be contrasted as those who have "got the point" of the Hebrew Bible versus those who have missed it, or those who read well versus those who read badly. The fulfillment of the scriptures is in Christ, not in the church, and (to quote Peter yet again)

> While the Christian reader must say that "Jesus Christ is the Messiah of Israel," no reader knows before the event of reading everything there is to say about the meaning of that sentence now, in the present moment of reading.[30]

Christians are called to read and reread, repairing and where necessary reforming their reading, as followers of Jesus Christ as Israel's Messiah. The God who is forming a people whose life together, as a reading of scripture, speaks God's triune name, is the God of Israel—and God has not reneged on God's promises.

Reading Together

In the light of all this, we can see Lindbeck's postliberal proposal as a proposal about the communities and inter-communal relationships within which Christian reading takes place. First, his proposal is an intervention in Lutheran-Catholic dialogues. It involves the attempt to define "*sola scriptura*" and "tradition" in ways that are not opposed, and so to construe the Lutheran Reformation as an embodied attempt at repair of the Catholic church's hermeneutical practices. "[T]he Reformation clarifies (and intensifies) the grammar of catholic Christianity," a grammar encapsulated in the three solas: "the heart of the Christian life is salvation by grace and faith alone in Christ alone as witnessed to by Scripture alone."[31]

> This hermeneutics . . . is catholic and ecumenical, not narrowly Reformation Protestant. The contribution of the Reformers . . .

28. Ochs, *Another Reformation*, 43.
29. Lindbeck, "Barth and Textuality," 375.
30. Ochs, *Another Reformation*, 44.
31. Lindbeck, "Reformation Heritage," 60.

was to clarify and intensify the hermeneutical implications of the pre-Reformation conviction that Scripture is primary and is to be christocentrically interpreted.[32]

Christians

need to place themselves within the total community of faith and read the authoritative sources as witnesses in their entirety to Jesus Christ who in his very humanity is Immanuel, God with us, and is alone to be trusted and obeyed in life and death.[33]

More generally, Lindbeck's postliberal proposal is a call to wider ecumenical reading together. It is an address to the whole divided church, calling its members to recognize that they are engaged in a constant christocentric rereading of scripture, reimagining in each new context what it means to witness to the Christ who is identified by the gospels as the Messiah of Israel. Christians inhabit the narrative world of the two testaments together, as those who have been grafted by God into the people of God. Their differences are to be read, insofar as it turns out to be possible, as diverse performances of this common task. The task of investigating Christian doctrine (including the reconciliation and repair of doctrinal systems) is central to this project. It is an exploration of the proper limits on diversity, but thereby also an exploration of the proper space for Christian diversity, and so of the differences that need not be church-dividing.

Finally, however, Lindbeck's proposal also acts as a call for Christians and Jews to read together (or rather, it calls for Christians to read with Jews, should there be analogous grounds on the Jewish side for reading with Christians). The claim that Jesus is the Messiah of Israel is not a Jewish claim, but it gives the church the Hebrew Bible as its Old Testament, and therefore gives it Jews as co-readers. From the postliberal Christian perspective, Jews and Christians together are the people of God, and together recipients of the scriptures, and "God may intend Jews and Christians to hear very different messages through one and the same text."[34] Indeed, we should beware "The erosion of distinctively Jewish and Christian interpretations" which will produce "a tastelessly lukewarm Judaeo-Christian tradition good for nothing except to be spewed out."[35]

However, it is possible that

---

32. Lindbeck, "Reformation Heritage," 73.

33. Lindbeck, "Reformation Heritage," 73.

34. Lindbeck, "Postmodern Hermeneutics," 111.

35. Lindbeck, "Postmodern Hermeneutics," 112.

both parties will find that both the distinctiveness and the depth
of their respective roots in the shared sacred text are increased
rather than diminished by their collaboration.[36]

Indeed, it is obvious to Lindbeck that, as Christians learn to reread the
scriptures after Christendom, after triumphalism, after supersessionism,
and as they learn to read as a fallible diaspora of the people of God in an
indifferent or hostile world, they will need to turn for instruction to Jewish
readers, who may see the patterns of reading appropriate to such a situation
much more clearly than do they.

It is, then, peculiarly fitting to find the patterns of Lindbeck's postliberal proposal offered back to the church by a Jewish colleague and friend—
one who digs deep, and makes of what he finds a gift.

Bibliography

Higton, Mike. "Reconstructing *The Nature of Doctrine*." *Modern Theology* 30.1 (2014)
    1–31.
Lindbeck, George. "Atonement and the Hermeneutics of Intertextual Social
    Embodiment." In *The Nature of Confession: Evangelicals and Postliberals in
    Conversation*, edited by Timothy Phillips and Dennis Okholm, 221–40. Downers
    Grove, IL: IVP.
———. "Atonement and the Hermeneutics of Social Embodiment." *Pro Ecclesia* 5.2
    (1996) 144–60.
———. "Barth and Textuality." *Theology Today* 43.3 (1986) 361–76.
———. "The Church." In *Keeping the Faith: Essays to Mark the Centenary of Lux Mundi*,
    edited by Geoffrey Wainwright, 179–208. London: SPCK, 1989. Reprinted in *The
    Church in a Postliberal Age*, 145–65.
———. "The Church as Israel: Ecclesiology and Ecumenism." In *Jews and Christians:
    People of God*, edited by Carl E. Braaten and Robert W. Jenson, 78–94. Grand
    Rapids: Wm. B. Eerdmans, 2003.
———. *The Church in a Postliberal Age*. Edited by James J. Buckley. Grand Rapids:
    Eerdmans, 2002.
———. "Confession and Community: An Israel-Like View of the Church." *The
    Christian Century* 107.16 (1990) 492–6. Reprinted in *The Church in a Postliberal
    Age*, 1–9.
———. "Dulles on Method." *Pro Ecclesia* 1 (1992) 53–60.
———. "Ecclesiology and Roman Catholic Renewal." *Religion in Life* 33 (1963) 383–94.
    Reprinted in *New Theology 2*, edited Martin Marty and Dean Peerman, 183–97.
    New York: Macmillan, 1965.
———. "Ecumenical Directions and Confessional Construals." *Dialog* 30.2 (1991)
    118–23.
———. "The Gospel's Uniqueness: Election and Untranslatability." *Modern Theology*
    13 (1997) 423–50. Reprinted in *The Church in a Postliberal Age*, 223–52.

36. Lindbeck, "What of the Future?" 365.

————. "Justification and Atonement: An Ecumenical Trajectory." In *By Faith Alone: Essays on Justification in Honor of Gerhard O. Forde*, edited by Joseph A. Burgess and Marc Kolden, 183–219. Grand Rapids: Eerdmans, 2004.

————. *The Nature of Doctrine: Religion and Theology in a Postliberal Age*. Philadelphia: Westminster, 1984.

————. "Postcritical Canonical Interpretation: Three Modes of Retrieval." In *Theological Exegesis: Essays in Honor of Brevard S. Childs*, edited by Christopher R. Seitz and Kathryn Greene-McCreight, 26–51. Grand Rapids: Wm. B. Eerdmans, 1999.

————. "Postmodern Hermeneutics and Jewish-Christian Dialogue: A Case Study." In *Christianity in Jewish Terms*, edited by Tikva Frymer-Kensky et al, 106–13. Boulder, CO: Westview, 2000.

————. "A Protestant View of the Ecclesiological Status of the Roman Church." *The Journal of Ecumenical Studies* 1 (1964) 243–70.

————. "The Reformation Heritage and Christian Unity." *Lutheran Quarterly* 2.4 (Winter 1988), 477–502. Reprinted in *The Church in a Postliberal Age*, 53–76.

————. "Reply to Avery Cardinal Dulles." *First Things* 139 (2004) 13–15.

————. "Response to Bruce Marshall." *The Thomist* 53.3 (1989) 403–6.

————. "Response to Michael Wyschogrod's 'Letter to a Friend.'" *Modern Theology* 11 (1995) 205–10.

————. "Scripture, Consensus and Community." In *Biblical Interpretation in Crisis: The Ratzinger Conference on Bible and Church*, edited by Richard John Neuhaus, 74–101. Grand Rapids: Eerdmans, 1989. Reprinted in *The Church in a Postliberal Age*, 201–22.

————. "Spiritual Formation and Theological Education." *Theological Education* 24, Supplement 1 (1988) 10–32. Reprinted in *Theological Perspectives on Christian Formation: A Reader on Theology and Christian Education*, edited by Jeff Astley, Leslie J. Francis, and Colin Crowder, 285–302. Grand Rapids: Eerdmans, 1996.

————. "The Story-Shaped Church: Critical Exegesis and Theological Interpretation." In *Scriptural Authority and Narrative Interpretation*, edited by Garrett Green, 161–78. Philadelphia: Fortress, 1987.

————. "What of the Future?" In *Christianity in Jewish Terms*, edited by Tikva Frymer-Kensky et al, 357–66. Boulder, CO: Westview, 2000.

Lindbeck, George, and Gerhard O. Forde. "Confessional Subscription: What Does it Mean for Lutherans Today?" *Word and World* 11.3 (1991) 316–20.

Ochs, Peter. *Another Reformation: Postliberal Christianity and the Jews*. Grand Rapids: Baker Academic, 2011.

16

Never a Liberal to Be "Post" It

(Re)learning to Be a Better Kind of Evangelical with Peter Ochs

—TOM GREGGS, University of Aberdeen

ALL THEOLOGIANS HAVE AN accompanying discipline to serve their theological enquiry. As a theologian, mine is history—the history of the church and her doctrines; Peter Ochs is a philosopher. No theologian exists outside of a faith context. As a church person, mine is Methodism of a particular evangelical form; Peter Ochs is Jewish. The contexts in which we are formed and grow shape our patterns of thinking and our lives of prayer. I am British; Peter Ochs in American. It is perhaps not a surprise that Peter Ochs and I can argue and disagree. But what may be a surprise is *how* we argue: we argue to hear one another—more specifically, we argue to hear one another well, to hear one another better. There is, indeed, no-one I would rather argue with in the world than Peter Ochs. He makes me think better, more clearly; and he provokes me to think more fully about my own theological identity and commitments. Yes, Ochs is a superb thinker and demanding writer. I have learned lots from him in ways I could not even begin to analyze in terms of drawing on his vast number of essays and books. But what I have learned most of all from Peter Ochs has been in the form of argument: he has continued to be a searching questioner of my work and approach, and all the more so (and the more importantly so) since the passing of another great mentor, Rev. Professor Daniel Hardy. The following is a theological reflection on a "conversation" (let the reader understand) which began on Friday afternoon and lasted well into Shabbat about the way I think of doctrine as a theologian. In the course of the "conversation" my identity as an evangelical rather than a post-liberal came to the fore, and the significance of starting points for theological dialogue was pronounced. I remember, in fact, when Ochs referred to me as a "post-liberal" what my reply was: "Peter, I have never been liberal to be 'post' it; my starting points and my concerns are just different." But in the course of the "conversation," I relearned what it meant for me to be an evangelical theologian, and learned how to be so better. In what follows, I seek to sketch some of this out (and can do little else in the space allowed), and in so doing offer a quiet dialogue with Ochs' own excellent work on *sola scriptura* and post-liberalism.

Sola Scriptura and the Untidiness of Scripture

Well over a decade of Scriptural Reasoning with Ochs has taught me to focus on the particularities and specifics of the plain sense of the texts in front of me. These have sometimes been tiny details which come to light in only the most careful of careful readings—disruptive, interruptive, and messy texts or pieces of texts that undermine the systematic presentation of doctrine which is so much a part of the life and thought of the Christian theologian. To attend to such texts is a reminder of the limits that need to be placed on doctrine, and on the danger of sanitizing or domesticating the text of Scripture in such a way that we miss the particularities and strangeness of the divine word as the Word *of God*. It is crucial in this to see the Word of God as that which is addressed to humanity, and as that which cannot neatly fit into categories of human making and cannot be smoothed out such that it says what the theologian desires for her given system. Karl Barth provides wise words in relation to the danger of arriving at the Bible with an answer and perspective already made up in terms of what we might find in Scripture—or, we might say, arriving at the text of the Bible with a system in place:

> The Bible says quickly, very clearly, and in a very friendly manner about the certain "versions" we make of it: "So this is you, but not me! Now this is what perhaps in fact fits you very well, your emotional needs, and your views, your schedules and your 'circles,' your religious or philosophical theories! See, you wanted to mirror yourself in me, and sure enough you have rediscovered your own image in me! But now go and search for me! Look for what is there!" The Bible itself, the certain implacable logic of its connection that drives beyond ourselves, regardless

of our worthiness or unworthiness, is what invites us to reach toward the final, highest answer, in which everything that can be said is said. And even if we barely comprehend it and can only stammer it out, that answer is: There is a new world in the Bible, the World of God.[1]

To read Scripture as an evangelical is to read Scripture in a manner in which we are constantly interrupted by the Bible's very strangeness, its very inability to be reduced to a formula or a system, to be tidied up. It is to read Scripture as the disrupter of doctrinal formulae. The interrogation of the text with Ochs has taught me what it means to speak of the Bible as the Word of God such that it cannot be captured finally or completely by dogmatic systems, but must be allowed to speak to those systems and to challenge and reshape them. This is the work that the Reformation principle of *ecclesia semper reformanda* must be allowed to do,[2] but this very work stems from a recognition of the divinely spoken Word of God's authority over the church and its doctrine: since no church or no church teaching can contain the Word of God (which can never be reduced), the church must be aware of its need always to reform itself, arising out of the humility that the Word of Scripture addressed to it must engender.

This instinct toward a church that is always reforming is one which stems from the Reformation principle of *sola scriptura*, therefore. The scripture principle is one that is nervous of the institution of the church claiming too much authority, and the danger of the church claiming too much certainty and authority in its presentation of the doctrines of the Christian faith. Scripture is not only the basis for all doctrine according to the scripture principle, but Scripture is also doctrine's limit—both in terms of the scope of doctrinal claim that must be measured for accuracy against Scripture, and also in terms of the limit of doctrine in relation to the particularities and undomesticated wildness of Scripture. The scripture principle is a principle about the Word of God ruling over the church such that the only appropriate and fitting posture that we can take in relation to it is that of being a church that is always reforming itself—not out of a desire to be an ever narrower and more exclusive organization, but out of the sense of humility which the foundational object of doctrinal claims (the Bible) engenders as the unsummarizable Word *of God*. There is a crucial

1. Barth, *Word of God and Theology*, 19.

2. This is a theme that Ochs discusses significantly throughout *Another Reformation*. It is situated within the post-liberal approach, and relates to ecumenical church unification. But this instinct should be one for the whole of the church which follows the Reformation. The church must be *reformata et semper reformanda*, and it is the latter because of the need to take seriously the words of Scripture.

hierarchy here. Scripture comes, for the Christian, from Christ, and as such, Scripture rules over the church, and over the churches' teachings and doctrinal claims. As Barth puts it,

> And the authority of His Word cannot be assimilated by the Church, to reappear as the divine authority of the Church. His Word—the same Word by which He imparts Himself to the Church, in which He lives in the Church, in which He Himself sets up His authority in the Church—is given to the Church in such a way that it is always His Word as against its word: the Word which it has to hear and proclaim and serve and by which it lives, but which in order that this may happen is prevented from being assumed or subsumed into the Church's word, which asserts itself over against it as an independent Word, as one which is always new to the Church in every age and has to be newly encountered by it. Its form as the word of the prophets and apostles is the safeguard of its independence and newness. It vests it with the healthy strangeness which it needs if it is to be said to the Church of every age as the Word of its Lord. It creates and maintains the healthy distance from the Church of every age which is needed if the Church is to hear it before and as it itself speaks, if it is to serve it before and as it takes its authority and promises on its own lips, if it is to live by it, before and as it lives its life as its own. Its form as the word of the prophets and apostles strengthens the differentiation in which alone the Church of every age can receive revelation and be the bearer of revelation. Because He has entrusted and commissioned His Word to His prophets and apostles, because He has made them the rock on which He builds His Church, the authority of Jesus Christ is a concrete authority. It stands over against the author-ity of the Church. It cannot be assumed and assimilated by it.[3]

Since Scripture rules over and governs the church, the church cannot (*even in its reception of the revelation Scripture offers and its interpretation of what Scripture offers*) claim for itself any authority of its own making. No church or dogmatic or doctrinal statement from the church can ever take precedence over the particularities of Scripture, and dogmatic or doctrinal statements can only be used as a light coda for the *sensus plenior* of the text. The very nature of a complex text made from sixty-six books in three languages spanning a thousand years with a multitude of authors and redactors determines that the activity of interpretation of the text (which is employed in doctrine) will only ever be one which points to the

3. Barth, *Church Dogmatics* I.2, 579.

otherness, the very strangeness and irreducibility, of the Bible's message. Indeed, even in relation to the life of Christ, the very existence of *four* gospels, with their distinctive emphases and their particular presentations, indicates the very irreducibility of the messages of Scripture. The rejection of Tatian's *Diatasseron* (which sought to harmonize the Gospels) or of Marcion's singular Gospel points to even the earliest church's focus on the nondomesticability of the biblical text.

Does this mean, then, that no doctrinal codification is ever possible? That we need only to let the text stand in its multivocity? Perhaps; this may well be the better propensity than those who wish always to neaten the revelation of God in God's Word, as if all reason did not flow from the divine Logos, and as if human-created reason were greater than the divine Logos. But Scripture is not read or given aside from a community who hears it: Scripture is given by God to be *heard* and *received* and *responded to*; it has a terminus in creation and in the community, and in their transformations. For evangelicals, doctrine concerns the teaching that the community offers as it gathers around the Word of God. But this is only a light and minimal teaching to aid the further reading of texts: it is offered so that those who read and hear the Word of God may read it better. But here there is a crucial cycle to be identified: the evangelical reader of Scripture receives the teaching of the church (which arises from the collective reading of Scripture; see below), to read Scripture again, and in that reading again of Scripture is to challenge and ensure that the doctrines offered never remove the divine otherness of the text or seek to reduce the text to propositional statements. Put otherwise, doctrines emerge as minimal codas from the reading of Scripture, to aid the reading of Scripture so that we can read it better, but in the process the doctrines themselves are always checked against the true authority which is the Biblical text. By virtue of this, evangelical readings of Scripture cannot ever be neat and tidy, but have to recognize the very otherness of the text in terms of its particularities and irreducible messages, and the very changeable historical contexts, in which these texts are received and interpreted. In this way, the doctrine of *sola scriptura* is a doctrine about hierarchies of authority to ensure that even in its reception of the biblical text the church does not confuse its interpretation of the text with the text itself: the community of interpretation exists always underneath the text; it can never be the final word on the text, and should be a minimal coda for the reading and hearing of the text. In this way, the *reformata* doctrine of *sola scriptura* requires, implies, and coexists alongside the need for the church to engage in *semper reformanda*.

Sola Scriptura and the Community

There is an important point to note in this hierarchy, however. *Sola scriptura* is about Scripture's authority over *the church* and only derivatively thereby over individuals, and *sola scriptura* requires *ecclesia* (not *homo*) *semper reformanda*. Since *sola scriptura* is about the sovereignty of Scripture over the church, it cannot ever be confused with a doctrine that gives priority to the hubris of an individual's interpretation over that of the whole communion of saints (both living and departed). Of course, the individual herself is a *part* of that communion and has an authority that exists within it, but (and this is crucial) the doctrine of *sola scriptura* must invest the evangelical with a sense of humility: if there is to be a sense of humility in relation to the authority of doctrine as stemming from the teaching of the church, there is to be an even greater sense of humility for the individual Christian confronted with the biblical text and its divine otherness. *Sola scriptura* is not an Enlightenment doctrine that gives authority and sovereignty to the individual; *sola scriptura* is an ecclesial doctrine that recognizes the awesome sovereignty of the Word of God.

In forming doctrine, the community collectively *reasons* around the text of scripture. Of course, in this, some voices will be heard more clearly than others: the doctors of the church are granted by the Spirit of God the illumination to read and reason with Scripture so as to teach the church how to read Scripture better through doctrine. There is no external authority afforded to these voices in themselves, but only an internal authority through the illuminating power of the Spirit in the reception of the Word of God. Put otherwise, the authority that the teachers of doctrine have and the doctrines themselves possess exist only insomuch as they reflect Scripture's own teachings; and they are a provisional statement about the texts which themselves contain the signs of the divine Word (signs of the signs of the Sign, we might think). The community may find better ways of expressing the messages of the biblical texts, and whether they are better or not depends on their capacity to hear the Word of God more clearly, and reason with it better; that is why the church is *semper reformanda*.

It is following this kind of logic that the Magisterial Reformers present their own reasoning on the traditional doctrines of the church (especially those present in the creeds). Doctrines (even the findings of ecumenical councils and the creeds, symbols and definitions that flow from them) are authoritative only insomuch as they are based solely on Scripture,[4] and earlier doctrinal settlements and judgments are meaningful not only in the contexts in which they take place, but also now and in the future since the

---

4. Calvin, *Institutes*, II.1178.

church still stands under the authority of Scripture.[5] In this way, the church's attempts at the doctrinal formulations which are offered in that councils, symbols, definitions, and creeds are exercises in biblical interpretation, in hermeneutics, in Biblical Reasoning (we might say!).[6] Furthermore, from an evangelical perspective, they are exercises in hermeneutics in which the church communally engages. The church's doctrinal statements are the ways in which they have variously formed themselves in relation to the interpretation of Scripture and their reasoning with it. In the most ancient creeds, we find modes of interpretation in which the church universally (catholically) engages. Whether these councils are correct in their doctrinal decisions still rests on the appropriateness of their biblical interpretation,[7] but the interpretations they offer are ones that arise not from the thoughts of an individual but from the negotiated reasoning of the whole body of the church with the biblical text: to be a member of the catholic church (small "c") is to read Scripture with other Christians in this way, to join in their patterns of reasoning. To engage with their dogmas and doctrines is to take seriously how the church has sought corporately to interpret Scripture; how the church has heard the Word of God; how it has formed itself in relation to reasoning with Scripture. This is why the doctrine of *sola scriptura* as described by the Magisterial Reformation did not do away with the early ecumenical councils and their interpretations of the text of the Bible. Instead, it is for the whole body of Christ collectively and ecclesially to discuss and interpret Scripture together, and to work out corporately the way in which Scripture should be understood. Put in more evangelical terms, we might say that the church is formed and created in its hearing of Scripture and in its collective interpretation of its meaning. Whatever reasoned doctrinal settlements are reached are always provisional because Scripture rules over the church, and the church is itself an historical and contingent entity in the conditions of temporal and geographical existence: there are no perfect, pure, abstracted reasons separated from the contemporary and past contingencies of spatio-historical creation. Furthermore, the role of doctrine is not to capture or domesticate Scripture but to stimulate and aid its further reading. However, crucially, the interpretation that gives rise to doctrine is

---

5. Calvin, *Institutes*, II.1173.

6. In this way, I wish to draw a stronger demarcation than Pannenberg does between Scripture and tradition; see Pannenberg, *Basic Questions in Theology*, 186. However, I agree with his argument later in the same piece that "later tradition is viewed not as completing the content of Scripture, but as having a purely hermeneutical function" (188).

7. Cf. Calvin, *Institutes*, 1176–79. For the Reformers, it is key that the councils can be wrong.

always corporate—both in terms of the church universal and in terms of the communion of saints across time.

Even if the formation of doctrine is an enterprise engaged in by particular people at particular times, the way in which members of the church hear and read Scripture is in itself a collective form of reasoning around Scripture. As Martin Luther once pointed out, the whole church engages together in judgment on the appropriate interpretation of texts by virtue of the church's affirmation of what is true in their acceptance of creeds and symbols: it is not that bishops and councils judge the church, but that all Christians judge the truthfulness of the claims of councils as they repeat the creed in liturgical settings. Symbols and creeds are supreme exercises, therefore, in ecclesial modes of scriptural reasoning (lower case) since they involve the *whole* church's (in the broadest and plainest sense) reading of Scripture, taking the power of interpretation away from religious professionals and academics, and placing the responsibility in the hands of the entire church. Thus, writes Luther: "bishops, popes, scholars, and everyone else have the power to teach, but it is the sheep who are to judge whether they teach the voice [i.e., the words] of Christ or the voice of strangers."[8] In this sense, *sola scriptura* is a fundamentally ecclesial-hermeneutical account of the existence of the church under Scripture (through the church's collective reasoning around the Word of God), and of the authority of creedal statements in relation to the church. There is a cycle here: Scripture is the authority on which any doctrine rests as it is negotiated by those who in the contingent conditions of space and time reason to the doctrine; this authority is recognized by the broader body of the church, whose collective assent is the true catholicity and authority of any dogmatic or doctrinal formula.

This issue of assent means that the church is formed in its reading and reasoning around Scripture, but it also means that the variegation within the church exists because of multiply complex dependent forms of biblical reasoning: since there is no perfect, pure, and a-contextual doctrine, there is scope for variegation. So, for example, the majority of Magisterial Protestant, Roman Catholic, and Orthodox (though not Oriental Orthodox who decry the Chalcedonian symbol) assent to the first seven ecumenical councils in their doctrinal settlements which arise from reasoning with Scripture so as to find a negotiated collective interpretation of the text in order to aid its continued reading. Within these parameters, the Orthodox and the Western Church separate over the *filioque* clause in 1054; and the Western Church itself separates at the Reformation. Within the Reformation, there is variance between Magisterial and Radical Reform around the interpretation

8. Luther, *Christian Assembly*, 307 (cf. 305–14).

of Scripture and so forth. Each form of the church is dependent immediately on another, and ultimately on the apostles because of shared and reasoned settlements on the reading of Scripture back to the ecumenical councils of the early centuries; and the particular doctrinal form each church takes is because of differently reasoned accounts of Scripture, which give rise to their particularized forms. There is unity that exists because the church reads the same Scripture and reasons with it in order to find the form the church should take in its faith and order in a particular historical and geographical context: at some points (however few!) there is complete agreement and at others difference. These differences should not be over-emphasized, however, since they are differences that arise from the sovereign rule of Scripture over the church, and since the Scripture, which is sovereign, is itself irreducible in the message(s) it gives. Diversity is part of the catholicity that exists within the church which stands under Scripture. The problem arises when any given form of the church in its diversity is considered absolute, such that the doctrine itself takes over the sovereignty of Scripture over the whole church. It is the *prohibition* of others' emphases, rather than the particular emphases we might have, which is the path to disunity: in such prohibition, we do not see doctrine as rightly conceived by the doctrine of *sola scriptura* but we find a doctrinaire church mistaking its own teachings with the Word of God which can never be captured ultimately in symbols, creeds, definitions, dogmas, and doctrines—however helpful these may be for the continued reading of Scripture necessary for a church that stands under its sovereignty and thereby needs always to be reforming.

Sola Scriptura: Why Make So Much of It?

In concluding this short piece, why do I make so much of *sola scriptura* and why tackle it in an essay in honor of Peter Ochs? It is a topic Ochs has addressed and which has formed his engagement with other faiths, so in that much I hope my reflections might be welcome. It is also a doctrine to which I assent in its more classical Magisterial Reformation form and which personal and intellectual engagement with Ochs has helped me form in relation to my particular understanding, and approach to doctrine—an approach similar to, but still distinct from, that of post-liberalism. But, neither of those reasons, while helpful, is good enough. Instead, let me end with three interrogations as reasons for this engagement.

   a. First, *sola scriptura* in the kind of form I seek to offer here should help to prevent evangelicals from arriving at the text of Scripture with all the answers in place. A true evangelical attitude should not be doctrinaire but humble. It should listen to the readings of others, and it should be careful not to confuse its own words with the Word of God. Such an attitude is one which Scriptural Reasoning in its Abrahamic form might help to develop further in evangelicals. My own engagement, for years, with Ochs around the Scriptural Reasoning table has, I hoped, helped me differentiate my own words from the words of the Word of God.

b. Second, Ochs' discussion of *semper reformanda* and *sola scriptura* has often been in relation to questions of supersession and its dangers in Christian theology. I might like to go on the record as saying the collective biblical reasoning of the early councils points toward the closing of the door to supersession. Its language is not used, and—crucial to the issue of Christian-Jewish relations—blame for the death of the Jewish man Jesus is laid squarely (even in the situation of attempted integration into the Roman Empire) at the feet of Pontius Pilate, at the feet of a Roman. The collective reasoning of the church has said this, even in a historical condition in which one might think the case might be papered over. Each week people in churches recite a creed that lays blame for the death of Jesus on a Roman. Any reading of the Bible that does not acknowledge this does not accept the catholic (small "c") reading of the Bible, and cuts itself off from ecumenical discourse. The church needs to relearn this: it should not be a *novum* or a *reformandus*; it should be a *ressourcement*.

c. Given the variegated forms of community formation around shared reading of Scripture, should the church now look further back than its ecumenical councils to the community with whom it shares the majority of its Scripture, and seek to read Scripture with the Jews for the sake of formation of its doctrine as well? Might a form of Scriptural Reasoning offer a deepening of the ecumenical discourse that currently exists? If ecumenism revolves around community formation and around reasoning with the texts of the Bible, should we not consider the place of Jewish interpretation in relation to the shared texts we have? What might a more basic doctrinal form around shared reading and reasoning with Scripture take? What form might this community take?

These are prompts and scattered thoughts, which I offer to my mentor, my friend, my teacher, Professor Peter Ochs, in the hope we might continue our conversations and open up new ones—conversations that will last all eternity at that great feast when many shall come from east and west to share in the banquet with Abraham, Isaac, and Jacob.

Bibliography

Barth, Karl. *Church Dogmatics, Volume 1 Part 2*. Translated and edited by T. F. Torrance, G. W. Bromiley et al. London: T&T Clark, 1957.

———. *The Word of God and Theology*. Translated by Amy Marga. London: T&T Clark, 2011.

Calvin, John. *Institutes of Christian Religion*. Edited by John T. McNeill. Translated by Ford Lewis Battles. Philadelphia: Westminster, 1960.

Luther, Martin. *That a Christian Assembly or Congregation Has the Right and Power to Judge All Teaching and to Call, Appoint, and Dismiss Teachers, Established and Proven by Scripture*. In *Church and Ministry I*, Luther Works Vol. 93, edited by Eric W. Gritsch. Philadelphia: Fortress, 1970.

Ochs, Peter. *Another Reformation: Postliberal Christianity and the Jews*. Grand Rapids: Baker Academic, 2011.

Pannenberg, Wolfhart. *Basic Questions in Theology: Collected Essays*. Vol. 1. Translated by George Kehm. Minneapolis: Fortress, 2008.

17

Who Is Israel?

Ochs, Barth, and Romans 9–11

—SUSANNAH TICCIATI, King's College London

WHO IS ISRAEL? THIS is a question that presses itself upon us in the context of debates concerning Christian supersessionism—broadly the claim that the church has replaced another people as the covenant partner of God. And its answer has far-reaching ramifications. Is Israel "the Jews"? God's eternal covenant people? The Church? The people replaced by the Church as God's covenant partner? Or several of the above at once? It is also a question that gains a variety of (conflicting) answers in the exegesis of Rom 9–11, and in particular Paul's claim in Rom 9:6b, that "not all Israel are Israel." In that context, moreover, it is complicated by the further question: Is there more than one Israel?

In this essay I offer an Ochsian critique[1] of Karl Barth's reading of Rom 9–11 (in the context of his doctrine of election),[2] which issues in turn a critique of Peter Ochs' account of Christian non-supersessionism. Both Ochs and Barth offer (multivalent, and in some ways implicit) answers to the question, Who is Israel? Their answers are bound up with their broader positions apropos of supersessionism. We will discover that while Ochs offers resources for the repair of Barth, Ochs' own account is in need of further repair in the light of his own criteria. The essay will culminate in

1. Drawing on Ochs, *Another Reformation*.

2. Barth, *Church Dogmatics* II/2, § 34, "The Election of the Community" (hereafter cited as *CD*). The paragraph is divided into four subparagraphs, each of which treats a section of Rom 9–11, which Barth follows sequentially.

some preliminary suggestions for a reparative rereading of Rom 9–11 itself, suggestions significantly informed by the recent work of Tommy Givens,[3] and by conversations with Daniel Weiss.

Peter Ochs on Supersessionism

I will begin by outlining the broad criteria for a Christian non-supersessionism offered by Ochs in *Another Reformation*, culled from the variety of postliberal Christian theologians he selects for examination. While embracing a familiar definition of supersessionism as "the Christian belief that with the incarnation of God in Jesus Christ, Israel's covenant with God was superseded and replaced by God's presence in the church as the body of Christ,"[4] Ochs goes on to diagnose the problem of supersessionism as primarily a *hermeneutical* one.[5] More specifically, supersessionism (on Ochs' reading of George Lindbeck) "[devalues] the scriptural story of Israel, [directing] the reader's attention away from the intrinsic theological value of the Old Testament text in its irreducible many layers of meaning" (51). A non-supersessionist Christian theology, by contrast, characterizes the gospel as "a perennial event of returning to the plain sense of Israel's story and rediscovering every day what it now means in the light of the Gospel narrative of Jesus Christ" (43). Ochs recapitulates these claims in his reading of David Ford. On a supersessionist account, Christ is understood to be the answer to the Old Testament in such a way that "the Gospel narrative . . . replaces rather than interprets the Old Testament," foreclosing its ability "to be read in different ways in different contexts." For Ochs this is effectively to claim that "Christ has come in place of Israel" (since Israel's history can be left behind in favor of its answer in Christ) (210).

Such a characterization of non-supersessionism is not first-order propositional in the sense that it does not rule out claims about the uniqueness of Christ—as the Messiah of Israel, as the one who "alone repairs contradictions in the Old Testament,"[6] or (more broadly) as the one who fulfills the scriptures. What matters is the manner in which these claims are made. On the one hand, they can be made with a finality or clarity of meaning which renders any further or alternative interpretation of Israel's

3. Givens, *We the People*.

4. Ochs, *Another Reformation*. From now on, where economical and unambiguous, page numbers will be included parenthetically within the main text.

5. Ochs, *Another Reformation*, e.g., 51 (in exposition of George Lindbeck) and 210 (in exposition of David Ford).

6. Ochs, *Another Reformation*, 245. This phrase is used by Ochs in the context of his critical discussion of John Milbank.

story superfluous. And this yields a logic of replacement in which Christ as locus of definitive meaning replaces an open-ended and provisional story of Israel. And insofar as the church lays claim to that definitive meaning, it becomes the fulfillment of Israel's ambiguous and provisional history in such a way as to replace the open-ended Israel of that history. This brings us back to the more familiar definition of supersessionism as belief in the replacement of Israel by the church.

On the other hand, claims for the uniqueness of Christ can be made vaguely, without spelling out how they are to be interpreted in advance of any new situation (since before the eschaton the finality of Christ's redemption is not fully realized[7]). Correspondingly, a non-supersessionist reading of the Old Testament treats the plain sense of Israel's story as vague: negatively, as patient of clear definition only for particular contexts beyond which such definition may not be applicable; positively, as open to a variety of contextual definitions. Putting these complements together: "[Christian] proclamation includes biblical Israel in a way that leaves vague (or not fully clarified) the scriptural meaning of Israel in relation to Christ in this time between the times" (254). Conversely, the vague gospel narrative and the vague story of Israel are (only) clarified in relation to one another on particular occasions of rereading. The reason, for Ochs, that such clarity is only possible for particular contexts is that God's word cannot be clearly defined by finite human beings in its universality, but only as it is addressed to them in particular times and places (254).

Within Ochs' account of Christian non-supersessionism, who then is Israel? Ochs neither poses nor answers this question explicitly. But it is possible to make a variety of inferences. First, at least two of the "American Protestant" postliberals discussed by Ochs make a case for an identification of the church as Israel. Indeed, the title of the chapter on George Lindbeck is "George Lindbeck and the Church as Israel." Oddly Ochs includes no explicit discussion of this identification. It is nevertheless worth showing how the latter is compatible with—and indeed concretely illustrates—Ochs' hermeneutical non-supersessionism.

According to Jenson, "'[s]upersessionism,' in the current semi-technical sense, is not the church's claim to be Israel. It is the theological opinion that the church owns the identity of Israel in such a fashion as to exclude any other divinely willed Israel-after-Israel."[8] In Ochs' terms, "the church is Israel" is a clear, context-specific claim, which because of its context-specificity does not rule out other context-specific claims such as "the Jewish people is Israel."

7. On Ochs' account of Robert Jenson, see Ochs, *Another Reformation*, 70.
8. Jenson, "Toward a Christian Theology of Judaism," 5.

Its context-specificity goes hand in hand with its reparative character. The problem to be repaired is Christian theological supersessionism, which it addresses in the first place by reuniting the church with its past in the history of biblical Israel, a history which the church continues rather than displaces; and second by acknowledging alternative (divinely willed) continuations of that history. The vague scriptural claim of which it is the context-specific complement is as follows: "Jesus . . . is in his own person the fulfillment of the promises to Israel."[9] This is vague because it does not specify what form such fulfilment will take, and is thus open to different construals in different contexts. In particular, it does not specify what the relation is between Jesus and Rabbinic Judaism. The church as Israel is one provisional form of this fulfilment, and can be no more than this, according to Jenson, because "until the Last Judgment and our resurrection, Christ has *not yet* come in the way that fully consummates Israel's history."[10]

Lindbeck adumbrates key aspects of Jenson's argument. He observes that there were two groups (early Christians and rabbinic Jews) that "lived in the world of Israel's story and Israel's God and claimed to be his chosen people." And he concludes that the Bible "is a capacious instrument of God's Spirit: it bestowed its unity-and-community-building power on both."[11] In Ochs' terms, its plain sense is inherently vague, and thus open to multiple interpretive possibilities. Like Jenson, Lindbeck characterizes supersessionism as the claim that "Christians alone are now the true Israel, the chosen people, because God rejected the Jews."[12] This is to reduce the vague plain sense of Israel's story to one clear meaning.

While quietly incorporating the proposals of Lindbeck and Jenson to identify the church as Israel, Ochs continues in his own voice to use "Israel" with the assumption that its primary reference is to "the Jews" (the subtitle of his book is telling in this regard). For example, Ochs comments on the fact that postliberal Christian theologians are led to "a new relationship with the Old Testament, with Israel's ancient covenant with God, and with the Jews as a religious people during the time of Jesus and into the rabbinic period that continues today." And he glosses this in terms of a "new relationship to *the people Israel*."[13] This identification of (biblical) Israel with "the Jews" is also implicit in the overall structure of *Another Reformation*.[14] It

---

9. Jenson, "Toward a Christian Theology of Judaism," 6.

10. Jenson, *Systematic Theology*, 2:336 (emphasis original).

11. Lindbeck, "Church as Israel," 87.

12. Lindbeck, "Church as Israel," 79.

13. Ochs, *Another Reformation*, 17–18 (my emphasis).

14. I am indebted to Nicholas Adams for this observation.

is divided into two parts, one treating American Protestant postliberalism, the other treating British postliberalism. The American postliberals have a christological, scriptural focus to their repair, which leads to the rediscovery of (biblical) Israel's story. The British postliberals have a pneumatological, worldly focus to their repair, which leads them to attend to Christian relations with Jews (as well as Muslims and potentially others).[15] Ochs envisages them as two wings of a bird, complementing and supplementing one another. But in doing so he implicitly equates the biblical Israel on the American side with the Jews on the British side, as becomes clear in his discussion of Daniel Hardy: "Like American postliberals, Hardy finds the Jews in the scriptural canon. . . . From this christological perspective, he overcomes supersessionism because the canon affirms God's promise to the Jews *a priori*. Hardy finds the Jews in a second way, however: in the Spirit's contingent actions in history that have led Jews and many others to the precincts of the Anglican Church . . ." (191). Those others include Muslims, and while "Americans and Anglicans" share "a modest [scriptural] basis for engagement with Muslims," the Americans largely lack the pneumatological basis (191). The implication is that the complementarity of the two wings in respect of the Jews is therefore stronger.

The equation assumed by Ochs here and throughout *Another Reformation* of Israel with "the Jews" will emerge in the light of an Ochsian critique of Barth as itself a dimension of Ochs' account which falls short of his criteria for non-supersessionism. To anticipate: to equate Israel with "the Jews" is prematurely to reduce the vagueness of Israel's story.

Barth on Rom 9–11

I turn now to Barth in order to sketch the contours of his exegesis of Rom 9–11, with a view to uncovering his answer to the question "Who is Israel?", and to assessing his account for its supersessionism, measured in Ochsian terms of vagueness and clarity. I will begin with the thorny Rom 9:6b: "For they are not all Israel which are of Israel" (Rom 9:6b).[16] This is a classic prooftext for a crude replacement theology, in which there are two Israels, one to be identified with the Israelites of whom Paul speaks in 9:4, his kinsmen according to the flesh (9:3), and the other a "true Israel," which the following verses will go on to characterize as children not of flesh but of promise (9:8–9), ultimately identifying them with the gathering of Jews

15. See Ochs, *Another Reformation*, 28 and 260–61.

16. As it reads in the English translation of Barth, *CD* II/2, 214. From now on, where clear, page numbers will be included parenthetically within the main text.

and Gentiles that we now know as the Church (9:24). Paul's argument, on this reading, is that the Israelites' rejection of Christ is not a sign that God's word has failed, since God did not have them in view but rather the Church. Thus the Church, as true, spiritual Israel, replaces Israel according to the flesh as the covenant partner of God.

Barth also finds two Israels here, but the relation between the two is worked out very differently: it is not a relationship of replacement but a dialectical relation which binds the two together as paired forms of the one elect community of God. Let us look at how he teases this out. Barth distinguishes between Israel as God's elect people (those of whom Paul speaks in 9:1–5) and God's special elect within Israel which eventually flower into the Church. Israel is characterized as the "race [*Stamm*] of Abraham," "Jews . . . by birth," distinguished by their "Jewish blood."[17] While "Israel" can be used with a variety of senses by Barth, when used without qualification it invariably refers to "the Jews." The Church is characterized, by virtue of its special election, as the true, spiritual Israel (214). However, far from replacing Israel, God's special election not only takes place *within* Israel, but thereby confirms the election of all Israel (216). Barth reads 9:6f as a display of the fact that God's election takes the form of *division* or *separation* (216–17), between those who witness to divine mercy on the one side (the special elect, or the preexistent Church within Israel) and those who witness to divine judgment on the other side (the rest). Crucially, both sides are included within the sphere of election. Thus, judgment is not to be equated with exclusion,[18] but is rather a necessary counterpart to the divine mercy, being ultimately for the sake of mercy (221).

17. *Pace* Katherine Sonderegger. The critical claim is the following one: "Not one of them is so by nature; not one in virtue of his Jewish blood; not one as a self-evident consequence of his membership of this people" (*CD* II/2, 214). I understand Barth to be describing God's special election here, as that which distinguishes "true Israel" from Israel, and thus (implicitly) to be affirming that Israel as an elect people is defined (among other things) by its blood. Sonderegger, by contrast, applies the claim to the election of Israel as such, concluding that Barth embraces the language of *volk* but not race (*That Jesus Christ Was Born A Jew*, 108 n. 31). While she is right to note that Barth avoids the term "*Rasse*," and no doubt to conclude that he distances himself from the racial theories of his time, her distinction between *volk* and race is arguably too clean, as evidenced by Barth's implicit embrace of the category of "Jewish blood" here. It is worth noting in Sonderegger's favor, however, that Barth later claims that "an idea of a specifically Jewish blood is pure imagination" (*CD* III/3, 213, cited in Sonderegger, *That Jesus Christ Was Born A Jew*, 156).

18. That is, exclusion from the one elect community of God. Barth does in fact say that "separation . . . means exclusion" (*CD* II/2, 217), but goes on to say that this does not mean forsakenness. I am wielding the terminology slightly differently for the sake of clarity.

Rom 9:6f narrates the historical beginnings of the one elect community of God in its twofold form as Israel and the Church, which has its eternal origins in the twofold determination of Christ as both the elect and the rejected. Israel is the community in its passing form, which hears the promise (only) and witnesses to the divine judgment, while the Church is the community in its coming form, which believes the promise and witnesses to the divine mercy (195). While figuring negatively, Israel performs an indispensable function within this pairing, witnessing to the rejection without which election cannot be had. In Christ, not only is rejection for the sake of election, but rejection is included in election and vice versa. Thus Israel's correspondence to rejection in Christ is inextricable from its ultimate election in Christ. Barth's pairs are never dichotomies or even straightforward distinctions; they are dialectical relations in which the opposite poles of a pair contain one another.

Barth's exegesis can conveniently be investigated under two headings: "the Church in Israel" and "Israel in the Church."[19] The first includes within its remit Israel's goal in the Church (a theme that has already begun to emerge in 9:6f), and the choice before Israel obediently to enter the church or disobediently to remain outside it as the Synagogue. Within the remit of the second, Barth maintains the Church's horizon in the election of Israel, affirms the uniqueness of Israel as the people of God, and considers the choice before the Church regarding its attitude toward Israel. Specifically, the Church comes under censure to the extent that it questions Israel's election. This becomes something of a refrain in Barth's exposition, and it is also the point at which Barth's otherwise apparently abstract theological considerations gain reparative traction. It will thus come in for special attention in the following.

We will return to Rom 9 for further exploration of "the Church in Israel." We have already established that the principle of election is inclusive division. But how does division within Israel, even inclusive division, result in a gathering of Jews *and Gentiles* (9:24)? How, in other words, can the goal of special election within Israel be the Church? Implicitly posing this question, Barth moves in the light of 9:24 from an Israel focus to a consideration of Israel's history from the perspective of the Gentiles. Serving merely as "the dark foil to Israel's history," they have appeared to have no share in the divine election even under the auspices of God's judgment. Barth finds them, however, to be introduced into Israel's history "at the eleventh hour," as they too become complicit, in the figure of Pontius Pilate, in the handing

19. See *CD* II/2, 210, for Barth's claim that "the Church lives in Israel," as well as his complementary claim that "Israel . . . lives in the Church."

over of Christ to death; and in this way "they participate concretely in the fulfilment of Israel's hope" (229). They do so, as is retrospectively revealed by the cross of Christ—which "unites what was divided, the elected and the rejected" (229)—as those who are paired with Israel as the rejected in relation to the elected. Israel's separation *from* the Gentiles, Barth implies, was itself a division of election, operating with the same logic as the divisions which were subsequently made *within* Israel. And as such, it was a division which included both poles within God's one elective purpose.

The shock of 9:24, on this reading, is not so much the inclusion of the Gentiles, but the reversal of the elect/rejected pair of Israel and the Gentiles to form the elect/rejected pair of the Church (as the "vessel of honor") and Israel (as the "vessel of dishonor"),[20] with Israel now figuring not on the side of mercy but on the side of judgment. What this reversal shows, among other things, is that all divine divisions beyond the central figure of Christ are provisional, merely witnessing to God's judgment and mercy as this has been definitively enacted in Christ. Indeed, Barth concedes that "[s]trictly speaking, He alone is Israel," in the sense of being God's special elect, and only in him can others be counted so (214). The vessel of mercy "is primarily the Lord Jesus Christ risen from the dead" (228), and the Church only "in virtue of its Head" (224).

The theological rationale behind the reversal of 9:24 will emerge only in Rom 11, but for now we may note its upshot: that Israel's goal is in the Church. In the coming of Christ and the formation of the Church with Christ as its Head and Lord, a choice is placed before Israel: will it obediently confess Christ as its Messiah, accepting him as its risen Lord and thereby becoming the Church? Or will it disobediently "[resist] its election by [refusing] to join in the confession of the Church," forming the Synagogue over against the Church and "[creating] schism" within the one community (208)? Jews who enter the Church continue to carry out their special witness to God's judgment, but now as "the undertone to the Church's witness about God's mercy" (208), thereby joining in the praise of the Church. But disobedient Israel, the "refractory synagogue" (221), "Israel in itself and as such" (210), witnesses only to judgment, thus witnessing to its divine election despite itself.

Barth's "Israel in the Church" theme finds its main development in his treatment of Rom 11:11f. In apparent reversal of the proposition that Israel's goal is in the Church, Barth asserts in his commentary on 11:11 that "God has so little forsaken [the hardened Jews] that it is for their sake that He has stretched out His hand to the Gentiles" (279). Similarly,

20. Rom 9:21; *CD* II/2, 224.

commenting on 11:13–14, Barth maintains that the Gentile Church has no *doxa* of its own, but "share[s] in the *doxa* of Israel by serving it" (281). He concludes that "the Church can be what it is . . . only as it is absolutely referred to Israel's future glory" (281). It is ultimately eschatologically that Barth holds together the twin themes of Israel's goal in the Church and the Church's subordination to the election of Israel. The Church in its present form, with the Synagogue outside it, is only provisional, while eschatologically it "is always both *all* Israel—not only the seven thousand but the hardened rest—and *all* the Gentile world, those who have already become believers and those who are yet to become so" (280). In a complementary fashion, Barth reads the "all Israel" of 11:26a as

> the community of those elected by God in and with Jesus Christ both from Jews and also from Gentiles, the whole Church which together with the holy root of Israel will consist in the totality of all the branches finally united with . . . it. (300)

Eschatologically, Israel and the Church are one.

But the eschatological horizon of their relation should not be an excuse to overlook real asymmetries in the present—which remain determinative for the kind of unity forged at the eschaton. The most persistent asymmetry in the present context, signaled by the fact that the Church has no glory of its own—that "its own election is indeed to some extent foreign to it" (282)—is the uniqueness of Israel as the people of God. This is first highlighted in Barth's exegesis of 9:4–5, Paul's list of Israel's privileges. Dependent on all these aspects of Israel's life, "the Church," concludes Barth, "leads no life of its own beside and against Israel" (205). The dark side of this assertion is that the Church, insofar as it "disputes Israel's election," commits a sin which is the "the Gentile repetition" of Israel's unbelief (205). Barth will make the stronger claim elsewhere that in doing so the Church "ceases to be the Church."[21] By contrast, Barth affirms "the eternal election of Israel" (204), implying that Israel cannot, even by its unbelief, undo its election, thereby ceasing to be Israel. We come up, for the first time here, against an intractable asymmetry between Israel and the Church: Israel has an enduring, empirical identity which is lacking to the Church.

The theme of Israel's uniqueness returns in force in the context of Barth's exegesis of the olive tree analogy developed by Paul in Rom 11:16–24. While he identifies the root with Jesus Christ (285), it is presupposed that the tree is Israel and its natural branches the Jews. While the Gentiles may be grafted in, becoming by grace what they were not by nature, and indeed "genuinely

---

21. *CD* II/2, 234. This is one instance of a refrain repeated in each of Barth's summary sections, and reiterated in different ways in the context of his exegesis.

[becoming] Israel" (297), even "true Israel" (288), that does not imply that "in place or beside Israel another of the world's peoples had now become the elected people. . . . [T]he election of Israel . . . cannot . . . be surpassed, supplanted or supplemented" (296). The Jews, "as ancestors and kinsmen of the one Holy One in Israel," are holy in a way that the Gentiles can never be (287). While Barth allows "Israel" to gain an expanded or transferred meaning, it does so exceptionally and only in the presence of a qualifier (e.g., "true" or "spiritual"). Thus Barth counterbalances any morphing of Israel by safeguarding the unqualified name "Israel" for the Jews, retaining the uniqueness of the people of Israel as the natural kinsmen of the Messiah.

The olive tree analogy is also an apposite context in which to develop the negative counterpart of that uniqueness: that in denying it the Church ceases to be the Church. The target of 11:16–24 is specifically Gentile Christians. Commenting on vv. 20b–21, Barth suggests that Gentile Christians who are presumptuous toward unbelieving Jews betray their own unbelief. Indeed, they "reject [Jesus Christ] by rejecting His ancestors and kinsmen the Jews" (292). He has suggested earlier that this Gentile Christian position is typical of "Christian anti-semitism" (290). And a little later in his comments on 11:22 Barth betrays that in this critique he has his eye on the church of his own day:

> How can they [Gentile Christians] arrive at the obscure distinction between "Judaism" and "Christianity" as between two separate religions and worlds succeeding one another? They can do so only as they themselves fail in the decision in which they see the Synagogue failing; only as they themselves become the Synagogue; only if they themselves are cut off and the same things happen in the Church as have happened in Israel. (293)

Having traversed some key moments of Barth's exegesis of Rom 11, we are now in a position to consider and appreciate Barth's answer to the theological conundrum of 9:24, which he arrives at in his exegesis of 11:25–27. Why does the Church of Jews and Gentiles become the vessel of mercy, over against recalcitrant Israel as the vessel of wrath? As Barth puts it: "it is highly abnormal that Gentiles suddenly obey and believe . . . by contrast to countless thousands who by descent and name seem to have the prior right" (288). According to Barth, the "mystery" Paul speaks of in 11:25 is the inversion in the natural ordering of events in respect of the conversion of Israel and the conversion of the Gentiles, the latter "incomprehensible thing" having been inaugurated while the former "natural and necessary thing" is still outstanding (299). And the reason for this inversion, according to Barth, is that the first shall be last and the last shall be first—*in order to show forth the divine mercy* (300). Grace can only be grace, Barth implies, if it is not nature.

This "solution" reveals an extraordinary tension in Barth's doctrine of election: between the absolutely gracious character of that election on the one hand, and the natural constitution of Israel as the elect people of God on the other hand. His account of election as division is arguably a creative way of dealing with just this tension, and we see him wrestling with it again in the context of the olive tree analogy. In paradoxical mode, Barth claims that "[even in] the existence of the natural root, holy in its natural-ness, we do not have an act of evolution but of creation. It is not nature which reigns, but grace" (296). Conversely, commenting on the uniquely beloved character of Israel as the kinsmen of Christ, he says that "it was nature too—nature created and preserved by grace but still nature—that all this was just here and only here" (297).

Barth's "solution" to the conundrum of 9:24 suggests that the only place a natural people can have—if grace is at the same time to be upheld—is as a rejected people, a people who reflect human incapacity and the sins of the world. In short, by insisting on the uniqueness and endurance of Israel as a natural people, Barth also singles this people out as uniquely rejected.

Vagueness and Over-determinacy in Barth

To assess Barth's exegesis apropos of supersessionism, let us begin by asking, in Ochs' terms, whether Barth "[returns] to the plain sense of Israel's story and [rediscovers] . . . what it now means in the light of the Gospel narrative of Jesus Christ."[22] There are some clear respects in which the answer to this is a resounding Yes! In the first place, Barth recovers the place of Israel as the people of God within the Christian story. Moreover, he definitively gives the lie to a standard replacement logic by affirming—"in defiance of all Gentile arrogance"—the eternal election of Israel.[23] In doing so Barth strikes at the roots of classic traditional Christian supersessionism. However, what gives his commentary its critical force is not this refiguring of tradition on its own. It is his repair of tradition in the light of the failures of the church of his own day—which in turn only become manifest as failures because of his immer-sion in the tradition. In this sense, Barth not only rediscovers Israel's story; he rediscovers what it means in the light of the gospel *now*.

As we have begun to indicate above, the mark of unbelief to which Barth repeatedly returns is, variously expressed, the church's antisemitism.

22. Ochs, *Another Reformation*, 43.
23. *CD* II/2, 204.

And he puts it no less strongly than to say that the church that becomes antisemitic "ceases to be the Church."[24] That he does not say this purely hypothetically, but with the church of his own day in mind, is evident from even the slightest acquaintance with his context: the church that ceases to be the church is, regrettably, far from being a hypothetical entity for him, but has substantial and horrifying reality in the German national church under Hitler—the *Deutsche Christen*. According to Tommy Givens, Barth not only writes his doctrine of election against the background of the rise of National Socialism—in which context the Jewish Question (*Die Juden-frage*) takes undeniably pressing form—but is responding to a wider political context of colonialism and racism in the aftermath of the First World War, in which Barth identifies the Jewish Question as *the* issue.[25] However, even apart from the light that contextual knowledge sheds, there are also intratextual signs of contemporary reparative bite.

First, as we saw above, Barth slides from talking about "Gentile Christian presumption" to talking about "Christian antisemitism."[26] He also refers to the erroneous distinction between Judaism and Christianity as religions succeeding one another, apparently attributing this error to Paul's Gentile audience.[27] The anachronism is evident, especially in the light of what we have now learned from the so-called New Perspective on Paul; but even for Barth who did not have the benefit of the latter, the specifically contemporary purchase of the categories of his critique would have been clear.

Second, Barth's attack on antisemitism within the church stands out not only because of its insistence—being a theme that recurs in every subsection of the overall paragraph, both within each summary section and at several places within the exegetical sections—but because it is the *only* mark of unbelief that he identifies. Barth's large-print summary sections that preface his exegesis of each section of Rom 9–11 follow a discernable pattern.[28] After naming Christ as the locus of God's election of the one community, he first identifies the special service of Israel within that community before he turns to the special service of the Church. At the same juncture within each iteration, just after having described Israel's special service, Barth emphasizes positively the fact that the Church needs Israel's contribution, and this becomes in turn the cue for his negative warning—which gains cumulative

24. *CD* II/2, 234.

25. Givens, *We the People*, 178–79.

26. See esp. *CD* II/2, 290.

27. *CD* II/2, 293.

28. This is true of the second, third, and fourth subsections of the paragraph (§33.2, 205f; §33.3, 233f., §33.4, 259f), but not the first (§33.1, 195f), which serves as a more general introduction to the themes of the paragraph as a whole.

force in its reiterations: "If [the Church forgets the unity of Israel and the Church] the Church is not the Church" (201); "If . . . the Church has become estranged from its Israelite origin . . . its name 'Church' may well be on the point of becoming sound and fury" (206); "A Church that becomes anti-Semitic or even only a-semitic . . . ceases to be the Church" (234); "Without Israel . . . [the Church] cannot continue to exist as the Church for a single moment" (260).[29] As we have already indicated, Barth (at a slightly later juncture within the pattern) identifies Israel's disobedience as its failure to join the Church, thereby creating schism within the one community. Antisemitism is the structural equivalent, within the Church, of Israel's unbelief, creating schism from the other side. It is not just one sin among others, but *the* sign of unbelief.

My suggestion is, to reiterate, that Barth's singling out of Christian antisemitism has reparative force—however much his critique is cloaked in the language of theological objectivity and abstraction. My further suggestion is that Barth's repair is enabled, in Ochs' terms, by the vagueness of his definition of the Church. Let me spell this out. First, Barth defines the Church (analytically) as that form of the community which by virtue of its belief in Christ witnesses to the divine mercy. But second, he refrains from exhaustively identifying the Church (as type) with a recognizable empirical entity. This is clear in his claim that "the Church ceases to be the Church." The latter claim assumes empirical reference: *something* (the empirical entity known as the Church) ceases to be the Church. But that something does not always coincide with the Church as ideal type. In that case while the empirical entity may endure, it is only erroneously called the Church. Such lack of coincidence goes together, in Barth, with a vague definition of the Church's belief: the shape that belief takes is open to contextual determination. It is neither the case that belief is fully defined in advance as an ideal (to which the empirical church may or may not live up), nor the case that belief is reduced to description of what an empirical church in fact exhibits (losing all normativity). Rather, belief is defined contextually, as Israel's story with its culmination in Christ comes into confrontation with the church of Barth's own day. The contours of belief become visible in respect of what that story *now* means. In Barth's case, those contours gain definition by way of their negative limit: antisemitism as a sign of unbelief. In other words, antisemitism is a contextual marker of unbelief. It contributes to a definition of belief in terms of its effects within Barth's context: belief rules out antisemitism.

29. And this is just within Barth's systematic summaries. Further critical references to Christian antisemitism under one name or another recur within his exegesis, too. See *CD* II/2, 204–5 (including the charge of antisemitism), 290–91 (exposing the classic argument for Christian antisemitism), 292–93 (critiquing Gentile presumption).

So far so good. But the vagueness of Barth's definition of the Church is not paralleled in Barth's definition of Israel, with the result that the reparative purchase of Barth's commentary is ineluctably one-sided. Again, let me spell this out. Barth defines Israel (analytically) as that form of the community which by virtue of its unbelief witnesses to the divine judgment. But unlike in the case of the Church, Israel as type necessarily coincides with Israel as empirical people. For Israel, even by its unbelief, cannot undo its election. Or in other words, as natural kinsmen of the Messiah, Israel cannot cease to be Israel. In short, the Church's precarious identity is not paralleled on the side of Israel. But Barth thus leaves himself no room for contextual definition of Israel's unbelief. Either it is defined in advance and imposed on the empirical people willy-nilly, or it is filled out by way of empirical description. In practice, Barth ends up with an unhappy combination of the two. As type, Israel's unbelief is fleshed out as its resistance to its election, its "refusal" to join the Church and consequent creation of schism (208), its character as "rebellious" (220) and "hardened" (228), being epitomized by the delivering up of its Messiah to death (226)—in all of which it embodies the wrath of God, witnessing to the divine judgment. But Barth also indulges in pseudo-empirical description, speaking of "Jewish or clerical phantasy and arrogance" (196), Israel's "sectarian self-assertion," "the spectral form of the Synagogue," "the [joyless] Jews of the Ghetto" (209), "Jewish obduracy and melancholy . . . caprice and phantasy" (236), and Israel's "carnal loyalty" (262).

If Barth had left himself room for contextual definition of "Israel's unbelief," he may have discovered that the synagogue does not fit his type, as a reality to which the Christian categories of belief and unbelief simply do not apply, revealing his Israel-type to be a Christianly devised foil for the Church. But as it is, Barth is not open to learning from the contingent realities of Jews and Judaism in his day (and indeed in the past); absorbed into his Christian framework they become a mere cipher. It follows that his critique of the Church can only be one-sided, since it is insulated from what it might learn from Jews as genuine others.

Let us return in the light of this one-sidedness to our assessment of Barth's supersessionism. We said that he overcame a standard replacement logic by his affirmation of the eternal election of Israel. This may be true as far as it goes. But it must now be qualified by our more subtle findings. The Israel that is not replaced is a fixed Israel: both a fixed type (witnessing to judgment) and a fixed people (defined as natural kinsmen of the Messiah). But is the establishment of this fixed Israel not itself the "replacement" of the living Israel of the Old Testament by a fixed form?

The ambivalence of Barth's (non-)supersessionism is exhibited power-
fully in his interpretation of Rom 9:25–26, in which Paul cites Hos 2:25 and
2:1 (Hb). Barth notes that Hosea's prophecy, fulfilled for Paul in the calling
of the Gentiles, originally concerned Northern Israel as the *Lo' 'Ammi* (not
my people) in contrast to Judah, who would one day again be addressed as
'Ammi (my people) (230). He continues:

> But we must not apply negatively against Israel Paul's indication
> of this overflowing fulfilment of prophecy in the calling of the
> Gentiles to the Church, as if the Hosea quotations were meant
> to say: "What was there prophesied for rejected Israel has now
> passed into fulfilment, not for it, but in its stead for the believing
> Gentiles. It no longer applies to them." (231)

Rather, he will elaborate, the prophecy's fulfilment in the Gentiles presup-
poses and anticipates its fulfilment in rejected Israel, as first becomes last
and last becomes first. On the one hand, this reading lends a multivalence
to Israel's story, understanding it to be fulfilled in the Church in addition to,
rather than in exclusion of, Israel. The Church does not replace Israel. On the
other hand, the Israel that is not replaced is Barth's fixed type: the mirror of
the Church whose election as paired with the rejected Gentiles has become
its rejection in pairing with the elected Church. Barth speaks in this context
of "the riddle of the Synagogue" and "the lost people Israel" (231).

To sum up, Barth defines the Church (and its belief) vaguely, while he
defines Israel (and its unbelief) over-determinately. This leads to a one-sided critique of the Church, which is closed to learning from Jews as genuine
others. But does this Ochsian critique of Barth shed any light in the other
direction on Ochs? We saw that Ochs, too, identified (biblical) Israel with
"the Jews" (albeit with acknowledgment of possible Christian definitions
of the church as Israel). There are two oddities in this identification. First,
Ochs appears to endorse a category ("the Jews") that sounds more at home
in the mouths of uninformed outsiders to Judaism, insofar as it homog-
enizes Jews who are temporally, geographically, and culturally diverse, and
potentially but anachronistically includes ancient Israelites, too. We have
seen that Barth does this too, equating Israel with "the Jews" on the basis of
their natural ancestral lineage. Second, Ochs identifies biblical Israel with
"the Jews" in the voice of *Christian* postliberal theologians. While there may
be a strong *Jewish* rationale for envisaging one's Jewish community as the
continuation of biblical Israel, narratively and liturgically (among other
ways) constructing one's community as Israel, this is not a rationale that can
be straightforwardly adopted by the Christian. To assume any such identification for the Christian, by contrast, is apparently to treat it as self-evident.

Again, Barth does so on the grounds of natural lineage, but this is a highly questionable category in the light not only of constructionist accounts of ethnicity, but also of the widespread phenomenon of Jewish proselytism, which undermines any putative purity of lineage.[30]

In both these ways, Ochs implicitly constructs "the Jews" as a people over against the church, in just the same way as Barth. To be sure, he does so more irenically, allowing both to exist side by side as contextually valid interpretations of biblical Israel's story today, which as vague can house them both even in their potential contradictoriness. But he nevertheless splits Israel into two: Israel and the church (which may or may not claim the name for itself). This replicates (as does Barth) the twofold character of the supersessionist readings of Rom 9:6 (to which we referred at the beginning), which find two Israels here (a fleshly and a spiritual Israel, say). My suggestion in conclusion is that such bifurcation over-determines the meaning of Israel in a way that falls foul of Ochs' definition of non-supersessionism. It does so in the following ways. First, it rules out other potential claimants to Israel by assuming just two Israels. Second, it hardens the relation between Christians and Jews into the relation between different Israels, which however much they are bridged will always retain a residual twoness.

An alternative, potentially reparative, approach is offered by Tommy Givens, who reads Romans 9:6f as about just one Israel, an Israel which includes Paul's kinsmen according to the flesh mentioned in 9:1–5.[31] This Israel, as Paul characterizes it in the light of Christ, is open-ended and hospitable to all potential participants, being defined by God's election rather than humanly policed borders. The ramifications for readers today, who find themselves in a situation very different from the one Paul encountered, are significant. Christians, as participants in God's elect people Israel, can acknowledge Jews as fellow participants in that elect people, while contesting their interpretation of what it means to be Israel. The oneness of the people, however much diversity and conflict it houses, is precisely the grounds for genuine argument and vital dispute, and thus mutual learning and criticism. The danger of the accounts of both Barth and Ochs is that the twoness—whether as two forms of the one people,

30. Givens is stridently critical of appeals to (what he calls) "ethnic" Israel (*We the People*, 244–56). He notes not only their recent ubiquity but also the fact they are made by some to guard against supersessionism and by others to reinforce it. Characterizing Israelite ethnicity as a "pure substance . . . passed on from parents to children . . . from a mythologically purified and common ancestor (i.e., Abraham)" (245), he exposes it as "a myth" (250).

31. For his detailed exegesis, see Givens, *We the People*, 345–411, in which Givens offers a reading of Rom 9–11 as a whole. See pp. 346–63 for his treatment of Rom 9:1–9 and his critique of "two Israels" readings.

or as distinctive interpretive continuations of the biblical Israel—erects a wall of incommensurability between Christians and Jews which hinders engagement with real purchase. My proposal, in conclusion, is that a truly Ochsian non-supersessionism must, with maximal vagueness, assume just one Israel, and thus an Israel hospitable to all.

Bibliography

Barth, Karl. *Church Dogmatics II/2.* Edited by G.W. Bromiley and T. F. Torrance. T&T Clark, 1957.

Givens, Tommy. *We the People: Israel and the Catholicity of Jesus.* Minneapolis: Fortress, 2014.

Jenson, Robert. *Systematic Theology.* Vol. 2. Oxford: Oxford University Press, 1999.

———. "Toward a Christian Theology of Judaism." In *Jews and Christians: People of God,* edited by Carl E. Braaten and Robert W. Jenson, 1–13. Grand Rapids: Eerdmans, 2003.

Lindbeck, George. "The Church as Israel: Ecclesiology and Ecumenism." In *Jews and Christians: People of God,* edited by Carl E. Braaten and Robert W. Jenson, 78–94. Grand Rapids: Eerdmans, 2003.

Ochs, Peter. *Another Reformation: Postliberal Christianity and the Jews.* Grand Rapids: Baker Academic, 2011.

Sonderegger, Katherine. *That Jesus Christ Was Born a Jew: Karl Barth's Doctrine of Israel.* University Park: Pennsylvania State University Press, 1992.

18

How to Be Theologically Funny[1]

—STANLEY HAUERWAS, Duke University

Analyzing humor is like dissecting a frog.
Few people are interested and the frog dies of it.

—E. B. WHITE[2]

1. I have many friends, but Peter Ochs is special. He is special because he is Peter Ochs. By that I mean few can match his intellectual energy and powerful personality. There is also the little matter that he is a Jew and I am a Christian. That difference makes our friendship different, but not in the way some might think. For it turns out, I often find Peter and I share more judgments than I share with other Christians. Of course, Peter knows more about Christianity than many Christians. I only wish I knew Judaism as well as Peter knows Christianity. Which brings me to the subject of this paper, or why I think this paper as a nonapologetic exercise in Christian theology is appropriate for Peter's festschrift. The main reason I think it appropriate is that I think Peter will like it. But I also think some of the remarks I make about the differences between Jews and Christians when it comes to humor are relevant to Peter's work. Peter is a funny guy and humor pervades his work. Therefore, I hope this paper pays due honor to this funny and profound man who honors me by claiming me as friend.

2. E. B. White's quote is from Hurley, Dennet, and Adams, *Inside Jokes*, 289. For those interested this book will tell you more than you want to know about how humor developed in the evolutionary process. To their credit the authors resist any reductive analysis of humor and along the way they make some enlightening suggestions about the role of humor for our lives as human beings. I call attention to their book as a way to indicate I am not trying to do what they have done.

1. Can or Should Theology Be Funny?
Beginning With a Joke

IT SEEMS THAT JOHN XXIII had an archeological expedition in the Holy Land. They made a great discovery that the head of the expedition thought presented certain theological problems. He called John XXIII, announcing he had some good news and some bad news. The good news was they had discovered the tomb in which Jesus was laid after the crucifixion. The bad news is that the body is in it. The head of the expedition thought he ought to alert John XXIII to the findings before they were generally known because it might entail some theological rethinking. John XXIII thanked the head of the expedition for letting him know because he did need to pray and think about this news. So he prayed and thought but was unsure what to say. Finally he said to himself, "My old friend Rudy Bultmann has thought long and hard about these matters. I will call him to see what he thinks." He called Bultmann, explaining he had some quite momentous news that he feared might upset Bultmann, but he needed Bultmann's help. John XXIII explained about the archeological expedition and the finding of the tomb. He then again warned Bultmann that what he had next to tell him he might find deeply disturbing but he had to tell him the truth if he was to get his help. So he said, "The body was in the tomb." There was a long silence on Bultmann's end. John XXIII waited and waited, fearing that Bultmann's faith had been shattered. Bultmann finally responded, "So he really existed."

This was the joke we told as seminarians at Yale Divinity School in 1965. At the time the joke certainly needed no "explaining." Bultmann was the New Testament historian/theologian we read. His presumption that we had little evidence to secure knowledge of the "historical Jesus" dominated discussions of New Testament scholarship. That Bultmann might be upset, or at least had to reconsider his views if the body was found, we thought to be quite funny. I confess I still find the joke not only funny but a nice commentary on the scholarship surrounding the New Testament when I was in seminary.

I suspect the story is not nearly so funny for current generations of seminarians. Bultmann simply does not dominate New Testament scholarship the way he did when I was a student. Indeed he can be read as a deeply conservative thinker about questions surrounding Jesus given developments in New Testament scholarship since he wrote. Better put, theologically, Bultmann never doubted that Jesus matters. But I suspect that for the joke to "work" for current students they will need some explanations that inform them about Bultmann and his scholarship. A familiar but often forgotten point about attempts to "be funny" is that humor is profoundly contextual, depending as it does on common presuppositions and habits.

I begin with an example of a joke but I take as my task in this paper to explore a more general question than the joke may suggest. I want to try to understand the role of humor in theology. Most of those who practice Christian theology think they are engaged in a serious science. That it is so should not be surprising given the reality that at the center of Christian theology is a crucified savior. Moreover any theology that is doing the work of theology well must deal with the fundamentals of life, that is, life, death, and all the stuff in between. Stuff like love and the betrayal of love. These subjects not only are serious but if truthfully addressed sentimentality and superficial nostrums must be avoided. Humor can be one of the ways that sentimentality and superficiality can be defied.

M. A. Screech, in his erudite and wise book *Laughter at the Foot of the Cross*, observes that "man is a laughing animal."[3] He traces that claim to Aristotle and Aquinas—a claim I might add I think to be more basic than the general characterization that the distinguishing character of being human is our rationality. I call attention to Screech's observation, an observation he develops by close attention to the work of Erasmus and Rabelais, in order to distinguish the question of whether and how theology can and should be funny from the question of the task of theology to provide an account of our humanity which entails our being funny. These questions are obviously interrelated, but they are not the same question. In this paper I am primarily concerned with the former.

By beginning with a joke, as well as using the description "funny," I mean to distinguish what I am about from attempts to characterize Christian theology in general by using genre categories such as tragedy or comedy. I have no reason to deny that general characterizations of Christianity as comedic can be quite informative. For example, in *The Comedy of Redemption: Christian Faith and Comic Vision in Four American Novelists*, Ralph Wood argues quite persuasively that the Christian vision of the world is fundamentally comic. Drawing on the insights of Karl Lowith, Wood observes that because Christians do not, as the ancients did, regard the universe as eternal or divine but as created, comedy is made possible by the acknowledgment of the sheer contingency of all that is. According to Wood, "What the Christian faith confesses is that God, in the Jews and Jesus, has perpetrated the most outrageous of tricks, a joke to end all jokes, a surprise beyond all surprises. He has upset our tragicomic equilibrium.

3. Screech, *Laughter at the Foot of the Cross*, 3.

In Israel and Christ he acts unilaterally to deliver the human race from its dialectical enslavement."[4]

I find Wood's account of the comic character of the Christian narrative to be quite insightful. I worry, however, that the use of tragedy and comedy to characterize the Christian worldview runs into the problem of diverse understandings of tragedy or comedy. The concepts of tragedy and comedy depends so heavily on the literature they are meant to characterize it is unclear how helpful those descriptions are when turned into general designations. Greek tragedy may have some resemblances to the tragedies of Shakespeare but the difference Christianity makes for Shakespeare's "tragedies" means to characterize the plays of the Greeks and Shakespeare as tragic may not be instructive but misleading.[5] I say this as someone who entitled an early book, *Truthfulness and Tragedy: Further Investigations Into Christian Ethics.*[6] In my defense I was using tragedy to avoid "lesser of two evils" arguments. I still think there may be something to that proposal, but that is a subject for another day.

Yet I do think, in spite of the considerable evidence to the contrary, that theology can and should be in some of its modes funny. Theology done right should make you laugh. Chris Huebner in a recent article on my work entitled, "Make Us Your Laughter: Stanley Hauerwas' Joke on Mennonites," makes some insightful comments about my use of laughter that I find extremely informative.[7] He, for example, calls attention to my poking fun at Mennonites in a sermon such as "On Milk and Jesus" as my way to help Mennonites recognize what a funny people they are.[8] Huebner observes that my use of laughter is my attempt to practice theology in a manner that refuses the attempt to manage the world. In short, my use of laughter is "an appropriate theological antidote to the Constantinian desire for control."[9]

Huebner argues it is important to note that my use of laughter does not mean I lack an appropriate seriousness. He suggests, I think rightly, that there is no contradiction between something at once being serious and funny. I

---

4. Wood, *Comedy of Redemption*, 32.

5. For example Sarah Beckwith, drawing on Stanley Cavell, suggests that Shakespeare's tragedies are the result of failures in acknowledgment due to the terrifying reality that to be loved as well as to love risks being known by another. Beckwith, *Shakespeare*, 6–7.

6. Hauerwas, *Truthfulness and Tragedy.*

7. Huebner, "Make Us Your Laughter."

8. "On Milk and Jesus" can be found in Hauerwas, *Disrupting Time*, 142–48. It was a sermon delivered at the installation of Dr. Gerald Gerbrandt as President of the Canadian Mennonite University in 2003.

9. Huebner, "Make Us Your Laughter," 362.

do, however, have a deep distaste for the cloying seriousness associated with some forms of pietism. But my use of laughter to counter what I regarded as feigned profundity is my attempt, as Huebner puts it, to offer "a response to the idolatrous temptation to take ourselves more seriously than God."[10]

Huebner calls attention to my self-designation as a "high church Mennonite" to illustrate how I use humor to make a serious theological point. He rightly suggests that I use that description as a joke. He doubts it is all that funny, but credits my use of the description as a way to raise theological questions about how we define our identities. Huebner argues I am trying, probably not very successfully, to call into question our preoccupation with identity. My use of "high church Mennonite" is but one expression of my general concern that "preoccupation with neatness tends to generate models of theological discourse that are methodologically egoistic."[11] Without laughter our speech about the strange, surprising, and funny God we worship threatens to become speech about ourselves.[12]

By calling attention to the importance of humor and laughter in theology I am trying to suggest that theology should be done in an entertaining manner. Humor is not the only mode of entertainment the discourse of theology can take but it is surely the case that we, and the "we" means most people, are often attracted to speech and writing that is funny. An observation that calls into question the presumption by some that if you want what you have to say to be entertaining then what you have to say cannot be serious. I have tried to defy that presumption by attempting to do theology in a manner that "tickles" the imagination.

For example, some years ago I wrote an essay entitled "A Tale of Two Stories: On Being a Christian and a Texan."[13] The essay begins by acknowledging I want to entertain my reader while doing what I take to be serious intellectual work. I wrote the essay first and foremost to honor my parents in the hope that if they read the essay they would recognize how deeply I valued the way they had formed me to be a Texan without regret.[14] I as-

10. Huebner, "Make Us Your Laughter," 365.

11. Huebner, "Make Us Your Laughter," 146.

12. Huebner suggests that Mennonites may not get the joke I am about, but Yoder did. For a fascinating analysis of the relation of humor and hope in Yoder see, Tran, "Laughing With the World."

13. The essay is the first chapter in my book *Christian Existence Today*, 25–45. I am grateful to Brazos Press for reprinting the book in 2001, though I continue to have the impression that the book is not widely read.

14. For a fuller account of my parents see my memoir, *Hannah's Child. Hannah's Child* was originally published in 2010. The paperback (with an afterword) was published in 2012.

sumed such training was the necessary condition to be a human being. I also wrote the essay for my own amusement because in it I was able to use William Humphrey's great novel, *The Ordways*, to elicit what it means to be a Texan. The novel, moreover, is filled with stories of Texans trying to make it in a hard land that are at once humorous and sad.

The serious intellectual work the essay was meant to do was to respond to the criticism that a focus on narrative as a basic grammar of Christian speech fails to appropriately acknowledge that no one narrative can or should constitute our lives. "On Being a Christian and a Texan" was my way to show how different stories work to shape our lives. I also wanted to show how the different stories that possess us can be judged more or less truthful by suggesting how the narrative(s) generally recognized as Christian makes how the stories of Texas must be told as well as lived. The great trick is how the injustice that is inherent in the stories that are Texas can be remembered without their being justified. I should like to think "A Tale of Two Stories" is not only entertaining but it is so exactly because it is serious theology.

Then, of course, there is my semi-famous essay, "Why Gays (as a Group) Are Morally Superior to Christians (as a Group)."[15] That short essay was meant to be funny by reframing the question of gay relationships in terms of their (at the time) doubtful status in the military. By raising the question about why Christians could not accomplish the feat of being banned from the military as a group I was trying to suggest how arguments about gays depended on the accommodated character of contemporary Christianity in America. But if Christians as followers of Christ found themselves banned from the military as a group then arguments about gay participation in the church would be quite different.

But enough about me. There is much more to be said about why theology needs to be funny. In particular I want to call attention to the theologian I think may be the "funniest" in the Christian tradition, namely, Karl Barth. Before doing so, however, I need to prepare the ground for Barth's humor by calling attention to a philosophical analysis of jokes. For it is by paying close attention to jokes we will be better able to understand that jokes are no joking matter.

I had once thought to entitle this paper "How to Tell a Theological Joke," but jokes are a more specific category than a story that is funny. Jokes are funny, but not everything that is funny is a joke. However, by attending to an analysis of jokes I hope to throw more light on what it means for theology to be funny. There is also the question of the relation between jokes, what is funny, and irony. It is probably the case that irony is a more inclusive category

15. The essay first appeared in my *Dispatches From the Front,* 153–55.

than either jokes or what is funny. Jokes often employ irony but irony is not always in the form of a joke nor is it necessarily funny. There is no reason to assume, nor is it crucial for the case I want to make, that these conceptual questions must be settled. I am content if the analysis of jokes I now will provide helps illumine what it means for theology to be funny.

The question of the relation of the theologian to their theology needs to be addressed. It is one thing to suggest that a theologian needs a sense of humor. It is quite something else to argue that their theology must be funny. I acknowledge the distinction, but I will maintain that not only should theologians know how to laugh at themselves but also their theology should also manifest the joy that reflects the glory of God. Of course joy is not the same as what makes something funny, but what is funny depends first and foremost on a joyful recognition that God is God and we are not. The joke is on us.

2. Ted Cohen on Jokes

Ted Cohen has written a very insightful and funny books on jokes. He entitled the book, *Jokes: Philosophical Thoughts on Joking Matters*.[16] "Philosophical thoughts" should not scare off any potential reader because the kind of philosophy Cohen represents does not need to call attention to itself. For example he confesses when he first began to write about jokes he thought they could be divided into pure and conditional jokes. A conditional joke would be those that only work with specific audiences. Cohen's exploration of jokes, however, has convinced him that there is no such thing as a pure joke (12). That is a philosophical point but Cohen does not reference or elaborate the philosophical sources that clearly inform his judgment that there are no "pure" jokes.

For example he tells a joke about the president of a small college who wants to improve the school's academic reputation. The president is told the best way to do that is to create a few first rank departments. He first focuses on the mathematics department because he is told to increase their quality would not be very expensive. After all the only things mathematicians need to do their work are pencils, paper, and wastebaskets. However the ambitious president then judges it might be even less expensive to make the philosophy department rather than the mathematics department better because philosophers do not need wastebaskets.

You do not need to be a mathematician or philosopher or even an academic to enjoy this joke but you do need some understanding of

16. Cohen, *Jokes*. Paginations to appear in text.

mathematician's demand for elegance as well as philosophers presumed professional license to say what they please because there is no way to prove
them right or wrong (14). Cohen notes that not all jokes require specialized
information or professional jargon, but they may require a little knowledge
about a specific subject. He provides as an example a response of a man who
is asked by a panhandler outside a theater for a handout. The man declined,
saying, "'Neither a borrower nor a lender be' —William Shakespeare." The
panhandler replied, "'Fuck you!' —David Mamet."

As I noted Cohen does not, as he might have done, call attention to
philosophical accounts of rationality that would support his argument that
there is no such thing as a "pure joke," but he does rightly argue that every
attempt to provide a general theory of jokes turns out to be wrong (43).
Of course some jokes draw on what we assume is general knowledge of
the human condition such as jokes about death and illness. But that some
jokes seem "to work" on the basis of such knowledge Cohen argues is not
sufficient to ground a general theory about jokes. Thus the "method" of his
analysis of jokes depends on exemplification.

For example the joke: "One good things about Alzheimer's disease is
that if you get it you can hide your own Easter eggs" (43) might be one anyone
could "get." But Cohen notes that some find such a joke disagreeable indicates
that how illness is experienced makes all the difference for how such a joke is
meant to work. The fact that those with the disease as well as those that care
for them are more likely to find the joke funny is but a further indication that
we do not need a general theory about jokes. Rather what we need is insight.
Thus the observation that those that find the joke funny do so because the
joke helps defeat the loneliness associated with the disease.

Cohen observes that he thinks what makes a successful joke successful
is "the sense held mutually by teller and hearer that they are joined in feeling" (25). That good jokes are concise is due to the fact that so much can go
unsaid because of what the teller and the hearers know in common. Cohen
even uses the language of intimacy to describe what he takes to be the effect
of a good joke. By intimacy he means a shared sense of community a joke
at once reflects and creates. Members know they are in such communities,
according to Cohen, to the extent they can identify (1) a shared set of beliefs, dispositions, prejudices, preferences, in short a common outlook on
the world and (2) shared feelings (28).

According to Cohen these two conditions of community that make
jokes possible can be cultivated and realized without jokes, but with jokes
our shared feelings are enhanced by our common outlook about the way
things are. When we laugh at the same thing something important is happening. That we laugh at all is, he suggests, noteworthy. This is true even

when we laugh alone, but when we laugh together we experience the satisfaction of "a deep human longing, the realization of a desperate hope. It is the hope that we are enough like one another to sense one another, to be able to live together" (29). Cohen argues, therefore, that when a joke is successful there is nothing to point to but the joke itself.

That is why you know if you have to explain a joke you have an indication that something has gone wrong that cannot be fixed by the explanation. When a joke is unsuccessful you cannot show that the joke is really an example of some other case that should be acknowledged as funny. The joke either works or it does not just as practical reason works or it does not. Cohen does not explicitly call attention to jokes as exemplifications of practical reason, but his account of how jokes work I take to be a compelling exemplification of how practical reason, at least practical reason as understood by Eugene Garver, works.[17] Jokes can be understood rhetorically as one of the means we have to make "common knowledge truly common."[18]

Just as practical reason extends its range by engaging problems that would not exist without our being the kind of people we are, so jokes can be created by imaging a problem for oneself. Any subject will do. Cohen, for example, asks, "What is Sacramento? It is the stuffing in a Catholic olive" (35). He acknowledges this is not a great joke, but one he and Richard Bernstein made up after having given themselves the challenge of making up a joke about pimiento. Perhaps a better example is that created by playing on certain words. Thus the eighty-five year old man's response to doubt about his claim to have sex almost every night: "For instance this week I had it almost on Monday, almost on Tuesday, almost on Wednesday . . . " (36).

Cohen observes that though it is stimulating to explore new topics to joke about it is even more stimulating when the topic is extremely specific. He uses as an example snail jokes. "What does a snail say when riding on the back of a turtle? 'Whee!'" Or a turtle was mugged and robbed by a gang of snails. When asked for a description of the robbers the turtle replied, "I'm sorry, but I just don't know. It all happened so fast." Cohen suggests such jokes' limits are comparable to Stravinsky's remark that the most strict and rigid musical forms, forms like the fugue, are the most liberating for the composer because they free one from the need to worry about too many possibilities and leave the composer to exploit his talent by being inventive within the confine of the form (39).

17. Garver, *For the Sake of Argument.*
18. Garver, *For the Sake of Argument,* 39.

Perhaps the most fundamental role of jokes, however, is their use to comprehend the unexpected and absurd aspects of life.[19] We laugh at that which defies our ability to make sense of events in our lives. According to Cohen such "laughter is an expression of our humanity, our finite capacity, our ability to live with what we cannot understand or subdue. We can dwell with the incomprehensible without dying from fear or going mad" (41). This role of jokes is particularly important for those who are under the control of others just to the extent jokes help those in such a situation to laugh at their oppressor and, if they are lucky and the joke is very good, make the oppressor laugh at themselves (44). Jokes often have a subversive character that cannot be acknowledged exactly because subversion is betrayed by being acknowledged.

Yet there is no escaping how jokes must deal with death. Death, moreover, is the subject Cohen suggests is the gateway for appreciating that particular tradition of jokes associated with Judaism. For Cohen Jewish joke telling reflects the Jewish acknowledgement of life's incomprehensibility.[20] Jewish jokes also manifest the sanctions internal to Judaism that are meant as a response to the incomprehensibility of life (45). Cohen provides a number of long Jewish jokes that underwrite certain Jewish stereotypes of themselves. For example, there was the elderly rabbi in Brooklyn whose piety was renowned but whose faith had begun to waver. Pondering his growing spiritual crisis he reasoned as well as prayed that if the Holy One would strengthen the rabbi's faith he would ensure that the rabbi would win the New York State Lottery. The rabbi waits for weeks and months continuing to pray that he will win the lottery. Finally standing alone in the synagogue he hears a rumbling and observes a brilliant light from which a beautiful melodious voice that seems to come from every direction says, "So *nu*, buy a ticket" (47).

Cohen thinks this kind of Jewish joke reflects the Jewish ability to laugh at absurdity as a way to negotiate the imponderables of life. Jewish humor reflects the conception of human decency found in the Hebrew Bible in which the mystification of the world is "a laughing acceptance, a kind of spiritual embrace" (51). Moses is the great exemplification of this response

19. In his illuminating book, *Redeeming Laughter,* Peter Berger drawing on Kierkegaard suggests that the comic exploits the inherent contradictions of our lives. According to Berger, therefore, the difference between tragedy and comedy is the tragic is the suffering of contradiction but the comical is painless contradiction (27). Though, as I suggested above I am skeptical of attempts to provide general accounts of tragedy or comedy, I suspect there is something to Berger's way of putting the matter.

20. Berger also provides an account of Jewish jokes that is quite similar and compatible with Cohen's analysis of Jewish humor. See his *Redeeming Laughter,* 87–98.

to the world as before the burning bush he answered "Here I am." That response is not funny, but Cohen suggests that Moses' response has a quality that pleases God. It pleases God because Moses turns aside to look at what he cannot comprehend. Cohen in a like manner argues that Abraham's and Sarah's response to the announcement they would have a child is paradigmatic for the development of Jewish humor.[21]

Such laughter, laughter that is a response to the incomprehensibility of the world is, nonetheless, an acceptance of that same world. "The world and its inhabitants are forever doing the damnedest things. It is one Jewish mode of acceptance and appreciation to receive things in their wonder. Then this laughter may be heard as the echo of faith" (60). This does not mean that Jews have a monopoly on jokes, yet there is a characteristic association of Jews with a joking spirit that Cohen argues is not accidental. It is the jokes of outsiders that exploit a deep and lasting concern and fascination with logic and language (60).

The obsession with language and its logic characteristic of Jewish humor Cohen suggests comes from the bilingual character of Jewish existence in America. Yet he argues that bilingualism is not sufficient to explain the Jewish fascination with language. The Jewish tradition of reasoning and argument developed in the study of Jewish texts Cohen thinks is crucial for understanding Jewish humor. For it is the character of Jewish tradition that debate is not only necessary but unending. For example Cohen tells the story from the Talmud of the debate between scholars about whether a cooking oven of a particular kind is ritually clean. The debaters call on God to support their judgments by dramatic actions which finally climaxes with a heavenly voice speaking in support of R. Joshua. The other Rabbis, however, were not impressed observing that a voice from heaven cannot trump what is written in the Torah. It is said that God laughed saying, "My sons have defeated Me. My sons have defeated Me" (56–57).

That much of Jewish humor is directed at themselves is an indication of the Jewish confidence in who they are. Yet Cohen raises the question of how far one can go in using humor to subvert oneself and still be oneself. Cohen thinks the Marx brothers managed to at once be Jewish but Americans by making American humor Jewish. Of course it is true that nothing could be more Jewish than entertaining judgments against the Jews, but Cohen worries that the negative judgments about Jews by people like Freud, Marx, and Wittgenstein may suggest a self-hate that is anything but Jewish.

21. For a wonderful account of the whole Isaac narrative as comic, see Kaminsky, "Humor and the Theology of Hope." Kaminsky observes that there is an intrinsic connection between humor and hope exemplified in the stories of Isaac, that is, both humor and hope suggest that the everyday necessarily has the final word.

Cohen, therefore, concludes his wonderfully short book by raising the question of when, if at all, a joke is inappropriate. He observes that the widespread conviction exists that some jokes on some occasions are morally objectionable. But it is not at all clear what makes a joke have this moral defect. He thinks it unlikely to be able to answer what makes a joke immoral by appealing to some moral theory. Given the "method" of his book, a method that clearly shows the influence of Stanley Cavell whom he claims as a friend, to appeal to a moral theory would betray the book. But just as important Cohen does not think any theory could provide what is needed because theories cannot help but oversimplify the diverse character of the comedic.

Most moral theories would try to show that immoral jokes harm someone or reveals or reduces the moral character of the one who tells the joke.[22] Cohen doubts that anyone can show these results obtain. Instead Cohen gives some "friendly advice." If you feel a joke is no damned good, express your feeling of moral disapproval. If you are asked to defend your judgment by giving moral-theoretical reasons for your negative judgment ask your interlocutor why you need to ground your judgments in theory. Rather what you must do is clarify matters for yourself and choose your words carefully, making sure that the words are really your words. We rightly feel disgust when exposed to jokes that are clearly racist, but crucial for the expression of that disgust is the availability of moral vocabulary to do the work that needs to be done (83). That is why Cohen's account of jokes is so compelling.

3. Theology Is Funny: The Case of Karl Barth

I have given an extensive account of Cohen on jokes because I find his analysis of jokes illuminating for thinking about why Christian theology should be funny. In particular I will try to make a case for how theology can and should be funny by calling attention to exemplifications of humor in the work of Karl Barth. I will end with a final brief look at some of my work. Before engaging Barth (or me), however, I want to explore a question Cohen's analysis of Jewish humor has raised for me. Why is there nothing in Christianity equivalent to Jewish humor?[23] As far as I know there is no

22. Screech puts the matter in as a succinct fashion as is possible when he observes, "What makes laughter good or evil is its target" (*Laughter at the Foot of the Cross*, 78).

23. I do not want to overlook that particular Christian traditions will develop their peculiar sense of humor. Martyn Percy, for example, argues that Anglicanism has developed a particular form of humor that is constitutive of Anglican ecclesiology. See his, "Joking Apart." Then there are the countless jokes about Southern Baptists. For example, "why do Baptists object so strongly to premarital sex? They're afraid it might

recognizable tradition of Christian humor comparable with Cohen's account of Jewish humor. Of course Christians can be quite funny, but they are seldom funny as Christians.[24] Is there something about the very content of the Christian faith that discourages Christians from having fun with our most fundamental convictions?

For example, consider the following:

> Jesus was walking down a dusty road when a woman ran toward him because she was being pursued by a mob of men calling her by slanderous names and bent on killing her by stoning her. As the woman approached Jesus he raised his arms, stopped the approaching men, and with eyes blazing stared at the women's pursuers and then said, "Let him who is without sin cast the first stone." Soon one man and then another man dropped their stones and begin to retrace their steps. It seemed clear that the men would disperse. But suddenly a rock from the back of the group of men came flying out, striking the woman on the head so that she fell to the ground. Jesus said, "Mother, sometimes you really piss me off."

This is clearly not a very funny joke. I suspect many Christians would find it distinctly offensive. You just do not make fun of the mother of Jesus. Jesus may have told his parents he must be about his Father's business, but Jesus is Jesus and we are not. What is it about the Gospel narratives and the letters of Paul that seem to inhibit the Christian sense of humor? Does the dramatic character of struggle against the powers of destruction at the heart of the Gospels mean that Christians simply have no place for making fun of themselves and the world? As I suggested above a story that has at its center a crucified savior just does not invite jocular commentary.

But there is the resurrection. I have always thought Thomas' recognition of Jesus profoundly comic. Jesus returns and offers his wounds to Thomas to touch so Thomas' demand for confirmation might be met. Thomas, and the text does not say he actually touched Jesus, says "My Lord

---

lead to drinking and dancing." Or: "How do you know Adam was a Baptist? Only a Baptist could stand next to a naked woman and be tempted by a piece of fruit."

24. Greg Jones reminds me that Christians do have a tradition of jokes about heaven and hell. For example there is the story of Reverend Jones, a Methodist minister, who had faithfully served the church over his life though he was appointed time after time to the worst churches in the conference. He approached Peter at the pearly gates only to be told his name was not on the books so he must go to hell. Later Peter was doing some book keeping and discovered Jones' name. He sent Gabriel to get Jones who was in a pool of brimstone up to his neck. On being told by Gabriel there had been a mistake Jones refused to leave to go to heaven. When asked why Jones observed he was standing on his bishop's shoulder. This is a very Methodist joke.

and my God." What an extraordinary response. You would have thought, given his worries about Jesus' actual return, he would have said something like, "Oh! You're back. Tell me about it." But he instead confesses that Jesus is Lord. That confession surely has the ring of joy if not laughter. The world will never be the same.[25]

In an extraordinary Easter sermon entitled, "One Day You Will Laugh," Sam Wells observes that laughter is often used in a defensive manner to help us deal with unpleasant realities who often turn out to be other people. But laughter can also be used in an attack mode to belittle. Thus jokes used to make us laugh at rather than with other people. In contrast Wells suggest that the laughter that is the resurrection is an infectious and irresistible laughter that overwhelms all who it encounters with joy.[26] If Wells is right about this, and I certainly think or at least hope he is, the question remains why Christians have failed to see the humor that pervades our scriptures and the lives of those who have preceded us.

It is not my intention to worry over this question about how the Gospel narratives may or may not inhibit or encourage what may be thought of as jokes, or at least funny stories. I certainly think Cohen is on to something by suggesting that the very character of Jewish debate around the law invites an imagination open to what might be called the grammar of the comedic. Could it be the very character of Christianity as a faith that one joins only by deep conviction inhibits a sense of humor about being a Christian? Jews do not choose to be Jews. To be a Jew simply comes with the territory known as their body. Such a stance invites a confidence that one has nothing to lose so that one can even complain that given the trials Jews have gone through over the centuries they can rightly wonder: "Is this what it means to be chosen?"

I suspect, however, far more significant for understanding the difference between Judaism and Christianity on matters comedic is Cohen's suggestion that the long history of Jews being outsiders has implanted in Judaism a distinct tradition of humor. Christians have sought to be in control of the worlds in which they have found themselves. If you desire to rule the world, the incomprehensibility of the world Cohen suggests is at the heart of Judaism must be denied or tamed. Constantinianism is but a name for the Christian attempt to make the world intelligible for Christian and non-Christian alike. What cannot be tolerated are forms of humor that might make the attempt to control a dangerous world absurd.

---

25. For my account of this passage from John see my *Cross-Shattered Church*, 27–32.
26. Wells, *Be Not Afraid*, 175–80.

The subversive character of humor often expressed in jokes is an unde-
niable reality. Those who use humor to subvert the pretentions of the powerful often have little to lose. One might think that the eschatological character
of the Christian faith would make Christians a people who have learned to
live "loose." To be able to so live is made possible by the recognition that the
use of humor in a defensive or attack mode is indicative of people enslaved by
their fears. Christians can risk being subversive because they believe that there
is a deeper reality than the world determined by fear.

There is, I believe, a close connection between the Christian justification of the use of violence to bring order in a disordered world and the
absence of humor among Christians. Christian nonviolence is surely an
absurd position requiring that you learn to live by your wits, which often
takes the form of your ability to talk your way out of tough situations. The
great surprise that Christians are called to witness, the surprise that God
became subject to our violence so that we might live nonviolently, is surely
the basis for the Christian identification with the Jews. If, as I suspect, we
are coming to the end of Christendom we may as Christians discover we
have a sense of humor.

I give as evidence of the possibility of that development the work of
Karl Barth. Karl Barth, the great enemy of cultural Christianity, I suspect
was "naturally" funny, but his humor was also a reflection of the character
of his theology.[27] Only a person with a profound sense of humor would
write *The Church Dogmatics*. Surely someone as intelligent and a lover of
all things human as Barth could have found other things to do with his life.
He could still have been a theologian. He just would not have assumed his
life needed to be dominated with the need to produce what surely must be
the most massive theological work by any Christian at any time. Yet Barth, I
think, rightly knew in our time we needed to have the *Dogmatics*.

In *With the Grain of the Universe: The Church's Witness and Natural
Theology* I have a footnote in which I discuss Barth's report of the exchange
between Harnack and Peterson in which Harnack challenged Peterson to
name which dogmas in which century and for which church should have
authority.[28] Deeply sympathetic with Peterson, Barth maintained that theology requires the theologian to identify with this or that confession of faith

27. I am certainly not the first to notice how funny Barth could be. For example,
Bernard Ramm called attention to the importance of Barth's humor in a chapter en-
titled "The Laughing Barth," in his book *After Fundamentalism*, 193–97. Ralph Wood
also has a wonderful chapter in his *Comedy of Redemption* entitled "Karl Barth as a
Theologian of the Divine Comedy," 34–56. More recently Jessica DeCou has written,
"Karl Barth: Comic Warrior."

28. Hauerwas, *With the Grain of the Universe*, 177–78.

in this or that branch of the church, together with this or that presupposed affirmation of the ancient church on which the confession rests. Yet Barth acknowledges that in the present day theology has no church behind her which has the courage to say unambiguously this is the highest concreteness. As a result Barth observes theologians are in a position dictated by King Nebuchadnezzar who demanded that his wise men tell him not only what his dream meant but what he dreamed. I observe that Peterson became a Roman Catholic. Barth wrote the *Dogmatics*. That he did so surely is a testimony to his profound sense of humor.

Jessica DeCou helpfully locates Barth's most extended discussion of humor in his *Ethics* which was originally published in 1928.[29] Barth did not publish the *Ethics* during his life time, one suspects, because in this book he was testing how to think about ethics, the results of which would receive mature expression in the *Church Dogmatics*. But I think DeCou is right to suggest that Barth's fundamental attitude about the significance of humor in theology he developed in the *Ethics* never changed. It did not change because in the *Ethics* Barth grounded humor in the eschatological character of the Christian faith which means it is incumbent on Christians to refuse to take the present with ultimate seriousness. Such a perspective elicits a "liberated laughter" that "derives from the knowledge of our final position—in spite of appearances to the contrary—with present reality."[30]

Barth observes that humor is fluid and flexible because it reflects what is done in time but from the standpoint of eternity. "Humor arises when the contrast between our eon is perceived and vitally sensed in what we do. Humor concerns the present as such with its strange connections and involvements. We cannot change the future into the present and the present into the future. We must persevere as best we can. We have humor when we do this."[31] Accordingly we must first laugh at ourselves so that we can laugh at others making possible the final test of being laughed at by them.[32] Barth concludes his account of humor by observing, an observation clearly meant to be funny, that a serious problem with Calvin is that he seems to have been unable to laugh.[33]

Barth does not deny that we must also live with an appropriate seriousness about the present, but we cannot take the present with ultimate seriousness. Humor that is genuine, however, is that which is appropriately serious.

29. Barth, *Ethics*, 510–12.

30. Barth, *Ethics*, 158.

31. Barth, *Ethics*, 510–11.

32. Barth, *Ethics*, 511

33. Barth, *Ethics*, 512.

Thus Barth's haunting remark: "Of humor, too, one may say that it is genuine when it is the child of suffering."[34] From Barth's perspective the great trick is to learn to live as a human being with the possibilities and limits that constitute our being human. Humor is liberation because it expresses an acceptance of our limitations in the light of our eschatological future.[35]

DeCou observes that Barth's complaint about humorlessness reflects his impatience with boredom. For example Barth's objections to natural theology are well known, but it is quite interesting that one of his most profound concerns about natural theology is too often work done in that name is "profoundly tedious and so unmusical."[36] In a similar fashion Barth found theological work done in the liberal tradition failed to take seriously what it means to be a human being exactly because of the absence of laughter in liberal theology. To describe faith as ultimate or unconditional concern is to take a far too serious view about what it means to be a human creature. For Barth we are fundamentally animals who laugh.

Humor pervades the *Dogmatics* but Barth explicitly discusses the significance of humor in his account of honor in *Church Dogmatics*, 3/4. Humor is a necessary attitude for any account of honor because a person can only be honorable as an expression of pure thankfulness that the honor that is due us comes from God. Accordingly the person honored by God finds himself oddly the object of such esteem. Thus Sarah laughed on being told of the birth of Isaac. Barth asks: "Is not the contrast between man himself and the honor done him by God really too great for man to take himself ceremoniously, and not to laugh at himself, in his quality as its bearer and possessor?"[37]

In the context of his discussion of honor Barth displays his characteristic humor by recounting a story of a person who is reported to have died because of a negative review of one of his books. Barth, clearly with tongue in cheek, declares "But he had no business to do this."[38] I do not know if Barth meant for his judgment that the man had no business to die to be funny, but it is hard to believe Barth did not recognize at once how silly as well as how funny it is for him to make such a judgment.

DeCou calls attention to John Updike's observation of Barth's "humor and love of combat" as evidence of Barth's being genuinely "indulgent of

34. Barth, *Ethics*, 511.

35. DeCou, "Karl Barth: Comic Warrior," 159.

36. Barth's observation can be found in *Church Dogmatics*, 2/1, 666.

37. Barth, *Church Dogmatics*, 3/4, 165.

38. Barth, *Church Dogmatics*, 3/4, 679. For my extended discussion of Barth (and Trollope) on honor see my *Dispatches From the Front*, 58–79.

the world."[39] Perhaps nowhere is that judgment better confirmed than in Barth's love of Mozart. For example in the "Preface" to *Church Dogmatics*, 3/4, and often Barth's self-deprecating humor is on display in his "Prefaces," Barth confesses while he still enjoys debate he has "gradually acquired more and more feeling for the affirmations by and with which we can live and die." "But," and you can hear the "but" coming, Barth observes that while he has gotten used to and does not respond to the criticisms of the Neo-Calvinists in the Netherlands who accuse him of being a "monist" they have finally gone too far and he must respond. Barth observes it is one thing to criticize him, but they have gone too far because they have tried to offend Barth by disparagement of W. A. Mozart. Barth observes that, of course, "in so doing they have shown themselves to be men of stupid, cold and stony hearts to whom we need not listen."[40]

Some years later in the "Preface" to *Church Dogmatics*, 4/2, Barth returns to his conflict with the Neo-Calvinists of the Netherlands. He begins by saying he needs to make some necessary amends. He observes the wrath of a man seldom does what is right in the sight of God. Responding to the publication of Berkouwer's book on Barth's theology, a book that treats Barth so fairly, Barth says he must withdraw his ill-founded words he unleashed against the Neo-Calvinists. So they will have nothing in the future to fear from Barth as long as "they do not say any more unseemly things about Mozart."[41]

Some may find Barth's love of Mozart odd given Barth's attack on all forms of cultural Christianity. But, as Ralph Wood has argued, exactly because Barth's theology was so sure of the victory of Christ he was free to enjoy the world. Barth, according to Wood, understood that the Bible contains the one ultimate cause for laughter and rejoicing. "Its joy is not cheap and easy but something deep-seated and lasting. Indeed, it often comes reluctantly. 'We may as well admit it,' Barth says of the believer, 'he has something to laugh at, and he just cannot help laughing, even though he does not feel like it.'"[42] From Barth's perspective Mozart, as many who are not necessarily Christian have done, "heard the harmony of creation to which the shadow also belongs."[43]

39. DeCou, "Karl Barth: Comic Warrior," 163.

40. Barth, *Church Dogmatics*, 3/4, xiii.

41. Barth, *Church Dogmatics*, 4/2, xii.

42. Wood, *Comedy of Redemption*, 55.

43. Wood, *Comedy of Redemption*, 73. The internal quote is from Barth, *Church Dogmatics*, 3/3, 298.

Barth was an energetic and spirited human being. Even if he had not become a theologian he would have been the kind of person you cannot help but find attractive. At least one of the reasons for such attraction would have been that he was genuinely funny. Stories abound about his humor and some of them may be true. For example, and I know this story is true, John Howard Yoder had written a very critical paper on Barth's view of war entitled, "Karl Barth and the Problem with War." Yoder being Yoder gave the paper to Barth a week or so before Yoder was to be examined for his PhD by Barth and other faculty at Basel. Barth began the exam observing "Herr Yoder, you Mennonites are so bellicose." Barth obviously not only respected Yoder's courage but he enjoyed the challenge.

Yet I have tried to show that Barth's humor is not a "personality quirk." Rather the way he taught himself to do theology is itself a testimony to the humor necessary if theology is to be a free discipline. I suggested above that when Christians think they must do theology in a manner that ensures that the way things are is the way things were meant to be the result cannot help but be the loss of humor. Barth was a free theologian because he thought theology that is a witness to God cannot help but manifest the sheer joy made possible by the recognition we are not alone.

4. Hauerwas One Last Time (at Least in This Chapter)

Which finally brings me back to me. A number of times, when being introduced before giving a lecture, the story is told of my encounter with a student at Harvard. It seems I was walking across Harvard looking for the library. Not sure I was going in the right direction I asked an undergraduate if he could tell me where the library is at. He responded by observing, "At Harvard we do not end sentences with a preposition." I am said to have responded, "Can you tell me where the library is at, asshole?" There is just one problem with that story; it did not happen. However, the story now seems to have reached a canonical stage so that it makes no difference whether it happened because the story confirms for many both negative and positive judgments about me.

I relate this phenomenon because the story also reflects the general presumption that I am a "funny guy." Some even think I have a gift for the one liner. It is not for me to claim to be funny, but I do hope that I have been able to do theology in a funny manner. I think my work is funny at least in two ways. First, I hope my work is really funny in the sense that people laugh out loud about something I have said or written. I know I laugh at what I often say and I see no reason that others should not laugh with me or about me. Secondly, my work is funny because I try to find ways to "do theology" in disguise. So I push the limits of presumptions about what theology is if it is to be "serious" in the hope that the difference might make a difference for how we live.

I think I am at my best as a humorist in prayers and sermons. So I think it appropriate to bring an end to this paper with this prayer:

> Funny Lord, how we love this life you have given us. Of course we get tired, bored, worn down by the stupidity that surrounds us. But then that stupid person does something, says something that is wonderful, funny, and insightful. How we hate for that to happen. But, thank God, you have given us one another, ensuring we will never be able to get our lives in order. Order is finally no fun, and you are intent on forcing us to see the humor of your kingdom. I mean really, Lord, the Jews! But there you have it. You insist on being known through such a funny people. And now us—part of your joke on the world. Make us your laughter. Make us laugh, and in the laughter may the world be so enthralled by your entertaining presence that we lose the fear that fuels our violence. Funny Lord, how we love this life you have given us. Amen[44]

Bibliography

Barth, Karl. *Church Dogmatics*, 2/1. Edinburgh: T & T Clark, 1957.
———. *Church Dogmatics*, 3/3. Edinburgh: T & T Clark, 1961.
———. *Church Dogmatics*, 4/2. Edinburgh: T & T Clark, 1958.
———. *Ethics*. Translated by G. W. Bromiley. New York: Seabury, 1981.
Beckwith, Sarah. *Shakespeare and the Grammar of Forgiveness*. Ithaca: Cornell University Press, 2011.
Berger, Peter. *Redeeming Laughter: The Comic Dimension of Human Experience*. New York: De Gruyter, 1997.
Cohen, Ted. *Jokes: Philosophical Thoughts on Joking Matters*. Chicago: University of Chicago Press, 1999.
DeCou, Jessica. "Karl Barth: Comic Warrior." In *World and World* 32/2 (Spring 2012) 157–65.
Garver, Eugene. *For the Sake of Argument: Practical Reasoning, Character, and the Ethics of Belief*. Chicago: University of Chicago Press, 2004.
Hauerwas, Stanley. *Christian Existence Today: Essays on Church, World, and Living in Between*. Durham: Labyrinth, 1988.
———. *A Cross-Shattered Church: Reclaiming the Theological Heart of Preaching*. Grand Rapids: Brazos, 2009.

44. Hauerwas, *Prayers Plainly Spoken*, 99–100.

———. *Dispatches From the Front: Theological Engagements With the Secular*. Durham: Duke University Press, 1994.

———. *Disrupting Time: Sermons, Prayers, and Sundries*. Eugene, OR: Cascade, 2004.

———. *Hannah's Child: A Theological Memoir*. Grand Rapids: Eerdmans, 2012.

———. *Prayers Plainly Spoken*. Downers Grove, IL: IVP, 1999.

———. *Truthfulness and Tragedy: Further Investigations Into Christian Ethics*. Notre Dame: University of Notre Dame Press, 1977.

———. *With the Grain of the Universe: The Church's Witness and Natural Theology*. Grand Rapids: Brazos, 2001.

Huebner, Chris. "Make Us Your Laughter: Stanley Hauerwas' Joke on Mennonites." *The Mennonite Quarterly Review* LXXXIV (July 2010) 357–74.

Hurley, Matthew, Daniel Dennet, and Reginald Adams. *Inside Jokes: Using Humor to Reverse-Engineer the Mind*. Cambridge: MIT Press, 2011.

Kaminsky, Joel. "Humor and the Theology of Hope: Isaac as a Humorous Figure." *Interpretation* (October 2008) 363–75.

Percy, Martyn. "Joking Apart: Exploring Comedy and Irony in Anglican Polity." *Ecclesiology* 1/1 (2004) 75–86.

Ramm, Bernard. *After Fundamentalism*. New York: Harper and Row, 1983.

Screech, M. A. *Laughter At the Foot of the Cross*. London: Penguin, 1997.

Tran, Jonathan. "Laughing With the World: Possibilities of Hope in John Howard Yoder and Jeffrey Stout." In *The New Yoder*, edited by Peter Dula and Chris Huebner, 253–70. Eugene, OR: Cascade, 2010.

Wells, Samuel. *Be Not Afraid: Facing Fear with Faith*. Grand Rapids: Brazos, 2011.

Wood, Ralph. *The Comedy of Redemption: Christian Faith and Comic Vision in Four American Novelist*. Notre Dame: University of Notre Dame Press, 1988.

19 _____

Mutual Intensities; Abductive Attraction; God

Thinking with Peter Ochs

—DAVID F. FORD

IT IS STRANGE THAT until the invitation to contribute to this Festschrift I had never tried to determine the influence of Peter Ochs on my thought and work. Once the question was raised, three things gradually (so gradually, indeed, that this whole essay has had to be completely rewritten four years after submitting a first draft to the editors) became clear: that his influence is so pervasive that separating it out is extremely difficult; that central to the difficulty is the fact that most of it has been through conversations in which others have taken part besides the two of us; and that it can only begin to be answered by a combination of narrative testimony and reference to key concepts (above all, abduction). The extreme compression necessitated by the word limit (amounting at times simply to naming things that can be pursued further in the writings given in the bibliography), means that key elements cannot be explored at any length. But this may be no bad thing. It may stimulate readers who do not know Peter in person to do the only thing that is likely to enable them to experience for themselves something like the transformations in thinking that Peter has helped me into: namely, to grapple with his writings—above all, perhaps, with three: the recent magnum opus, *Religion Without Violence: The Practice and Philosophy of Scriptural Reasoning*[1]; his essay on Jewish

1. Ochs, *Religion Without Violence*. My foreword to the book sums up my appreciation of it.

Morning Prayer;[2] and what I regard as the most extraordinary and generative of all, the chapters he wrote in the name of Daniel Hardy in *Wording a Radiance: Parting Conversations on God and the Church*.[3]

In what follows I distill from our twenty-eight-year friendship some of the thought generated through seven events and a great deal else surrounding them. Associated with each event will be a reference to the Gospel of John—I have been working on a theological commentary on John since 2000, and have spent many hours studying and discussing it with Peter.

1. At a Lake: Intensive Conversation between Friends

I first met Peter when we were both members of the Center of Theological Inquiry in Princeton in 1992. The Director of the Center, Daniel (Dan) Hardy, my father-in-law, introduced us. Peter invited us two Christians to sessions of the Textual Reasoning group of Jewish text scholars, philosophers, and theologians that met on the fringe of annual meetings of the American Academy of Religion. Within a couple of years some of that group had joined with ourselves and other Christians, and some Muslims led by Basit Koshul, to begin the practice of Scriptural Reasoning.

We were all taken by surprise by this practice of studying and discussing together short passages from the Tanakh, Bible, and Qur'an. As we did more of it and reflected on it there was a flood of questions. What were we now part of? How understand it from within each tradition? What about languages and translations, Talmud, hadith, tafsir, doctrines, and liturgies? What about scholarship, hermeneutics, philosophy, ethics, theology, the human and natural sciences? What about the very different, and controversial, roles of scriptures and concepts of revelation within each tradition? How relate Textual Reasoning to Scriptural Reasoning? How cope with the diversity within Judaism, Christianity, and Islam? What were we learning from each other? How describe the new relationships being formed, both individual and collegial? What were we learning that could help others engage fruitfully in the practice? How best nurture Scriptural Reasoning beyond the academy? What were the implications for relations between Jews, Christians, and Muslims now? How understand and encourage practical implications beyond the Abrahamic communities—for the academy, or for multi-faith societies? What about conflict situations in which Jews, Christians, or Muslims were involved? How should we organize ourselves? And many more.

2. Ochs, "Morning Prayer."

3. Hardy, *Wording a Radiance.*

Dan Hardy's family had a house on a lake in woods near Salisbury, Connecticut. Dan, Peter, and I gathered there during several summers in the 1990s and early 2000s. The intensive conversation went on morning, afternoon, and evening, day after day, with time for swimming, walking, and meals. They ranged widely, but the recurrent theme was the emergent practice of Scriptural Reasoning and the questions it was raising. We tried to distill what we, and a range of participants from several academic disciplines, cultures, and backgrounds, were discovering. From the avalanche of ideas, here I select just two.

One was what might be called the "betweenness" of fresh thinking drawing on the three scriptures and much else. Again and again in Scriptural Reasoning, and between the three of us, ideas were generated that could not be ascribed to just one person or tradition. They arose between us, through intensive study, thought, and conversation. That might be a relatively common experience,[4] but part of the distinctiveness here was that before our time Jews, Christians, and Muslims have rarely, if ever, engaged together year after year in shared study in settings not dominated by any single tradition. And among the participants now were Peter and Dan, each able to draw on a range of disciplines and on long engagement with the history of philosophy and theology, and each finding that Scriptural Reasoning was being generative in new ways—often challenging deeply embedded habits and concepts, not least about individualized cognition. On what I am calling "betweenness," Peter's book on Scriptural Reasoning, *Religion Without Violence*, gives his mature thought, which can be followed through references in the index to, for example: community, concept, Descartes, and Cartesian, difference, fellowship, habit, inquiry, intellect, judgement, knowing, language, logic (including abduction), Peirce, practice, individual, pragmatism, reasoning, relational, relations, sign, truth, social, and Western. A good example is the thinking about abductive attraction (see below) between Dan and Peter in *Wording a Radiance*.

The second is the idea of a university, and, more widely, of the sort of collegiality needed to pursue meaning, knowledge, truth, and wisdom through research and teaching in our complexly multi-religious and multi-secular world. Peter's thinking about this, and in particular about teaching and cognition, is also well summed up in *Religion without Violence*. Again and again our discussions at the lake returned to our own institutional commitments and our vocations as academics and teachers. Seeds were sown for the development of undergraduate and postgraduate courses,

---

4. In fact, it may be that the noteworthy thing is how and why so many have come to have an individualist conception of thinking.

first in the University of Virginia and later elsewhere; for the Society for Scriptural Reasoning; for founding the Cambridge Inter-faith Programme in the University of Cambridge in 2002; for the Rose Castle Foundation (now hosting the website www.scripturalreasoning.org); and for a range of projects and programs in institutions around the world, from the Center of Theological Inquiry, the University of Birmingham, and the Free University of Amsterdam to Minzu University in China and Dev Sanskriti Vishwavidyalaya in India.

As I reflect on those times at the lake in Connecticut in relation to the Gospel of John, I especially recall the rich exchanges between Peter and Dan about C. S. Peirce and the deeply Johannine Samuel Taylor Coleridge, which were to culminate in the conversations between them recorded in *Wording a Radiance*. The theological center of these conversations was the dynamic integration of Word and Spirit. I have come to read John's Gospel as the most profound biblical expression of this, with the aim of drawing readers into the fullness of God and into relationship with all creation. "For Coleridge we are being attracted to God, 'drawn toward the true center,' through particularity (Jesus Christ) and its relating universally (Holy Spirit). We can be led into the truth (John 16:13), which means stretching the mind and imagination and often the will, too, since some truth is only known through action, above all through love."[5]

2. At an Inauguration: God

In 2004, when Iain Torrance was inaugurated as President of Princeton Theological Seminary, he invited Peter Ochs, Aref Ali Nayed and myself to give lectures on Scriptural Reasoning.[6] It was an extraordinary experience, spending time over several days with Iain and with two of the seminal figures in Scriptural Reasoning. Besides the festivities, there were long conversational walks by day, followed by intensive conversations far into the night with Peter and Aref. Again, there was an avalanche of ideas, of which I choose just one: occasionalism.[7]

I have come to appreciate more and more Peter's fascination with occasionalism. His conception of it has not so much been in line with any of the specific thinkers in various traditions who have been associated with

5. Hardy, *Wording a Radiance*, 118.

6. See Ford, "Reading Scripture with Intensity"; Ochs, "Reading Scripture Together"; and Nayed, "Reading Scripture Together."

7. At the opposite extreme from deism, in which God creates and then leaves creation to itself, occasionalism sees God as in continual, intensive engagement with creation, free to spring surprises.

occasionalism as it has been a reference point for strong concerns about how to begin to do justice to the reality and freedom of God in dialogue with scripture, philosophy, and current science.

In the lake conversations, Peter's concerns resonated with those of Dan Hardy, above all in their desire to move away from any general concept of divine life, activity, and determination of regularities, in the direction of a radical particularism, God as freely interacting, split second by split second, with each element of creation, including each person. The regularities are real because God is faithful in each instant, not because there is some predetermined framework; but the faithfulness is accompanied by a transcendent freedom that allows for endless new creation, novelty, and improvisation. This God is utterly and intimately involved with creation and also freely transcendent. Alertness to this living God is therefore inseparable from living a full life as part of creation. Prayer, thanks, and praise are intrinsic to such a life, as is loving God with all one's mind as well as one's heart, soul, and strength, and all this overflowing into love of neighbor and creation.

In the Princeton conversations Aref Nayed gave an Islamic complement to this. He is an Ash'arite in theology, a tradition (also associated with Al-Ghazali) that is often called occasionalist, conceiving of God as utterly sovereign and free, moment by moment, to rearrange the very atoms that make up the world. Aref also complemented Peter and Dan in his thinking about logic, mathematics and the sciences. His education was as an engineer and philosopher of science, before doing extensive research in hermeneutics,[8] and later engaging in both the hardware and software sides of information technology. One of the recurring topics of conversation between Peter and Dan in our times at the lake had been quantum theory. This, they agreed, opens fresh ways not only of conceiving physical reality and our relationship with it, but also, analogously, of understanding how God might relate to creation intensively, freely, and yet noncoercively. Aref was also thinking through the implications of quantum mechanics; he added further thinkers, both Western and Islamic, to the conversation (Ahmed al-Rifa'i was the one we concentrated on most during these days); and he also repeatedly drew on practices of recitation, prayer, and singing.

These conversations at the lake and in Princeton were sustained examples of minds, dedicated to and fascinated by God, being stretched by each other in unprecedented ways towards fuller understanding. Occasionalism, enhanced by the Jewish-Christian-Muslim interplay in scriptural interpretation, theology, philosophy, and hermeneutics, by immersion in diverse practices of prayer and worship, by knowledge of current science

8. See Nayed, *Operational Hermeneutics.*

and technology, and by critical appreciation of the contemporary universi-ty, proved to be the least unsatisfactory traditional conceptuality[9] to bring into interplay with other elements.

Above all, the concentration on God rang true with what for many of us involved in Scriptural Reasoning had become increasingly clear. There can be all sorts of genuine motives, and combinations of motives, for tak-ing part in Scriptural Reasoning—intellectual, ethical, personal, cultural, political, theological, educational, and more—but the healthiest primary motive is to do it for God's sake. As Jews say, it is to be done "*l'shma*," for the sake of the Name.

I have found that collegial discussion drawing on resources from Judaism, Christianity, and Islam, together with a range of contemporary intellectual discourses, has helped me to appreciate both the mutual illumi-nation possible between the three traditions and, simultaneously, the ways in which my Christian faith is distinctive, beyond any possibility of inter-religious agreement that I can imagine. Perhaps the single biblical text that best exemplifies this is the Gospel of John, with its doctrine of incarnation and its leading role in inspiring the doctrine of God as Trinity. Its God-centeredness is inseparable from being centered on Jesus Christ as the full, free, living, eternal self-expression God, and from the self-giving of God in the Holy Spirit. Yet for John this God of Jesus Christ is also the God of Abraham and Moses, there are strong resonances with occasionalism (for example, in core Johannine concepts of creation through the Word, eternal life, light, God's continual working, the dynamic of glorifying, and, above all, the Holy Spirit), and there is the prospect of being led into all the truth that encourages an openness to more and more illumination and the sur-prises that will bring. And the remarkable engagement of Peter Ochs with Christian theology of the Trinity (I do not know of any other Jewish thinker who has had such a fruitful conversation with modern Christian thought) has itself been a generative illumination for many.[10]

9. It is worth noting how Peter often gives traditional concepts and practices a re-parative rather than a substantial, constative role. He is not suggesting they give the full answer, but rather that they can help resource a diagnosis of where thinking has gone wrong, becoming deeply entrenched in ways that can be healthily challenged by earlier ways. His work on Jewish Morning Prayer is a good example of this.

10. Cf. Ochs, *Another Reformation*.

3. In a Poet's Attic: Thanks for Texts and Practices

I think it was in 2005, some time after Micheal O'Siadhail had published *The Gossamer Wall: Poems in Witness to the Holocaust*,[11] for which Peter Ochs had found him an American publisher, that Micheal, Peter, and I met for a day in Micheal's attic study in Dublin.[12] It was a one-off—the three of us had not met together before, and we have not met for three-way face to face conversation since.

What a time! Peter suggested two experiments: in liturgical reasoning and poetic reasoning.

Peter had been writing on Jewish Morning Prayer, and with us he decided to study the first prayer that many Jews say on first waking up each morning. In translation it goes: "Thanks I give to You, living and eternal King, for giving me back my soul with compassion—great is Your faithfulness."[13] In my memory, that day is distilled into three interwoven elements: the first word, "Thanks," which sparked discussion for over two hours;[14] intensive attention to two short texts, that prayer and one of Micheal's poems; and clearer recognition of how urgently we need to be connected (for nourishment, for *ressourcement*, and for the healing of what has gone wrong) with the depths of the past for the sake of the present and future.

Fifteen years later, Micheal and I still, every morning, pray that prayer, learned in Hebrew from Peter, and it has been a generative moment for many a day. Such liturgy carries within it the concentrated wisdom of a tradition in which practice is primary. The sustained practice of prayer and worship is especially significant for the sustained practice of studying and interpreting scripture. Together they open up depths that have resourced many generations, and that continue to shape people and communities around a world in which it is easy to forget that over 80 percent of the population are directly involved with a religion. The inattention and amnesia with regard to prayer, scripture, and much else with premodern roots, that has so often been characteristic and formative in high and late modernity—perhaps especially exemplified by leading universities—cannot be mended without transformative practices of many sorts. The environmental crisis and the coronavirus pandemic are very sharp reminders of the systemic nature of both our ecology and our health, and of how these are inseparable

11. O'Siadhail, *Gossamer Wall*. Also published in O'Siadhail, *Collected Poems*.

12. Aref Nayed had intended to be there but had to cancel.

13. My translation, modifying and blending those in Sacks, *Authorised Daily Prayer Book*, 5; and *Forms of Prayer*, 28.

14. Some sense of it is given in Peter's essay on Jewish Morning Prayer, Ochs, "Prayer as Redemptive Thinking."

from deeply embedded practices—individual, social, political, economic, artistic, and meaning-seeking. They are also sharp reminders of the pathologies to which all these practices can succumb, and the multidimensional complexity of the required healing.

Since being a co-founder of Textual Reasoning, Peter has continued to improvise imaginatively on Jewish textual study practices, beginning with Scriptural Reasoning. Texts are one of the main channels through which the meaning of the past can inform the present and stimulate our wisdom-seeking now. "Poetic reasoning" has been just one of his further improvisations, which have also included "contemplative reasoning," and forms of peacebuilding inspired by both Textual Reasoning and Scriptural Reasoning. Peter's pragmatic passion, suggested by the title of *Religion Without Violence*, is for healing the tragic pathologies of our world.

The more I have studied the Gospel of John the more I have read it as offering an education in how to read scripture, and especially the text he himself has written, and, at the same time, inviting readers to pray this text.[15] John was steeped in the Septuagint, the translation of the Hebrew Bible into Greek that became the Bible of the Greek-speaking Jewish authors of the New Testament. John is also himself wanting to write scripture, and so how he reads the Septuagint is his way of teaching his readers how to read his own text. He reads imaginatively, improvising in the Spirit, within the open horizon of God and all reality, and centrally concerned with the practice of loving as Jesus loved. Reading and rereading well connects not only with following Jesus in the way of love but also with praying well: the climax of the Farewell Discourses is the final prayer of Jesus (John 17), which for me is the deepest and most challenging chapter in the Bible. Peter's passion for reasoning through reading and rereading texts, and through praying, is at the root of his (and my) way of seeking to heal as well as appreciate current intellectual and religious habits.

4. Dan Hardy's Parting Conversations: Abduction

The most unusual and most intellectually and spiritually adventurous book I have ever been part of was *Wording a Radiance: Parting Conversations on God and the Church*. During the final six months of Dan's life, from May till November 2007, when he was suffering from incurable cancer in Cambridge (and living next door to my wife Deborah and myself), Peter telephoned him at length almost daily from Charlottesville in order to elicit from him what became the central chapters of that book. Peter also joined Dan, Deborah, and

---

15. See the remarkable, neglected book by Ecclestone, *Scaffolding of Spirit*.

myself at the lake in Connecticut that summer for an extraordinary few days of conversation. After Dan's death, Peter, Deborah, and I shared with each other what Dan had shared with each of us during that six months. The book distills the results of our conversations both with Dan and with each other. Again, I choose here just one element: abduction.

Abduction is a way of describing how we can come by fresh imaginative and rational thinking, inventing ways of approaching problems, and conceiving new hypotheses—in logical terms, moving beyond deduction and induction. In *Wording a Radiance* I tried to describe what resulted from Dan Hardy's conversations about abduction with both Peter and myself.[16] The mutual illumination of Peter's development of Peirce's concept of abduction and Dan's improvisation on Coleridge's concept of abduction (which above all emphasizes being attracted to and by God through Word and Spirit) is there combined with my attempt to explore abduction through the New Testament texts of the Letter to the Ephesians and the Gospel of John. Dan and I saw those texts condensing, respectively, the matured theology of the Pauline tradition and the matured Gospel tradition.

Taking up here just the Gospel of John, it has more to say about the Holy Spirit than any of the other gospels, and the promise that "when the Spirit of truth comes, he will guide you into all the truth" (John 16:13) can be read as an invitation into theological abduction. John both practices abduction—the most obvious examples are his Prologue (1:1–18) and the prayer in John 17, which daringly go beyond the other Gospels—and inspires it, above all by the account of Jesus breathing the Holy Spirit into his disciples and saying, "As the Father has sent me, so I send you" (John 20:21). Time and again in John that "as . . . so . . ." pattern recurs (e.g. 10:14; 13:14–15, 34; 15:9, 12–13; 17:21–23, 26). It is an invitation to imaginative, analogical thinking that goes ever deeper into who Jesus is and what he said and did, and then improvises upon all this in new situations. This capacious Johannine "as" opens up a horizon of continual abduction, living in the Spirit of Jesus, open to being led further and further into discerning and living the truth in love. The Holy Spirit in John exemplifies the abductive logic of both Peirce and Coleridge as interpreted by Ochs and Hardy, with leaps of hypothetical, imaginative thinking coming together with the attraction exercised by the Word and Spirit of God.

16. See especially Hardy, *Wording a Radiance,* 116–18.

5. Pain, Polemics, and Peace

The trauma of the Shoah (his preferred term for the Holocaust) has weighed extremely heavily on Peter. He is acutely alert to pain, suffering of all sorts, violence, dissonance and discord, deception, fault lines, pathologies, false binaries, distortions, "breaks," foolishness, and other signs of people, their thinking, their societies, their systems, and their religions going wrong. I try to do justice to those too, but have written more on such themes as joy, praise, flourishing, wisdom, love, and glory. Peter and I have had a long series of engagements (some rather painful) around these matters.

The fullest engagement in print by me[17] with Peter's thought is in *Christian Wisdom*.[18] Wisdom as "the discernment of cries" was for me a key insight. The cries were not only of suffering, disorientation, and lament but also of joy, wonder, and delight. But how to do some justice to the weight of suffering, sin, evil, and death? My way was to grapple with the book of Job, Peter's thought, and Micheal O'Siadhail's poetry on the Shoah.

I had intended to treat all the wisdom literature of the Bible, but Job took over. That amazing text interweaves wisdom as the discernment of cries with two other key insights. Susannah Ticciati[19] suggested this second key insight: that the theological and hermeneutical key to Job, as to Scriptural Reasoning, is relating to God for God's sake. Job is tested as to whether, in the words of Satan, he "fears God for nothing" (Job 1:9) or whether he is in the relationship for the sake of health, or wealth, or children, or social standing, or the advantages of being moral and religious. And a third key insight is into the nature of mature faith. Such faith is not just about affirmations of belief, or obedience to imperative commands. It is also about radical, daring questioning; imaginative, experimental exploration; and passionate desire. All those are there in Job, with the latter, his unquenchable longing for God and God's response, as the core dynamic, even as the mystery of God always remains.

I recognized all five of those elements in the Gospel of John's pedagogy of mature faith—the core affirmations, as in the "I am" statements of Jesus; the two fundamental, interrelated commands, to wash feet and love as Jesus has loved; the repeated questions, beginning with the first words of Jesus, "What are you searching for?" (1:38); the encouragement to think

---

17. Peter's fullest engagement in print with me is "Wisdom's Cry: David Ford's Reparative Pneumatology," chapter 7, in Ochs, *Another Reformation*, 195–221. Dan and I were moved by the dedication of this book: "For the Ford and Hardy families, in deep friendship, at the lake."

18. Ford, *Christian Wisdom*, chapter 4 and chapter 8.

19. See Ticciati, *Job and the Disruption of Identity*.

imaginatively, not only through intertextual resonances, and through big symbols such as light and darkness, wine and vines, water, wind, bread, sheep and shepherd, and fish, but also through those capacious ". . . as . . . so . . ." statements and the abductions they encourage; and the whole gospel as an education of desire, stretching from those first words of Jesus to his first disciples, through his passionate final prayer, "Father, I desire . . ." (17:24), to the question of the resurrected Jesus to Mary Magdalene, "Whom are you searching for?" (20:15).

But also in John there is bitter conflict. So sharp and pervasive is it that there is a large literature about accusations of anti-Semitism against John, and the Christian reception history of John has a shocking amount of supersessionism and polemic against Jews. This Gospel has been used to support the horrendous persecution of Jews by Christians. The event I want to focus on here is in 2015, when my engagement with Peter about this came to a head. He was giving his Stanton Lectures in Cambridge University, and stayed in our home for three weeks, while I was giving the Bampton Lectures in Oxford University over several months on the theme, *Daring Spirit: The Gospel of John Today*,[20] and was preparing for one that faced the question of John on "the Jews." Our study and conversation centered on John 8, and led to many insights, but two are primary.

John 8 is often read as anti-Jewish or antisemitic in its harsh polemic by Jesus, and his characterization of his opponents as, for example, children of the devil. Its difficulties did not disappear in our reading (my commentary tries to deal with these), but the perspective changed as Peter noted many parallels to John in the polemics that accompanied the genesis of Rabbinic Judaism, which overlapped with the genesis of Christianity. Both traditions related to the same scriptures (and claimed to be in continuity with them) and to an internally divided, fragmented Second Temple Judaism, and they were born amidst bitter intra-Jewish polemic and violent, traumatic events. They also developed a polemical relationship to each other, and their conflictual separation was maintained through an often tragic and violent history. But at root this is a Jewish "family quarrel," with all the bitterness such quarrels can generate.

The second insight is into the possibility of healing the reception history of John, and enabling a better one in future. Is it possible to reread John so as to help repair that history? My experience with Peter (and with Scriptural Reasoning more widely) gives a "yes" to that question. It also warns us Christians not to try, as we often do, to address the question only among

20. These have not been published but are deposited in the Bodleian Library.

ourselves, necessary though that is.[21] A more radical challenge is to address it with Jews, in ongoing relationships that seek wisdom through reading, discussing, and arguing together.[22] In such ways, the history of reception can be both grappled with and taken in new directions.

But Peter's thinking with texts, and his concern with conflict and polemics, reach beyond religious and interreligious matters. As response to the Shoah necessitates, he is also concerned with religion's interrelationships with the rest of social, cultural, and political reality, and the pathologies of our civilization. For some years we were involved with Global Covenant Partners (now, at the time of writing, merging with the Rose Castle Foundation), focused on religion-related violence in the contemporary world and on how to act with nonreligious players at all levels—top-down, bottom-up, and middle-out. I have watched in fascinated admiration as Peter has developed in the University of Virginia courses and interdisciplinary research on religion and conflict. The culmination so far in his writing about this is in *Religion Without Violence*, which can be read as a diagnosis of pathological dimensions of our civilization, with a prescription for practices and associated thinking that hold out some hope for a healthily plural and peaceful world.

6. One of Twenty-five Points: Flourishing around the Break

In May 2018 Deborah and I spent several days with Peter and Vanessa in Charlottesville, the last physical meeting I have had with Peter before writing this during a time of coronavirus lockdown. Again, there was a superabundance of thinking in many directions, culminating in a four-hour conversation until the early morning hours, which began with Peter

21. Many Christians (and whole Christian denominations) in the aftermath of the Shoah have sought to do this, repenting of the record of Christian persecution, and rethinking doctrines and practices relating to Jews. Peter Ochs has himself been in the forefront of the Jewish response to this Christian development (especially in his cofounding of Scriptural Reasoning and his leadership of the *Dabru Emet* initiative in 2000 and coediting of the associated volume, *Christianity in Jewish Terms*).

22. The most satisfactory sustained example of this that I have taken part in has been the project of the Council of Christians and Jews in England in which over twenty of us met over several years and eventually produced Bayfield, *Deep Calls to Deep*. In relation to the Gospel of John, Muslims too have many fundamental issues, and analogous projects are needed; and Scriptural Reasoning has shown the fruitfulness of all three traditions being brought into conversation together around such texts. In January 2014 the McDonald Agape Foundation sponsored a symposium in Cambridge on the Gospel of John in which a number of Christians were joined by Peter Ochs and the Muslim Qur'anic scholar Maria Dakake for a vigorous discussion of these questions, the paper on John 8 being given by the Archbishop of Canterbury, Justin Welby.

saying that he had twenty-five points to make about me, himself, and our relationship. He did!

I choose just one of the points, what Peter called "flourishing around the break." "The break" signifies an event of suffering, trauma, breach of trust, disruption of relationship (with God, between people, with the created world, within oneself), false dichotomy, wounding, and so on—anything that cries out for repair, for mending, for healing. Peter has been more concerned with the break, I with flourishing, yet each also with each. And just as the otherness in our respective Judaism and Christianity has not been able to be synthesized, "reconciled," brought within some single framework or truth or practice, so neither can the otherness of "break" and "flourishing." There is something utterly intractable, a depth of wounding, an ongoing darkness (for all the fact that light shines in it), a tearing and unravelling of the fabric of life beyond imaginable mending, the reality of the tragic, the persistence of cries of anguish, and the unavoidability of living within earshot of those cries even when they are not our own. Peter has testified to this in many ways, and that night in Charlottesville spoke of the teaching that emerges at the point at which "the system is permanently wounded."

For me, writing in Holy Week as Good Friday and Easter Sunday approach, it is about the wounds shown by the crucified and resurrected Jesus (John 20:19–29)—permanent wounds? This is not the place to go further into that, but I do want to follow through one of Peter's lines of thought that night: any hope of "flourishing around the break" cries out for a quality of coming together with others, of solidarity, mutuality, shared discernment, compassion, and joint commitment. And this coming together has to be able to take on profound levels of anguish, wounding, disappointment, and hostility. This is a hope now in the midst of the coronavirus emergency. It is a hope that goes beyond conversation or even collaboration toward long-term covenantal relationships (including friendships) across differences, and the organizational and institutional expressions of these relationships. Who is up to this? Without the sharing, in mutual intensities, of our deepest resources and involvements, such developments are unimaginable. But so are the pain and the cost: as Peter said, "I fight with those I love."

7. Shabbat

The seventh event is appropriately the Sabbath. It is also appropriate that I have reached my word limit. Anyone who has celebrated Shabbat with Peter and Vanessa will know what I mean by seeing it as a sign of flourishing that is not overshadowed by the break. *Modeh ani. . .* In terms of the

Gospel of John I think of the invitation by Jesus in his final appearance: "Come and have breakfast" (21:12).

Bibliography

Bayfield, Tony. *Deep Calls to Deep. Transforming Conversations between Christians and Jews.* London: SCM, 2017.

Clemson, Frances, and David F. Ford, eds. *Interreligious Reading after Vatican II.* Oxford: Wiley-Blackwell, 2013.

Ecclestone, Alan. *The Scaffolding of Spirit: Reflections on the Gospel of John.* London: Darton, Longman and Todd, 1987.

Ford, David. *Christian Wisdom: Desiring God and Learning in Love.* Cambridge: Cambridge University Press, 2007.

———. "Developing Scriptural Reasoning Further: Reflections on Scripture, Reason, and the Contemporary Islam-West Encounter." In David F. Ford, *Shaping Theology: Engagements in a Religious and Secular World.* Oxford: Blackwell, 2007.

———. "An Inter-Faith Wisdom: Scriptural Reasoning between Jews, Christians and Muslims." In *The Promise of Scriptural Reasoning,* edited by David Ford and C. C. Pecknold, 1–22. Oxford: Blackwell, 2006.

———. "Reading Scripture with Intensity: Academic, Ecclesial, Interfaith, and Divine." *The Princeton Seminary Bulletin* 26.1 (2005) 22–35.

———. *Self and Salvation: Being Transformed.* Cambridge: Cambridge University Press, 1999.

———. "The Theological and Educational Promise of Scriptural Reasoning." In *Schools of Faith: Essays on Theology, Ethics and Education in Honour of Iain R. Torrance,* edited by David Fergusson and Bruce McCormack, 235–47. New York: Bloomsbury Academic, 2019.

Ford, David, and C. C. Pecknold, eds. *The Promise of Scriptural Reasoning.* Oxford: Blackwell, 2006.

Forms of Prayer. London: Movement for Reform Judaism, 2008.

Hardy, Daniel W., with Deborah Hardy Ford, Peter Ochs, and David F. Ford. *Wording a Radiance: Parting Conversations on God and the Church.* London: SCM, 2010.

Nayed, Aref Ali. *Operational Hermeneutics: Interpretation as the Engagement of Operational Artefacts.* Dubai: Kalam Research and Media, 2011.

———. "Reading Scripture Together: Towards a Sacred Hermeneutics of Togetherness." *The Princeton Seminary Bulletin* 26.1 (2005) 48–53.

Ochs, Peter, et al., eds. *Christianity in Jewish Terms.* Boulder: Westview, 2000.

Ochs, Peter. *Another Reformation: Postliberal Christianity and the Jews.* Grand Rapids: Baker Academic, 2011.

———. "Morning Prayer as Redemptive Thinking." In *Liturgy, Time, and the Politics of Redemption,* edited by Chad Pecknold and Randi Rashkover, 50–90. Grand Rapids: Eerdmans, 2006.

———. *Peirce, Pragmatism and the Logic of Scripture.* Cambridge: Cambridge University Press, 1998.

———. "The Possibilities and Limits of Inter-Religious Dialogue." In *The Oxford Handbook of Religion, Conflict, and Peacebuilding,* edited by R. Scott Appleby, et al., 488–515. Oxford: Oxford University Press, 2015.

————. "Reading Scripture Together in Sight of Our Open Doors." *The Princeton Seminary Bulletin* 26.1 (2005) 36–47.

————. *Religion Without Violence: The Practice and Philosophy of Scriptural Reasoning.* Eugene, OR: Cascade, 2019.

O'Siadhail, Micheal. *Collected Poems.* Tarset: Bloodaxe Books, 2013.

————. *The Gossamer Wall: Poems in Witness to the Holocaust.* Tarset: Bloodaxe Books, 2002.

Sacks, Jonathan, trans. and ed. *The Authorised Daily Prayer Book of the United Hebrew Congregations of the Commonwealth.* 4th ed. London: Collins, 2007.

Ticciati, Susannah. *Job and the Disruption of Identity: Reading beyond Barth.* New York: T&T Clark, 2005.

Contributors

Nicholas Adams is Professor of Philosophical Theology at the University of Birmingham.

Rumee Ahmed is Associate Dean in the Faculty of Arts and Associate Professor of Islamic Law at the University of British Columbia.

Emily Filler is Assistant Professor in the Study of Judaism at Washington and Lee University.

Jim Fodor is Professor of Theology at St. Bonaventure University.

David F. Ford is Emeritus Regius Professor of Divinity at the University of Cambridge.

Robert Gibbs is Professor of Philosophy and Religion at the University of Toronto.

Jacob L. Goodson is Associate Professor of Philosophy at Southwestern College.

Tom Greggs is the Marischal Professor of Divinity at the University of Aberdeen.

Stanley Hauerwas is the Gilbert T. Rowe Professor Emeritus of Divinity and Law at Duke Divinity School.

Mike Higton is Professor of Theology and Ministry at Durham University.

Mark Randall James is an independent scholar.

Steven D. Kepnes is the Murray W. and Mildred K. Finard Professor of Jewish Studies and Religion at Colgate University.

Basit Bilal Koshul is Associate Professor in the Department of Humanities and Social Sciences at the Lahore University of Management Sciences.

Shaul Magid is the Distinguished Fellow in Jewish Studies at Dartmouth College.

Rachel Muers is Professor of Theology at the University of Leeds.

Randi Rashkover is the Nathan and Sofia Gumenick Chair in Judaic Studies at the College of William & Mary.

Susannah Ticciati is Lecturer in Systematic Theology at King's College London.

Daniel H. Weiss is Polonsky-Coexist Senior Lecturer in Jewish Studies at the University of Cambridge.

Elliot R. Wolfson is the Marsha and Jay Glazer Endowed Chair in Jewish Studies at the University of California, Santa Barbara.

Laurie Zoloth is the Margaret E. Burton Professor of Religion and Ethics at the University of Chicago Divinity School.